Gegenwartsliteratur 24/2025

Graphic Novels

Herausgeberin/Editor-in-Chief
Friederike Eigler

Herausgeberin für Rezensionen/Book Review Editor
Anke Biendarra

Mitverantwortliche Herausgeberin/Assistant Editor
Astrid Weigert

DE GRUYTER

Wir danken dem German Department der Georgetown University in Washington DC sowie der Max Kade Foundation in New York für die Unterstützung des Jahrbuchs.

Gegenwartsliteratur ist Mitglied des Council of Editors of Learned Journals (CELJ); www.celj.org

Herausgeberin/Editor-in-Chief
Friederike Eigler (gegenwartsliteratur.yearbook@gmail.com)

Herausgeberin für Rezensionen/Book Review Editor
Anke Biendarra (abiendar@uci.edu)

Mitverantwortliche Herausgeberin/Assistant Editor
Astrid Weigert

Assistentin/Editorial Assistant
Katie Lightfoot

ISBN 978-3-11-914384-4
e-ISBN (PDF) 978-3-11-221863-1
e-ISBN (EPUB) 978-3-11-221915-7
ISSN 1617-8491
DOI https://doi.org/10.1515/9783112218631

[CC BY-NC-ND]

Dieses Werk ist lizenziert unter der Creative Commons Namensnennung - Nicht-kommerziell - Keine Bearbeitungen 4.0 International Lizenz. Weitere Informationen finden Sie unter https://creativecommons.org/licenses/by-nc-nd/4.0/.

Die Creative Commons-Lizenzbedingungen für die Weiterverwendung gelten nicht für Inhalte (wie Grafiken, Abbildungen, Fotos, Auszüge usw.), die nicht im Original der Open-Access-Publikation enthalten sind. Es kann eine weitere Genehmigung des Rechteinhabers erforderlich sein. Die Verpflichtung zur Recherche und Genehmigung liegt allein bei der Partei, die das Material weiterverwendet.

Library of Congress Control Number: 2025941340

Bibliografische Information der Deutschen Nationalbibliothek
Die Deutsche Nationalbibliothek verzeichnet diese Publikation in der Deutschen Nationalbibliografie; detaillierte bibliografische Daten sind im Internet über http://dnb.dnb.de abrufbar.

© 2025 bei den Autorinnen und Autoren, Zusammenstellung © 2025 Friederike Eigler, publiziert von Walter de Gruyter GmbH, Berlin/Boston, Genthiner Straße 13, 10785 Berlin
Dieses Buch ist als Open-Access-Publikation verfügbar über www.degruyter.com.

Einbandabbildung: Nikada/iStock/Getty Images Plus
Satz: Integra Software Services Pvt. Ltd.

www.degruyterbrill.com
Fragen zur allgemeinen Produktsicherheit:
productsafety@degruyterbrill.com

Editorische Notiz / Editorial Note

Das Jahrbuch *Gegenwartsliteratur* beschäftigt sich mit der Literatur der drei letzten Jahrzehnte in der Bundesrepublik Deutschland, Österreich und der deutschsprachigen Schweiz. Die Beiträge, die von promovierten Literaturwissenschaftler:innen auf Englisch oder Deutsch verfasst werden, können jederzeit bei der Herausgeberin unter der Mailadresse des Jahrbuches eingereicht werden und werden umgehend beantwortet (gegenwartsliteratur.yearbook@gmail.com).

Das Jahrbuch ist ein „refereed journal", d. h., die eingereichten Beiträge werden, soweit sie wissenschaftliche Standards erfüllen, von Fachgutachter:innen bewertet. Das Evaluierungsverfahren ist anonym. Weitere Informationen zu *Gegenwartsliteratur* finden Sie auf der Webseite *gegenwartsliteratur.org*.

Das Schwerpunktthema für das *Jahrbuch Gegenwartsliteratur* 2026 heißt „Räume & Orte erzählen – erinnern – imaginieren / Narrating – Remembering – Imagining Spaces & Places". Außerdem wird es einige Beiträge zum Thema „(Neue) Medien & Mediendynamiken im Kontext der deutschsprachigen Gegenwartsliteratur" geben sowie, wie gewohnt, Einzelanalysen zu anderen Aspekten der deutschsprachigen Gegenwartsliteratur.

Friederike Eigler, Georgetown University
Washington, D.C., Sommer 2025

Inhaltsverzeichnis / Table of Contents

Editorische Notiz / Editorial Note —— V

Friederike Eigler
Vorwort zum Jahrbuch 2025 —— 1

Anna Kinder/Sandra Richter
Gegenwartsliteratur im Deutschen Literaturarchiv Marbach: Sammeln für und in die Zukunft —— 5

I Schwerpunkt/Focus: Graphic Novels

Andreas Platthaus
Durchsetzungsvermögen. Wie der Begriff „Graphic Novel" das Verständnis von Comics verändert hat —— 19

Christian Klein
„Nicht nur Fakten runterbeten" – Spielräume biographischen Erzählens im Comic am Beispiel von Reinhard Kleists Graphic Novel *Der Boxer* —— 31

Paul M. Malone
Nils Oskamp's *Drei Steine* (2016) and the Void in Germany's *Erinnerungskultur* —— 51

Anna Karina Sennefelder
Ökokrieger:innen. Ästhetik und ökokritisches Potential einer neuen Figur am Beispiel von George Millers *Mad Max: Fury Road*, Olivia Viewegs *Endzeit* und Frauke Bergers *Grün* —— 75

Kalina Kupczyńska
Autorinnenschaft im Comic – das Selbstbild als Autorin bei Marie Marcks und Birgit Weyhe —— 103

Lynn Marie Kutch
Gender, Race, and the Silenced Asian Other in Olivia Vieweg's *Huck Finn: Die Graphic Novel* —— 125

Andreas Stuhlmann
Anke Feuchtenberger's Graphic Novel *Genossin Kuckuck* as Palimpsest: History, Memory, Violence, and Transformation —— 149

II Einzelanalysen/Individual Analyses

Katrin Sieg
"Theater of Ir/reconciliation: Empathy and Anger in Decolonial Theater" —— 173

Caroline Schaumann
***Haarbüschel*, *Pausbacke*, and *Fledermaus*: Christopher Kloeble's Recasting of the Schlagintweit Expedition in *Das Museum der Welt* (2020) —— 203**

Hanna Maria Hofmann
Dinçer Güçyeters *Unser Deutschlandmärchen* im Dialog mit Scheherazade, Loreley und Dorothea Viehmann —— 223

III Rezensionen/Book Reviews

Harald Gschwandtner
Aust, Robin-M. „Im Grunde ist alles, was gesagt wird, zitiert". Die kreative und intertextuelle Thomas-Bernhard-Rezeption —— 251

Necia Chronister
Brockmann, Stephen. *The Freest Country in the World: East Germany's Final Year in Culture and Memory* —— 255

Roberto Di Bella
Catani, Stephanie und Christoph Kleinschmidt (Hg.). *Popliteratur 3.0. Soziale Medien und Gegenwartsliteratur* —— 259

Michael Braun
Jürgensen, Christoph und Michael Scheffel (Hg.). *Günter Grass Handbuch* —— 263

Dora Osborne
Meyer, Christine und Anna Gvelesiani (Hg). *Postmemory und die Transformation der deutschen Erinnerungskultur* —— 267

Anna Seidel
Pasewalck, Silke (Hg.). *Shared Heritage – Gemeinsames Erbe. Kulturelle Interferenzräume im östlichen Europa als Sujet der Gegenwartsliteratur* —— 269

Anna Horakova
Pinkert, Anke. *Remembering 1989: Future Archives of Public Protest* —— 273

Namensregister/Index of Names —— 277

Friederike Eigler
Vorwort zum Jahrbuch 2025

Nach dem erfolgreichen Verlagswechsel zu De Gruyter im letzten Jahr erscheint das Jahrbuch *Gegenwartsliteratur* nun zum zweiten Mal nicht nur in Druckfassung, sondern ist auch weltweit über „open access" zugänglich. Dies entspricht der internationalen Ausrichtung des Jahrbuchs, das sich als Publikationsorgan für Wissenschaftler:innen aus allen Kontinenten versteht.

Es freut mich sehr, dass ich Sandra Richter, Leiterin des Deutschen Literaturarchivs Marbach (DLA), und Anna Kinder, Leiterin des DLA-Forschungsreferats, für einen gemeinsamen Beitrag gewinnen konnte. Unter der Devise „Sammeln für und in die Zukunft" stellen sie die Forschungsschwerpunkte des DLA unter besonderer Berücksichtigung der Gegenwartsliteratur vor. Damit ist der Beitrag auch eine Einladung an Literatur- und Kulturwissenschaftler:innen aus aller Welt, von den vielfältigen und stetig wachsenden Beständen des DLA aktiv Gebrauch zu machen.

Das Schwerpunktthema für das Jahrbuch 2025, „Graphic Novel", wird eröffnet von Andreas Platthaus, Chef des Ressorts „Literatur und literarisches Leben" der *Frankfurter Allgemeinen Zeitung* und Initiator des Comic-Blogs auf FAZ/NET. Neben einer Skizzierung der Geschichte des in den USA entstandenen Genres zeigt er auf, wie sehr sich im deutschsprachigen Bereich das Marketing und damit die Verbreitung und Rezeption des Genres durch die Umbenennung von „Comic" in „Graphic Novel" vor etwa 15 Jahren verändert hat (in beiden Fällen wird der englische Begriff verwendet). Eine erstaunliche Entwicklung, die, wie er deutlich macht, auch Räume für ästhetische Innovationen eröffnet hat. In gewisser Weise schildert Platthaus damit auch die „backstory" für die zunehmende Etablierung der Forschung zu Comic und Graphic Novel in den Literaturwissenschaften.

Einen Einblick in dieses spannende Forschungsgebiet – hier vornehmlich mit Fokus auf die Germanistik und German Studies – bieten sechs literaturwissenschaftliche Beiträge zum Schwerpunktthema, die in diesem Jahrbuch erscheinen. Die beiden ersten Artikel beschäftigen sich mit biographisch bzw. autobiographisch orientierten Graphic Novels, die sich als formal wie inhaltlich sehr unterschiedliche Beiträge zur deutschen Erinnerungskultur verstehen lassen. Mit Blick auf Reinhard Kleists *Der Boxer*, der das Leben des polnischen Holocaust-Überlebenden Hertzko Haft als Vorlage nimmt, untersucht Christian Klein das Verhältnis von faktualen und fiktionalen Darstellungsstrategien. In dem Artikel zu Nils Oskamps *Drei Steine* (2016), der den Widerstand gegen Neo-Nazis thematisiert, zeigt Paul M. Malone sowohl die Stärken wie die Schwächen dieses Comics auf,

Friederike Eigler, Georgetown University

Open Access. © 2025 bei den Autorinnen und Autoren, publiziert von De Gruyter. Dieses Werk ist lizenziert unter der Creative Commons Namensnennung - Nicht-kommerziell - Keine Bearbeitungen 4.0 International Lizenz.
https://doi.org/10.1515/9783112218631-001

der von der Bundeszentrale für politische Bildung für den Schulunterricht empfohlen wird.

In den beiden folgenden Beiträgen geht es um Fragen weiblicher bzw. queerer Handlungsmacht und Autorschaft. Mit Bezug auf den Film *Mad Max: Fury Road* (R: George Miller) sowie die Graphic Novels *Endzeit* (Vieweg) und *Grün* (Berger) identifiziert Anna Karina Sennefelder eine neue und revolutionäre Figur der „Ökokrieger:in", die gegen das „Petro-Patriarchat" und für neue Formen des Zusammenlebens kämpft. Kalina Kupczyńska untersucht dann die visuellen Formen der Selbstdarstellung bei Marie Marcks und Birgit Weyhe – Comic-Autorinnen, die zwei unterschiedliche Generationen repräsentieren. Ging es in der Forschung diesbezüglich bisher nur um männliche Comic-Künstler, wird hier die Darstellung weiblicher und queerer Autorschaft – und die Thematisierung genderspezifischer Arbeitsbedingungen – analysiert.

In den beiden letzten Beiträgen zum Schwerpunktthema stehen zwei weitere prominente Comic-Autorinnen im Mittelpunkt. In der kritischen Analyse der Twain-Adaption von Olivia Vieweg in *Huck Finn: Die Graphic Novel* argumentiert Lynn Marie Kutch, dass Vieweg die (umstrittene) Figur des versklavten Jim bei Twain durch eine ebenfalls problematische, da auf Stereotype zurückgreifende Darstellung einer asiatischen Sexarbeiterin ersetzt. Schließlich steht mit Anke Feuchtenberger, die „grande dame" des Comics im Zentrum. Andreas Stuhlmann untersucht in seinem Beitrag die Entstehungsbedingungen und Kompositionsprinzipien von Feuchtenbergers Graphic Novel *Genossin Kuckuck*, ein komplexes und umfangreiches Werk, das an die feministische Avantgarde der 1990er Jahre anknüpft.

Auch die auf das Schwerpunktthema folgenden Einzelanalysen beschäftigen sich mit Entwicklungen – hier in Literatur und Theater – die so ästhetisch innovativ wie gesellschaftspolitisch relevant sind. In ihrer Auseinandersetzung mit aktuellen Beispielen dekolonialen Theaters kontrastiert Katrin Sieg zwei sehr unterschiedliche Versionen des Theaterstücks *Hereroland* – eine Inszenierung in Hamburg (2019) und eine in Nambia (2023). Sie argumentiert, dass gerade die ausbleibende „Versöhnung" in der namibischen Inszenierung einen Raum für noch zu leistenden öffentlichen Debatten offenhält. Wie Caroline Schaumann in dem folgenden Beitrag zeigt, lässt sich auf andere Weise auch Christopher Kloebles Roman *Museum der Welt* (2020) als Kritik an kolonialer Praxis verstehen – hier im Kontext einer historisch verbürgten Expedition nach Indien: Mit Hilfe der pikaresken Figur des indischen Gehilfen stelle der Roman koloniale Machtverhältnisse auf den Kopf. In dem abschließenden Artikel nimmt Hanna Maria Hofmann dann den postmigrantischen Roman *Unser Deutschlandmärchen* (2023) von Dinçer Güçyeters in den Blick und analysiert, wie der Autor mit Hilfe intertextueller und interkultureller Märchenmotive ein migrantisch-kritisches Gegennarrativ zu dominanten nationalen Diskursen entwirft.

Das Jahrbuch schließt wie immer mit Rezensionen wichtiger literaturwissenschaftlicher Neuerscheinungen zur Gegenwartsliteratur ab, die unter der sachkundigen Leitung von Anke Biendarra ausgesucht und zusammengestellt wurden.

Auch in diesem Jahr geht mein großer Dank an eine Reihe von Personen: an die zahlreichen, hier ungenannten Gutachter:innen (darunter einige Mitglieder des Internationalen Beirats), die maßgeblich zur Qualität der publizierten Artikel beigetragen haben; und ganz besonders an mein Editorial Team: an meine Assistentin Katie Lightfoot, die zum ersten Mal mit dabei ist und sich schnell die erforderlichen Kenntnisse angeeignet hat; und an Astrid Weigert, die mir seit dem Beginn meiner Herausgeberschaft mit Rat und Tat – und mit Adleraugen bei der Lektoratsarbeit – zur Seite steht.

Anna Kinder/Sandra Richter

Gegenwartsliteratur im Deutschen Literaturarchiv Marbach: Sammeln für und in die Zukunft

Abstract: Der Beitrag stellt die Sammlungen des Deutschen Literaturarchivs Marbach (DLA) zur Gegenwartsliteratur in ihrem Potential für die Forschung vor und beleuchtet die Strategien, mit denen das Archiv auf die Herausforderungen des Sammelns von Gegenwartsliteratur reagiert. Als Archiv, dessen Sammelauftrag der neueren deutschen Literatur gilt, sammelt das DLA in die Zukunft. Die Bestände des DLA sind, solange es Literatur gibt, unabgeschlossen. Die Sammlungsstrategie des DLA steht damit immer in einem spannungsvollen und dynamischen Verhältnis zu ihrem Gegenstand, der Gegenwartsliteratur, die sich in ihrer Archivwürdigkeit erst noch beweisen muss. Das Archiv befindet sich in einem ständigen Aushandlungsprozess darüber, was in den Kanon aufgenommen werden soll.

I

Saša Stanišić, Träger des Preises der Leipziger Buchmesse (2014), des Deutschen Buchpreises (2019) und sicherlich eine der bekanntesten Stimmen der deutschsprachigen Gegenwartsliteratur, ist sich seiner Archivwürdigkeit bewusst. Bevor er seine Social-Media-Aktivitäten einstellte, gab er in einem Post bekannt, eine E-Mail gelöscht zu haben, da „Marbach", also das Deutsche Literaturarchiv Marbach (DLA), immer schon mitlese. Er demonstrierte damit das, was man in der Forschung seit einigen Jahren Nachlassbewusstsein (vgl. Spoerhase und Sina) nennt: Das Bewusstsein darüber, dass Dokumente, die man gegenwärtig erstellt, in der Zukunft möglicherweise von Archivar:innen bearbeitet und von Forschenden gelesen werden. Die Archivierung und der damit möglich werdende öffentliche Zugriff sind schon im Schreiprozess präsent, die erhoffte Unverstelltheit und Unverfälschtheit von Archivdokumenten im Moment ihrer Entstehung passé. Das Phänomen ist kein Neues, es ging vielmehr mit der Schärfung des Konzepts des Nachlasses im 19. Jahrhundert einher, als sich ein Verständnis durchsetzte, das jenseits eines „werkfixierten und publikationsorientierten Interesses" (Spoerhase 25) mit Nachlass auch das mit meint, was über das Werk im engeren Sinne hinaus überliefert wurde. Ging es bis dahin primär darum, noch Unpubliziertes ans Licht zu bringen, so tritt mit Entstehung der Neuphilologie der Nachlass als epistemische Formation auf den Plan: Das Feld der textuellen Genese verschafft den nachgelassenen Papieren ein Recht in eigener Sache und sorgte auch bei den Autor:innen für entsprechendes Relevanzbewusstsein – denken wir an Goethe, der seinen Nachlass zu Lebzeiten vorbereitete und selbst darüber wachte, dass „eine reinliche, ordnungsgemäße Zusammenstellung aller Papiere" (Archiv des Dichters 27) erfolgte, oder an Thomas Mann, der bewusst einige seiner Tagebücher zerstörte.

Gleichwohl hat sich das Nachlassbewusstsein mit dem Aufkommen des sogenannten „Vorlass"-Handels noch verschärft. Archive treten vermehrt mit Autor:innen selbst in Kontakt und verhandeln die Übernahme der späteren Nachlasspapiere. Dies hat nicht nur zur Folge, dass die Autor:innen selbst autorisieren, was sie übergeben (vgl. Grond-Rigler), sondern auch dass die Materialien bereits zu Lebzeiten der Forschung zur Verfügung stehen. So konnte das DLA in den letzten Jahren etwa die Vorlässe von Hildegard Brenner, Hans Magnus Enzensberger, Julia Franck, Barbara Honigmann, Christoph Hein, Anna Rheinsberg und Martin Walser übernehmen. Barbara Köhler übereignete dem DLA noch vor ihrem Tod (2021) ihr persönliches Archiv.

Als Literaturarchiv, dessen Sammelauftrag „der neueren deutschen Literatur im umfassenderen Sinne" (Satzung Deutsche Schiller Gesellschaft) gilt, sammelt das DLA in die Zukunft. Die Sammlungen des DLA sind, anders als die etwa historisch konturierter Archive, bei denen es in der Erwerbung vor allem um Bestandsergänzungen geht, unabgeschlossen: „The German Literature Archive's collections have the potential to continue expanding forever or for as long as literature exists" (Richter 2023a, 8). Die Sammlungsstrategie des DLA steht damit in einem spannungsvollen und dynamischen Verhältnis zu ihrem Gegenstand, der Gegenwartsliteratur. Die Literatur muss sich behaupten und beweisen und das Archiv steht in einem ständigen Aushandlungsprozess darüber, was in den Kanon aufgenommen werden soll, „[...] the question must be asked which contemporary literature is so consistent, yet so distinctive, so topical and yet simultaneously so ahead of its time that it can continue to be relevant into the future" (Richter 2023a, 8).

Mit der Bewertung und dem Erwerb von Gegenwartsliteratur, deren Kanonizität sich noch nicht über einen längeren Zeitraum erwiesen hat, geht das Archiv immer auch eine Wette auf die Zukunft ein, darauf, „dass mit dem Tod der vorlassgebenden Person eine Nachfrage von Seiten der Forschung eintreten wird, durch die sich die Investition in die Archivierung langfristig amortisiert" (Engelmeier 33).

Die Verständigung darüber, was für das Archiv auszuwählen ist, was mithin als kulturelles Erbe überliefert wird, erfordert ein offenes Verständnis von Literatur und einen kontinuierlichen und kritischen Reflexionsprozess. So befindet sich auch das DLA im ständigen Gespräch und Austausch mit Autor:innen ebenso wie mit der internationalen Forschung und Akteur:innen des Literaturbetriebs, um gemeinsam über gegenwärtige Formen des Literarischen nachzudenken, wie etwa über Comics oder digitale Literatur in all ihren Ausprägungen, von Games über KI-generierte Literatur und Netzliteratur bis hin zu Fanfiction (vgl. Çakir, Kinder und Richter; Möring; Gunser et al.; Rohleder; M. Y. Müller; Bendt). Mitunter bedeutet dies auch eine Erweiterung des Sammlungsprofils, wie es etwa jüngst auch mit Blick auf mehrsprachige Bestände geschehen ist. Die bestehenden und umfangreichen Sammlungen des DLA zur Exil- und Migrationsliteratur haben ihren Ursprung in der Zeit der Shoah, wobei der Schwerpunkt auf deutschjüdischen Autor:innen liegt. Seit den 1960er Jahren und vor allem seit 1989 sind kontinuierlich Bestände zu Schriftsteller:innen aus zahlreichen wirtschaftlich oder politisch prekären Ländern der Welt hinzugekommen. Um diesen Literaturen gerecht zu werden, wurde der Sammelauftrag explizit auch auf Literatur ausgeweitet, die einen Bezug zu Deutschland bzw. zur deutschen Kultur hat, jedoch nicht zwangsläufig in deutscher Sprache verfasst ist, wie etwa Literatur von Autor:innen, die in Deutschland im Exil leben, aber nicht auf Deutsch schreiben.

Entsprechend versteht und dokumentiert das Literaturarchiv Literatur in einem umfassenden, mehrdimensionalen und facettenreichen Sinne. Es umfasst sowohl die literarischen Texte selbst als auch die Produktions- und Rezeptionskontexte, in denen Literatur entsteht, wahrgenommen und bearbeitet wird. Erfasst werden damit auch Literaturkreisläufe und literarische Zirkulationen. Dieses Verständnis liegt auch dem Forschungsprogramm des DLA zugrunde, insbesondere den fünf Forschungslinien, die der Vielschichtigkeit der Literatur im Archiv Rechnung zu tragen und zugleich etablierte und neue Ansätze ausgehend vom Material zu prüfen und weiterzuentwickeln suchen: (1) Wie Literatur entsteht: Literatursoziologie, (2) Lesespuren: Leserpsychologie, Textverstehensforschung und Literaturpolitologie, (3) Literaturvertonungen: Audioanalyse der Literatur, (4) Literaturdaten: Digitale Sammlungsforschung und (5) Schreibwerkzeuge, Literaturträger und literarische Objekte: Materiale Hermeneutik.

II

(1) Wie Literatur entsteht: Literatursoziologie

Das DLA beherbergt 55 Verlagsarchivbestände, darunter die Archive der Verlage Cotta, Hanser, S. Fischer, Insel, Luchterhand, Piper, Reclam, Rowohlt und Suhrkamp, sowie zahlreiche Redaktionsarchive, u. a. zu den Zeitschriften *Alternative*,

Merkur, *text + kritik*, *Die Wandlung*, *Westermanns Monatshefte* und denen des Cotta-Archivs (vgl. Bürger et al.; Kinder und Richter 2024b). Besonders erwähnenswert ist eine der jüngsten Erwerbungen des DLA, die des digitalen Kultur- und Büchermagazins „Perlentaucher", das seit dem 15. März 2000 täglich als Meta-Feuilleton Literaturkritik und kulturelles Leben spiegelt. Übergeben wurde dem Archiv ein digitaler Abzug, der alle gespeicherten Seiten seit der Gründung von 25 Jahren bis zur Datenübernahme am 28.02.2025 umfasst.[1]

Diese Sammlungen, die teils bis an die unmittelbare Gegenwart heranreichen, können darüber Auskunft geben, wie Literatur gemacht und rezipiert wird, welche Akteur:innen jenseits der Autorinnen und Autoren daran beteiligt sind und welcher Prozesse es zu diesem Zweck bedarf. Literatursoziologische Ansätze, die im französischen Sprachraum durch das Werk von Pierre Bourdieu und im amerikanischen Sprachraum durch eine aktive Kultursoziologie einige Prominenz genießen, hierzulande aber bislang nur wenig entwickelt sind, helfen weiter, um das Entstehen von Literatur aus Verlags- und Zeitschriftenarchiven zu beschreiben. Wer sich für das Entstehen von Literatur interessiert und in ein Verlagsarchiv blickt, trifft auf eine komplexe und vielschichtige Gemengelage und auf zahlreiche Akteur:innen, die dazu beitragen, dass Leserinnen und Leser mit Büchern versorgt werden. Die Formel von der Entstehung eines Werkes im Kopf und am Schreibtisch eines Autors greift, das wird schnell klar, zu kurz. Vielmehr spielen die ökonomischen, kulturellen, politischen und sprachlichen Rahmenbedingungen eine entscheidende Rolle dafür, wann und weshalb bestimmte Titel erscheinen und sich durchsetzen können. Neben die Autor:innen treten eine Reihe weiterer Akteur:innen, wie etwa Verleger:innen, Lektor:innen, Agent:innen, Scouts, Übersetzer:innen, Kritiker:innen, Leser:innen, Vertriebs- und Pressepersonen, die ebenfalls Einfluss darauf haben, wie und ob ein Buch das Licht der Welt erblickt. Exemplarisch aufgezeigt hat dies Clayton Childress in seiner Untersuchung *Under the Cover. The creation, production and reception of a novel* (2017), systematisiert hat den Befund Gisèle Sapiro in ihrer *Soziologie der Literatur* und zahlreichen weiteren Beiträgen und dabei die Dimensionen des literarischen Marktes vermessen (Childress; Sapiro 2014). Einzelne Buchtitel werden damit zum Ergebnis kollektiver Anstrengungen. Verlagsarchive dokumentieren all diese Prozesse in ihren Ablagen und fungieren hier gleichsam als „Knotenpunkte, an denen sich die an der Literaturproduktion und -zirkulation beteiligten Akteure und Institutionen in ihrer Interaktion beobachten und beschreiben lassen"

---

1 Vgl. die Podcast-Folgen aus dem Blog des DLA: blog.dla-marbach.de/2025/04/01/anja-seelinger-und-thierry-chervel-im-gespraech-folge-1/; https://blog.dla-marbach.de/2025/04/01/25-jahre-perlentaucher-anja-seelinger-und-thierry-chervel-im-gespraech-folge-2/.

(Kinder und Richter 2024b, 6–7). Verlagsarchive, die nicht nur, etwa in ihren Lektoratsakten, die literarische Arbeit am Text, sondern auch die Rahmenbedingungen dokumentieren, eröffnen damit die Möglichkeit, auch nach der wirtschaftlichen und politischen Verfasstheit von Literatur und der Rolle des weltweiten Rechte- und Lizenzhandels zu fragen. Die literatur- wie buchwissenschaftliche Forschung ist diesen Spuren in den letzten Jahren verstärkt nachgegangen, so in spezialisierten Einzeluntersuchungen zu einzelnen Akteur:innen des Literaturbetriebs oder zu einzelnen Phänomenen (vgl. Ajouri; Amslinger; Barner; Cottenet; Kinder und Richter 2024a; Nebrig; Norrick-Rühl und Razakamanantsoa; Sapiro 2015; Schmuck et al.; Sprengel). In der Natur von Verlagsarchiven liegt es dabei auch, dass sich der Radius immer auch ins Internationale und auf einen globalen Markt erstreckt, ist die internationale Vermarktung und Platzierung von Literatur doch genuines Interesse von Verlagen. Dies schlägt sich in der Vielsprachigkeit der Bestände nieder, die damit für die verschiedensten Philologien von Interesse sind und enormes Potential für eine globale Literatur- und Kulturgeschichte bieten (vgl. Kemper et al.; G. Müller; Sneis und Spoerhase 2023a, b, 2024).

(2) Lesespuren: Leserpsychologie, Textverstehensforschung und Literaturpolitologie

Lesespuren zählen seit jeher zu den großen Themen des DLA. Sie finden sich an unterschiedlichen Orten im Archiv: in den zahlreichen Autor:innen-, Gelehrten- und Sammler:innenbibliotheken, in Korrespondenzen von Autor:innen und in den beiden Marbacher Museen, dem Schiller Nationalmuseum und dem Literaturmuseum der Moderne, wo die Besuchenden nicht nur betrachten, sondern auch lesen. Diesen Spuren geht das DLA seit einigen Jahren in Kooperation mit dem Leibniz-Institut für Wissensmedien Tübingen (IWM) genauer nach. Die Verbindung von Ansätzen der Leserpsychologie und der Textverstehensforschung erweisen sich dabei als besonders ertragreich. In dem seit Januar 2024 laufenden Forschungsprojekt „»WR-AI-TING«: Kreatives Schreiben mit KI-Tools in Schul- und Museumskontexten", gefördert durch das Bundesministerium für Bildung und Forschung (BMBF), wird im Zusammenspiel von Literaturwissenschaft, Museumspädagogik, Schreibdidaktik, Kreativitätsforschung und Computerlinguistik untersucht, welche Rolle sprachliche KI im Kontext kultureller Bildungs- und künstlerisch-kreativer Prozesse spielen kann.[2]

---

[2] Vgl. dla-marbach.de/forschung/forschungsprojekte/wr-ai-ting/.

In den letzten Jahren hat insbesondere das wissenschaftliche Interesse an Autor:innenbibliotheken stark zugenommen, die Einblicke in die literarische Arbeitswerkstatt ermöglichen. Zu den meistbenutzten Autoren- und Gelehrtenbibliotheken im Deutschen Literaturarchiv Marbach gehören die Büchersammlungen von Gottfried Benn, Hans Blumenberg, Paul Celan, Ernst Jünger, Reinhart Koselleck, Siegfried Kracauer, Martin Heidegger, Hermann Hesse und W. G. Sebald. Zu den jüngsten Erwerbungen zählt die Bibliothek von Barbara Köhler, die zahlreiche autographe Lesespuren und Einlagen (Fotos, Briefe, Klebezettel u. a.) für die Forschung bereithält. Die umfangreiche und wachsende Sammlung eröffnet die Möglichkeit, poetische und wissenschaftliche Arbeitspraktiken des 20. und 21. Jahrhundert zu erforschen. Individuelle Provenienzexemplare mit ihren Lese- und Gebrauchsspuren erlauben gleichsam den Blick über die Schulter und geben Auskunft über Lese- und Schreibpraktiken, über Prozesse des „Auswählens, Wahrnehmens und Aufnehmens, des Verstehens, Erinnerns, (Wieder-)Erkennens, Vergleichens, Übertragens und des Um- oder Neu-Gestaltens" (Pott 192–193; vgl. ferner Jaspers und Kilcher; Jessen; Découltot und Zedelmaier). Produktiv gemacht wurden zudem Fragen einer literaturwissenschaftlichen Provenienzforschung, die den Blick auf die ›Herkünfte‹ und Wege von Handschriften, Büchern und Sammlungen richtet und die Zusammenhänge zwischen Handel, Sammlung und Forschung bei der Untersuchung ihres Gegenstandes einbezieht (vgl. Gaber, Höpfner und Hundehege).

(3) Literaturvertonungen: Audioanalyse der Literatur

In der Öffentlichkeit wenig bekannt, aber seit Jahrzehnten gepflegt ist der Bereich der auditiven Medien der Literatur im DLA. Dieser Sammelbereich umfasst aktuell 51.400 Hörfunk- und Fernsehmanuskripte literarischer Sendungen seit 1975 und 62.000 Audio- und Videomaterialien mit Dichterstimmen, Hörspielen, Literaturverfilmungen und -vertonungen (von der Schellackplatte bis zur Audiodatei). Hinzu kommt die Audiodatenbank dichterlesen.net, die Mitschnitte historischer und aktueller literarischer Veranstaltungen zum kostenfreien Anhören anbietet.

Die Sammlung bietet damit reichlich Potential für Forschungsvorhaben, die, nicht zuletzt angeregt durch die Sound Studies, die Aufmerksamkeit auf akustische Phänomene, also auf die unterschiedlichen Bedeutungen und Funktionen gesprochener und gesungener Stimme legen, als Gestaltungsmerkmal wie als Gegenstand von Literatur (vgl. Richter 2021). Das vorhandene Tonmaterial bietet hierfür eine reichhaltige empirische Basis, ebenso wie für die Untersuchung intermedialer und multimodaler Ausdrucksformen von Literatur. Die Materialien, von der Notenhandschrift bis zur Rezitation, eröffnen einen breiten Forschungshorizont und erlauben Einsichten a) in die Aura der Autorenstimme in ihrer Symbolfunktion oder in ihrer Zeugenschaft und in ihrem Verhältnis zum Text, b) in historische Formen des Deklamierens, der Artikulation und Modulierung, c) in die Medienspezifik von Tonaufnahmen, d) in das Verhältnis von Vertonung und Text (Akzent, Sprachmelodie, Rhythmus usf.) und e) in multimodale Kunstformen wie die Oper, das Kabarett oder in neuere Liedformen des ausgehenden 20. und frühen 21. Jahrhunderts (z. B. Neue Deutsche Welle, Rap). (Richter 2021, 313)

Im Rahmen des Projekts „textklang. Mixed-Methods-Analyse von Lyrik in Text und Ton" konnte die Frage nach der Beziehung zwischen literarischen Texten und der Interdependenz ihrer lautsprachlichen Realisierung bei Rezitation, gesungener Darbietung und musikalischer Aufführung exemplarisch ausgelotet werden (vgl. Richter et al.).

(4) Literaturdaten: Digitale Sammlungsforschung

Die digitalen Bestände des DLA, die in allen Bereichen des Archivs – in Form von digitalen Vor- und Nachlässen ebenso wie in unterschiedlichen Formen digitaler Literatur – stetig und schnell wachsen, sind Gegenstand digitaler Sammlungsforschung. Das DLA reagiert dabei auch auf die Bedeutung des Internets als (experimentellen) Publikationsraum. Das Projekt „Netzliteratur" hat 2013 die Sammlung „Literatur im Netz" durch den Aufbau eines in technischer und ästhetischer Hinsicht typologisch beispielhaften Grundstocks an Quellen ausgebaut.[3] Fortgesetzt wurde die Arbeit im Rahmen des Forschungsverbunds Marbach Weimar Wolfenbüttel, der seit 2019 in der zweiten Phase durch das Bundesministerium für Bildung und Forschung gefördert wurde, im Science Data Center for Literature wie auch im Konsortium Text +.[4] Aus Literaturkreisläufen werden hier Literaturdatenkreisläufe. Dabei gilt es zum einen, die Datenqualität des aufgenommenen Materials durch entsprechend gründliche Sacherschließung sicherzustellen, zum anderen aber auch, die ‚datafication' der Literatur für die Forschung zu nutzen. Einzelne Fallstudien, insbesondere zum digitalen literarischen Medium Computerspiel und zu digitalen Autorennachlässen, sondierten Praxis und Reflexion digitaler Schreib-, Speicher-, Sammlungs-, Ordnungs- und Auswertungsarbeit (vgl. Çakir und Holz). Seit 2024 wird die Sammlung um soziale Medien, Podcasts, Autorenhomepages, digitale Feuilleton und das Genre Fanfiction erweitert. Die Herausforderungen, die sich mit dem Eintritt ins digitale Zeitalter und dem damit verbundenen

---

3 Vgl. https://www.dla-marbach.de/bibliothek/projekte/aufbau-eines-quellencorpus-fuer-die-seit-den-1990er-jahren-entstehende-literaturgattung-netzliteratur/.
4 Vgl. mww-forschung.de/; sdc4lit.de/; text-plus.org.

Medienwandel für das Archivieren von Gegenwartsliteratur ergeben, können exemplarisch anhand von Verlagsarchiven veranschaulicht werden, hat sich doch auch die Verlagsarbeit in den letzten Jahrzehnten rapide verändert. Auf der Produktions- wie auf der Rezeptionsseite kommen nach und nach neue Technologien zum Einsatz, die die Art und Weise, wie Literatur entsteht, vermarktet, rezipiert und archiviert wird, verändern. Autor:innen, Verleger:innen, Lektor:innen und Übersetzer:innen kommen über E-Mails, SMS und Kurznachrichtendienste in Kontakt. Die Textproduktion durch Autor:innen, Lektorat und Herstellung verläuft mitunter simultan vermittels webbasierter Software und kollektiver Produktionsplattformen, wobei digitale Produktions- und Rezeptionsmöglichkeiten (z. B. Social Media Plattformen, Blogs) das Schreiben beeinflussen; Pressearbeit und Vertrieb sind durch die sozialen Medien, Rezensions- und Marketingportale wie Goodreads und durch heterogene Vertriebsplattformen mit Leserbewertungen und stetigen Buchrankings einer gravierenden Umwälzung unterworfen (vgl. Kinder et al.). Mit der zunehmenden Umstellung aller Prozesse ins Digitale kommt diese Ablagepraxis an ihre Grenzen, im Verlag ebenso wie im Archiv. Seit 2000 ist die Geschichte des Verlegens in Deutschland bislang nur fragmentarisch erforscht, und zwar nur, insofern bestimmte digitale Formate wie Rezensions- und Marketingportale oder Vertriebsplattformen, Social-Media-Kommunikationen und konventionelle Zeitschriftenartikel zugänglich sind. Der Grund für die erhebliche Forschungslücke liegt nur zum kleineren Teil an rechtlichen Schwierigkeiten. Stärker ins Gewicht fällt der Umstand, dass der Medienwandel zu Lücken in den Sammlungen und einem Mangel, der noch stark am Analogen orientierten Erschließung und Zugänglichmachung geführt hat. Gegenwärtig bemühen sich sammelnde Einrichtungen, teils in enger Absprache mit Verlagshäusern, hier Abhilfe zu schaffen und Prozesse für eine verlässliche Langzeitarchivierung zu entwickeln.

(5) Schreibwerkzeuge, Literaturträger und literarische Objekte: Materiale Hermeneutik

Das DLA beherbergt Literatur in ihren unterschiedlichen materiellen Produktions- und Darbietungsformen, gegenwärtig über 450.000 bildliche und gegenständliche Sammlungsstücke seit 1750 sowie die größte Porträtsammlung zur deutschen Literatur- und Geistesgeschichte seit dem 18. Jahrhundert mit Schwerpunkt auf den Künstlern des württembergischen Klassizismus und der Klassischen Moderne. Die Sammlung umfasst Skulpturen (Büsten, Statuetten und Reliefs), Totenmasken, Gemälde und Miniaturen, Zeichnungen, Druckgraphiken und Scherenschnitte, Fotografien, Plakate, historische Buchumschläge sowie verschiedenste Erinnerungsstücke (u. a. Schreibgeräte, Möbel, Porzellan, Textilien). Einen besonders umfangreichen Sammlungsschwerpunkt stellen Fotokonvolute und Alben aus Schriftsteller:innennachlässen und Verlagsarchiven mit mehr als 360.000 Einzelfotografien dar.

Diese Objekte lassen sich mit Hilfe der Material Studies als eigenständige Objekte beschreiben und erforschen. Das besondere Potenzial des Archivs liegt dabei darin, sie zugleich mit den Autor:innen und den literarischen Werken, auf die sie sich beziehen, in Verbindung zu bringen, sodass sich Objekt und Literatur wechselseitig erhellen. Seit 2024 kooperiert das DLA im Rahmen dieser Forschungslinie mit dem Exzellenzcluster „Understanding Written Artefacts" an der Universität Hamburg. Desiderat sind neue Erschließungs- und Forschungsprojekte und virtuelle Forschungsräume zu bestimmten Objektgruppen (z. B. Schreibgeräte, Buchumschlagsentwürfe oder Totenmasken).

III

Für die Erforschung der Literatur ab etwa 1990 ergibt sich mit den Beständen des DLA eine besonders reizvolle Ausgangssituation, kann doch die Forschung nicht nur auf einen großen Fundus an Vor- und Nachlässen, Verlags- und Redaktionsarchiven zurückgreifen, sondern durch die eigenen Forschungsinteressen und -ergebnisse auch einen aktiven Beitrag zur Diskussion um das, was künftig ins Archiv wandern soll, leisten. Relevanzabschätzungen und Valorisierungsfragen gilt es im internationalen und interdisziplinären Dialog auszuloten und damit das Potential von Sammlungen – analog wie digital – unter Beweis zu stellen.

Literaturverzeichnis

Ajouri, Philip, Hg. *Die Präsentation kanonischer Werke um 1900. Semantiken, Praktiken, Materialität.* De Gruyter, 2017.
Amslinger, Tobias. *Verlagsautorschaft. Enzensberger und Suhrkamp.* Wallstein, 2018.
Barner, Ines. *Von anderer Hand. Praktiken des Schreibens zwischen Autor und Lektor.* Wallstein, 2021.
Bendt, Jutta, Hg. *Netzliteratur im Archiv. Erfahrungen und Perspektiven.* Wallstein, 2017.
Bürger, Jan, et al., Hg. *Verlagsarchive im Deutschen Literaturarchiv. Sammeln und Forschen.* Deutsche Schillergesellschaft, 2024.
Çakir, Dîlan C. „Überlegungen zu Born-digitals-Beständen von Gamesautor:innen im Deutschen Literaturarchiv Marbach". *Sammlungsforschung im digitalen Zeitalter. Chancen, Herausforderungen und Grenzen.* Hg. von Katharina Günther und Stefan Alscher. Wallstein, 2024, S. 43–54.
Çakir, Dîlan C. und Alex Holz. „Born-Digital Data and Literature Archives". *Articulations. Peer-reviewed articles on „Temporal Communities"*, 2024, articulations.temporal-communities.de/contributions/born-digital-data/. 31. März 2025.

Çakir, Dîlan C., Anna Kinder und Sandra Richter. „Computerspiele und Literatur. Schnittmengen, Unterschiede und offene Fragen". *Text+Kritk. Sonderband: Digitale Literatur II*. Hg. von Hannes Bajohr und Annette Gilbert. Edition Text+Kritik, 2021, S. 77–88.

Childress, Clayton. *Under the Cover. The creation, production and reception of a novel*. Princeton/Oxford UP, 2017.

Cottenet, Cécile. *Literary agents in the transatlantic book trade. American fiction, French rights, and the Hoffman Agency*. Routledge, 2017.

Décultot, Elisabeth und Helmut Zedelmaier, Hg. *Exzerpt, Plagiat, Archiv. Untersuchungen zur neuzeitlichen Schriftkultur*. Mitteldeutscher Verlag, 2017.

Deutsche Schillergesellschaft. „Satzung der Deutschen Schillergesellschaft (DSG)". *Deutsches Literaturarchiv Marbach*, dla-marbach.de/fileadmin/redaktion/Ueber_uns/DSG/Satzung_DSG_Stand_2018.pdf. 28. März 2025. 31. März 2025.

Engelmeier, Hanna. „Selbsteinlieferung oder: Vorlass nach Marbach!". *Merkur* 830 (2018): S. 33–46.

Eschenbach, Gunilla, Hg. *Singen! Literatur und Lied*. Deutsche Schillergesellschaft, 2023.

Gaber, Sarah, Stefan Höpfner und Stefanie Hundehege, Hg. *Provenienz: Materialgeschichte(n) der Literatur*. Wallstein, 2024.

Goethe, Johann Wolfang von. „Archiv des Dichters und Schriftstellers [1823]". *Goethes Werke, hg. im Auftrag der Großherzogin Sophie von Sachsen. Weimar 1903. Fotomechanischer Nachdruck der Ausgabe*. Abt. I, Bd. 41.2. Deutscher Taschenbuch Verlag, 1987, S. 25–28.

Grond-Rigler, Christine. „Im Dialog mit der Nachwelt. Auktoriale Inszenierung in Vorlässen". *Archive für Literatur. Der Nachlass und seine Ordnungen*. Hg. von Petra-Maria Dallinger, Georg Hofer und Bernhard Judex. De Gruyter, 2018. S. 163–179. doi.org/ 9783110594188-011.

Gunser, Vivian Emily, et al. „The Pure Poet: How good is the subjective credibility and stylistic quality of literary short texts written with an artificial intelligence tool as compared to texts written by human authors?" *Proceedings of the Annual Meeting of the Cognitive Science Society* 44 (2022): S. 1744–1750.

Jaspers, Anke und Andreas Kilcher, Hg. *Randkulturen. Lese- und Gebrauchsspuren in Autorenbibliotheken des 19. und 20. Jahrhunderts*. Wallstein, 2020.

Jessen, Caroline. „Die Autorenbibliothek als Bestand. oder: Vom spielerischen Umgang mit einer heuristisch problematischen Kategorie". *Zeitschrift für Bibliothekswesen und Bibliographie* 68.1 (2021): S. 10–19.

Kemper, Dirk, Paweł Zajas und Natalia Bakshi, Hg. *Kulturtransfer und Verlagsarbeit. Suhrkamp und Osteuropa*. Wilhelm Fink, 2019.

Kinder, Anna, et al. „Verlagsarchive und Digitalisierung". *Handbuch Verlag. Geschichte – Aufgaben – Perspektive*. Hg. von Alexander Nebrig, Corinna Norrick-Rühl und Erika Thomalla. Springer, 2025 [im Druck].

Kinder, Anna und Sandra Richter. „Literatursoziologie der Übersetzung. Übersetzernachlässe und Mehrfeldertheorie". *Übersetzungen im Archiv. Potenziale und Perspektiven*. Hg. von Lydia Schmuck et al. Wallstein, 2024a. S. 17–25.

Kinder, Anna und Sandra Richter. „Wie Literatur entsteht. Der Blick hinter die Kulissen". *Verlagsarchive im Deutschen Literaturarchiv. Sammeln und Forschen*. Hg. von Jan Bürger et al. Deutsche Schillergesellschaft, 2024b. S. 4–11.

Möring, Sebastian. „Why collect computer games in a literary archive of the future?". *The Literature Archive of the Future. Statements and Perspectives*. Hg. von Sandra Richter. Wallstein, 2023. S. 37–42.

Müller, Gesine. „Die Konstruktion von Weltliteratur und Verlagspolitiken. Der Lateinamerika-Nachlass des Suhrkamp Verlags". *Buchmarkt, Buchindustrie und Buchmessen in Deutschland, Spanien und Lateinamerika*. Hg. von Mario Bossard. LIT Verlag, 2015. S. 147–160.

Müller, Marie Yvonne. „Überall Mäuse. Zur Tagung ‚Comic und Graphic Novel. Erzählen in Bildern'". *Deutsches Literaturarchiv Marbach*, blog.dla-marbach.de/2024/12/09/zur-tagung-comic-und-graphic-novel-erzaehlen-in-bildern/. 31. März 2025.

Nebrig, Alexander. *Für alle Länder. Deutsche Literatur im interlingualen Lizenzraum*. Springer, 2025.

Norrick-Rühl, Corinna und Miaïna Razakamanantsoa. „‚Your eyes and ears on this side of the ocean'. Complicating S. J. Greenburger's Role as Literary Scout and US Representative for Rowohlt Verlag in the 1960s". *Authorship* 11.1 (2022): doi.org/10.21825/authorship.85418.

Pott [Richter], Sandra. „Lesen, poetisches Lesen und poetischer Text. Rainer Maria Rilkes Auseinandersetzung mit Oswald Spenglers Untergang des Abendlandes (I, 1918)". *IASL* 30.1 (2005): S. 188–213.

Richter, Sandra. „Die Literatur und ihre Stimmen. Einleitung". *Jahrbuch der Deutschen Schillergesellschaft* 65 (2021): S. 311–314.

Richter, Sandra. „The Archive Paradox, or: How to Archive Disruptive Energy. Nine Hypotheses About Literature in a Literature Archive". *The Literature Archive of the Future. Statements and Perspectives*. Hg. von Sandra Richter. Wallstein, 2023a. S. 7–12.

Richter, Sandra, et al. „Der Klang der Lyrik. Zur Konzeptualisierung von Sprecher und Stimme, auch für die computationelle Analyse". *Poema. Jahrbuch für Lyrikforschung/Annual for the Study of Lyric Poetry/La recherche annuelle en poésie lyrique* 1 (2023b): S. 39–51, 2023. doi.org/10.38072/2751-9821/p4.

Rohleder, Daniela. „‚Lest ihr noch oder schreibt ihr schon?' Fanfiction im Archiv. Workshop im DLA." *Deutsches Literaturarchiv Marbach*, blog.dla-marbach.de/2025/03/31/fanfiction-im-archiv/. 31. März 2025.

Sapiro, Gisèle. *La sociologie de la littérature*. La Découverte, 2014.

Sapiro, Gisèle. „Translation and Symbolic Capital in the Era of Globalization. French Literature in the United States". *Cultural Sociology* 9.3 (2015): S. 320–346.

Schmuck, Lydia, et al., Hg. *Übersetzungen im Archiv. Potenziale und Perspektiven*. Wallstein, 2024.

Sneis, Jørgen und Carlos Spoerhase, Hg. „The Consecrating Power of the Nobel Prize in the Global Literary Field". *Special issue of Poetics* 100.101 (2023a).

Sneis, Jørgen und Carlos Spoerhase, Hg. „World Literature in the Nobel Era". *Special issue of the Journal of World Literature* 8.4 (2023b).

Sneis, Jørgen und Carlos Spoerhase, Hg. „World Literature in the Nobel Era – Part II". *Special issue of the Journal of World Literature* 9.1 (2024).

Sprengel, Marja Christine. *Der Lektor und sein Autor. Vergleichende Fallstudien zum Suhrkamp Verlag*. Harrassowitz, 2016.

Spoerhase, Carlos und Kai Sina, Hg. *Nachlassbewusstsein. Literatur, Archiv, Philologie 1750–2000*. Wallstein, 2017.

Spoerhase, Carlos. „Neuzeitliches Nachlassbewusstsein. Über die Entstehung eines schriftstellerischen, archivarischen und philologischen Interesses an postumen Papieren". *Nachlassbewusstsein. Literatur, Archiv, Philologie 1750–2000*. Hg. von Carlos Spoerhase und Kai Sina. Wallstein, 2017. S. 21–48.

Zajas, Paweł. *Verlagspraxis und Kulturpolitik. Beiträge zur Soziologie des Literatursystems*. Wilhelm Fink, 2019.

I **Schwerpunkt/Focus: Graphic Novels**

Andreas Platthaus
Durchsetzungsvermögen
Wie der Begriff „Graphic Novel" das Verständnis von Comics verändert hat

Abstract: Der Beitrag diskutiert Aspekte der Gattung im US-amerikanischen und im deutschsprachigen Kontext unter besonderer Berücksichtigung der so unterschiedlich konnotierten Gattungsbezeichnungen „Comic" und „Graphic Novel". Während sich in den USA der Begriff „Graphic Novel" durch die Initiative des Comicautors Will Eisner schon seit Ende der 1970er Jahre für anspruchsvollere Comics durchzusetzen begann, etablierten eine Reihe deutscher Comicverlage erst vor gut 15 Jahren den (englischen) Begriff „Graphic Novel", was zu einer Aufwertung der Gattung und einer breiteren Vermarktung führte. Außerdem stellt der Beitrag eine Reihe besonders erfolgreicher und künstlerisch innovativer Graphic Novels aus unterschiedlichen sprachlichen und kulturellen Kontexten vor; eine Experimentierfreudigkeit, so die These, die nicht zuletzt durch den Marketingbegriff „Graphic Novel" angeregt wird.

Heute ist alles Graphic Novel, was als Comic Anspruch für sich in Anspruch nehmen will. Der Siegeszug dieser Bezeichnung ist bemerkenswert, vor allem wenn man bedenkt, dass sie in Deutschland erst seit etwas mehr als fünfzehn Jahren etabliert ist. Und dass sie hierzulande als reiner Marketingbegriff begann: gedacht zur Imageverbesserung für einen anderen Anglizismus, eben die „Comics", in denen auf Deutsch noch mehr als im Englischen das Komische anklingt (die zu Beginn des zwanzigsten Jahrhunderts in den Vereinigten Staaten noch allgemein gängige Rede von *funnies* statt *comics* verlor sich in den dreißiger Jahren, als die amerikanischen Zeitungen vermehrt Abenteuergeschichten als Comic Strips druckten, und die sich dann erst durchsetzende Bezeichnung „Comics" ging auf die Selbsttitulierung britischer Karikaturenblätter des neunzehnten Jahrhunderts zurück, hatte also eine ernsthaftere Konnotation als „Funnies"). Es war in gewisser Weise Pech, dass mit der Nachkriegspopularität amerikanischer Comics in Deutschland die vorher übliche Gattungsbezeichnung „Bildergeschichte" verloren ging, weil der englische Terminus moderner klang. In der NS-Zeit war das Wort „Comics" noch als Kampfbegriff eingesetzt worden, um die Minderwertigkeit der in den Vereinigten Staaten populären Erzählform gegenüber der deutschen Bildergeschichtentradition zu belegen: Was schon so „komisch" klang, musste doch Ernsthaftigkeit und damit deutsche Tiefe vermissen lassen. Die terminologische Gegenentwicklung in den fünfziger Jahren war dann auch eine Entnazifizierung der Sprache, doch sie bürdete dem nun positiv gemeinten Begriff „Comic" nolens volens den alten pejorativen Beiklang mit auf. Was schon so „komisch" klang, musste man doch wohl immer noch nicht ernst nehmen.

Um gegen dieses hartnäckige Vorurteil anzukämpfen, setzten deutschsprachige Comicverlage vor anderthalb Jahrzehnten in enger Absprache miteinander eine andere Bezeichnung für ihre Publikationen im Buchhandel durch: Graphic Novel. Bezeichnenderweise waren dabei die treibenden Kräfte jene Unternehmen, die sich schon lange bemüht hatten, den Leserkreis für Comics zu erweitern: hin zu Erwachsenen. 2009 brachte der schon ein halbes Jahrhundert alte Carlsen Verlag gemeinsam mit den deutlich jüngeren Kleinverlagen Avant, Cross Cult, Edition 52, Edition Moderne und Reprodukt ein Faltblatt heraus, für das einer der damals erfolgreichsten jüngeren deutschen Zeichner, Sascha Hommer, einen kurzen Comic anfertigte, der den Begriff „Graphic Novel" vorstellte. Der Text dieser illustrierten Erläuterung hob so an: „Graphic Novels sind Comics mit Themen, die sich nicht mehr nur an Kinder und Jugendliche, sondern an erwachsene Leser richten." Interessant an dieser Formulierung war einmal der Verzicht auf das eigentlich logisch notwendige Wort „auch" im letzten Satzteil, denn während zuvor noch davon die Rede war, dass „nicht nur" jüngere Leser als Publikum angestrebt seien, wurden plötzlich nur noch Erwachsene als Zielgruppe definiert. Und außerdem interessant war die Wahl des neutralen Begriffs „Themen" bei der inhaltlichen Beschreibung. Damit konnten Graphic Novels alle Stoffe umfassen, insofern sie nur „erwachsen" genug waren. Die klare Einschränkung der englischen Bezeichnung, die mit der Wortwahl *novels* nur auf fiktive Handlungen abstellte, wurde im deutschen Imagefaltblatt von 2009 bewusst ausgeblendet.

Es ist dieses hiesige trennunscharfe Verständnis von Graphic Novels, das bis heute die Verständigung darüber erschwert, was denn überhaupt als eine solche zu gelten habe. Doch gleichzeitig ist es auch die Ursache für den immensen Erfolg, den der neu etablierte Begriff auf dem deutschen Buchmarkt verzeichnen darf. Je schwammiger eine Bezeichnung ist, desto mehr kann man darunter fassen, und wenn sie dann erst einmal bei den Käufern positiv besetzt ist, profitieren davon auch Produkte, die im strengen Sinne gar nicht dazugezählt werden dürften.

Als da wären autobiographische Comics (die im Englischen mittlerweile als *graphic memoir* bezeichnet werden), Sachcomics (*graphic non fiction*) oder Reportagecomics (*graphic journalism*). All das wird im deutschen Sprachraum einheitlich als Graphic Novel, also wörtlich übersetzt „gezeichneter Roman", bezeichnet. Dass dadurch die inhaltliche Analyse erschwert wird, liegt auf der Hand – was dem kommerziellen Aspekt keinen Abbruch tut. Unter Graphic Novels werden hierzulande auch autobiographische Comics wie Art Spiegelmans *Maus* eingereiht oder die Reisebeschreibungen von Guy Delisle, die jeweils schon im Titel als Chroniken ausgewiesen sind. Ho Che Andersons Comic-Biographie von Martin Luther King, Will Bingleys und Anthony Hope-Smiths Comic-Lebensbeschreibung des Schriftstellers Hunter S. Thompson oder Sid Jacobsens und Ernie Colóns gezeichnetes *Leben von Anne Frank* dienen als Beispiele für Graphic Novels, obwohl die jeweiligen Verlage sie klugerweise als „grafische Biografien" bezeichnen. Und was ist mit Jacobsens und Colóns *9/11 Report*, einem Sachbuch in Comicform, das trotzdem als Graphic Novel gilt? Der Fiktionszwang, der in der Genrebezeichnung „Novel" zu stecken hätte, ist aufgehoben. Die Werbewirksamkeit des Begriffs für das, was als „Comic" im Verständnis vieler Menschen als leichtgewichtig gilt, ist zu verlockend für Presseabteilungen, Buchhändler und nicht zuletzt auch für die Leser selbst. Ehre, wem Ehre gebührt: Sie schauen sich nun keine Comics mehr an, sie lesen Graphic Novels.

Dadurch wurde das Gefühl vermittelt, man hätte es hier mit einer neuen Qualität, wenn nicht gar einer ganz neuen Erzählform zu tun, und plötzlich öffnete sich der deutschsprachige Buchhandel für Comics. Zuvor waren diese vor allem Kioskware, von wenigen Ausnahmen wie *Tim und Struppi* (des Klassikerstatus wegen) und *Asterix* (der Absatzzahlen wegen) abgesehen. Und natürlich mit der Ausnahme von Spiegelmans *Maus*, dessen erster Teil 1989 bei Rowohlt herausgekommen war und nicht nur deshalb einen Durchbruch für Comics im deutschen Buchhandel bedeutete, weil sich damit ein hochangesehener literarischer Verlag auf diesem Gebiet betätigte – das hatte Rowohlt schon zuvor mit Comics von Ralf König und Keiji Nakazawa getan und zwar auch bereits mehr (König) oder minder (Nakazawa) erfolgreich abseits des Kioskvertriebs –, sondern weil bei Spiegelmans Comic eine Assoziation mit Komik unmöglich war, ja geradezu frivol wirken musste. Es ist eine der pikanten Pointen der Comicgeschichte, dass *Maus* heute als Inbegriff dessen gilt, was eine Graphic Novel ausmacht, ihr Autor diese Bezeichnung aber vehement ablehnt, weil er sein Werk in die von ihm bewunderte Traditionslinie der Comics gestellt sehen will und jede andere Titulierung als bloße Bedeutungshuberei ablehnt.

Etabliert hat den Begriff „Graphic Novel" allerdings jemand, dem auch Spiegelman seinen Respekt nicht verweigert: ein anderer Großmeister des amerikanischen Comics, der Zeichner Will Eisner. Wobei schon dessen gängige Einordnung als Zeichner etwas berührt, was für die Entstehungsbedingungen der Bezeichnung „Graphic Novel" wichtig war. Eisner hatte tatsächlich in seinen Anfangsjahren vorrangig als Zeichner gearbeitet, weil in den „Shops" oder „Studios" genannten Arbeitsgemeinschaften der dreißiger und vierziger Jahre, als sich in den Vereinigten Staaten mit dem Aufkommen von Comic-Heften die serielle Produktion von dafür benötigten Geschichten durchsetzte, das organisatorische Prinzip einer strikten Arbeitsteilung galt. Es gab Autoren, die lediglich Szenarios, also die Handlungen von Comics, verfassten, dann Zeichner, die diese Vorlagen in Bilder umsetzten und zwar in abgestuften Funktionen wie Vorzeichner, Tuschezeichner und Schriftenzeichner, gegebenenfalls auch noch Kolorist, wobei diese Aufzählung eine absteigende Hierarchie beschreibt. Eisner war in seinem Studio, das er 1936 als Neunzehnjähriger gemeinsam mit Jerry Iger gegründet hatte, der Vor-, also auch der Chefzeichner. Erst später begann er, auch selbst Szenarios zu verfassen, und als er lange nach der Auflösung des Studios und einer daran anschließenden Karriere als Auftragsillustrator von Comics in den siebziger Jahren wieder eigene Geschichten anfertigte, tat er es schließlich vollständig allein – als Autor im literarischen Verständnis der Berufsbezeichnung, dem also die komplette Ausfertigung eines Textes von der Idee bis zur letztgültigen Formulierung obliegt. Der erste Band dieser Eisnerschen „Autorencomics" erschien 1978. Er hieß *A Contract With God and Other Tenement Stories*, und diese Mietshausgeschichten, die auf Eisners eigene Jugenderlebnisse in der New Yorker Bronx zurückgingen, also eigentlich eine Erzählungssammlung, trugen als Genrebezeichnung „A Graphic Novel by Will Eisner". Danach war dieser Begriff in aller Munde.

Allerdings hatte ihn Eisner erst in die Paperback-Ausgabe seines Buchs einfügen lassen; die gebundene Erstausgabe verzichtete noch auf ihn. Die Gründe für diese Ergänzung sind unbekannt, doch es spricht einiges dafür, dass die überaus positive Aufnahme von *A Contract With God* bei Kritik und Lesern den Verfasser in seiner Annahme bestätigte, es sei nun endlich der Moment für anspruchsvolle Comic-Erzählungen gekommen, und da Eisner zeit seines Lebens für die künstlerische Anerkennung der eigenen Profession stritt, bediente er sich eines Begriffs, der das, was er tat, auf bewusst sachliche Weise und einigermaßen abstrakt beschrieb: Die Rede von „graphischen Romanen" legt auch im Englischen das jeweilige Werk weniger fest, als es die Bezeichnung als „Comic" täte; zumal seit den fünfziger Jahren ein erbitterter Streit in den Vereinigten Staaten darüber ausgetragen worden war, ob Comics die Jugend verderben könnten. Für Romane war das nicht zu befürchten, selbst wenn es sich um gezeichnete handelte.

Will Eisner hat aber die Bezeichnung „Graphic Novel" nicht erfunden; ihr erster Gebrauch ist zwei Jahre vor *A Contract With God* nachgewiesen und zwar unabhängig voneinander bei gleich drei amerikanischen Comicpublikationen, die von Zeichnern stammten, die kaum geeignet waren, ein Bildungsbürgertum vom Reiz ihrer jeweiligen Bücher zu überzeugen: dem Fantasyzeichner Richard Corben, der für „Bloodstar" eine Pulp-Geschichte aus der Zwischenkriegszeit adaptierte, dem Undergroundzeichner George Metzger, der für *Beyond Time and Again* eine surreale Erzählweise gewählt hatte, und dem Superheldenzeichner Jim Steranko, der mit *Chandler* einen Hard-Boiled-Krimi illustrierte. Aber da es sich dabei jeweils nicht um Comics nach gängigem Schema handelte, die sich an ein minderjähriges Publikum gerichtet hätten, wurden sie von den Verlagen als „Graphic Novels" beschrieben – in der Hoffnung, damit die angestrebte erwachsene Leserschaft zu ködern. Aber erst Eisners *Contract With God* flößte dieser Zielgruppe so viel Achtung ein, dass der Neologismus sich an breiter Front durchsetzte: weil er in diesem Fall tatsächlich etwas Neuartiges bezeichnete.

In seinen später erschienenen theoretischen Analysen des eigenen Metiers, *Comics and the Sequential Art* und *Graphic Storytelling*, verwendete Eisner den neuen Terminus dann konsequent als Oberbegriff für alle Geschichten, die Texte mit gezeichneten Bildern kombinierten; wortlose Bildgeschichten wie etwa die des Belgiers Frans Masereel aus den zwanziger Jahren galten ihm als „totally graphic story". Die Rede von *novel* nahm Eisner also sehr ernst; nicht eine romanhafte Erzählweise, sondern die Form des Romans selbst als geschriebener Text war für sein Verständnis einer Graphic Novel entscheidend.

Noch wichtiger aber war die unausgesprochene Erwartung, dass sich eine Graphic Novel genau wie ein normaler Roman nicht in vorgegebene kommerzielle Muster pressen ließe. Denn das war die Grunderfahrung amerikanischer Comicautoren: strenge Vorgaben betreffs Format und Umfang ohne jeden eigenen Entscheidungsspielraum. Ein Heft als die seit dem Zweiten Weltkrieg gängige Publikationsform von Comics hatte 32 Seiten und ein genormtes Format; beides schränkte die Freiheit des Erzählens massiv ein. Eisner verband mit der Rede von „Graphic Novel" eine Emanzipation von diesen vertriebstechnischen Beschränkungen: Ein *graphic novelist* sollte sich wie ein klassischer Romanautor jeweils den Raum nehmen, den er für seine Geschichte brauchte. In diesem Sinne waren allerdings schon etliche Graphic Novels erschienen, bevor *A Contract With God* herauskam; für Europa wird dabei immer wieder *Die Südseeballade* genannt, die der italienische Comicautor Hugo Pratt zwar als Fortsetzungsgeschichte in standardisierten Heften vorabdrucken ließ, aber in so vielen Kapiteln anlegte, dass schließlich eine mehr als hundertsechzigseitige Publikation dabei herauskam, die alle Maßstäbe sprengte, die bis dahin für einzelne Comicalben gegolten hatten. Eisners erste Graphic Novel erreichte dann einen ähnlichen Umfang und wurde zudem in einem Format gedruckt, das aus dem üblichen Schema von Heften und Alben herausfiel: Er strebte ein klassisches Romanformat an und legte deshalb seine Seiten kleiner an, als es sonst üblich war. Zugleich vergrößerte er die Einzelbilder, so dass *A Contract With God* aus weitaus weniger Panels bestand, als man gemeinhin erwarten sollte. Aber auch Erzählrhythmus und Seitenarchitektur unterlagen in Eisners Vorstellung ausschließlich den Bedürfnissen der Geschichte, nicht den Vertriebsüberlegungen eines Verlags oder gar den Lesegewohnheiten des Publikums.

Interessieren soll uns fortan also weniger, was Graphic Novels inhaltlich von anderen Comics unterscheidet, denn nahezu alle gängigen Erzählformen waren auch unter den Bedingungen strikter formaler Festlegung schon aufgetaucht, ehe man von Graphic Novels sprach – man sehe sich nur die Comics von Autoren wie Pratt, André Franquin oder Carl Barks an (um nur die brillantesten und vielseitigsten Erzähler zu nennen). Oder das, was Alan Moore im klassischen Superheldenheftformat mit *Swamp Thing*, *Watchman* oder *Promethea* geleistet hat, nachdem man längst von Graphic Novels sprach.

Freiheit sollte für einen Comicautor nach dem Willen Eisners natürlich auch in der Frage von Farbigkeit bestehen – nicht umsonst legte er *A Contract With God* gegen alle Erwartungen des amerikanischen Comicmarkts der siebziger Jahre schwarzweiß an. Er wollte damit gerade jene Authentizität beschwören, die von historischen Schwarzweißaufnahmen ausging, denn es handelte sich bei den Geschichten des Bandes ja um eine Dokumentation der eigenen Jugendeindrücke. Auch diese Eisnersche Forderung nach Entscheidungsfreiheit beim Kolorieren – undenkbar in den ersten acht Jahrzehnten des Comicgeschäfts – ist mittlerweile durchgesetzt. Gerade weil er selbst in seiner ersten Graphic Novel so konsequent gegen alle Vorstellungen eines normalen Comics verstieß, setzte sich ja deren Gattungsbezeichnung durch: als Sammelbegriff für Comics, denen die Individualität ihrer Schöpfer nicht nur an der Graphik und Inhalt, sondern an allen Entscheidungen formaler Art abzulesen waren.

Je selbstbewusster die Autoren wurden, desto genauer achteten sie etwa auf drucktechnische Details. Ein Musterbeispiel dafür ist die 2009 erschienene Graphic Novel *Asterios Polyp* von David Mazzucchelli. Der Amerikaner schrieb nicht nur allen fremdsprachigen Verlegern vor, dass sie seinen Band in derselben Ausstattung (vom Halbleineneinband über die Blindprägung des Buchdeckels bis zur Verwendung von Recyclingpapier) wie die Originalausgabe zu drucken hatten – er machte auch die Verwendung seines eigenen Schriftfonts zur Pflicht. Dass sich dadurch exorbitante Herausforderungen an die Übersetzer stellten, die ja die Sprechblasen adäquat zu füllen hatten, also diese weder überfüllen noch zu leer lassen durften, ohne dabei aber den Gehalt des Textes verändern zu können, das zeigt einmal mehr die für den Comic konstitutive Untrennbarkeit von Form und Inhalt. Bei einem übersetzten Roman macht es nichts, wenn in der deutschen Fassung gegenüber der Originalausgabe ein paar Seiten mehr herauskommen; bei einer Graphic Novel dagegen ist der Umfang des Buchs durch die Zahl gezeichneter Seiten festgelegt, von der Größe der Sprechblasen gar nicht zu reden.

Ein anderes, jüngeres Beispiel für solche Herausforderungen ist die international erfolgreichste Graphic Novel einer deutschen Künstlerin: *Heimat* von Nora Krug (die allerdings in New York City lebt und auch die amerikanische Staatsbürgerschaft besitzt), erschienen 2018. Untertitelt als „Ein deutsches Familienalbum", erschien der Band zuerst auf Englisch als *Belonging*, und Krug hatte ihn auch auf Englisch konzipiert, weshalb die deutsche Übersetzung erst später entstand. Da der Band Comic- und Bilderbuchelemente kombiniert, stellte er unterschiedliche Anforderungen an die Gestaltung der übersetzten Textpassagen: Beschränkung auf Sprechblasen und Textkästen in den – weniger zahlreichen – Comicsequenzen und Einpassung in die Freiräume rund um die Illustrationen auf den Bilderbuchseiten. Dazu kamen aber auch noch in die Erzählung integrierte in möglichst authentischer Gestalt wiedergegebene Familiendokumente, die für die Originalausgabe ins Englische gebracht worden waren und nun wiederum als deutschsprachige Faksimiles Aufnahme fanden. Man sieht: Die Übersetzung von Graphic Novels hält besondere Herausforderungen bereit. Dem Siegeszug von *Heimat*, das außer auf Englisch und Deutsch noch in einem Dutzend weiterer Sprachen erschienen ist, tat das keinen Abbruch, und auch Nora Krugs Nachfolgebände, die von ihr illustrierte Ausgabe von Timothy Snyders Essay „On Tyranny" (deutsch „Über Tyrannei") und „Diaries of War" („Im Krieg"), für den sie die von ihr angeregten Tagebuchaufzeichnungen eines Russen und einer Ukrainerin nebeneinander in Bilder setzte, fanden international große Beachtung. Mit ihnen hat man angesichts der illustrativen Freiheiten, die die (Bilder-)Autorin sich dabei nimmt, und des klaren Übergewichts der Texte Beispiele für Graphic Novels, bei denen man nicht notwendig von Comics sprechen müsste. Die Übersetzung ist hier nicht allein eine sprachliche, sondern auch eine gestalterische Herausforderung, die sich bei jedem Schriftsystem anders beantworten lassen muss.

Genug der herstellerischen Fragen. Gibt es auch ein zeichnerisches Charakteristikum für Graphic Novels? Im Falle von *Asterios Polyp* fällt die Antwort scheinbar leicht: der Reichtum an graphischen Formen, den Mazzucchelli bietet. Comics ändern ihren Zeichenstil im Regelfall nicht in der Geschichte, aber genau das ist Mazzucchellis Prinzip. Er erzeugt eine Stilvielfalt, die durch die Veränderung der Form inhaltliche Aussagen trifft: Wenn der Titelheld im Stil einer Oskar-Schlemmer-Figur dargestellt wird, assoziiert man bei seinem Auftritt größere Sachlichkeit als im Falle einer anderen Zeichnung, die dann in der Manier von Piranesi gehalten ist. Das ist jedoch keine spezifische Errungenschaft von Graphic Novels. Comic-Strip-Pioniere der ersten Hälfte des zwanzigsten Jahrhunderts wie Frank King (*Gasoline Alley*) oder George Herriman (*Krazy Kat*) haben diesen Kunstgriff gleichfalls angewandt, und wenn es überhaupt so etwas geben soll wie graphische Romane, dann trifft diese Bezeichnung auf Kings und Herrimans epische Erzählungen mehr zu als auf alle anderen Comics. Sie sind die Entsprechungen zu Charles Dickens und James Joyce auf dem Feld der graphischen Literatur.

Generell gilt, dass erzählerischer Anspruch ästhetischen Einfallsreichtum provoziert. In Marjane Satrapis *Persepolis*, einem von 2000 bis 2003 erschienenen vierbändigen autobiographischen Comic über Kindheit und Jugend dieser iranischstämmigen Autorin, entspricht die schlichte Linienführung bei Einsatz intensiver Schwarzflächen ganz dem naiven Blickwinkel der jungen Erzählerin. Gleichzeitig aber durchsetzt Satrapi ihren Comic mit symbolistischen Elementen und Zitaten der traditionellen persischen Kunst. Die scheinbare Unvereinbarkeit der Stilebenen ist für Comiczeichner ein geringeres Problem als für Vertreter anderer Kunstformen, weil die Comics eine notwendig hybride Ausdrucksform sind – will sagen: Wenn man schon Text und Bild nicht nur zu-, sondern auch ineinander geführt hat, schreckt die Aussicht, verschiedene Bildästhetiken miteinander zu kombinieren, kaum noch. Weitere Beispiele von als Graphic-Novel-Meilensteine gefeierten Comics, die zeichnerisch ähnlich agieren, sind David B.s „Heilige Krankheit" (1996 bis 2004, laut Satrapi das erklärte Vorbild für Stil und Tonfall von *Persepolis*), *Die Sternenwanderer* von Moebius (1988 bis 2004) oder die *Acme Novelty Library* von Chris Ware (1993 bis 2010).

Ware ist zweifellos der graphisch einflussreichste Comiczeichner der Gegenwart, wobei er unter Designern und Architekten die größten Bewunderer findet. Diese Berufsgruppen schätzen seine unerschöpfliche Experimentierfreude bei der Organisation des Seitenraums. Die von Ware im Alleingang produzierte *Acme Novelty Library*, eine Comicserie mit wechselnden Protagonisten und Publikationsformaten, ist eine solche Fundgrube für graphische Darstellungsformen, dass sie eher als Lehrbuchsammlung denn als Geschichtenzyklus wahrgenommen wird. Was Ware darin mit den Seitenarchitekturen anstellt, ermöglicht ganz neue Methoden der Leseführung durch Bildsequenzen. Und nebenbei ist der Autor auch noch einer der originellsten zeitgenössischen Erzähler, was seinen Comics Eingang in hochliterarische Anthologien wie *McSweeney's* oder *Virginia Quarterly Review* verschafft hat.

Wenn man denn auch nur eine Graphic Novel benennen sollte, die ihre Bezeichnung als Roman wirklich verdient hat, dann wäre das Chris Wares *Jimmy Corrigan, the Smartest Kid on Earth* von 2000. Für diesen fast vierhundertseitigen querformatigen Comic, in dem keine Seite im Bildaufbau der anderen gleicht und doch dank Wares an Computerstilisierung erinnernde, aber komplett handgezeichnete Graphik ein höchst homogenes Erscheinungsbild herrscht, fasste der Autor zahlreiche Episoden aus seiner *Acme Novelty Library* zusammen, ergänzte sie um neues Material und schuf so einen fiktiven Lebenslauf seines Titelhelden, der in bester postmoderner Manier Ironie und Tragik, Zitat und Verwandlung, Epik und Pointe mischte. 2019 wiederholte er dieses Erfolgsrezept mit einer weiteren biographischen Fiktion: *Rusty Brown*, doch bei Ware von „Wiederholung" zu reden, ist unzulässig, weil er vielmehr immer wieder neue Pfade graphischer Erzählweisen beschreitet. So ist denn auch sein Buchprojekt *Building Stories* (2012), das er zwischen den beiden biographischen Graphic Novels fertigstellte, ganz anders ausgefallen: Vierzehn Comics unterschiedlichsten Formats, in einer Box zusammengefasst, erzählen Geschichten rund um ein Haus – *Building Stories* eben. Was aber auch zu lesen ist als „Geschichten aufbauen". Ebendas tut Chris Ware immer wieder anders. Nur darin liegt die Wiederholung in seinem Werk.

Was Ware aus seiner Lehrzeit bei Art Spiegelmans Anthologie *Raw* gelernt hat, ist die Vereinbarkeit der unterschiedlichsten Formen in der Bastardkunst des Comics.

Dabei ist ausgerechnet Spiegelmans eigenes Meisterwerk, *Maus* (1981 bis 1992), ein Beispiel für größte graphische Strenge und Stiltreue. Trat der amerikanische Comic-Avantgardist, der zugleich zu den größten Kennern seiner Kunstgattung zählt, vor und nach *Maus* als Eklektiker reinsten Wassers (wenn das Paradox gestattet ist) auf, so wählte er für die Darstellung der Geschichte seines Vaters, eines Auschwitz-Überlebenden, die denkbar kompromissloseste Form. Schwarzweiß im Kleinformat (die einzelnen Kapitel waren als separate Publikationen den überformatigen Ausgaben von *Raw* beigeheftet), meist im klassischen Vierreihenschema pro Seite gehalten und mit Figuren im Stil der *funny animals* à la Disney erzählt, schuf *Maus* einen Eindruck von einerseits nostalgischer Comic-Erzählung (was dem historischen Stoff zupass kam) und andererseits absoluter Zeitlosigkeit durch seine graphische Allgemeingültigkeit (was Spiegelmans Intention der Bewahrung seiner Familiengeschichte entsprach). Die Lektüre ist unvergesslich, und das liegt nicht allein an der Intensität des Inhalts, sondern auch an der ästhetischen Kargheit.

Maus ist dadurch jenes Beispiel für den Anspruch von Graphic Novels geworden, das auch die größten Verächter von Comics anerkennen – sehr zum Leidwesen von Spiegelman, der nach Erscheinen der Buchausgabe noch durch persönliche Intervention bei der *New York Times* dafür gesorgt hatte, dass man seinen Band von der Bestsellerliste für Romane herunternahm und auf die für Sachbücher setzte. Es ist aber genau diese Ununterscheidbarkeit – eine weitere in der Hybridform Comic –, die am besten dazu geeignet scheint, den Reiz von Graphic Novels festzumachen: Die bedeutendsten unter ihnen weisen stets sichtbare Vermengungen von Fiktion mit Realität auf.

Das geht über das Prinzip des literarischen Realismus hinaus. Denn Comics sieht man buchstäblich an, wie nahe sie an der Wirklichkeit sind. Ob Ulli Lust ihre autobiographisch grundierte Graphic Novel *Heute ist der letzte Tag vom Rest deines Lebens* (2009) in einem bewusst skizzenartigen Stil zeichnet, um die Authentizität der Schilderungen ästhetisch zu beglaubigen, oder ob Mazzucchelli in *Asterios Polyp* die Kunstgeschichte des zwanzigsten Jahrhunderts auf die Oberfläche seiner Bilder bringt, während ansonsten der ästhetische Diskurs zwischen den Figuren subkutan verläuft – die Intensität der Darstellung ist jeweils tatsächlich sichtbar. Und deshalb ist der Marketingbegriff „Graphic Novel" doch hilfreich, insofern er die Erwartung weckt, ungewöhnliche Formate geboten zu bekommen. Um dieser Erwartung zu entsprechen, variieren die Comic-Autoren sowohl ihre Darstellungsweisen als auch die Erscheinungsformen für ihre Geschichten. Und somit öffnen sich ihnen neue Wege zur Gestaltung, die nicht begangen worden wären, wenn man weiter dem bequemen Pfad der standardisierten Publikationen gefolgt wäre. Schön, dass manchmal aus merkantilen Interessen Herausforderungen an die Kunst entstehen.

So muss man die Marketing-Initiative der deutschsprachigen Verlage im Jahr 2009 dafür loben, dass sie auf die Übersetzung der englischen Bezeichnung „Graphic Novel" zu „Comicroman" verzichtete und in weiser Voraussicht den fürs hiesige Publikum und vor allem für den Buchhandel allgemeineren Begriff wählte, unter dem dann eben alles subsumiert werden konnte, was Anspruch auf Anspruch erhob. Da konnte vieles auch als Graphic Novel auftreten und plötzlich reüssieren, was vorher schon dagewesen, aber weniger wirkungsvoll rubriziert war. Es war ja nicht so, als ob es in den Jahrzehnten zuvor hierzulande keine anspruchsvollen Comicpublikationen gegeben hätte. Pratts *Südseeballade* war 1983 bei Carlsen auf Deutsch erschienen, sogar mit moderatem Erfolg, und *Maus* bewies dann 1989 und mit dem Erscheinen des zweiten Teils 1992 endgültig, dass sich die Comicrezeption auch in Deutschland bei Presse und Publikum wandelte. Aber in die klassischen Buchhandlungen zog davon nur wenig ein, vielmehr gründeten sich Spezialgeschäfte für Comics, über die der größte Teil an „literarischen Comics" verkauft wurde.

Die normalen Buchhändler wurden dann durch ein ganz anderes Phänomen darauf aufmerksam, dass sich Comics auch für sie lohnen könnten: Bereits zehn Jahre bevor hierzulande die Graphic-Novel-Offensive einsetzte, begann der Manga-Boom, also die Begeisterung einer jungen Generation für japanische Comics. Damit wurde dasselbe Distinktionsschema bedient, das die Eltern der Manga-Leser ehedem dazu gebracht hatte, sich als Jugendliche für klassische Comics zu begeistern: in Abgrenzung zur älteren Generation, die damit nichts anfangen konnte, ja häufig die ganze Erzählform in Bausch und Bogen verteufelte. Genauso geschah es nun wieder: Manga mit ihren ungewohnten Codes und Stilen irritierten die mittlerweile erwachsen gewordenen und saturierten Comicleser, und umso zuverlässiger fanden deren Kinder darin einen provozierenden Lesestoff und entbrannten für die fremde Form. Doch weil auch das etablierte Vertriebssystem in Deutschland (Kioske oder Comic-Fachhandel) mit den Manga nichts anfangen konnte, kamen nun jene Buchhandlungen ins Spiel, die zuvor Comics vernachlässigt hatten, aber nun bereitwillig Manga-Bestellungen annahmen und angesichts des daraus resultierenden Umsatzes und einer neuen jungen, vor allem weiblichen Klientel sogar eigene Abteilungen dafür einrichteten, deren Mitarbeiter dann Kompetenzen im Umgang mit graphischer Literatur erwarben.

Diese frischgewonnene Offenheit gegenüber gezeichneten Geschichten nutzte dann der Graphic-Novel-Initiative, zumal auch damit ein neues Publikum erreichbar wurde: literarisch anspruchsvolle Leser, die nunmehr auch für Comics bereit waren, Preise wie bei Romanen zu zahlen. Jahrzehntelang schien die Zwanzig-

Mark-Grenze für Comics unüberwindbar; heute sind umfangreiche Comics bisweilen teurer als die dicksten Romane. Damit wurde das ganze Segment für den Buchhandel attraktiver, und es traten plötzlich Verlage auf den Plan, die nie zuvor einen Gedanken an die Publikation von Comics verschwendet hatten: Kiepenheuer & Witsch, S. Fischer, Suhrkamp, Aufbau. Sie alle wurden aber auch vom Begriff „Graphic Novel" verführt, denn bei etwas, das ein „Roman" sein wollte, hielten sie sich für kompetent. Dass etliche Hoffnungen aufs Massengeschäft, das die mit Comics unerfahrenen literarischen Verlage von diesem Segment erwarteten, enttäuscht wurden, hat aber erstaunlicherweise nicht dazu beigetragen, das ganze Feld zu diskreditieren. Vielmehr entwickelten die Verlage langsam Gespür für die Qualität von Comics, so dass jüngere Meisterwerke der Erzählform bei anderen als den etablierten deutschen Comicverlagen erschienen sind: Riad Sattoufs sechsteilige autobiographische Serie *Der Araber von morgen* etwa bei Penguin, *Asterios Polyp* von David Mazzucchelli bei Eichborn oder Richard McGuires *Hier* bei DuMont.

Die Traditionshäuser für Comics in Deutschland haben sich also selbst einen Teil ihres Monopols abgegraben, als sie ihre neue Bezeichnung „Graphic Novel" propagierten, die auch neue Konkurrenz auf den Plan rief. Zugleich hat die Popularisierung von Graphic Novels die Rezeption von Comics begünstigt: Das Feuilleton verlor seine lang gehegten Berührungsängste; heute genießen wichtige Neuerscheinungen anspruchsvoller Comics ebenso breite kritische Aufmerksamkeit wie Romane (im Jahr 2011 war Nicolas Mahlers Comic-Adaption von Thomas Bernhards *Alten Meistern* nach Judith Schalanskys Roman *Der Hals der Giraffe* der zweitmeistrezensierte Suhrkamp-Titel). Und auch eine rezensorische Nebenaktivität wie das wöchentliche Comic-Blog des Verfassers dieser Zeilen auf FAZ/NET findet erfreulich große Aufmerksamkeit. Nur die Literaturpreise verweigern sich immer noch der Erkenntnis, dass Graphic Novels doch auch für Romanauszeichnungen in Frage kommen müssten. Aber immerhin ist beim englischen Booker-Preis schon 2018 erstmals ein Comic auf die Longlist gekommen: *Sabrina* des amerikanischen Autors Nick Drnaso, und der Preis der Leipziger Buchmesse hat mittlerweile sowohl in der Sachbuchrubrik als auch bei der Belletristik Graphic Novels berücksichtig: 2022 *Rude Girl* von Birgit Weyhe und 2024 *Genossin Kuckuck* von Anke Feuchtenberger.[1] Da hat der Deutsche Buchpreis noch Nachholbedarf, von Büchner- oder gar dem Literaturnobelpreis ganz zu schweigen. Aber der Begriff „Graphic Novel" wurde ja auch nicht an einem Tag durchgesetzt.

---

1 Siehe dazu den Beitrag von Andreas Stuhlmann zu Feuchtenberger in diesem Band.

Literaturverzeichnis

B., David. *Die heilige Krankheit* (*L'ascension du Haut Mal*). Übers. von Kai Wilksen. 2 Bde. Edition Moderne, 2006.
Drnaso, Nick. *Sabrina*. Drawn and Quarterly, 2018.
Eisner, Will. *Ein Vertrag mit Gott und andere Mietshausstories aus New York* (*A Contract with God and Other Tenement Stories*). Übers. von Carl Weissner. Zweitausendeins, 1980.
Feuchtenberger, Anke. *Genossin Kuckuck*. Reprodukt, 2023.
Krug, Nora. *Heimat. Ein deutsches Familienalbum*. Penguin Verlag, 2018.
Krug, Nora. *Im Krieg. Zwei illustrierte Tagebücher aus Kiew und St. Petersburg* (*Diaries of War*). Übers. von Alexander Weber. Penguin Verlag, 2024.
Lust, Ulli. *Heute ist der letzte Tag vom Rest deines Lebens*. Avant, 2009.
Mahler, Nicolas. *Alte Meister*. Suhrkamp, 2011.
Mazzucchelli, David. *Asterios Polyp*. Eichborn, 2009.
McGuire, Richard. *Hier* (*Here*). Übers. von Stephan Kleiner. DuMont, 2014.
Moebius [Jean Giraud]. *Die Sternenwanderer* (*Le Monde d'Edena*). 6 Bde. Carlsen, 1988–2004.
Platthaus, Andreas. faz.net/aktuell/feuilleton/buecher/comic-kolumne/. 1. Juli 2025.
Pratt, Hugo. *Corto Maltese. Die Südseeballade* (*Una Ballata del Mare Salato*). Carlsen Verlag, 1983.
Satrapi, Marjane. *Persepolis*. 2 Bde. Edition Moderne, 2004.
Sattouf, Riad. *Der Araber von morgen. Eine Kindheit im Nahen Osten* (*L'Arabe du futur. Une jeunesse au Moyen-Orient*). Übers. von Andreas Platthaus. 6 Bde. Penguin Verlag, 2015–2024.
Snyder, Timothy. *Über Tyrannei. Zwanzig Lektionen für den Widerstand* (*On Tyranny. Twenty Lessons from the Twentieth Century*). Übers. von Andreas Wirthensohn. Illustriert von Nora Krug. C.H. Beck, 2021.
Spiegelman, Art. *Maus. Die Geschichte eines Überlebenden. Bd. 1: Mein Vater kotzt Geschichte aus* (*Maus. A Survivor's Tale. vol. 1: My Father Bleeds History*). Übers. von Christine Brinck und Josef Joffe. Rowohlt, 1989.
Spiegelman, Art. *Maus. Die Geschichte eines Überlebenden. Bd. 2: Und hier begann mein Unglück* (*Maus. A Survivor's Tale. vol. 2: And Here My Troubles Began*). Übers. von Christine Brinck und Josef Joffe. Rowohlt, 1992.
Ware, Chris. *Jimmy Corrigan. The Smartest Kid on Earth*. Pantheon, 2000.
Ware, Chris. *Building Stories*. Pantheon, 2012.
Ware, Chris. *Rusty Brown*. Pantheon, 2019.
Weyhe, Birgit. *Rude Girl*. Avant, 2022.

Christian Klein

„Nicht nur Fakten runterbeten" – Spielräume biographischen Erzählens im Comic am Beispiel von Reinhard Kleists Graphic Novel *Der Boxer*

Abstract: Auch wenn Comics häufig gerade mit solchen Elementen assoziiert werden, die mit unserer Wirklichkeit nicht viel zu tun haben, zählen faktuale Erzählungen von Anfang an zum Kernbestand des Comics. Unter den faktualen Comics sind Comic-Biographien besonders prominent vertreten. Dabei stehen biographische Comics vor besonderen Herausforderungen: Sie müssen überzeugend kommunizieren, dass sie zuverlässig außersprachliche Wirklichkeit repräsentieren, können dies aber notwendigerweise nur in einer Art und Weise, die über den Modus der Darstellung permanent auf die Diskrepanz zwischen Vorbild und Abbild verweist. Der Beitrag diskutiert, wie Reinhard Kleist, einer der prominentesten deutschen Comic-Autoren der Gegenwart, mit diesen Herausforderungen in seiner biographischen Graphic Novel *Der Boxer* (2012) umgeht, in der er das Leben des polnischen Holocaust-Überlebenden Hertzko Haft verarbeitet. Zu zeigen ist am Beispiel Kleists, wie biographische Comics einen eigenständigen Beitrag zur Auseinandersetzung mit kultureller Erinnerung leisten, indem sie die Schnittstellen von dokumentarischer Faktizität, subjektiver Perspektivierung und künstlerischer Imagination sichtbar machen.

I

Am Beginn der analytischen Beschäftigung mit biographischen Comics steht ein Rezeptionsparadox. Als faktuale Erzählungen werden biographische Comics so gelesen, dass sie außersprachliches Geschehen – im Falle biographischer Comics also: das Leben der biographierten Person – zuverlässig präsentieren. Zugleich wird aber beim ersten Blick in einen biographischen Comic erkennbar, dass die erwartete Repräsentation von ‚objektiver' Wirklichkeit durch die Subjektivität der Comic-Zeichner geprägt ist. Zwar ist jede biographische Erzählform beeinflusst von der Individualität des Biographen, denn biographisches Erzählen bedeutet, dass der Biograph aus überlieferten Details auswählen und diese zu einer kohärenten und überzeugenden Geschichte kombinieren muss und sich so als Selektions- und Organisationsinstanz einbringt. Aber im Unterschied zu anderen biographischen Erzählformen wie dem dokumentarischen Biopic, in dem die Subjektivität des Zugriffs hinter die vermeintliche Objektivität der Originaldokumente zurücktreten kann, können Comic-Biographien die Subjektivität des Vermittlungsaktes nicht vergessen machen. Auch wenn biographische Comics das Leben realer Personen zuverlässig zu schildern beabsichtigen, wird die Art und Weise der Repräsentation bestimmt durch den persönlichen Stil des Comic-Künstlers. Comic-Biographien müssen daher Darstellungsweisen finden, die als (ggf. auch verfremdende) bildliche Repräsentationen einer ‚objektiven' Wirklichkeit überzeugen und stellen dabei die Subjektivität des Zugangs und die ‚Gemachtheit' der Darstellung notwendigerweise von Anfang an explizit aus (vgl. Mikkonen 195). Biographische Comics verhandeln also nicht nur das Leben der biographierten Person, sondern auf einer Metaebene auch, wie der:die Biographierte von einer anderen Person erinnert, repräsentiert und interpretiert wird (vgl. Warley und Filewood 154). Umso wichtiger scheint vor diesem Hintergrund die Frage, mithilfe welcher Signale Comics den Leser:innen kommunizieren, dass sie einen faktualen Geltungsanspruch erheben und mithilfe welcher Strategien der Eindruck vermittelt wird, dass der Comic diesen Geltungsanspruch auch einlöst.

Als Erzählung ist der Comic geprägt von Selektion, kann er doch nur einen kleinen Teil der Informationen, die für das Verständnis der Geschichte notwendig sind, durch (bildliche oder sprachliche) Zeichen repräsentieren – den Rest müssen die Leser:innen im Rahmen der Lektüre ergänzen. Verschiedentlich wurde darauf hingewiesen, dass Comics gerade durch das Aussparen von Details oder Ereignissen im Bild ihre besondere Wirkung erzielen (vgl. Lefèvre 2000). Aussparungen zählen aber auch sehr konkret zu den konstitutiven Merkmalen von Comics, denn die Bilderfolgen des Comics bestehen bekanntlich aus einer Reihe von Einzelbildern (Panels genannt), die durch Zwischenräume, meist schmale weiße Streifen, voneinander getrennt sind (vgl. zum Folgenden Abel und Klein 84–87). Der Comic-Zeichner und -theoretiker Scott McCloud hat für diese Zwischenräume die Bezeichnung „Gutter" (im Deutschen auch: „Rinnstein") aus der Druckersprache übernommen, und er sieht im „Gutter" einen der wichtigsten Bestandteile des Comics: Hier finde das Eigentliche des Comics statt, weil die Leser:innen zwei separate Bilder in einen Gedanken überführten (vgl. McCloud 66). Die Überbrückungsleistung der Leser:innen, die aus den Einzelbildern des Comics (als ‚sequenzieller Kunst') eine zusammenhängende Geschichte macht, bezeichnet McCloud als „closure" (also „Schließung", im Deutschen meist als „Induktion" übersetzt): „Comic panels fracture both time and space, offering a jagged, staccato rhythm of unconnected moments. But closure allows us to connect these moments and mentally construct a continuous, unified reality" (McCloud 67). Insofern sei es falsch, den Comic einfach als eine Mischform aus Literatur und Bild zu verstehen, denn der „Rinnstein" und die von ihm provozierte Rezeptionsleistung ist für McCloud ein originäres Element des Comics (McCloud 66).

Ausgehend von bestimmten Vorannahmen, die die Leser:innen eines biographischen Comics in die Lektüre mit einbringen, konstruieren sie im Akt der Rezeption eine zusammenhängende (Lebens-)Geschichte. Zu diesen Prämissen zählt etwa die Annahme, dass eine Figur, die in verschiedenen Panels wieder auftaucht, dieselbe Figur zu unterschiedlichen Zeitpunkten ist. Es gehört ferner zu den Voraussetzungen einer gelingenden Comic-Lektüre, dass die Leser:innen wissen, dass die Platzierung der Panels auf der Comicseite nicht zufällig erfolgt, sondern die Einzelbilder auf bestimmte Art und Weise angeordnet sind und Verknüpfungen zwischen den einzelnen Panels bestehen (vgl. Lefèvre 2000). Erwartet wird zumeist, dass die Abfolge der Bilder mit einer chronologischen und kausalen Beziehung einhergeht (vgl. Lefèvre 2000; Groensteen 13) – auch wenn natürlich Vor- und Rückblenden möglich sind oder Comics gerade aus dem Unterlaufen der antizipierten Korrelation von Bildanordnung und Handlungsverlauf erzählerischen Mehrwert schlagen können. In diesem Sinne setzen die einzelnen Bilder narrative Stimuli, die im Akt der Lektüre zu einem Handlungsverlauf zusammengeführt werden, der mit einem spezifischen kognitiven Schema korreliert und somit von den Leser:innen in Muster der eigenen Lebenspraxis eingepasst wird (vgl. Schüwer 37). Berücksichtigt man die zentrale Bedeutung von Aussparungen im Comic (auf Einzelbild-, aber auch auf Sequenzebene) und bezieht die Überlegungen der literaturwissenschaftlichen Rezeptionstheorie (Ingarden; Iser) mit ein, dann ist es die konstitutive Funktion von Unbestimmtheit im Comic, die die Leser:innen besonders intensiv an der Sinnkonstitution des Geschehens mitwirken lässt, weil Leerstellen im Rahmen der Lektüre in Abgleich mit den eigenen realweltlichen oder auch literarisch vermittelten Erfahrungen gefüllt werden. Die Ausgestaltung des Wechselspiels zwischen Unbestimmtheit und konkretisierender Veranschaulichung dürfte wesentlich dazu beitragen, ob die jeweilige biographische Comic-Erzählung als plausibel und überzeugend wahrgenommen wird.

Festzuhalten ist, dass sich biographische Comics aufgrund der Notwendigkeit zur Selektion in der Regel auf ausgewählte Stationen aus dem Leben der Biographierten konzentrieren, die für deren Denken und Handeln als zentral erachtet werden. Entsprechend formuliert Reinhard Kleist sein Vorgehen im Entstehungsprozess einer Comic-Biographie:

> Ich lese mich erst einmal ein und erstelle dann verschiedene Script-Entwürfe, schreibe also kurze ein- bis zweiseitige Texte, in denen ich ausprobiere, wie ich die Geschichte mit einer Rahmenhandlung versehen könnte. Da stehen dann Fragen im Zentrum wie: Wer ist mein

> Erzähler? Wie erzähle ich? Worauf will ich mich thematisch konzentrieren? Was ist nicht so wichtig für die Geschichte? Bei einer Biographie habe ich natürlich immer einen Berg von Fakten und dann muss ich entscheiden, welche ich brauche und welche ich getrost beiseite lassen kann. (Kleist 2019, 123)

Im Rahmen der Präsentation im Comic sollen sich die einzelnen Fakten und Episoden dann – unter aktiver Beteiligung der Leser:innen im Rahmen des *Closure*-Prozesses – zu einer interessanten Geschichte kombinieren lassen, die den faktualen Geltungsanspruch einzulösen verspricht. Dabei ist ‚Faktualität' keine ontologische Kategorie, sondern ein Zuschreibungsphänomen, das sich nicht ‚notwendigerweise' aus dem Schaffen des Comic-Autors als Selektions- und Organisationsinstanz ergibt, sondern Ergebnis von spezifischen Kommunikationsprozessen ist. Wie aber schaffen es biographische Comics, den Leser:innen den Eindruck zu vermitteln, dass ein faktualer Geltungsanspruch evoziert und zufriedenstellend eingelöst wird? Hierzu stehen eine Reihe von Techniken und Strategien zur Verfügung, die über bestimmte Texteigenschaften die Rezeption lenken und im Falle biographischer Comics den Text als Aussage über Wirklichkeit wahrnehmen lassen (vgl. hierzu und zum Folgenden Klein 2022).

II

Spätestens seit Mitte der 1990er Jahre gibt es eine ausführlichere Debatte über Comics in der Geschichtswissenschaft. In diesem Kontext haben Pandel (1994) und Gundermann (2007) Typologien vorgelegt, die ausgehend vom jeweiligen „Authentizitätsgrad", der einem Comic zugeschrieben wird, unterschiedliche Typen von „Geschichtscomics" unterscheiden. Ungeachtet verschiedener Kritikpunkte im Einzelnen (vgl. hierzu Dolle-Weinkauff 30–32) legen diese Typologien nahe, dass auch auf dem Feld der faktualen Comics und damit auch der Comic-Biographien ein (mindestens) ebenso großer Spielraum für die konkrete Ausgestaltung der jeweiligen biographischen Text-Bild-Erzählung existiert wie etwa auf dem Feld der reinen Text-Biographien. So können auch Comic-Biographien solche Textstrategien und Darstellungsverfahren einsetzen, die gemeinhin eher fiktionalen Comics vorbehalten scheinen. Doch müssen biographische Comics über spezifische Werkeigenschaften ihren Geltungsanspruch als referentialisierbare Erzählungen kommunizieren, damit das aufgerufene Kommunikationsmodell ‚Biographie' erkannt und die Erzählung angemessen rezipiert werden kann. Das Funktionieren des Kommunikationsmodells ‚Biographie' setzt mithin ein komplexes Zusammenspiel von Textstrukturen und pragmatischen Bedingungen voraus, das von Signalen, die auf Kommunikationskonventionen beruhen (Gattungsbezeichnung etc.), initiiert wird.

Mit anderen faktualen Erzählungen teilen biographische Comics die zentralen *Faktualitätssignale auf der paratextuellen Ebene*. Als Paratexte bezeichnet man die Gesamtheit jener rezeptionssteuernden Elemente, die den ‚eigentlichen' Text umgeben und ein Buch erst zum Buch machen – etwa Titel, Umschlag, Klappentext, Motto etc. (vgl. Genette 1987/2001). So finden sich auch in biographischen Comics besonders häufig *explizite Statusmarkierungen*, wenn Autoren etwa durch Gattungsbezeichnungen den faktualen Status ihrer Erzählung anzeigen. Eine weitere Signalart, die auf paratextueller Ebene oft zu finden ist, sind *Transparenzmarker* in Vor- oder Nachworten, also z. B. Reflexionen zum eigenen Vorgehen, Überlegungen zu den Begrenzungen des subjektiven Zugriffs etc. Indem sich Biographen etwa in einer Nachbemerkung selbstreflexiv über die Eingeschränktheit ihres Sichtfeldes, die Lückenhaftigkeit ihres Quellenmaterials o. ä. äußern, suggerieren sie den Rezipient:innen, dass die eigentliche biographische Erzählung (im Rahmen der Möglichkeiten) zuverlässig ist. Die transparente Ausstellung der Bedingungen und Begrenztheiten des Zugriffs erhöht den Eindruck der Glaubwürdigkeit der präsentierten Biographie.

Fragt man nach comic-spezifischen Faktualitätssignalen, dann wird man vor allem im Hinblick auf die *Faktualitätsindizien auf der textuellen Ebene* fündig. Ungeachtet der unterschiedlichen Möglichkeiten der Beziehung zwischen Text- und Bildelementen kommt der visuellen Komponente in Text-Bild-Erzählungen eine besondere Bedeutung zu, denn Text-Bild-Erzählungen müssen *zeigen*, wovon sie *erzählen* (vgl. Mikkonen 77). Entsprechend zentral ist in biographischen Comics die Präsentation einer *empirisch triftigen erzählten Welt*, das heißt die Präsentation einer Diegese, die mit den *Vorstellungen* der Rezipient:innen vom realweltlichen Referenzgeschehen korrespondiert, die ihnen mithin ‚authentisch' erscheint (vgl. Gundermann 2018, 263–270). Wobei auch ‚Authentizität' hier keine feststellbare Eigenschaft ist, sondern ein Effekt, der sich im Zug der Rezeption einstellt und seinerseits durch Textstrategien evoziert wird.

Zur Evokation eines solchen Effekts haben sich eine Reihe von ‚*Referenzankern*' auf Geschehens- und Darstellungsebene etabliert, die die Faktualität des Dargestellten indizieren. Hierzu zählen etwa die Präsentation von referentialisierbaren räumlichen Settings (bekannten Gebäuden etc.) oder bestimmten historischen Ereignissen. In biographischen Comics spielen naheliegenderweise Personen eine besondere Rolle. Figuren, die in biographischen Comics auftreten, werden als mimetische Repräsentationen von Menschen aus dem ‚wirklichen Leben' interpretiert. Sofern die Vertrautheit mit den Ereignissen oder Persönlichkeiten bei der intendierten Leserschaft vorausgesetzt werden kann, müssen sie zwar wiedererkennbar sein, können ansonsten aber in relativ freier Gestaltung aufgerufen werden. Sind Ereignisse oder Personen unbekannt, wird die Möglichkeit zur Referentialisierung häufig mitgeliefert. Dies geschieht dann etwa durch die Präsentation von Referenz-*Materialien* (Briefen, Fotos etc.), die z. B. im Nachwort im Original abgedruckt werden.

Aber auch diesseits der Paratexte spielt das Zeigen von Quellen im Kontext von faktualen Text-Bild-Erzählungen eine große Rolle – und zwar inhaltlich und formal. So werden oft Informationsträger präsentiert, die visuell als *dokumentarische Belege* inszeniert werden (vgl. Gundermann 2018, 270–273). Besonders häufig werden in diesem Kontext gezeichnete Briefe und vor allem gezeichnete Fotografien in biographischen Comics präsentiert. Diese Darstellungen suggerieren über ihre spezifische Präsentationsweise – indem sie konventionalisierte mediale Codes aufrufen – eine Art Dokumentcharakter und beglaubigen damit die Referenzqualität des Dargestellten. El Rafaie spricht in diesem Kontext von „Authentication through documentation" (158). Da in Bezug auf zeitgenössische Vorstellungen der visuellen Repräsentation von ‚Realität' fotografischer Realismus ungeachtet aller technischen Entwicklungen noch immer ein dominierendes Paradigma konstituiert (vgl. Mickwitz 29), fungiert der *Einsatz von Bildkonventionen der Fotografie* auch ganz allgemein im Kontext von faktualen Comics als Authentizitätsindiz (vgl. El Rafaie 159) – unabhängig von der Referentialisierbarkeit der Darstellungen (vgl. Schmitz-Emans). Ein Beispiel aus der Comic-Biographie über Anne Frank von Sid Jacobson (Text) und Ernie Colón (Bilder) soll das komplexe Zusammenspiel von fotografischen Dokumenten und Erzählung im Kontext biographischer Comics veranschaulichen.

Die Comic-Biographie über Anne Frank (Jacobson und Colón) richtet sich vornehmlich an jugendliche Leser:innen und funktionalisiert Fotos zur Etablierung eines Referentialisierbarkeitsmodells. Die Biographie kommuniziert ihren faktualen Status zunächst über paratextuelle Angaben, z. B. den Untertitel „eine grafische Biographie". Den vorderen und hinteren Buchdeckel zieren allerdings auch zahlreiche Zeichnungen, die als Fotografien gestaltet sind und den Eindruck eines Fotoalbums wecken, genauer: des privaten Fotoalbums von Anne Frank, in das die Leser:innen nun einen Blick werfen dürfen. Auf diese Weise indiziert der Buchumschlag über das Aufrufen spezifischer Darstellungskonventionen den Dokumentcharakter des im Inneren Dargestellten und stiftet so einen Referenzrahmen, der die komplette Erzählung prägt.

Im Verlauf der Erzählung wird der faktuale Geltungsanspruch des Textes regelmäßig durch gezeichnete ‚Dokumente' bekräftigt, z. B. neben Fotografien auch durch eine maschinengeschriebene Liste oder einen Stadtplan (Jacobsen und Colón 2018, 67, 77). Zudem werden Darstellungskonventionen eingesetzt, die die intendierten Leser:innen aus faktualen Textsorten kennen, mit denen sie alterstypisch aus Geschichtslehrbüchern vertraut sind (vgl. Gundermann 2018, 275). So werden einzelne Übersichten im Stile sogenannter „Geschichtskarten" (vgl. Jacobson und Colón 2018, 66) präsentiert, also solche Karten zitiert, die erst im historischen Rückblick erstellt werden können, und durch Legenden etc. ebenso historische Einordnungskompetenz ausstrahlen wie der Stammbaum (Jacobson und Colón 11), der im Stile von Passfotos Darstellungen der Familienmitglieder zeigt. Auch das Stilmittel der Zeitleiste oder Zeittafel wird im Anhang genutzt, um paratextuell die erzählte individuelle Geschichte zu kontextualisieren. In der Zeittafel werden dann Originalfotos abgedruckt, die im Text selbst als Zeichnung auftauchen. Das so gestiftete wechselseitige Referenzverhältnis von Foto und Zeichnung wird systematisch genutzt, da die ersten Kapitel von Zeichnungen von im Anhang abgedruckten Fotos eingeleitet werden (Jacobson und Colón 9, 33, 149). Diese referentialisierbaren Vignetten kommunizieren aufgrund ihrer prominenten Platzierung stellvertretend für das jeweilige Kapitel die Triftigkeit der Darstellung und die Zuverlässigkeit des Dargestellten. Da diese Kapitelrahmungen zu Beginn des Buches stattfinden, wird den Leser:innen nahegelegt, das so etablierte Referenzverhältnis auf die Gesamterzählung zu generalisieren.

III

Reinhard Kleist zählt zu den renommiertesten und erfolgreichsten Comic-Autoren Deutschlands. Bekanntheit erlangte er insbesondere mit seinen zahlreichen biographischen Graphic Novels u. a. zu Johnny Cash, Fidel Castro, Nick Cave und David Bowie.[1] Zwar konstatiert Kleist in einem Interview: „Eine 1:1-Abschilderung des Lebens finde ich nicht sehr reizvoll, zumal man sich so etwas wie einer biographischen ‚Wahrheit' ohnehin nur annähern kann" (Kleist 2019, 122). Doch er nutzt gekonnt die umfangreichen formalen und erzählerischen Mittel, um den faktualen Geltungsstatus seiner Texte zu untermauern, wie bei einer Analyse seiner Graphic Novel *Der Boxer. Die wahre Geschichte des Hertzko Haft* von 2012 besonders deutlich wird (vgl. auch Albiero).

In *Der Boxer* erzählt Kleist die Geschichte des polnischen Juden Hertzko Haft, der als Jugendlicher die Besetzung des Landes durch die Nationalsozialisten erlebt und im Alter von sechzehn Jahren nach Auschwitz deportiert wird. Dort wählt ihn ein SS-Aufseher dazu aus, als Boxer in Schaukämpfen, die zum Vergnügen der SS-Offiziere veranstaltet werden, buchstäblich um sein Leben zu kämp-

---

1 Vgl. *Johnny Cash – I See a Darkness* (2006), *Castro* (2010), *Der Traum von Olympia. Die Geschichte von Samia Yusuf Omar* (2015), *Nick Cave – Mercy on me* (2017), *Knock Out!* (2019) oder zuletzt die zwei Bände seiner Biographie über David Bowie: *Starman. David Bowie's Ziggy Stardust Years* (2021) und *Low. David Bowie's Berlin Years* (2024). Kleists vielfach preisgekrönte Bücher wurden in zahlreiche Sprachen übersetzt.

fen, denn die Unterlegenen dieser Kämpfe werden unmittelbar in die Gaskammern geschickt. Auf einem der berüchtigten Todesmärsche gelingt Haft die Flucht und er beschließt, nach Amerika zu emigrieren, um dort seine große Liebe Leah wiederzufinden, von der er durch die Umstände getrennt wurde. Haft beginnt eine Karriere als Profi-Boxer in den USA, die er wegen des Einflusses der Mafia auf den Ausgang der Kämpfe an den Nagel hängt, um im Anschluss einen Gemüseladen in Brooklyn zu eröffnen und mit einer anderen Frau eine Familie zu gründen, auch wenn er feststellen muss, dass die Erinnerung an Leah zwar verblasst, aber nicht verschwindet (*Boxer* 170).

Die Komplexität von Hafts Leben spiegelt sich in ihrer Vielschichtigkeit schon auf der Ebene der Erzählanlage der biographischen Graphic Novel. Denn an der Nahtstelle von biographischer Vergangenheit und (Erzähler-)Gegenwart setzt die Comic-Biographie mit einer Rahmenhandlung ein, in der Haft im Auto mit seinem Sohn sitzt, plötzlich an den Straßenrand fährt und weint, was der Sohn ebensowenig einzuordnen weiß, wie die Leser:innen. Mit der Ankündigung: „Eines Tages werde ich dir alles erzählen" (*Boxer* 7) wird in die Binnenhandlung übergeleitet, die letztlich als lange aufbauende Rückwendung zu verstehen ist und erklärt, wie es zu dieser Eingangssituation im Auto gekommen ist. Die Binnenerzählung führt also die Einlösung des väterlichen Versprechens vor, die das Vorliegen der gedruckten Graphic Novel auf materieller Ebene zu beglaubigen scheint.

Die Binnenerzählung besteht aus drei (sehr unterschiedlich langen) Abschnitten. Der erste Abschnitt der Biographie (*Boxer* 9–115) ist ein langer Rückblick auf Hafts Leben von seiner Kindheit über die Zeit, die er in den Konzentrationslagern verbringt, bis zu seiner Flucht und Befreiung und seiner endgültigen Entscheidung, in die Vereinigten Staaten zu emigrieren, um dort seine große Liebe Leah zu suchen. Hafts Leben in New York steht im Mittelpunkt des zweiten Abschnitts (*Boxer* 117–170), der seine Karriere als Profiboxer bis zu dem Punkt zeigt, an dem die Mafia ihn unter Druck setzt, seinen letzten Kampf zu verlieren. Der kurze dritte Abschnitt der Biographie (*Boxer* 172–182) schildert Hafts Begegnung mit Leah, nachdem er einen Hinweis auf ihren Aufenthaltsort in Florida erhalten hat. Als Haft schließlich Leah, die mit Ehemann und Tochter in Miami lebt, in Begleitung seines Sohnes besucht, findet er sie an Krebs erkrankt und vom Tod gezeichnet vor und weiß auf der Rückfahrt, dass das Wiedersehen ein Abschied war. Mit der Rückfahrt von dieser Begegnung endet das Buch, und die Erzählung ist in die Rahmenhandlung und zum Ausgangspunkt des Buches zurückgekehrt.

Der Boxer ist damit nicht nur eine Comic-Biographie, die die Auswirkungen der Traumata eines Holocaust-Überlebenden zeigt, für den selbst das vermeintliche Happy End des Wiedersehens mit der großen Liebe vor allem den Schmerz über ein verhindertes gemeinsames Leben bereithält, sondern auch ein Zeugnis dessen, was Marianne Hirsch im Hinblick auf Art Spiegelmans bahnbrechende

Comic-Auto-/Biographie *MAUS* als „Postmemory" bezeichnet hat, denn Spiegelman erzählt nicht nur die Geschichte seiner Eltern, die den Holocaust überlebten, sondern auch, wie sein eigenes Leben durch die Traumata der Eltern geprägt ist:

> ‚Postmemory' describes the relationship that the ‚generation after' bears to the personal, collective, and cultural trauma of those who came before – to experiences they ‚remember' only by means of the stories, images, and behaviors among which they grew up. But these experiences were transmitted to them so deeply and affectively as to seem to constitute memories in their own right. (Hirsch)

Die prägende Bedeutung der Erfahrungen und Erinnerungen des Vaters für die zweite Generation der Holocaust-Überlebenden wird in *Der Boxer* erzähltechnisch dadurch unterstrichen, dass der Erzähler der Rahmenhandlung Hafts Sohn Alan ist und die Binnenhandlung die Lebensgeschichte des Vaters erzählt, die dieser zu Beginn der Rahmenhandlung ankündigt.

Fragt man nach den paratextuellen Signalen, die den Geltungsanspruch kommunizieren, zuverlässige Aussagen über außersprachliche Wirklichkeit zu präsentieren, fällt zunächst der Untertitel des Buches auf, der „Die wahre Geschichte des Hertzko Haft" verspricht und damit im Sinne einer expliziten Statusmarkierung die Glaubwürdigkeit der Erzählung zu untermauern versucht. Das Nachwort des Sportjournalisten Martin Krauß über „Boxen im KZ", in dem dieser das individuelle Schicksal Hafts historisch kontextualisiert, verstärkt die Glaubwürdigkeit der geschilderten Handlung. Im Anhang abgedruckte Quellen – auf die unten noch genauer einzugehen ist – unterstreichen die Zuverlässigkeit der Darstellung ebenso wie das Betonen der Wissensgrenzen des Biographen. Indem Kleist offenlegt, dass er sich bisweilen auf seine Imagination verlassen musste, um biographische Lücken zu füllen, er aber immer begründete Vermutungen präsentiere, erhöht dieses Eingeständnis insgesamt seine Glaubwürdigkeit als Biograph.

Darüber hinaus werden die Bildkonventionen der Fotografie in *Der Boxer* vielfältig genutzt, um den Referentialisierbarkeitsanspruch des Dargestellten zu stützen. Eine besondere Rolle spielen Fotos, die einerseits im Sinne dokumentarischer Belege eingesetzt, aber auch in einem spezifischen Wechselverhältnis mit von Kleist imaginierten Passagen funktionalisiert werden. Gezeichnete Figuren werden im biographischen Comic als – mehr oder weniger verfremdete – mimetische Rekonstruktionen von Menschen aus dem wirklichen Leben interpretiert. Der Comic-Forscher Kai Mikkonen weist allerdings darauf hin, dass das Medium Comic der Wiedererkennbarkeitserwartung, die die Lektüre biographischer Comics mitbestimmt, eigentlich entgegenstehe:

> The demands of graphic drawing and style, the use of caricature, and the rich symbolic language of comics, easily compromise the sense of life-likeness in characters. [...] [P]hotorealistic characterisation and reality-building has the potential to undermine idiosyncratic cartooning

that draws on the cartoonist's individual style of the graphic trace–a strong expectation in the medium. (Mikkonen 195–196)

So muss der Comic-Biograph einer doppelten Erwartungshaltung gerecht werden: Zum einen muss die Zuverlässigkeit der Darstellung von realen Personen gewährt, zum anderen der persönliche Zeichenstil erkennbar bleiben. Kleist nutzt eine Art exemplarische Beglaubigungsstrategie, die im Lektüreprozess generalisiert wird. Im Nachwort zu *Der Boxer* werden einige historische Porträtfotos der realen Person Hertzko Haft und Schnappschüsse abgedruckt, die zunächst vor allem die Triftigkeit der Präsentation und die Zuverlässigkeit der Darstellung belegen sollen: Der gezeichnete Hertzko Haft sieht dem historischen tatsächlich ähnlich. In der Comic-Erzählung selbst werden zu einigen der Fotos die Entstehungssituationen gezeigt. Auch wenn die Quellen ggf. mit Kontext überliefert wurden (so zeigt laut Bildunterschrift im Nachwort einer der Schnappschüsse das erste Rendezvous Hertzkos mit seiner späteren Frau; *Boxer* 188), so muss die konkrete Darstellung der Situation im Comic (Gesprächsverlauf vor Betreten des Lokals, Frage des Fotografen, Gedanken des Protagonisten etc.; *Boxer* 165–166) doch als von Kleist imaginiert betrachtet werden. Durch die Einbettung in einen möglichen, aber letztlich imaginierten Handlungsverlauf verleiht Kleist den vereinzelten historisch-realen Schnappschüssen Relevanz für die Handlung – er bettet sie in die Geschichte ein. Damit stehen Foto und Zeichnung in einem wechselseitigen Referenzverhältnis: Die gezeichnete Entstehungsszene unterstreicht die Referenz-Qualität des Fotos, denn erst indem das Foto damit ‚tatsächlich' zur Geschichte gehört, besitzt es Dokumentcharakter. Gleichzeitig indiziert das Foto die Referenz-Qualität der Zeichnung, sodass die Leser:in annimmt, dass die Zeichnung wirklich Haft in einer ‚echten' Situation zeige, da man das ‚Ergebnis' (das Foto) ja kenne. Indem die Biographie für einige Zeichnungen entsprechendes Referenzmaterial anbietet, etabliert sie, wie oben erwähnt, ein grundsätzliches Referentialisierbarkeitsmodell, das auch die Wahrnehmung der anderen Zeichnungen und damit des Comics insgesamt beeinflusst, ohne deshalb die produktiven Entfaltungsmöglichkeiten zu beschneiden oder dem persönlichen Zeichenstil im Wege zu stehen.

Der Comic-Forscher Pascal Lefèvre weist allgemein darauf hin, dass viele biographische Comics einige prototypische Codes und Konventionen des Dokumentarischen auf kreative Weise einsetzen, indem sie etwa die Möglichkeiten von Fotografien oder historischen Dokumenten nutzen (Lefèvre 2013, 51–52). Kleist weist im Interview darauf hin, dass er einzelne Panels bewusst an bekannte historische Fotografien anlehnt: „Ja, eine Reihe von Bildern im *Boxer* beruhen auf Fotografien, an denen ich mich orientiert habe – zum Beispiel das berühmte Foto, auf dem einem Juden im Ghetto der Bart abgeschnitten wird, oder die Fotos von der Rampe in Auschwitz" (Kleist 2019, 124). Kleist ruft hier also Szenen und Räume auf, die über historisch verbürgte und weit verbreitete Fotografien im kollektiven Bildgedächtnis abgespeichert sind. Der exemplarische Bezug auf historische Fotografien behauptet die Referenzqualität des Dargestellten weit über jene konkreten Panels hinaus, die sich auf historisch verbürgte Szenen beziehen. Die punktuelle Beglaubigung der Comic-Zeichnungen mittels überlieferter Fotografien funktioniert als Authentifizierungsstrategie, die im Rahmen der Lektüre generalisiert wird und die die Zuverlässigkeit der biographischen Comic-Erzählung insgesamt untermauert.

Kleist spielt in *Der Boxer* aber auch mit den Konventionen der Biographik und bewegt sich geschickt zwischen dokumentarischer Genauigkeit und künstlerischer Freiheit. Einerseits legt er großen Wert darauf, dass er recherchiert und historische Quellen – insbesondere die Biographie Hafts aus der Feder seines Sohnes Alan – verarbeitet hat, worauf schon zu Beginn des Buches verwiesen wird, heißt es doch im Innentitel: „Nach dem Buch *Eines Tages werde ich alles erzählen* von Alan Scott Haft." Kleist positioniert seine Figuren im historischen Kontext, wodurch sie in ihrem zeitlichen und gesellschaftlichen Umfeld verankert werden, was er durch die Art und Weise der Darstellung bekräftigt. Andererseits erlaubt er es seiner Erzählung bisweilen, Fakten und Fiktionen zu kombinieren. In seiner künstlerischen Auseinandersetzung mit der Biographie vermischen sich die dokumentierten Ereignisse zwangsläufig mit erfundenen Elementen, um die Lücken des Quellenmaterials zu überbrücken, aber auch, um zu einer anderen Ebene der Realität vorzudringen, will er doch auch die emotionale Wirklichkeit der Zeit einfangen und vermitteln (vgl. Kleist 2019, 122). So gelingt es Kleist, die Lebensgeschichten seiner Figuren anschaulich und greifbar zu machen, ohne jedoch die Rückbindung an deren existenzielle Erfahrungen aus den Augen zu verlieren. Er nutzt die Freiheiten des Mediums, um narrative Lücken zu füllen und komplexe Persönlichkeiten zu formen, die mehrdimensional sind und die Leserschaft in ihren Bann ziehen (Kleist 2019, 122). Zugleich hinterfragt Kleist nicht nur traditionelle biographische Erzählweisen, sondern erweitert sie um neue Perspektiven und erzählerische Möglichkeiten.

Die Gründe, warum das Leben einer Person zum Gegenstand einer Biographie wird, können ebenso mannigfaltig sein wie die Ansätze, die der biographischen Arbeit jeweils zugrunde liegen, oder die Schwerpunkte, die verschiedene Biographien setzen. Sehr verallgemeinernd könnte man sagen, dass ein Leben zum Gegenstand einer Biographie wird, weil es entweder so einzigartig ist bzw. die Person Einzigartiges hervorgebracht hat, oder weil es so typisch ist bzw. die Person stellvertretend für eine bestimmte Gruppe von Menschen steht. Olaf Hähner spricht im Fall der Perspektivierung ‚typischer Leben' von paradigmatischen Biographien und im Fall ‚besonderer Leben' von syntagmatischen Biographien (vgl. Hähner). Ob es sich um eine paradigmatische oder syntagmatische Biographie handelt, hat Auswirkungen auf die Art der Darstellung und damit die Legitimationstechniken des biographischen Schreibens. Während eine paradigmatische Biographie vor allem auf die Übereinstimmung mit parallelen Lebensverläufen abhebt und das Gemeinsame betont, wird eine syntagmatische Biographie vor allem die Differenz zwischen dem Leben des Biographierten und zeitgleichen Lebensläufen herausstellen und besonderes Augenmerk auf die Andersartigkeit der individuellen Handlungen legen. Den Fokus der paradigmatischen Biographie bildet folglich die *Egalität*, den der syntagmatischen Biographie die *Originalität*.

Reinhard Kleists Comic-Biographie über Hertzko Haft versteht es, mittels spezifischer Darstellungsverfahren beide Zugriffe miteinander zu verbinden und zu verdeutlichen, dass das präsentierte herausragende individuelle Schicksal ungeachtet aller Einzigartigkeit stellvertretend für die Leidenswege vieler anderer stehen kann. Kleist entwirft Hertzko Haft in seiner Biographie als einsamen Charakter, doch gleichzeitig fällt die Vielzahl der Figuren auf, die Haft umgeben. Besonders eindrücklich ist in diesem Kontext Seite 118, die die Verbindung von Hafts Schicksal mit dem seiner Leidensgenossen vor Augen führt (Abb. 1).

Gezeigt wird Haft schlafend auf dem Deck des Schiffes, das ihn in die USA bringt, und der Geruch des Rauchs aus den Schiffsschornsteinen ruft in ihm die Erinnerungen an seine Arbeit an den Krematoriums-Öfen in Auschwitz auf. Wie in einem erstickenden Albtraum erscheinen ihm im oberen Panel Kolonnen von Menschen, die in die Öfen marschieren. Auf dem untersten Panel der Seite sieht man im Rauch aus dem Schornstein die Gesichter jener Menschen, die er zurücklassen musste, was als intertextuelle Referenz auf die berühmten Verse aus Celans *Todesfuge* („dann steigt ihr als Rauch in die Luft / dann habt ihr ein Grab in den Wolken da liegt man nicht eng") zugleich belegt, dass Kleist nicht nur auf Fotografien, sondern auch Texte rekurriert, die im kulturellen Gedächtnis gespeichert sind und unsere Wahrnehmung des Holocausts prägen. Indem Kleist hier das durch Celans breit rezipiertes Gedicht bekannte sprachliche Bild visualisiert, verbindet er Hafts Schicksal nicht nur mit den Menschen, die er zurücklassen musste, sondern passt es zugleich in gemeinsame Vorstellungswelten der Rezipient:innen ein. In *Der Boxer* wird mithin die Verquickung von individueller Lebensgeschichte und kollektivem Trauma metareflexiv immer wieder herausgestrichen. *Der Boxer* zeigt, dass Hafts persönliche Geschichte nicht isoliert gelesen werden kann, sondern mit den Schicksalen vieler anderer Menschen verbunden ist, die in der Erzählung auftauchen, aber am Rande bleiben. Auf diese Weise erscheint die Geschichte des Protagonisten exemplarisch für die Leiden und Traumata der von den Nationalsozialisten verfolgten und ermordeten Juden.

Ausgehend von den Schilderungen des Sohnes Alan erschafft Kleist eine vielschichtige Figur, die die Leser:innen emotional herausfordert und nicht durchweg Sympathie weckt. Haft, der Protagonist, ist eine ambivalente Gestalt, die so-

Abb. 1: Reinhard Kleist. *Der Boxer. Die wahre Geschichte des Hertzko Haft*. Carlsen, 2012, S. 118: „Hertzko Haft auf der Überfahrt in die USA".

wohl Täter als auch Opfer ist. Im Laufe der Erzählung verübt er verschiedene Gewalttaten, darunter Diebstahl und Mord. Später wird er auch seiner eigenen Familie gegenüber gewalttätig. Kleist macht deutlich, dass Haft tief von seiner Vergangenheit, von den traumatischen Erfahrungen geprägt ist. Das hinterlässt in

Kleists Darstellung nicht nur psychische, sondern auch physische Spuren, die Haft charakterisieren. Denn fragt man nach der Wiedererkennbarkeit von Figuren in biographischen Comics, dann sind es in der Regel einzelne phänotypische Besonderheiten, die darstellerisch akzentuiert werden. Bei Haft sind es vor allem Stirnfalten, die Kleist besonders hervorhebt. Die Falten sind weniger Zeichen des Alters, sondern repräsentieren das Grauen und das Leid, das Haft aushalten musste. So bleibt Haft selbst in einem Zustand äußerster Entkräftung, ausgemergelt und ohne Haare, für die Leser:innen wiedererkennbar. Die erlittene Gewalt und die erlebten Leiden haben sich erkennbar in seine Physis eingeprägt. Dass sie darüber hinaus aber auch sein Verhalten bestimmen, wird im Laufe der Erzählung deutlich, denn Kleist präsentiert Haft als gequälte Figur, die gleichermaßen Opfer und Täter ist, was ein allzu schnelles moralisches Urteilen verunmöglicht.

Im Hinblick auf die Zuverlässigkeit der biographischen Erzählung ist auf stilistischer Ebene zu betonen, dass Kleist einen zeichnerischen Stil verwendet, der gleichermaßen andeuten wie verbergen kann. So kann es die Glaubwürdigkeit der Darstellung paradoxerweise gerade untermauern, dass Kleist Gewalttaten, an denen Haft beteiligt ist, zwar darstellt, aber ihre detaillierte Visualisierung ausspart und den Leser:innen die Aufgabe überlässt, die Lücken zu füllen. In Momenten extremen Grauens wirkt der Stil besonders abstrakt, fast schon expressionistisch, so etwa auf Seite 51 als Haft im Krematorium in Auschwitz arbeiten muss (Abb. 2).

Die Figuren verlieren ihre unverwechselbaren Züge, die sie als Individuen erkennbar machen, es werden verzerrte Gesichter gezeigt, die durch Kleists Stil wie gespenstische Fratzen erscheinen. Das Grauen, das Haft an den Öfen erlebt, lässt ihn schließlich zusammenbrechen und die Dramatik dieser Grenzerfahrung spiegelt sich in der Darstellung, wenn die existenzielle Emotionalität durch Zacken repräsentiert wird, die die einzelnen Panels expressiv durchschneiden. Das erlittene Trauma manifestiert sich im Laufe der Erzählung wiederkehrend im Rahmen von Flashbacks (etwa *Boxer* 89), die schon stilistisch eine Brücke zur Arbeit im Krematorium herstellen.

Kleists Stil, der dunkle Farben und verschiedene Formen der Verzerrung verwendet, erlaubt es ihm, auf die Präsenz von Gewalt in der Geschichte zu verweisen und dabei die vollständige, realistische Darstellung zu vermeiden. So wird auf Seite 81 eine Szene gezeigt, die darauf rekurriert, dass es in Auschwitz angeblich zu kannibalistischen Übergriffen gekommen sei, worauf Kleist im Nachwort auch noch einmal explizit durch Quellenmaterial verweist (Abb. 3).

Die entsprechenden Panels arbeiten allerdings mit extremen Schwarz-Weiß-Kontrasten und sind insgesamt so dunkel gehalten, dass sie das Geschehen mehr andeuten als zeigen. Die Betrachtenden müssen sehr genau hinschauen und kön-

Abb. 2: Reinhard Kleist. *Der Boxer. Die wahre Geschichte des Hertzko Haft*. Carlsen, 2012, S. 51: „Das Grauen an den Öfen der Krematorien von Auschwitz".

Abb. 3: Reinhard Kleist. *Der Boxer. Die wahre Geschichte des Hertzko Haft.* Carlsen, 2012, S. 81: „Andeutungen statt Ausdeutungen".

nen auch dann nur ahnen, was auf den Panels zu erkennen sein könnte. So wird den Leser:innen ein Spielraum eröffnet, in dem ihnen selbst überlassen bleibt, das dargestellte Geschehen auszudeuten oder ggf. auch nur zu überfliegen, wenn es ansonsten vielleicht emotional überwältigen würde. Damit sind die Leser:innen gezwungen, an der Sinnkonstitution des Geschehens aktiv mitzuwirken, indem sie die Leerstellen, die die Darstellung absichtlich offenlässt, im Rahmen des Spielraums füllen.

IV

Die möglichen Signale, mit denen Comics das Kommunikationsmodell ‚Biographie' aufrufen und einen entsprechend faktualen Geltungsanspruch evozieren können, sind äußerst vielfältig. Sie reichen von Statusmarkierungen und Transparenzmarkern über Referenzanker bis zur Funktionalisierung solcher Darstellungsweisen, die gemeinhin mit Quellenmaterial und Dokumenten verbunden werden und so den Eindruck von ‚Authentizität' hervorrufen, wobei die Ästhetik von Fotografien eine besondere Rolle spielt. Die Beispiele aus dem Comic von Kleist haben gezeigt, dass der punktuelle Einsatz spezifischer Authentifizierungsstrategien Referentialisierbarkeitsmodelle etablieren kann, die im Zuge einer Generalisierung die Rezeption der Comic-Erzählung insgesamt beeinflussen.

Kleist verankert die Figuren in *Der Boxer* über die mimetische Konstruktion und Repräsentation fest in der Welt ihrer Erzählungen, während ein Set von Paratexten den faktualen Geltungsanspruch der Biographie betont. Dabei verzichtet Kleist auf die Verherrlichung seines Protagonisten, stellt dessen Agieren in aller Widersprüchlichkeit aus und legt den Fokus auf die tragischen Erfahrungen, die nicht nur Haft zeitlebens prägten, sondern auch das Erleben seiner Angehörigen mitbestimmten.

Die Analyse von Kleists Graphic Novel *Der Boxer* verdeutlicht exemplarisch zentrale Herausforderungen und Potenziale biographischer Comics. Biographische Comics stehen im Spannungsfeld zwischen faktualem Geltungsanspruch und künstlerischer Subjektivität. Gerade weil die zeichnerische Darstellung notwendigerweise von der individuellen Stilistik der Künstler geprägt ist, unterstreicht das Medium Comic, dass Faktualität kein inhärentes Textmerkmal ist, sondern ein spezifisches Kommunikationsangebot, das im Rahmen der Rezeption realisiert wird.

Biographische Comics reflektieren somit nicht nur das Leben der Biographierten, sondern auch die Bedingungen und Grenzen biographischen Erzählens selbst. Gerade die notwendige Offenlegung des Vermittlungsaktes – die unauflösbare Verbindung von Faktizität und künstlerischer Interpretation – wird zur signifikanten Aussage solcher Werke über die Konstruktionsbedingungen historischer Erinnerung.

Durch die erzählerische Grundanlage seiner Graphic Novel sowie die Art und Weise der Darstellung gelingt es Kleist, die unvermeidlichen biographischen Lücken plausibel zu überbrücken, ohne seinen Leser:innen deswegen jedes Detail in Text oder Bild auszubuchstabieren. Vielmehr fordert er sie zur aktiven Lektüre auf, indem sie durch das Füllen von Leerstellen zur Sinnkonstitution der Erzählung beitragen. In seiner Comic-Biographie findet Kleist einen Weg, nicht nur die Fakten aus dem Leben Hafts zu vermitteln, sondern auch einen Einblick in dessen Gefühlswelt zu ermöglichen und zugleich das biographische Erzählen selbst zu reflektieren, indem er die notwendige Subjektivität des biographischen Zugriffs offen ausstellt. So entsteht eine eigenständige Erzählung aus Fakten und Fiktionen, die die Grenzen zwischen ‚Wahrheit' und Erfindung bewusst verschwimmen lässt, ohne deshalb den faktualen Status der Erzählung insgesamt zu unterminieren.

In dem oben zitierten Interview zeigt sich Reinhard Kleist sehr reflektiert im Hinblick auf den Einsatz der verschiedenen Verfahren und Techniken, die den faktualen Status seiner biographischen Comics kommunizieren können, auch wenn er bezogen auf seine biographischen Comics betont: „Ich wollte nicht nur Fakten runterbeten" (Kleist 2019, 122). Einige Faktualitätsindizien verwendet er in *Der Boxer* bewusst nicht: „Es war mir beispielsweise nicht wichtig, mit Textkästen zu signalisieren, dass die Zeichnungen dem historischen Geschehen tatsächlich entsprechen. Da vertraue ich auf die Überzeugungskraft der Geschichte, dass das beim Lesen klar wird" (Kleist 2019, 124). Ziel des Beitrags war es, aufzuzeigen, dass eben diese angestrebte Überzeugungskraft ein Rezeptionseffekt ist, der aus dem Einsatz einer Vielzahl von erzählerischen Mitteln resultiert, die Kleist in der Präsentation der Geschichte von Hertzko Haft kunstvoll funktionalisiert. Vor diesem Hintergrund ist Kleists Vertrauen auf die Überzeugungskraft keineswegs eine naive Hoffnung, sondern selbstbewusster Ausdruck des Wissens um die eigenen Fähigkeiten als Comic-Biograph.

Literaturverzeichnis

Abel, Julia und Christian Klein. „Leitfaden zur Comicanalyse". *Comics und Graphic Novels. Eine Einführung.* Hg. von Julia Abel und Christian Klein. J. B. Metzler, 2016. S. 77–106.

Albiero, Olivia. „When Public Figures Become Comics. Reinhard Kleist's Graphic Biographies". *DIEGESIS. Interdisciplinary E-Journal for Narrative Research / Interdisziplinäres E-Journal für Erzählforschung* 8.1 (2019): S. 6–23.

Dolle-Weinkauff, Bernd. „Was ist ein ‚Geschichtscomic'? Über historisches Erzählen in Comic, Manga und Graphic Novel". *Comparativ – Zeitschrift für Globalgeschichte und vergleichende Gesellschaftsforschung* 24.3 (2014): S. 29–46.

El Refaie, Elisabeth. *Autobiographical Comics: Life Writing in Pictures*. UP of Mississippi, 2012.
Genette, Gérard. *Seuils*. Editions du Seuil, 1987. (dt. *Paratexte. Das Buch vom Beiwerk des Buches*. Suhrkamp, 2001.)
Groensteen, Thierry. *Comics and Narration*. UP of Mississippi, 2013.
Gundermann, Christine. „Inszenierte Vergangenheit oder wie Geschichte im Comic gemacht wird". *Ästhetik des Gemachten: Interdisziplinäre Beiträge zur Animations- und Comicforschung*. Hg. von Hans-Joachim Backe et al. De Gruyter, 2018. S. 257–283.
Gundermann, Christine. *Jenseits von Asterix. Comics im Geschichtsunterricht*. Wochenschau-Verlag, 2007.
Hähner, Olaf. *Historische Biographik. Die Entwicklung einer geschichtswissenschaftlichen Darstellungsform von der Antike bis ins 20. Jahrhundert*. Lang, 1999.
Haft, Allan Scott. *Eines Tages werde ich alles erzählen. Die Überlebensgeschichte des jüdischen Boxers Hertzko Haft*. Die Werkstatt, 2009.
Hirsch, Marianne. „An Interview with Marianne Hirsch". *Columbia University Press*, cup.columbia.edu/author-interviews/hirsch-generation-postmemory. 6 Apr. 2025.
Ingarden, Roman. *Vom Erkennen des literarischen Kunstwerks*. Niemeyer, 1968.
Iser, Wolfgang. „Die Appellstruktur der Texte. Unbestimmtheit als Wirkungsbedingung literarischer Prosa". *Rezeptionsästhetik. Theorie und Praxis*. Hg. von Rainer Warning. Wilhelm Fink, 1975. S. 228–252.
Jacobson, Sid und Ernie Colón. *Das Leben von Anne Frank. Eine grafische Biographie*. Carlsen, 2018.
Klein, Christian. „Biographische Comics und Graphic Novels". *Handbuch Biographie. Methoden – Traditionen – Theorien*. Hg. von Christian Klein. 2., akt. und erw. Auflage. J. B. Metzler, 2022. S. 275–283.
Kleist, Reinhard. *Der Boxer. Die wahre Geschichte des Hertzko Haft*. Carlsen, 2012.
Kleist, Reinhard. „'Eine 1:1-Abschilderung des Lebens finde ich nicht sehr reizvoll'. Der Comic-Zeichner Reinhard Kleist im Interview". *DIEGESIS. Interdisziplinäres E-Journal für Erzählforschung / Interdisciplinary E-Journal for Narrative Research* 8.1 (2019): S. 121–126.
Lefèvre, Pascal. „Narration in Comics". *Image & Narrative. Online Magazine of the Visual Narrative*, 1.1 (2000): imageandnarrative.be/inarchive/narratology/pascallefevre.htm. 6. April 2021.
Lefèvre, Pascal. „The Modes of Documentary Comics". *Der dokumentarische Comic – Reportage und Biografie*. Hg. v. Dietrich Grünewald. Ch. A. Bachmann Verlag, 2013. S. 50–60.
McCloud, Scott. *Understanding Comics. The Invisible Art*. 2. Aufl. HarperPerennial, 1994.
Mickwitz, Nina. *Documentary Comics. Graphic Truth-Telling in a Skeptical Age*. Palgrave Macmillan, 2016.
Mikkonen, Kai. *The Narratology of Comic Art*. Routledge, 2017.
Pandel, Hans-Jürgen. „Comicliteratur und Geschichte. Gezeichnete Narrativität, gedeutete Geschichte und die Ästhetik des Geschichtsbewußtseins". *Geschichte lernen* 37 (1994): S. 18–26.
Schmitz-Emans, Monika. „Photos im Comic". *Comics intermedial: Beiträge zu einem interdisziplinären Forschungsfeld*. Hg. von Christian A. Bachmann, Véronique Sina und Lars Banhold. Ch. A. Bachmann Verlag, 2012. S. 55–74.
Schüwer, Martin. „Visuelle Aspekte der erzählerischen ‚Sprache des Comics': Senso-motorisches Bild und Zeit-Bild". *Erzählen im Comic. Beiträge zur Comicforschung*. Hg. von Otto Brunken und Felix Giesa. Ch. A. Bachmann Verlag, 2013. S. 33–48.
Warley, Linda und Alan Filewod. „Visual Silence and Graphic Memory. An Interdisciplinary Approach to *Two Generals*". *Picturing Life Narratives*. Hg. von Candida Rifkind und Linda Warley. Wilfrid Laurier UP, 2016. S. 153–175.

Paul M. Malone
Nils Oskamp's *Drei Steine* (2016) and the Void in Germany's *Erinnerungskultur*

Abstract: Originally produced with a grant from the German Family Affairs Ministry, Nils Oskamp's graphic novel *Drei Steine* (2016) describes the young Oskamp's conflict with Holocaust-denying Neo-Nazis in his Dortmund *Realschule* in 1983. The comic thus consciously conforms to Germany's official *Erinnerungskultur*. However, like that *Erinnerungskultur* itself, and due in part to the institutional contexts of its production, *Drei Steine* is hampered not only by the relative absence of Jews – the primary historical victims – in the daily lives of both its protagonist and of its contemporary young readers, but also by its appropriation of Jewish suffering as a vehicle for the non-Jewish protagonist's character development. Against a background of increasing racism and antisemitism both within Germany and in Europe more broadly, however, the graphic novel's conception as part of a broader pedagogical strategy to dissuade young people from accepting extremist propaganda provides some scope to mitigate these problems.

I

Nils Oskamp's comic *Drei Steine* (2016), designated in German as a *Graphic Novel* despite its autobiographical basis,[1] recounts Oskamp's teenage years in 1983 Dortmund-Dorstfeld (North Rhine-Westphalia), where he comes into conflict with a local Neo-Nazi group recruiting among his schoolmates. After mocking their antisemitism and standing up to them, he endures several beatings and an attempted shooting. He receives no support from his family, who are distracted by other problems and do not believe he is in any danger; his school, where one of the teachers is an unrepentant Nazi; or the police, who dismiss his concerns. Aided only by Tom, a friend of his older brother Jonas, young Nils tries to fight back, but following a near-fatal beating he forsakes violence and takes several assailants to court. After lengthy proceedings they are acquitted or receive minor penalties, but they are deterred from further attacks. At the story's end, Nils finishes *Realschule* and throws his schoolbooks into the river. These events, told in pictures dominated by cold blue-grey – with bright red

---

[1] The publisher's website, for example, describes the book as a "Ergreifende Graphic Novel gegen rechte Gewalt mit autobiografischen Zügen" ("Drei Steine," at Panini's website).

splashes whenever blood flows (*Drei Steine* 90–91, 105–108) – are set within a framing story toned in warm sepia and set in 2011 (*Drei Steine* 6–9, 56–58, 116–118): the older Oskamp, working on the graphic novel, tries to explain the period to his young son Tom, named after Oskamp's school friend. The book's title is inspired by the stones of remembrance or 'visitation stones' traditionally left by visitors at Jewish graves (*Drei Steine* 121–122). The young Nils takes three of these stones from a grave in Dorstfeld's neglected Jewish cemetery, and they structure the plot: he throws the first stone at an attacker (*Drei Steine* 66); almost fatally strikes his main antagonist with another, but thinks better of it and only frightens him by striking the ground instead (*Drei Steine* 90–93); and ultimately, three decades later, places the third at the Pillar of Heroism, the monument to resistance fighters at Yad Vashem (*Drei Steine* 120). Oskamp himself glosses this development: "Der erste Stein wird zur Waffe, der zweite Stein zum Symbol dafür, nicht zu töten, und der dritte Stein verweist dann wieder zurück auf das Gedenken" (*Drei Steine* 121). Despite its suspenseful story and social relevance, *Drei Steine* took almost a decade to produce, during which its publication often seemed unlikely. Its eventual appearance was enabled by the confluence of several social-institutional contexts; these same contexts, however, also affected the comic's final form. In their anthology *Was war, ist, wird Comicforschung – für uns?* Christina Meyer, Vanessa Ossa and Lukas R.A. Wilde describe the interdependence between comics and the contexts of their production:

> Verstanden als heuristischer Überbegriff für gezeichnete populäre Standbilder existieren Comics daher nicht außerhalb von medialen Kontexten; *sie sind maßgeblich in Medienökologien, sozialsystemische Institutionen und partizipative Netzwerke eingebunden*, in denen sie einerseits unentwegt von Akteur:innen, Technologien und Institutionen in gesellschaftlichen Spannungsfeldern 'formatiert' werden und andererseits selbst an den Ausgestaltungen und Transformationen dieser Kommunikationsgemeinschaften beteiligt sind. (Meyer et al. 6; emphasis added)

The following describes several institutional contexts of *Drei Steine*, including the media-ecological context of the contemporary German comics industry; the broader social-systemic context of the *Erinnerungskultur* or "culture of remembrance" developed in Germany as a continuance of (or, as Peter Kuras would claim, a replacement for) *Vergangenheitsbewältigung*[2]; and the participatory networks of active political education. As will be argued below, at least some of the perceived weaknesses of *Erinnerungskultur* are reflected in Oskamp's graphic novel, despite its good intentions. However, its service in the necessary project of resisting growing tendencies toward an openly chauvinistic nationalism also counteracts some of these problematic tensions.

---

2 As Kuras argues: "Only, in other words, when the generation who lived through World War II began to die out did talk of the culture of memory begin."

II

Throughout *Drei Steine*, the young protagonist's main weapon against flourishing Neo-Nazi graffiti in his school is his artistic talent: he disarms their messages by turning swastikas into little square houses (24) and supplements the command "Deutschland erwache" with "Frühstück ist fertig" (38; Fig. 1). These scenes are revisited in the present-day scene of Oskamp drawing the comic itself (56), demonstrating that the younger Nils' weapon has become the adult artist's career and main vehicle of expression.

Fig. 1: Nils uses his artistic skills to defuse Nazi graffiti, to the chagrin of one of the Neo-Nazis and the laughter of their unseen classmates (*Drei Steine 38*).

After finishing *Realschule*, Nils Oskamp studied graphic design at the Ruhrakademie in Schwerte (North Rhine-Westphalia) and animation at the Animation School Hamburg. Oskamp began his career in illustration and advertising, and his work appeared in mass-market magazines, including *Der Spiegel*, *Auto-Bild* and *Hörzu* (Ihme 110). He also sought to process his childhood experiences and as a visual artist and comics fan (his lifelong love of René Goscinny and Albert Uderzo's *Astérix* is alluded to twice in *Drei Steine*: 11–12, 57–58), he chose to do so in comic form. Knowing the time required for such a project – in his own words, "An einer Graphic Novel arbeitet man circa zwei Jahre, und in dieser Zeit muss der Lebensunterhalt gesichert sein" (Neubauer 35) – he began applying for funding in 2007. Over subsequent years, Oskamp collected over forty rejection letters from various funding agencies (Ihme 107).

In 2014, however, provocateur Siegfried Borchardt, known as "SS-Siggi," was elected to Dortmund's city council as a member of the party *Die Rechte*, and the media began to focus on the city's far-right milieu.³ As a result, Oskamp finally received a grant from the Federal Ministry for Family, Seniors, Women and Youth (Ihme 107; Neubauer 35), officially recognizing the project as a contribution to *Erinnerungskultur*; but the grant was time-limited, and so the work was rushed (Neubauer 35). *Drei Steine* was first published in 2016 as a 96-page softcover album, with a print run of 5,000 copies (see the companion website, Oskamp, *Drei Steine: Graphic Novel gegen rechts*, www.dreisteine.com). This edition was given away at schools as a *Leseprobe* by the Amadeu Antonio Stiftung, founded in 1998 by East Berlin teacher Anetta Kahane and devoted to strengthening democratic civil society and combatting far-right extremism.⁴

In fostering *Drei Steine*, the Amadeu Antonio Stiftung followed an established tradition: as Ralf Palandt notes, "politisch motivierte Sachcomics" in Germany date back to the late 1970s (Palandt 32).⁵ Through the 1980s and '90s, independent and underground comics criticized both historical and resurgent Nazism via original comics anthologies and unauthorized pastiches of *Astérix*, *Lucky Luke* and *Donald Duck* facing off against racist skinheads (Palandt 32–34). Moreover, as Christine Gundermann argues, the 1989 publication in German of Art Spiegelman's *Maus* (originally published in 1986) marked a turning point and laid "die diskursive Grundlage [. . .] für ein intensives Nachdenken über den Einsatz von Comics und Graphic Novels im Geschichtsunterricht" (Gundermann 152).

In the early 1990s, a wave of far-right violence against foreigners in reunified Germany – including the murder of Amadeu Antonio – inspired state governments and non-governmental organizations to publish comics aimed at preventing the radicalization of young people: in 1993, for example, Mecklenburg-Western Pomerania's Interior Ministry published the funny-animal comic *Leo mischt mit*, whose protagonist becomes entangled with Neo-Nazi violence against his will (Palandt 35).⁶

---

3 Borchardt had also been one of Oskamp's attackers three decades previously. He appears in *Drei Steine* as "SS-Michi" (Oskamp 99).
4 The foundation is named after Amadeu Antonio, an Angolan who had come to the former German Democratic Republic as a contract worker in 1987. Antonio became an early victim of right-wing violence following German reunification when he was murdered by Neo-Nazis in Eberswalde (Brandenburg) in November 1990 ("Die Amadeu Antonio Stiftung").
5 The first such comics were imports from abroad, such as Eduardo "Rius" del Rio Garcia's *Marx für Anfänger* (Rowohlt, 1979), which inspired further such comics from Rowohlt Verlag and other publishers (Dolle-Weinkauff 303–305). In 1983, for example, Rowohlt's political "Quer-Comics"-series published Wolfgang Wimmer and Gabriel "Tschap" Nemeth's *Sklaven*, describing German firms' exploitation of concentration camp prisoners under the Nazi regime (Palandt 32).
6 Klaus Wilinski's studio published several *Leo* comics during the 1990s in the service of state or municipal governments.

Palandt describes *Andi*, published by North Rhine-Westphalia's Interior Ministry between 2005 and 2009, as the best-known of these pedagogical comics. Each of *Andi*'s three issues, drawn in naive style by Peter Schaaff, shows Andi's multicultural group of schoolmates confronting a different extremist ideology: first Neo-Nazism, then radical Islam, then left-wing *Autonome*. The *Andi* comics are still updated and available online from the state ministry's website. Palandt criticizes the series, however, for not showing the characteristically violent aspects of far-right groups in the initial issue, while depicting the left movement as violent vandals in the third issue – a portrayal that prompted vehement rebuttals from some left-wing organizations, who responded with unofficial *Andi* comics rewriting the offending issue, or showing Andi confronted with police violence against the left (Palandt 38–40).[7]

Because the *Andi* series deals with contemporary radicalism in the same province, North Rhine-Westphalia, rather than historical Nazism or the Holocaust, it serves as a useful point of comparison with *Drei Steine*. In its didactic instrumentalization, *Andi* is a precursor to the later graphic novel. *Drei Steine* explicitly portrays Neo-Nazism as intrinsically violent and takes as its starting point the centrality of antisemitism and Holocaust denial to far-right ideology, whereas *Andi* depicts its Neo-Nazis simply as obnoxious, broadly racist nationalists – antisemitism is mentioned only in the supporting textual material (32–33, 35, 37).[8]

Moreover, while *Andi* was disseminated non-commercially as a public service by the North Rhine-Westphalia government, *Drei Steine* also came out in a longer hardcover commercial edition of 144 pages by Panini Verlag (the publisher who had also printed the Antonio Stiftung version without the publisher's logo on the cover). Thanks to a scheduling error, however, the two versions appeared simultaneously in the spring of 2016. Although the Panini edition was published amid the publicity of the biannual International Comic Salon in Erlangen – which put even more pressure on Oskamp to finish the book (Neubauer 35) – the free edition undercut the sales of the longer version, at least in the short term.

If, on the one hand, the themes of *Drei Steine* corresponded with the mission of the non-profit Amadeu Antonio Stiftung, then on the other, they were also suited to the commercial publishing program of Panini Verlag. The tiny German-language comics publishing market is dominated by a mixture of older foreign-owned multinationals, primarily focused on foreign licenses (Carlsen Verlag and

---

[7] For a defense of *Andi* against left-wing criticism (though one that ignores Palandt's specific objection), see Grumke 188; Grumke was the series' author (Palandt 39).
[8] Antisemitism plays a larger role in *Andi*'s second issue, whose topic is radical Islam: antisemitic ideas are uttered by characters in the plot as well as explicitly criticized in the supplementary material (*Andi 2* 22).

Egmont Ehapa Verlag, for example, both founded in the 1950s as offshoots of Danish firms); and smaller, younger, local firms in Germany and Switzerland, specializing in avant-garde or counterculture comics foreign and homegrown, such as Berlin's Avant-Verlag and Reprodukt, or Edition Moderne in Zurich (Malone 21–24). The Italian firm Panini is an outlier: old, large and global, but a relative latecomer to comics publishing. Originally founded in 1961 as Edizioni Panini Modena to manufacture collectible football stickers, Panini was briefly owned by the American Marvel Entertainment Group in the 1990s, entering the comics market throughout Europe and Latin America. Reacquired by its Italian management, by 2001 its German branch distributed such popular American licenses as the Marvel and DC superheroes, *Star Wars* and *The Simpsons*, as well as many popular Japanese manga. These foreign comics were lucrative enough that in its initial decade on the German-language market, unlike its competitors, Panini was the only firm that did not publish works by German-language creators.[9]

In the last decade, however, Panini has focussed on socially relevant non-fiction themes for its German-language projects: if Panini's imported superheroes, popular culture tie-ins and manga are its cash cows, its non-fiction "graphic novels" are hardcover prestige products.[10] As Panini Deutschland editor Steffen Volkmer said in 2015, "Graphic Novels sind im Moment DER Wachstumsmarkt" (emphasis in original), attracting new readers and entering bookstores rather than selling at kiosks (Marquardt), and reflecting what Gundermann had two years earlier called "ein starker Trend zum Sachcomic und zur Comic-Biografie" (Gundermann 154).

More specifically, before *Drei Steine*, Panini had published several graphic novels on related Jewish or Israeli themes, such as Sarah Glidden's *Israel verstehen – In 60 Tagen oder weniger* (2011), Luca Enoch and Claudio Stassi's *Die Stern-Bande* (2014), and Boaz Yakin and Nick Bertozzi's *Jerusalem: Ein Familienporträt* (2015).[11] Oskamp's *Drei Steine* thus fit well with Panini's programming at the time,

---

9 Panini Deutschland editor Steffen Volkmer admitted as late as 2015 that although the firm was Germany's leading comics publisher with forty titles every month, "Die Anzahl deutscher Künstlerinnen und Künstler ist bei uns im Vergleich zur Anzahl amerikanischer Künstler verschwindend gering" (Marquardt).
10 For instance, Christian Hardinghaus and Markus Friese's *Großväterland* (2016) collects eye-witness accounts of Second World War horrors; Stefan Dinter and Adrian Richter's *Crystal.Klar* (2020; based on Dominik Forster's 2015 autobiographical novel), concerns meth addiction; and Daniela Schreiter's *Schattenspringer: Wie es ist, anders zu sein* (2014) and its sequels *Schattenspringer 2: Per Anhalter durch die Pubertät* (2015) and *Schattenspringer 3: Spektralfarben* (2018) detail the author's life with Asperger's syndrome. Only Schreiter's books remain in print.
11 These were originally the American *How to Understand Israel in 60 Days or Less* (DC/Vertigo, 2010); the Spanish *Banda Stern* (Norma, 2013); and the American *Jerusalem: A Family Portrait*

at least superficially due to its ostensibly Jewish reference point. It was at least as well suited to Panini as it was to Reprodukt, for example, arguably the German-language publishing specialist in both autobiographical and political comics (Ditschke 272). At the end of 2016, *Drei Steine* won the Rudolph Dirks Award for best biography at Dortmund's German Comic Con, and with the comic in its fifth edition as of late 2024, Oskamp's work must also be considered a commercial success (Ihme 108).[12]

III

Despite this accolade and success, however, and despite Stephan Ditschke's observation in 2009 that "die feuilletonistische Kulturkritik" was paying increasing attention to comics (265), most of the press coverage of *Drei Steine* – some of which is available through the "Medienspiegel" section of Oskamp's website – is reportage, rather than aesthetic or cultural criticism. While laudatory regarding the comic's pedagogical mission (for example, Sterk; Betzholz), the media coverage remains blandly descriptive or totally silent about its aesthetic qualities.[13] Even the *Frankfurter Allgemeine Zeitung*'s comics expert, Andreas Platthaus, whom Ditschke singles out for an exemplary focus on "das genuine narrative Mittel des Comics [. . .], die Panelstruktur" (273), confined his reaction to a terse plot synopsis, stressing that the story would hardly be believable if Oskamp "nicht mit so großer Verve für die Authentizität der von ihm erzählten Geschichte einstehen [würde]."[14]

Among the few reports that mentioned formal qualities, Götz Piesbergen of *Splashcomics* approved of the realistic drawing style as most appropriate to the comic's message, and especially commended the coloring (Piesbergen), which in-

---

(First Second, 2013). All three are out of print from Panini; Glidden's *Israel verstehen* was reissued by Reprodukt in 2018.

12 The Rudolph Dirks Award was a jury-adjudicated prize awarded in over thirty categories to comics creators from around the world; although the German Comic Con (now the German Film Comic Con) has returned after being interrupted by the COVID-19 pandemic, the Dirks Award has not been given out since 2020.

13 Had *Drei Steine* been published by Reprodukt or Carlsen, rather than superhero-oriented Panini, it might have been received differently.

14 Platthaus's "review" appeared not in the *FAZ* itself, but rather in one of its several blogs. Some of the *FAZ* blogs – inaccessible from the newspaper's main web page – were integrated as columns into the main website in summer 2023. Others have lain dormant since 2018. There is no way to search older blog posts (*Fazblog – Blogs der FAZ*).

deed effectively both separates the story's time periods and creates a fitting atmosphere for each.

In general, the most negative reactions were those that saw the comic's aesthetic problems as obstacles to its didactic efficacy. An anonymous reviewer in the *Antifaschistisches Infoblatt*, however, declared, "Auf der ästhetischen Ebene verbleibt der Comic auf einem niedrigen Niveau." Nonetheless, the review concluded, "In Hinblick auf die Thematisierung rechter Gewalt im Schulunterricht ist der Comic jedoch eine gute Möglichkeit Schüler*innen zu sensibilisieren" ("Rezensionen: Drei Steine").

Moritz Honert granted no such concession in the *Tagesspiegel*, where he found many plot turns unresolved or illogical, while Nils' utter isolation from school, state and family "wirkt auf Dauer nicht ergreifend, sondern unglaubwürdig und ermüdend" (Honert). In terms of aesthetics, Honert criticized inconsistencies in the drawing style, with raw, unfinished panels appearing next to smooth, apparently digitally polished images. Honert's negative review later became a point of discussion in Oskamp's interview with Frank Neubauer for *Zack*, another specialist magazine for comics readers. In *Zack*, Oskamp defended his work as autobiographical and described in detail his working out a plot structure through interactions with Cédric Fortier, Paul Derouet, Reinhard Kleist and Uli Oesterle as testimony to the degree of artistic intervention that even a "rein autobiografisch [er]" text can undergo.[15] In fact, the pedagogical *Begleitmaterial* on Oskamp's website describes the graphic novel's plot structure in terms of the well-known "Hero's Journey" attributed to Joseph Campbell ("Begleitmaterial" 3–6). Yet even the more sympathetic Neubauer agreed with some of Honert's criticisms, likewise describing the art as inconsistent and declaring that the recruitment of Thomas by Neo-Nazis did not seem convincing to him.[16]

Among personal blogs, reactions similarly focussed on *Drei Steine*'s message rather than its form. In the blog *Litterae Artesque*, for example, Uwe Rennicke praised the book's coloring but described the drawing style only as "sehr genau gezeichnet." Against the background of rising extremism and *Fremdenfeindlich-*

---

[15] Cédric Fortier (1980–) is a French comics artist; Paul Derouet (1947–) is a French comics translator and talent agent headquartered in Hamburg; Reinhard Kleist (1970–) and Uli Oesterle (1966–) are German comics writers/artists known for their biographical or autobiographical works (e.g., Oesterle's *Vatermilch*, in two volumes; Carlsen Verlag, 2020–2023; Kleist's biographical comics are mentioned above).

[16] The Neo-Nazis' attempt to recruit Tom is in fact explained in the graphic novel – they admire his fighting spirit and mistake him for a nationalist despite his aiding Nils – to which Oskamp's further statements to Neubauer add little (*Drei Steine* 70; Neubauer 35–36).

keit, he considered the comic "ein interessantes Unterrichtsmittel für deutsche Geschichte bzw. die politische Bildung an Schulen" ("Dresdner Bücherjunge"). Vanessa Nagel, in the librarian-oriented blog *LibTips*, focused briefly on the narrative, which she found lacking in depth, yet concluded that Oskamp nevertheless succeeds in telling a story of "Hoffnung und Umbruch" ("v"). Frank Lang lamented in his blog *Der Büchernarr* that "mit dem Erstarken der rechten Szene in Deutschland wird [das Buch] leider wieder sehr aktuell," but also declared the character design to be lacking, making it difficult to differentiate between characters and thus to interpret what was happening.[17]

While many of these observations are subjective, the quality of the artwork was certainly affected by the rush to finish the project. For example, not only some of the minor characters, but also Nils and Tom are often difficult to tell apart, other than their differing haircuts. The size of characters' heads relative to their bodies also varies from panel to panel, making the protagonists magically appear a few years older or younger than their putative age of thirteen. Keeping characters on-model generally proves to be a challenge: the antagonistic teacher Frau Kunz, for instance, first appears as a realistic if stereotypical "old maid" (*Drei Steine* 12), but sixteen pages later she is an outright witch, with a sharper nose and chin and completely different hairdo (*Drei Steine* 28–29).[18] This portrayal seems more to conform with the depictions of the other antagonistic figures – the elderly teacher who glorifies Stalingrad (*Drei Steine* 48–55), or "der alte Fritz," a former SS-officer who now recruits young hooligans (*Drei Steine* 59–60, 72–75) – whose features are more clearly caricatured than the other characters, to a degree that does not always seem well integrated with the otherwise realistic style throughout.

Many of Oskamp's action scenes also seem stiffly posed (for example, the extended battle on pages 39–42), and even scenes of normal conversation occasionally show characters gesticulating almost comically (such as Nils's outraged father's speech, 35).

---

[17] Personal blogs often take longer to react to publications than commercial press organs. Rennicke's post is from August 2016, shortly after *Drei Steine*'s publication, but Nagel's is over three years later (November 2019) and Lang's is almost exactly four years later.

[18] Nils's mother is the only other female character who speaks, incidentally, with a total of three utterances (*Drei Steine* 22, 32–33). Nils's few female Pantheon characters, and the Nazi Fritz's wife is clearly forbidden to speak (*Drei Steine* 73, 75). This is a stark contrast with the active female figures in *Andi* (set in the "present" of the early 2000s), where Andi is romantically interested in his assertive hijabi friend Ayshe, and even the ardent Neo-Nazi student Magda bristles at her mentor figure Müller's condescending sexism (Grumke and Schaaf 19).

However, there are also many well-drawn, expressive panels, particularly closeups, demonstrating Oskamp's talent as an artist, and it seems unlikely in any case that the comic's young target audience is invested in artistic virtuosity at the expense of a gripping story.

There are indeed narrative gaps as well: for example, while the neglect shown by Nils's parents is partly justified by the father's academic job in distant Kiel and the mother's grief at her own father's death (*Drei Steine* 33–35), Nils's brother Jonas disappears completely after only two pages (*Drei Steine* 30–31), with no explanation for the contempt he shows not only Nils, but also his own friend Tom (who simply becomes Nils' friend instead).[19] This situation also leads to the comic's most awkward piece of dialogue, when Tom interrupts a gang of Neo-Nazis about to beat Nils with a few swift blows and the line: "Keiner schlägt hier den Bruder meines Kumpels" (*Drei Steine* 40), snarled like a *bon mot* from an action movie. Notably, none of Oskamp's family members or teachers appear after the halfway point of the plot, making the young protagonist seem isolated to the point of active abuse and raising serious questions about the Oskamp family dynamic – including the question of whence Nils derives a moral certitude and uprightness that nobody else in his family demonstrates.[20] Again, however, the narrative's swift pace is engaging enough that these instances are no obstacle to enjoying the suspense, and it may well be that some teenage readers sympathize even more strongly with Nils' feelings of isolation and with the touch of melodrama in the dialogue.

IV

A controversial aspect of the graphic novel is its appropriation of Jewish suffering as a vehicle for the non-Jewish protagonist's character development – which it does in a manner fully consonant with the prevailing German *Erinnerungskultur*.

If the inciting plot incident of *Drei Steine* – in terms of the "Hero's Journey" and the "Ruf des Abenteuers" ("Begleitmaterial" 5) – is Nils' classmate Andreas dismissing a lesson on the Holocaust as "eine reine Propagandalüge der Besatzungsmächte, um deren eigene Kriegsverbrechen zu vertuschen!" (*Drei Steine* 13),

---

[19] Oskamp was later able to reconcile with his father, who died just as *Drei Steine* was about to be published (Neubauer 36); however, Oskamp is estranged from his brother, who repeatedly attempted to stop the graphic novel's publication while relativizing the Holocaust and, during the COVID-19 pandemic, embracing conspiracy theories (Ihme 111).

[20] The instructor who teaches the lesson on the Holocaust that sets off the plot, and who at least seems to take his job seriously (Oskamp 13), also never appears again.

followed by Nils's ridicule of him – "Massenmörder verehren. Du bist doch bekloppt!" (*Drei Steine* 14), then its first plot point, marking the point of no return for Nils, comes at the end of that day. After using judo to fend off another classmate's attack, Nils rides his bicycle home past a Jewish cemetery (which he seems to have never previously noticed), dismounting to find it vandalized, with toppled headstones and antisemitic graffiti. Here he sees the eponymous three stones on one of the headstones, and muses, "Es gibt keine Gräber nach 1938 . . . Wenn es hier seit 45 Jahren kein jüdisches Leben mehr gibt, . . . wie kann man dann behaupten, dass es den Holocaust nie gegeben hat?" (*Drei Steine* 20), as he puts the stones in his pocket and leaves (Fig. 2). With this gesture, Nils takes up the burden of remembrance and appropriates the act of Jewish mourning, riding his bicycle toward the distant horizon.[21]

Nils' experience here is believable: in 1980, only three years before the events of *Drei Steine*, American academic Lisa Kahn, fearing "dass der Holocaust so gut wie vergessen ist in Deutschland – trotz Fernsehsendung" (Kahn),[22] travelled to Unterbalbach (Baden-Württemberg), about 350 km southeast of Dortmund, to visit a Jewish cemetery. Once she located both the graveyard and a reluctant, deaf caretaker with its keys, she found it neglected (though not vandalized). With similar thoughts to those Oskamp describes in his younger self, Kahn expresses reflections on this experience as follows:

> Die letzten drei Steine,[23] groß, fast prächtig, die Schrift wohlerhalten, müssen für angesehene Bürger gewesen sein, zumindest für wohlhabende. Sie datieren vom 17. Dezember 1937, 4. Februar 1938, 12. März 1938. Gingen zu diesen letzten Begräbnissen noch viele mit? Gab es nach dem 12. März 1938 keine Alten, keine Gebrechlichen mehr, die man in ihrer Heimat hätte sterben lassen können? Wurden sie alle, alle abtransportiert? (Kahn)

The particular grave that Kahn sought is never named; she could not find it on the overgrown grounds: "Es ist doch her stürzend [sic], daß im Land des Wirtschaftswunders –, und die Wohlhabenheit der Bürger schaut doch aus all ihren Knopflöchern heraus! – immer noch jüdische Friedhöfe völlig verwildern, sei es aus Mangel an Teilnahme, an bewilligten Mitteln oder beidem" (Kahn). If Kahn's

---

21 In his own *Begleitmaterial*, Oskamp places the cemetery visit between "Aufbruch, Schritt über die Schwelle" and "Prüfung, Verbündete und Feinde" stations of the "Hero's Journey" ("Begleitmaterial" 5–6).
22 This refers to the West German broadcast of the 1978 American television miniseries *Holocaust*, directed by Marvin J. Chomsky. The German-dubbed version was transmitted on WDR and in ARD's *Drittes Fernsehprogramm* in January 1979, leading to intense public discussion of German historical responsibility for National Socialist atrocities.
23 The *Steine* here are simply *Grabsteine*; visitation stones are not mentioned.

Fig. 2: Nils encounters the three stones in the Jewish cemetery (*Drei Steine* 20).

experience in Unterbalbach only increased her anxiety that the Holocaust was being forgotten, however, Nils Oskamp leaves the cemetery further convinced that it should be remembered; and yet, after this scene, the words *Jude, jüdisch* and *Holocaust* are never mentioned again within the comic proper (as opposed to the prose afterword that explains the significance of the three stones, and the lengthy documentary account of Neo-Nazism in Dortmund by Alice Lanzke that serves as the comic's appendix; 121–122, 125–139).[24]

Again, the absence of Jews is plausible in the historical context and certainly reflects Oskamp's real-life experience: Dortmund's tiny Jewish population numbered 351 in 1970 and only 337 in 1989 ("Dortmund") of a total population of around 600,000.[25] The Jewish population of Westphalia as a whole, including Lippe, was only 2,049 in 1987 (Aschoff 44), and thus half the size of the Jewish community in Dortmund alone in 1933: 4,108 – though by the dates on the last gravestones in 1938, that number had shrunk to 2,600 ("Dortmund"). It is thus unsurprising that Nils has no Jewish schoolmates in the 1980s, and that not a single living Jewish person appears in the story.[26] This is consistent with the experience of many German students between that era and the present who, like their American and British counterparts, have experienced decades of Holocaust education and yet still have little or no direct contact with Jewish fellow citizens – to the extent that in 2020, the *Zentralrat der Juden in Deutschland* established a "Meet a Jew" program to enable non-Jewish Germans to encounter Jews face to face (Horn; Solomon).[27]

This absence of lived Jewish experience has also been observed in other visual media, such as the cinema. In *Framed Visions*, Gerd Gemünden says of the avant-garde filmmaker Herbert Achternbusch, who often used fantasy images of Native Americans in his films:

> . . . in [Achternbusch's] Indian fantasies the Jew is everywhere, not as a physical reality but as an absence that demands recollection . . . . They are virtually extinct in Germany, and, according to Achternbusch, contemporary Germany has made no effort to preserve those traces of Jewish life the Nazis had not managed to eradicate, thus continuing the politics of the final solution. In his films real Jews are as absent as real Native Americans; for Achtern-

---

24 The one exception is a mention of "die jüdische Weltverschwörung" as the Neo-Nazi ring tries to recruit Tom (*Drei Steine* 74).
25 Dortmund's population shrank from 639,000 in 1970 to 591,000 in 1989 ("Dortmund, Germany"), likely due to the economic downturn that Oskamp depicts as background to the rise of far-right movements (*Drei Steine* 22).
26 In Düsseldorf in the early 2000s, the eponymous hero of the *Andi* comics likewise has no Jewish schoolmates, although his best friends are Muslim and he has one Asian friend (*Andi 1* 18).
27 Even in 2021, one of the interviewees speaking with Solomon reports, the most common question asked was "There are still Jews in Germany?" – not much better than the American students who ask, as one Texas teacher told Horn, "Are any Jews still alive today?" (Solomon; Horn).

busch both are imaginary people who can be represented only by the void they have left in our cultures and whose remembrance is therefore an act of mourning. (Gemünden 125)[28]

In Oskamp's *Drei Steine*, Jews are likewise only represented by a void ("Wenn es hier seit 45 Jahren kein jüdisches Leben mehr gibt"), at best metonymically by the gravestones in a few panels, and in fact their absence is taken as the guarantee that the Holocaust really happened (*Drei Steine* 20). This is not the story of defending those Jews – for that it is too late – but nor do any living Jews enter the picture. Rather, the absent Holocaust victims symbolize in their very absence the humanistic and democratic values that must be defended from resurgent Nazism. The fact that the *drei Steine* are specifically part of a funerary tradition, representing the void the dead have left, thus gives the title a macabre resonance.

V

If the inaction of the authority figures in *Drei Steine* seems implausible to today's reader, that is a sign of progress: The plot takes place at the beginning of Helmut Kohl's chancellorship (1982–1998), which started with attempts to distance the West German state from the original Nazi regime's crimes, claiming – falsely, as *Drei Steine* bears witness – that the lessons of history had been learned. Over the course of the long Kohl era, however, the tide turned toward acknowledging the Holocaust's long shadow. As Jacob Eder puts it in a critical overview of the inconsistencies of German *Erinnerungspolitik*:

> Stieß Kohl also in den 1980er Jahren mit "Schlussstrich"-Projekten wie der Versöhnungszeremonie mit Ronald Reagan auf dem Soldatenfriedhof in Bitburg oder seinen Plänen für eine zentrale Gedenkstätte in Bonn, die nicht genauer zwischen Opfern der Deutschen und deutschen Opfern differenzieren sollte, auf heftige Gegenwehr innerhalb der deutschen Gesellschaft, so sprach er zum Ende seiner Regierungszeit mit großer Selbstverständlichkeit vom Holocaust als "Kern unseres Selbstverständnisses als Nation." Ohne Zweifel spielte politisches Kalkül hier eine Rolle, was jedoch einen genuinen Gesinnungswandel und langfristige Lernprozesse nicht ausschließt. (Eder)

Adam Sutcliffe claims that this increasing emphasis on the Holocaust as a defining factor of German identity coincided with the rise throughout the West of "a new, non-ideological, emotionally resonant, and hopeful framework for learning from the past," a framework "largely met by enshrining empathy with Holocaust

---

[28] Gemünden consistently uses the term "Indian" in the context of "Indian fantasies": "Indians" are fictionalized representations of Native Americans, not the real people.

victims as the locus classicus of morally improving engagement with the horror of history" (Sutcliffe 223).

In recent years, however, Germany's *Erinnerungskultur* has become increasingly contested (see, for example, Kuras; Buck; Cronin). According to political scientist Dirk Moses, this has resulted in a focus on the Holocaust as a uniquely evil event that beggars comparison with, for example, the massacres of African natives under German colonialism, or the Nazi regime's attempts to exterminate other ethnic or social groups – and also obligates unquestioning German support for Israel and condemnation of anti-Zionism. Moses controversially labelled this relationship to the Holocaust "Der Katechismus der Deutschen," claiming that it had led to an "erlösender Philosemitismus" meant to negate the National Socialist mindset, but in practice allowing non-Jewish Germans to police the opinions of migrants, foreigners and even Jews and Israelis critical of current governments in Israel (Moses).

At the same time, this *Erinnerungskultur* did not displace other aspects of German identity. When William Noah Glucroft asked in 2020 why German state media, funded by fees incumbent on all households, allotted time for broadcasting Christian church services, he "was told that Christianity is part of Germany's *Selbstverständnis* . . . and therefore a key component of their public service mission." Glucroft points out that ever more Germans are in fact becoming non-believers, but the state's public embrace of Christianity "sends a powerful signal about who is, and is not, considered part of the nation" (Glucroft). In practice,

> When Jews, Muslims, and other groups fall victim to far-right violence, the German response is couched in the language of tolerance, not acceptance. State protection is afforded on the basis of human rights, not German rights, because these groups are considered outsiders *even though in many cases they are not*. (Glucroft; emphasis added)

By failing to displace the German *Selbstverständnis* as a Christian culture, the rise of a *Selbstverständnis* based on *Erinnerungskultur* has done little to prevent a growing antisemitism threatening contemporary German Jews, as rising attacks on synagogues and Jewish individuals demonstrate (nor has it countered increasing Islamophobia or secured Muslim Germans' safety). Rather, it has only turned Moses's "erlösender Philosemitismus" into what Sutcliffe reframes as "redemptive anti-antisemitism" that

> draws its underlying emotional power, as did redemptive antisemitism for the Nazis, from the fact that it rests on a largely unspoken messianic conception of history, which rests in turn on deep-seated connections in Western thinking between Jewish suffering and world-historical transformation. (Sutcliffe 233)

And indeed, against this background, *Drei Steine* is the story of young Nils' personal development through "redemptive anti-antisemitism," as he forsakes responding to the Neo-Nazis' violence with violence of his own. This process begins when he hesitates to bring the second of the three stones down on his antagonist Andreas's head, thinking: "Du sollst nicht töten. Das hatte ich noch einige Zeit vorher von meinem Pastor im Konfirmandenunterricht gehört" (91; Fig. 3).[29]

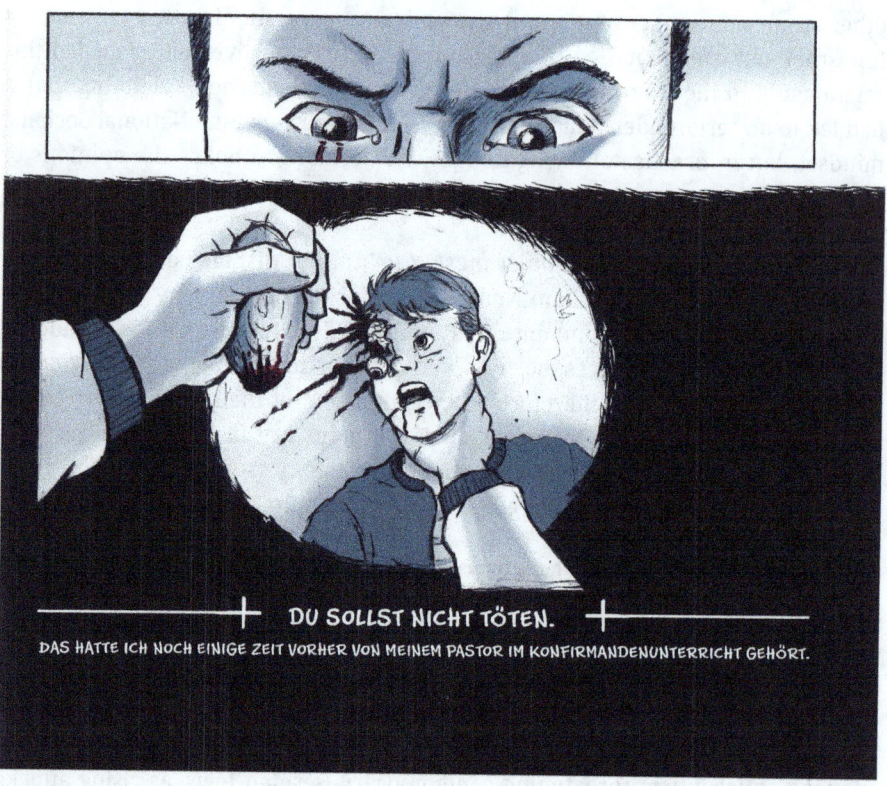

Fig. 3: Nils thinks better of using the second stone to kill his adversary (*Drei Steine* 91).

Nils' development continues when the tables are turned and Nils is badly beaten by the Neo-Nazi gang under SS-Michi's direction: Nils lies in a bright red pool of his own blood, with his school folder bearing a picture of James Dean, captioned ". . . denn sie wissen nicht, was sie tun" (*Drei Steine* 106–107; Fig. 4).

---

29 In terms of the "Hero's Journey," Oskamp sees this as "Der Weg zurück" ("Begleitmaterial" 5–6).

Fig. 4: Nils, beaten almost to death, juxtaposed with James Dean (*Drei Steine* 107).

The cinematic iris-in effect that frames the unconscious Nils within a growing black circle recapitulates the earlier subjective shot of Nils's violent revenge fantasy, where the black circle represents Nils' focus.[30] Likewise, the first Biblical reference (to the Old Testament's Ten Commandments) is echoed in a quotation from the New Testament, specifically from Christ's passion – here in the form of a film poster: . . . *denn sie wissen nicht, was sie tun* is the German title of the 1955 film *Rebel Without a Cause* (released in West Germany in March 1956). Nils, whose letterman jacket or *Collegejacke*, here juxtaposed with Nils' red blood, recalls the iconic red jacket worn by Dean's character Jim Stark, is a rebel *with* a cause, and he now turns that cause away from violence.[31]

---

[30] The significance of these two events is marked by their departure from an otherwise conventional and functional panel layout throughout.

[31] *Rebel Without a Cause* was retitled with a Biblical quotation in Germany because Dean's previous film, *East of Eden* (1955), had been a hit under the title *Jenseits von Eden*. On the two occa-

Lying in his hospital bed, Nils tells Tom that he no longer wants to fight the Neo-Nazis in the streets: "Nein, ich will das nicht, wenn wir jetzt nicht damit aufhören, wird noch jemand sterben" (*Drei Steine* 113), turning to the legal system for recourse instead despite his skepticism – which turns out to be justified. In the "Hero's Journey" schema, this recovery and renunciation form the "Wiederauferstehung" ("Begleitmaterial" 5–6). And Nils' process of redemption concludes thirty years later in Yad Vashem, when he once more turns the final stone into a visitation stone at the resistance fighters' memorial (*Drei Steine* 120).[32] Oskamp labels this action "Rückkehr mit dem Elixir" ("Begleitmaterial" 5–6), indicating both the hero's completed resurrection/purification and the healing of his land.

In the summer of 2016, as *Drei Steine* had just been published, Oskamp was interviewed by Ralf Hutter for the newspaper *Neues Deutschland* and remarked on the topic of victimhood:

> "Es gibt sonst keine Geschichte aus Opfersicht," begründet der Autor die Wichtigkeit seines Buches. Trotz der immensen Nazi-Gewalt der letzten Jahrzehnte kennt Oskamp als Zeugnis aus Opfersicht nur das 2013 erschienene Buch von Semiya Şimşek, der Tochter des vom Nationalsozialistischen Untergrund (NSU) 2000 in Nürnberg ermordeten Enver Şimşek. (Hutter)

Although the graphic novel's entire plot is initiated by contradicting a schoolmate's Holocaust denial, the *Opfer* of whom Oskamp speaks are not the Jews murdered by the Nazis – to say that there are no accounts from this viewpoint, even among comics alone, would clearly be false – but rather the victims of modern Neo-Nazism. The suffering of those who died in the Shoah plays no part in the story of Oskamp's own *via dolorosa* at the hands of a new generation of perpetrators. Dennis Betzholz, writing in *Welt am Sonntag* three months after Hutter's article, clearly recognizes this when he writes of Oskamp, "Dabei liegt *das Martyrium, das er erlebt hat,* 33 Jahre zurück" (Betzholz 3; emphasis added).[33] Oskamp himself revealed to Frank Neubauer that the theological aspect of his story had only become clear to him in the last stage of working on the story and that at that

---

sions that I have taught *Drei Steine* in a graduate-level course, however, none of the German native-speaker graduate students – admittedly a very small sample – recognized the Biblical reference, though they knew the film.

32 Jewish tradition recommends that visitation stones be placed with the left hand, but the photograph shows Oskamp holding and laying this final stone with his right hand. This is doubly curious because on the facing page with the book's *Nachwort*, he draws a Biblical-era Jew laying a stone on a grave with his left hand (121); and at several points throughout *Drei Steine*, we see that Nils is himself left-handed (*Drei Steine* 24, 38, 56). Various sources indicate, however, that laying stones is an informal, relatively recent tradition, neither codified nor uniformly observed.

33 The visual reference to James Dean, who, like many short-lived celebrities, is seen as a kind of martyr (Springer 25, 35), further reinforces this sense of sacrifice.

point a circle had closed for him. With regard to the historical perpetrators, he stated: "Ob ich den Tätern von damals vergeben kann, wird wohl eine meiner nächsten Prüfungen sein" (Neubauer 35).

The displacement of the historical Jewish victims into the void to make room for Oskamp and others in the present is required by the structures of redemptive anti-antisemitism, as Sutcliffe points out:

> Like the caged canary whose death indicates that the mine must be evacuated because lethally poisonous gas is present, Jewish suffering from the gas of racist hatred provides an early warning that others must take action so that they do not meet the same fate . . . . The instrumentalist and Christological sacrificial logic of this metaphor highlights redemptive anti-antisemitism's deep theological resonance. (Sutcliffe 229–230)

As Dara Horn says, however, "using dead Jews as symbols isn't helping living ones"; and placing a stone from a Jewish German's grave at Yad Vashem's Pillar of Heroism, though it may be purifying for the protagonist, is hardly "returning the elixir" if it does nothing to heal Germany.

VI

None of these objections should be taken to impugn Oskamp's sincerity or disparage his efforts. As mentioned above, he works within the existing context of the social and media structures at hand – it would be even more difficult to obtain financial support if he did not. He has also faced ongoing threats of retaliation from Neo-Nazi groups, including twenty death threats, since *Drei Steine* was published; all the more because his wife Maria Zarada, a photographer whom he met in 2013, is a Sicilian of Sinti background whose own family was decimated under the Nazis in the 1940s. The couple is forced to keep secret their address in Hamburg, and Zarada has nonetheless faced physical assault on the street (Ihme 110). Illustration jobs have tailed off – not only for Oskamp, but in general – and he makes his living mainly as a political educator touring schools (Ihme 110), facilitated through frameworks such as the Projekt CleaRNetworking, supported by the *Bundeszentrale für politische Bildung* ("Mit Comics gegen rechts!"), and the *Landeszentrale für politische Bildung* of North Rhine-Westphalia ("Drei Steine: Publikationen").

However valid some of the criticisms of *Drei Steine* as a standalone work may be, its intended function within a broader and more interactive pedagogical strategy serves to mitigate many of the comic's weaknesses. This strategy, elucidated on Oskamp's website (dreisteine.com), involves interactive readings and multimedia presentations at schools by the author, which also serve to advertise both *Drei*

Steine – increasing the graphic novel's commercial viability – and Oskamp's forthcoming projects. In the context of this participatory pedagogy, many of *Drei Steine*'s apparent weaknesses become teaching opportunities: for example, one question to be workshopped with students asks who did or did not help Nils ("Pädagogisches Begleitmaterial"). Supplementary materials detail the historical development and features of far-right groups and the form of their arguments, as well as provide online information resources ("Begleitmaterial" 11). They even explain how to lay charges against extremists and follow the court process ("Pädagogisches Begleitmaterial"). Some of the materials Oskamp uses are still supplied by the Amadeu Antonio Stiftung (Ihme 108), in line with its mission to promote "bundesweit Projekte, die sich für eine demokratische Zivilgesellschaft stark machen. Besonders im ländlichen Raum" ("Amadeu Antonio Stiftung"). These materials facilitate various creative projects, including street art, filmmaking, poster making and, of course, making comics ("Begleitprogramm").[34] As he tells Ihme, Oskamp has so far spoken to about 150,000 young people during over 370 readings and more than 250 workshops, despite the interruption caused by the COVID-19 pandemic and subsequent funding cuts in the field of political education (Ihme 108).

One result of the focus on Holocaust education in Western Europe and North America, however, has been an increasing weight of evidence that Holocaust education, as it has been carried out, does little to eradicate antisemitism (e.g., Pearce, Foster and Pettigrew; Hänel; Solomon; Horn). Against this background, Sutcliffe describes the tensions caused by rising criticism of Israel's actions in Gaza in 2009: "The widespread perception of Israeli responsibility for Palestinian suffering clashed jarringly with the paradigm of redemptive anti-antisemitism, which associated Holocaust remembrance and Jewish history with drawing morally elevating lessons from victimhood" (Sutcliffe 235). These tensions have only become more extreme, in Germany and elsewhere, since the Hamas invasion of Israel in October 2023 and Israel's reprisal, with unforeseeable consequences for the maintenance of Germany's already-embattled *Erinnerungskultur* or for Oskamp's pedagogical project, which is heavily intertwined with that culture and apparently entirely uncritical of it.

Despite such uncertainty, *Drei Steine* is being expanded for an even longer, redrawn international edition in both German and English. Meanwhile, Oskamp and Zarada have traveled through Europe to produce a photographic book, *Memorial Sites of Nazi Terror in Europe*, whose production will form the basis of his

---

34 Many of the pedagogical strategies used with *Drei Steine* had already been used with the *Andi* comics, among others; see Grumke's and Schaaff's contributions to the Palandt anthology.

next graphic novel, *Die Halbierung* – titled in part after the many friends and family members who disowned Oskamp as a result of his activities (Ihme 110). Although the projects were supposed to be published to coincide with the eightieth anniversary of the concentration camps' liberation in 2025, Oskamp had already begun collecting rejection letters from funding agencies in early 2024 (Ihme 107), and no forthcoming formal publication had been announced as of early 2025. Nonetheless, Oskamp remains as impassioned as he was in a 2017 interview: "Wenn eine jugendliche Person eine Neonazigruppierung an ihrer Schule hat und sich aufgrund der Geschichte überlegt, den Blödsinn nicht mitzumachen, hat sich die ganze Arbeit schon gelohnt" ("Ruben" 28).

The comics medium, as Véronique Sina writes in 2023, "hat sich . . . [d]ank seiner Darstellungsvielfalt und seines erzählerischen Potenzials als wertvoller Teil der Erinnerungskultur etabliert" (Sina 7).[35] With far-right chauvinist parties such as the *Alternative für Deutschland* (*AfD*) encroaching ever more on mainstream politics and emboldening even more extreme groups, Oskamp's work and his activity in political education remain an important counterbalance despite the weaknesses of Germany's *Erinnerungskultur*. Given Oskamp's difficulties in acquiring financial support in the last decade and a half, however, it might become yet more challenging to apply for funding under either a federal or state government that includes the *AfD* in a coalition, or even in opposition. In either case, Oskamp's future career as an artist and educator will be worth examining for further developments.

Works Cited

Aschoff, Diethard. "The Current State of the Study of Jewish History in Westphalia." *Shofar*, vol. 15, no. 4, 1997, pp. 41–58. jstor.org/stable/42942651. Accessed 31 Oct. 2024.

Betzholz, Dennis. "Von Gewalt gezeichnet." *Welt am Sonntag*, 9 Oct. 2016, p. 3.

Buck, Tobias. "The Fight for Germany's 'Memory Culture.'" *Financial Times*, 9 Mar. 2024, ft.com/content/3ecdaff5-23b3-4afa-8cd7-3123ddabd2fa. Accessed 15 Oct. 2024.

Cronin, Joseph. "Germany's Holocaust Memory Problems." *Georgetown Journal of International Affairs*, 20 Apr. 2022, gjia.georgetown.edu/2022/04/20/germanys-holocaust-memory-problems%ef%bf%bc/. Accessed 15 Oct. 2024.

"Die Amadeu Antonio Stiftung stellt sich vor." *Amadeu Antonio Stiftung*, amadeu-antonio-stiftung.de/ueber-uns/. Accessed 28 Oct. 2024.

---

[35] Note, however, that Sina's frame of reference is "die internationale Comiclandschaft," with a particular focus on Spiegelman's *Maus* (Sina 8–14) and other directly Holocaust-related comics. None of the other works she discusses briefly are of German origin, although several have been published in German translation.

Ditschke, Stephan. "Comics als Literatur: Zur Etablierung des Comics im deutschsprachigen Feuilleton seit 2003." *Comics: Zur Geschichte und Theorie eines populärkulturellen Mediums*, edited by Stephan Ditschke, Katerina Kroucheva and Daniel Stein, Transcript Verlag, 2009, pp. 265–280.

Dolle-Weinkauff, Bernd. *Comics: Geschichte einer populären Literaturform in Deutschland seit 1945*. Beltz, 1990.

"Dortmund." *Jewish Virtual Library*, jewishvirtuallibrary.org/dortmund. Accessed 29 Oct. 2024.

"Dortmund, Germany Metro Area Population 1950–2024." *Macrotrends*, macrotrends.net/global-metrics/cities/204310/dortmund/population. Accessed 29 Oct. 2024.

"Drei Steine." *Panini.de*, https://www.panini.de/shp_deu_de/drei-steine-yddrei001-de01.html. Accessed 7 May 2025.

"Drei Steine: Publikationen der Landeszentrale für politische Bildung Nordrhein-Westfalen." *Lpb.nrw*. politische-bildung.nrw.de/publikationen/titelverzeichnis/details/print/drei-steine/. Accessed 18 Nov. 2024.

"Dresdner Bücherjunge" [Uwe Rennicke]. "Oskamp, Nils: Drei Steine." *Litterae Artesque*, 6 Aug. 2016, litterae-artesque.blogspot.com/2016/08/oskamp-nils-drei-steine.html. Accessed 27 Oct. 2024.

Eder, Jacob. "Der Weg ist das Ziel: Deutsche Erinnerungspolitik und ihre Widersprüche." *Geschichte der Gegenwart*, 23 June 2021, geschichtedergegenwart.ch/jacob-eders-text/. Accessed 15 Oct. 2024.

Fazblog – Blogs der FAZ, FAZ.net, blogs.faz.net/. Accessed 27 Oct. 2024.

Gemünden, Gerd. *Framed Visions: Popular Culture, Americanization, and the Contemporary German and Austrian Imagination*. U of Michigan P, 1998.

Glucroft, William Noah. "Germany's Inadequate Culture of Remembrance." *Berlin Policy Journal*, 21 Jan. 2020, berlinpolicyjournal.com/germanys-inadequate-culture-of-remembrance/. Accessed 15 Oct. 2024.

Grumke, Thomas. "*Andi* – Bildungscomic für Demokratie und gegen Extremismus." *Rechtsextremismus, Rassismus und Antisemitismus in Comics*, edited by Ralf Palandt, Archiv der Jugendkulturen Verlag, 2011, pp. 182–191.

Grumke, Thomas, and Peter Schaaff. *Andi 1*. Innenministerium des Landes Nordrhein-Westfalen, 2005.

Grumke, Thomas, and Peter Schaaff. *Andi 2*. Innenministerium des Landes Nordrhein-Westfalen, 2007.

Gundermann, Christine. "Abschied von Farbe und Fiktion? Comics in der politisch-historischen Bildung." *Wissen durch Bilder: Sachcomics als Medien von Bildung und Information*, edited by Urs Hangartner, Felix Keller and Dorothea Oechslin, Transcript, 2013, pp. 149–169. doi.org/10.1515/transcript.9783839419830.149. Accessed 28 Jan. 2025.

Hänel, Lisa. "Antisemitismus trotz Erinnerungskultur." *Deutsche Welle*, 6 May 2020, dw.com/de/antisemitismus-trotz-erinnerungskultur/a-53342458. Accessed 15 Oct. 2024.

Honert, Moritz. "'Drei Steine' von Nils Oskamp: Deutsche Jugend in Schwarzweiß." *Tagesspiegel*, 3 July 2016, tagesspiegel.de/kultur/comics/deutsche-jugend-in-schwarzweiss-3735520.html. Accessed 15 Oct. 2024.

Horn, Dara. "Is Holocaust Education Making Anti-Semitism Worse?" *The Atlantic*, 3 Apr. 2023, theatlantic.com/magazine/archive/2023/05/holocaust-student-education-jewish-anti-semitism/673488/. Accessed 13 Oct. 2024.

Hutter, Ralf. "Allein im Nazi-Sumpf." *Neues Deutschland*, 20 July 2016, p. 7, nd-aktuell.de/artikel/1019253.allein-im-nazi-sumpf.html. Accessed 18 Oct. 2024.

Ihme, Burkhard. "'Den Schneeball kann man noch zertreten, die Lawine hält keener mehr auf': Interview mit Nils Oskamp." *Comic! Jahrbuch 2024*, edited by Burkhard Ihme, Interessenverband Comic e.V. ICOM, 2024, pp. 106–112.

Kahn, Lisa. "Vergessene Gräber: '. . .'s gibt ja keine Juden mehr.'" *Zeit Online*, 12 Sept. 1980, zeit.de/1980/38/s-gibt-ja-keine-jude-mehr. Accessed 28 Oct. 2024.

Kuras, Peter. "Germany's Holocaust Remembrance Is Turning Upside Down." *Foreign Policy*, 20 Feb. 2021, foreignpolicy.com/2021/02/20/germanys-holocaust-remembrance-is-turning-upside-down/. Accessed 15 Oct. 2024.

Lang, Frank. "[Graphic Novel] Drei Steine." *Der Büchernarr*, 19 Aug. 2020, buechernarr.org/graphic-novel-drei-steine/. Accessed 28 Oct. 2024.

Malone, Paul M. "A Periphery Surrounded by Centres: The German-Language Comics Market, Transnational Relationships, and Graphic Novels." *Journal of Graphic Novels and Comics*, vol. 11, no. 1, 2020, pp. 10–30. doi:10.1080/21504857.2019.1629506.

Marquardt, Sylvia. "Steffen Volkmer – Panini." *Tötlëgër*, totleger.org/interviews/interviews-mit-verlagen/steffen-volkmer-panini/. Accessed 30 Oct. 2024.

Meyer, Christina, Vanessa Ossa and Lukas R.A. Wilde. "Was war, ist, wird Comicforschung–für uns? Zur Einleitung." *Was war, ist, wird Comicforschung–für uns? 10 Jahre ComFor e.V. als eingetragener Verein*, edited by Christina Meyer, Vanessa Ossa and Lukas R.A. Wilde, Gesellschaft für Comicforschung, 2024, pp. 5–10.

"Mit Comics gegen rechts! – Lesung und Workshop mit Nils Oskamp." *Clearing-Schule.de.*, clearing-schule.de/mit-comics-gegen-rechts-lesung-und-workshop-mit-nils-oskamp/.

Moses, Dirk. "Der Katechismus der Deutschen." *Geschichte der Gegenwart*, 23 May 2021, geschichtedergegenwart.ch/der-katechismus-der-deutschen/. Accessed 28 Oct. 2024.

Neubauer, Frank. "'Der Schoß ist fruchtbar noch': Interview mit Nils Oskamp." *Zack*, Sept. 2016, pp. 35–36.

Oskamp, Nils. "Begleitmaterial." *Drei Steine: Graphic Novel gegen rechts*, dreisteine.com/wp-content/uploads/2022/09/Begleitmaterial-DREI-STEINE-Oskamp_10-1.pdf. Accessed 31 Oct. 2024.

Oskamp, Nils. "Begleitprogramm." *Drei Steine: Graphic Novel gegen rechts*, dreisteine.com/begleitprogramm/. Accessed 31 Oct. 2024.

Oskamp, Nils. *Drei Steine*. Panini, 2016.

Oskamp, Nils. *Drei Steine: Graphic Novel gegen rechts*. dreisteine.com. Accessed 31 Mar. 2025.

Oskamp, Nils. "Pädagogisches Begleitmaterial." *Drei Steine: Graphic Novel gegen rechts*, dreisteine.com/wp-content/uploads/2020/01/A4_Lernmaterialien_UmgangBasic.pdf. Accessed 31 Oct. 2024.

Palandt, Ralf. "Einleitung: Rechtsextremismus, Rassismus und Antisemitismus in Comics." *Rechtsextremismus, Rassismus und Antisemitismus in Comics*, edited by Ralf Palandt, Archiv der Jugendkulturen Verlag, 2011, pp. 5–60.

Pearce, Andy, Stuart Foster and Alice Pettigrew. "Antisemitism and Holocaust Education." *Holocaust Education: Contemporary Challenges and Controversies*, edited by Stuart Foster, Andy Pearce and Alice Pettigrew, UCLP, 2020, pp. 150–170.

Piesbergen, Götz. "Comic-Besprechung – Drei Steine." *Splashcomics*, 18 Aug. 2016, splashcomics.de/php/rezensionen/rezension/23790. Accessed 28 Oct. 2024.

Platthaus, Andreas. "Blogs – Comic: Dortmund im Schatten des Hakenkreuzes." *Frankfurter Allgemeine*, 15 Aug. 2016, faz.net/blogs-1/blogbeitraege/blogs-comic-dortmund-im-schatten-des-hakenkreuzes-14388654.html. Accessed 28 Oct. 2024.

"Rezensionen: Drei Steine – Nils Oskamp." *Antifaschistisches Infoblatt*, 14 Oct. 2016, antifainfoblatt.de/aib111/drei-steine. Accessed 28 Oct. 2024.

"Ruben." "Drei Steine: Graphic Novel von Nils Oskamp über die rechte Szene im Dortmund der 1980er Jahre." *BLATT: Magazin des BDP [Bund Deutscher Pfadfinder_innen]*, no. 1, 2017, pp. 26–28, bundesverband.bdp.org/drei-steine. Accessed 28 Oct. 2024.

Schaaff, Peter. "'Kein Auftrag wie jeder andere' – Über die Arbeit am Bildungscomic *Andi*." *Rechtsextremismus, Rassismus und Antisemitismus in Comics*, edited by Ralf Palandt, Archiv der Jugendkulturen Verlag, 2011, pp. 192–203.

Sina, Véronique. "Comics und Erinnerungskultur: Zur Thematisierung der Shoah in der sequenziellen Kunst." *theologie.geschichte – Zeitschrift für Theologie und Kulturgeschichte*, vol. 18, edited by August H. Leugers-Scherzberg, Katharina Maria Peetz and Lucia Scherzberg, 2023, pp. 1–26. doi.org/10.48603/tg-2023-art-2. Accessed 3 Feb. 2025.

Solomon, Erika. "Germany's Remembrance Culture Fails to Protect Present Day Jews." *Financial Times*, 3 Mar. 2021, ft.com/content/0bf3b0ea-a4b9-4da7-a3b7-a65138692a69. Accessed 30 Oct. 2024.

Springer, Claudia. *James Dean Transfigured: The Many Faces of Rebel Iconography*. U of Texas P, 2007.

Sutcliffe, Adam. "Whose Feelings Matter? Holocaust Memory, Empathy, and Redemptive Anti-Antisemitism." *Journal of Genocide Research*, vol. 26, no. 2, 2024, pp. 222–242, doi.org/10.1080/14623528.2022.2160533. Accessed 30 Oct. 2024.

"v" [Vanessa Nagel]. "Nils Oskamp – Drei Steine." *LibTips*, 24 Nov. 2019, libtips.de/2019/11/24/nils-oskamp-drei-steine/. Accessed 28 Oct. 2024.

Anna Karina Sennefelder
Ökokrieger:innen
Ästhetik und ökokritisches Potential einer neuen Figur am Beispiel von George Millers *Mad Max: Fury Road*, Olivia Viewegs *Endzeit* und Frauke Bergers *Grün*

Abstract: Vorliegender Beitrag verfolgt die These, dass sich aktuell eine revolutionäre Figur transmedial durchsetzt, die ich als Ökokrieger:in bezeichne. Diese unterscheidet sich in ihrer Agentialität und Ästhetik stark von den heteronormativ geprägten Wissenschaftlerinnen aus der Speculative Fiction der 2000er und 2010er Jahre und zeichnet sich durch den bewussten Einsatz konvivialer *tools* im Sinne des frühen Technologiekritikers Ivan Illich aus. Ziel der Ökokrieger:innen ist eine konviviale Gesellschaftsordnung, d. h. eine Form des Zusammenlebens, die auf Rücksichtnahme und Selbstbegrenzung basiert; ihr Kampf richtet sich deshalb spezifisch gegen das Petro-Patriarchat und seine Akteure. Die Ökokrieger:innen sind von sozial- und materiell-ökofeministischen Überzeugungen inspiriert, gehen in ihrem kriegerischen Einsatz aber weit über diese hinaus. Am Beispiel der Figur Furiosa aus dem Film *Mad-Max: Fury Road* (2015) wird die neue Figurenästhetik erläutert, um auf Basis dieser Erkenntnisse die Graphic Novels *Grün* (2018/2019) von Frauke Berger sowie *Endzeit* (2018) von Olivia Vieweg zu analysieren und die Ökokrieger:in damit erstmals konzeptuell und ästhetisch im medienkomparatistischen und ökokritischen Diskurs der Gegenwart zu verorten.

I

Welche Akteure, welche Werkzeuge und welche Formen des gesellschaftlichen Miteinanders sind erforderlich, um das Überleben von Menschen und Nicht-Menschen auf der Erde zu sichern? Inmitten dieser bekannten Fragen des Anthropozäns und seiner multiplen Krisen lässt sich zur Zeit das Entstehen einer revolutionären Figur beobachten, die sowohl ästhetisch als auch gesellschaftspolitisch immenses Potential birgt und die ich als Ökokrieger:in bezeichne. Zu diesem Typus gehörige Figuren kontrastieren mit der Trope der „sidelining women" (Kac-Vergne) die sich seit den 1990er Jahren in der Science Fiction re-etablieren konnte, und das, obwohl gerade dieses Genre zuvor Figuren wie Ellen Ripley und

Sarah Connor[1] hervorgebracht hatte. Kac-Vergne führt diese Entwicklung vor allem darauf zurück, dass „die Allgegenwart des Postfeminismus in der Populärkultur und die Vorstellung, dass Frauen jetzt gleichberechtigt sind, in Wirklichkeit zu einer Tilgung des Feminismus sowie zur Marginalisierung von Frauen im zeitgenössischen Science-Fiction-Film geführt hat"[2] (Kag-Vergne 10–11), weshalb die Erscheinung der Ökokrieger:in auch kulturgeschichtlich mit Blick auf diese Zäsur in den 90er Jahren aufschlussreich für den feministischen Diskurs der Gegenwart ist. Die Ökokrieger:innen unterscheiden sich aber nicht nur von den seltsam saturierten Frauenfiguren der 1990er Science-Fiction, sie haben auch keinerlei Gemeinsamkeiten mehr mit den stereotypen Wissenschaftlerinnen aus dem Ökothriller der 2000er und 2010er Jahre, obwohl sie mit diesen das endgültige Ziel teilen, die Erde als bedrohten Lebensraum vor der totalen Zerstörung zu schützen. Der Ökothriller, der sich bis heute auch im deutschsprachigen Raum großer Beliebtheit erfreut, zeichnet sich durch eine extrem schematische Figurenkonzeption aus. Die weiblichen Protagonistinnen sind hier als naturverbundene und damit ‚ursprünglichere' Wesen angelegt, die instinktiv das Richtige tun, um ‚Mutter Erde' zu schützen, während die ihnen antagonistisch zugeordneten Männer als handlungsmächtige Wissenschaftler nach dem Schema des *Homo Faber* inszeniert werden, letztlich aber auf das ‚weibliche Prinzip' angewiesen sind, um nicht auszusterben. Besonders anschaulich lässt sich diese stereotype Rollenverteilung am Erfolgsökothriller *Der Schwarm* (2004) von Frank Schätzing demonstrieren. Die weiblichen Figuren erliegen hier reihenweise dem Charme des Meeresbiologen Sigur Johanson und werden, dem *male gaze* entsprechend, von Beginn an entweder auf ihre körperliche Attraktivität reduziert – „Nackt sah Karen Weaver aus wie eine Bronzeskulptur, mit schimmernder Haut, unter der sich beeindruckende Muskelstränge entlangzogen" (Schätzing 248–249) – oder sie sind militante Psychopathinnen, die die Destruktion der eigenen Welt billigend in Kauf nehmen (vgl. Schätzing 447–448). Diese auffällige und aus heutiger Perspektive doch erstaunlich banale Figurenzeichnung hängt auch mit der narrativen Struktur dieser Subgattung des Thrillers zusammen:

> Die Technikzukünfte sind im Ökothriller aufgrund seines konventionellen Musters vielleicht noch etwas markanter geschlechtlich codiert als in anderen Technikromanen. Besonders im

---

[1] Ellen Ripley ist die Protagonistin der renommierten *Alien*-Filmreihe und wurde von der bekannten Schauspielerin Sigourney Weaver verkörpert. Seit der Veröffentlichung des ersten Films der Reihe 1979 unter der Regie von Ridley Scott ist Ellen Ripley zu einer ikonischen Figur avanciert, die für ihre Autonomie, ihre Persistenz und Resilienz berühmt ist. Sarah Connor rangiert in derselben Kategorie berühmt gewordener Science-Fiction Frauenfiguren: sie ist die Mutter des Widerstandskämpfers John Connor in der *Terminator*-Filmreihe.
[2] Eigene Übersetzung aus dem Englischen.

> Gegenspiel von Natur and Technik wird ein Gegenspiel zwischen Frau und Mann konstruiert, in dem Ersterer oftmals die Rolle der Mahnerin, Warnerin und des moralischen Gewissens zukommt. (Schneider-Özbek 2018, 235)

Interessanterweise trifft dieser Befund aber auch heute noch auf den populären deutschsprachigen Ökothriller zu, und das, obwohl in den letzten „zehn bis fünfzehn Jahren" etliche Science-Fiction-Romane erschienen sind, „die die gesellschaftspolitische Umweltdebatte nicht nur aufgreifen und verarbeiten, sondern darüber hinaus die genretypischen Eigenschaften der Science-Fiction nutzen, um Probleme weiterzudenken" (Maciejewski 98). Trotz dieser positiven Entwicklung, die den Ökothriller grundsätzlich diverser, umweltkritischer und geschlechtssensibler gemacht hat, bleibt zu vermerken, dass aktuelle Bestseller im Bereich Climate Fiction wie etwa Marc Elsbergs *°C-Celsius* von 2023 oder Christina Sweeney-Bairds *The End of Men* von 2022 noch immer wesentlich mit den binären Geschlechterschemata des Ökothriller aus den 2000er Jahren operieren. So ist etwa die kluge Klimaforscherin in Elsbergs Roman eine Nigerianerin, die mit ihrer Familie in Berlin lebt und mit ihrem Ehemann eine gleichberechtigte Aufteilung von Erwerbs- und Care-Arbeit zu leben versucht. Doch neben den Parametern ‚of color, beruflich erfolgreich und selbstbewusst' verbleibt die Figur im profanen Muster der ‚sexy scientist', die zwar smart und eigenständig erscheint, sich aber letztlich im männerdominierten Machtkampf nicht ausreichend durchsetzen kann. Und auch in Sweeney-Bairds Geschlechterdystopie, in der fast sämtliche Männer der Weltbevölkerung einem Virus erlegen sind, agieren die Frauen innerhalb des neuen Machtvakuum eher mit männlich kodierter Ruchlosigkeit. So entscheidet etwa Lisa, Professorin für Virologie an der Universität Toronto, auf Anraten ihrer Partnerin, den von ihr entdeckten Impfstoff keinesfalls der vom Aussterben bedrohten Menschheit kostenlos zur Verfügung zu stellen, sondern diesen an die kanadische Regierung zu verkaufen. Lisa ist innerhalb der Romanhandlung insofern keineswegs Sympathieträgerin, vielmehr wird sie als egoistisch kalkulierend und ‚bossy' charakterisiert, als jemand, der den persönlichen Vorteil über das politische Ziel stellt.

Ein erster Befund zu gegenwärtigen Öko-Dystopien lautet also, dass zwar mit starren cis-hetero-normativen Normen gebrochen wird, indem etwa die klügsten Köpfe der erzählten Welt auf weiblichen Körpern sitzen und auch Hauptfiguren homosexuell oder *of color* sind, im Grunde aber gibt es noch immer ein „fundamentales Problem", das darin besteht, dass die zentralen Figuren „jenseits von Cyborg und böser Heldin" (Schneider-Özbek 2016, 169) angelegt sind und damit traditionellen Rollenvorstellungen verhaftet bleiben. Die Ökokrieger:innen zeichnen sich vor diesem Hintergrund umso mehr als narrativ und ästhetisch innovative Figuren ab, wie bei der Analyse ihrer Geschlechterkodierung, Handlungsmacht und ihres ökokritischen Potentials im Folgenden gezeigt wird.

II

Verglichen mit den oben besprochenen Wissenschaftlerinnen in zeitgenössischen populären Öko-Dystopien agieren die Ökokrieger:innen wesentlich autonomer, meist sogar gänzlich autark und zeichnen sich durch eine auffällige Figurenästhetik aus. Diese definiere ich als markante Mischung, bei der einerseits ökofeministische Perspektiven auf das Anthropozän gestärkt werden (vgl. Grusin), andererseits aber auffällig retro-ästhetische Werkzeuge zum Einsatz kommen, die ich unter Bezug auf den frühen Technologieskeptiker Ivan Illich als „konviviale Werkzeuge" verstehe (vgl. Abschnitt IV). Bevor die Ökokrieger:innen und ihre Werkzeuge in den beiden deutschsprachigen Graphic Novels[3] *Endzeit* (2018) und *Grün* (2018/2019) analysiert werden, sei die spezifische Ästhetik der Ökokrieger:in zunächst am Beispiel der Figur Furiosa aus George Millers Science-Fiction Film *Mad Max: Fury Road*[4] veranschaulicht, die innerhalb meiner Argumentation den Idealtypus einer Ökokrieger:in verkörpert und deshalb als konzeptuelle und visuelle Referenz für die nachfolgend diskutierten Beispiele fungiert.

Die einarmige, mit einer hochfunktionalen Prothese ausgerüstete Furiosa kann als Ökokrieger:in par excellence verstanden werden. Sie nimmt es in ihrer erzählten Welt – einer von degenerierten und brutalen Warlords dominierten Wüstendystopie – nicht nur mit dem Despoten auf, der dank Monopolstellung die gesamte Bevölkerung kontrolliert, sondern setzt sich zudem für die Befreiung der zur Reproduktion versklavten Frauen ein. Furiosas Krieg richtet sich damit gegen das Petro-Patriarchat als Gesamtkonstrukt: Sie will nicht nur einen gerechten und bewussten Umgang mit den letztverbleibenden Ressourcen – in der Welt von *Mad Max* sind das bezeichnenderweise nur noch Wasser, Öl und Muttermilch – sondern riskiert auch ihr eigenes Leben im Kampf gegen die patriarchale Unterdrückung und sexuelle Ausbeutung der Frau. In der Forschung wurde das kritische Potential dieser Figur bislang kaum gewürdigt und in den wenigen Bespre-

---

[3] Mit der Einordnung als Graphic Novel beziehe ich mich auf die Terminologie von Abel und Klein, nach welcher sich die Graphic Novel, jenseits von Marketing- und Instrumentalisierungsfragen, dadurch auszeichnet, dass sie sich als „Teil des Literaturbetriebs" permanent „neu erfindet" (Abel und Klein 36). Als Graphic Novel verstehe ich entsprechend eine Subform der Gattung Comic, die im Besonderen auf „innovative Ästhetik" und „Selbstreflexivität" setzt (Abel und Klein 156–157).
[4] Im Folgenden zitiert mit *Fury Road*.

chungen vor allem darauf hingewiesen, dass der für seine Action-Ästhetik bekannte Regisseur George Miller mit *Fury Road* eine unerwartete Dekonstruktion des *male gaze* vorlege. Die entsprechenden Szenen im Film, in denen normschöne, dünne, glatthäutige, langhaarige und leichtbekleidete Frauen zu sehen sind, dienten nämlich nicht dazu, dem *male gaze* zu entsprechen, sondern würden diesen vielmehr entlarven. Diese feministische Botschaft ist indes so unmissverständlich, dass sie auch vom oppositionellen Lager sofort als Provokation verstanden wurde, was sich nicht zuletzt daran zeigt, dass manch anti-feministisches Organ sogar zum Boykott von *Fury Road* aufrief. Man(n) beschwerte sich über das „trojanische Pferd", das Miller hier im Sinne der „Feministinnen und Hollywood-Linken" verwende, „um (vergeblich) auf der Trope zu bestehen, dass Frauen in allen Dingen den Männern gleich sind, einschließlich Körperbau, Kraft und Logik" (vgl. Reglińska-Jemioł 110). In der Tat lässt Miller keine Sekunde lang Zweifel an der mentalen und physischen Überlegenheit seiner Heldin aufkommen. Er inszeniert Furiosa durchgängig als souveräne, lässige, mutige und geschickte Figur, die meiner These nach aber viel mehr repräsentiert als eine „weibliche Kriegerin", die an den „Archetypus der Amazone" anknüpft (Reglińska-Jemioł 114).

Furisoa, deren Namenssemantik nicht zufällig die kulturpolitisch vielfach diskutierte und auch literarisch verhandelte ‚weibliche Wut', den *female furor* (vgl. Rauschenberger; Henkel; Fallwickl) evoziert, hält das sprichwörtliche Rad Fortunas bereits von der ersten Filmminute an in der einen, ihr noch verbleibenden Hand. Ihr Auftritt erfolgt nach einer rasanten Action-Jagd, bei der Max Rockatansky, früherer Alleinheld der *Mad Max*-Filmreihe, von den blassen Warboys des Alleinherrschers Immortan Joe gefangen genommen und als *universal donor*, d. h. als lebende Bio- und Blutreserve, im ganz wörtlichen Sinne, mittels einer glühenden Eisenstange, gebrandmarkt wurde. Die Zuschauer:innen sehen Furiosa das erste Mal von hinten, die Kamera folgt ihrem langsam schlendernden Gang und fokussiert ein Lenkrad, das sie in der einen Hand trägt. Im nächsten Moment rammt sie dieses mit einem plötzlichen Ruck in die Lenkvorrichtung eines mordsmäßig motorisierten Tanklasters. Erst nach dieser hochsymbolischen Geste zeigt die Kamera das erste Mal das Gesicht der Figur mit kurzrasiertem Haar und einer auffälligen schwarzen Bemalung über den Augen. Kompakter und eleganter als in dieser Auftrittsszene kann eine postapokalyptische Kriegerin, die es mit einem auf Öl und Waffen basierenden Patriarchat aufnimmt, kaum eingeführt werden. Denn was die Zuschauer:innen in diesen wenigen Bildern zu sehen bekommen, ist nichts Geringeres als die Rückeroberung der zur Wüste verkommenen Welt durch eine Frau, die das Petro-Patriarchat stürzen will, indem sie sich die Waffen des Systems erst zu eigen macht und anschließend gegen dieses wendet. Sie nimmt das Steuer selbst in die Hand, sie bringt den Tanklaster vom vorgesehenen Kurs ab und setzt damit die kriegerische Handlung in Gang. Denn im Inneren des Tanklasters befinden sich nicht nur „Aqua Cola" – wie Wasser in *Mad Max* ironischerweise genannt wird – und Muttermilch als wertvolle Rohstoffe, die in „Gas Town" gegen Öl und an der „Bullet Farm" gegen Waffen eingetauscht werden sollen, sondern Furiosa hat darin auch fünf junge Frauen versteckt, die bis dahin in einem Tresorraum gefangen gehalten wurden (vgl. Abb. 1) und denen sie nun zur Flucht verhelfen will. In diesem maximal antagonistischen Setting agiert Furiosa als autarke Ökokrieger:in, denn anstatt Wasser und Muttermilch – Stoffe, die im kulturellen Ökofeminismus existenziell feminin gedeutet werden – gegen die maskulin-kodierten Rohstoffe Öl und Munition zu tauschen, entzieht sie dem Patriarchen seine wertvollste Ressource: den jungen weiblichen Körper, mittels dessen er das Fortbestehen seiner Gewaltherrschaft zu sichern versucht. Auch diese eindeutige Geste wird zusätzlich mit filmischen Mitteln betont, wenn Immortan Joe den leeren Tresorraum im Innersten seiner Zitadelle betritt und dort eine Nachricht der befreiten Frauen vorfindet:

Abb. 1: Immortan Joe im Tresorraum, *Fury Road*, 14:07.

Die Bildsprache ist provokativ, plakativ und unmissverständlich: die zur Reproduktion gezwungenen Frauen entziehen ihrem Unterdrücker die Kontrolle über ihre Körper und den Nachwuchs und ritzen als Befreiungsgeste die Botschaft „Our Babies will not be Warlords" in den Boden ihres Gefängnisses, die um eine Struktur herum angeordnet wird, die an ein riesiges Spermium erinnert (vgl. Abb. 1). Dieser visuell eindeutige sexuelle Subtext knüpft dabei an die Einführungsszene von Immortan Joe an. In dieser verteilt er, in einem phallischen Gestus absoluter Macht, große Mengen Wasser über einer erwartungsvoll wartenden Menschenmenge, indem er mechanische Hebel umlegt, woraufhin das Wasser sich aus riesigen Röhren auf die Menschen ergießt (vgl. *Fury Road* 8:59–9:15). In seinem ersten Auftritt verschwendet Immortan Joe also die kostbarste Ressource, um seine Macht zu demonstrieren wobei er sprichwörtlich am ‚längeren Hebel' sitzt, den er nutzt, um das von ihm kontrollierte Wasser wie Ejakulat über der lechzenden Menschenmenge zu verspritzen. Bereits nach wenigen Filmminuten wird den Zuschauer:innen damit klargemacht, dass in der Welt von *Mad Max* die Petromaskulinität regiert. Daggett beschreibt mit ihrer Wortkreation „petromasculinity", wie engmaschig die Ausbeutung fossiler Brennstoffe und weißes Patriarchat miteinander verflochten sind und wie leicht die vieldiskutierte toxische Männlichkeit in klimafaschistische Tendenzen kippen kann. Ihre Theorie zu Männlichkeit und Öl eignet sich insbesondere für die Welt von *Mad Max*, weil sie über eine spezifisch männliche Frustration spricht, die zu der Überzeugung führt, ein vermeintlich durch den Klima- und Genderdiskurs bedrohtes ‚Terrain' verteidigen zu müssen. So führt sie aus, dass Trump-Anhänger dessen ostentativ sexistisches Gebaren zelebrieren können und dabei zugleich selbst Enthaltsamkeit predigen. Die rechtsextremen „Proud Boys" etwa werben mit dem Slogan „no wanks" (Daggett 2018, 38). Prüde Rigidität und Trump-Verehrung, ein eigentlich eklatanter Widerspruch, wird kurzerhand zum politischen Programm, was Daggett mit einem Stellvertreter-Mechanismus erläutert: Die „Proud Boys" und ähnliche rechtsextreme Gruppen vertreten die Ansicht „Trump alone can flow" (Daggett 2018, 38), was bedeutet, dass das eigene sexuelle Begehren maximal unterdrückt wird. Dadurch wird indes die Sehnsucht nach anderweitiger Enthemmung umso größer und schließlich stellvertretend übernommen von Trump oder anderen Demagogen. George Miller hat mit *Fury Road* gewissermaßen für das, was Daggett 2018 beschrieben hat, bereits 2015 eine fulminante Bildsprache gefunden. Bei ihm ist es allein ‚Immortan Joe who can flow'. Er ist der Autokrat, der auf dem Öl thront und die sexuelle Unterdrückung der Frau durchsetzt. Offen bleibt aber in *Fury Road*, was nach dem Sturz des Petro-Patriarchats kommen soll. Furiosa lenkt zwar den Tanklaster hinaus aus der Welt der fossilen Brennstoffe und der männlichen Gewaltherrschaft, aber ihr Weg – die titelgebende „Straße" – führt keineswegs zu einer idyllischen Gegenwelt, auch wenn der Plot das zu Beginn suggeriert. Das „grüne Land der vielen Mütter", jener von Furiosa angesteuerte Fluchtort, ist zerstört und die wenigen Frauen, die überlebt haben, vagabundieren ziellos mit den letzten Samentütchen durch die Wüste. Furiosa bleibt deshalb nichts anderes übrig als zurückzukehren, den Autokraten zu stürzen und zu versuchen, ein neues System zu etablieren. Die Suche nach einem ökofeministischen Utopia führt also bei Miller in eine Sackgasse, weshalb die implizit-ökokritische Botschaft lautet: wir müssen die vorhandenen Ressourcen unseres Planeten möglichst nachhaltig und im Sinne des Gemeinwohls einsetzen, denn einen rettenden Ort ‚grüner Mütterlichkeit' gibt es nicht.

Als Zwischenfazit lässt sich festhalten, dass die drei zentralen Figuren in *Fury Road* zunächst genrekonforme Typen repräsentieren. Max führt als *lonesome warrior* einen in der Science-Fiction vielfach erzählten Überlebenskampf, bei dem er auf bewährte Mittel setzt: Motoren, Muskelkraft und radikalen Egoismus. Immortan Joe verkörpert den mächtigen *pater familias*, der die wertvollsten Ressourcen besitzt, verschwendet und dabei die Petromaskulinität in Reinform repräsentiert. Er ist der weiße,[5] autoritäre Sexist, der in einer beinahe völlig zerstörten Welt noch immer auf Waffen, Öl und Gewalt setzt. Und Furiosa schließlich wirkt durch ihre androgyne Erscheinung und die auffällig inszenierte mechanische Armprothese zunächst wie eine visuelle Übersetzung der Cyborg aus Donna Haraways berühmten Manifest (vgl. Haraway 1991). Die visuellen Codes, die zur Einführung der drei zentralen Figuren genutzt werden, sind also eindeutig, zugleich aber wird diese vermeintliche Simplizität genutzt, um die neue Figurenästhetik der Furiosa besonders zu markieren. Denn sie ist eben nicht ‚nur' eine Cyborg, die sich für die fragilen Abhängigkeitsbeziehungen zwischen den noch lebenden Menschen, dem verbleibenden technologischen Wissen und den letzten Ressourcen einsetzt, sondern auch durch und durch Ökokrieger:in mit einer klaren Vision: Die befreiten Frauen will sie ins „grüne Land der vielen Mütter" bringen, an einen utopischen Gegen-Ort zu Immortan Joes Wüstenfestung. Für diese Mission riskiert sie nicht nur ihre privilegierte Stellung und ihr eigenes Leben, sondern macht sich die Waffen des Petro-Partriarchats zunutze, um das System zu Fall zu bringen: Sie penetriert mit ihrem eigenen Steuer den Tanklaster und pervertiert damit den Akt vollendeter männlicher Eroberungsphantasie. Sie bezwingt das mächtigste Symbol von Petromaskulinität, einen überdimensionierten und mit Waffen hochgerüsteten Tanklaster, mit ihrer eigenen Lenkstange und bringt diesen auf neuen Kurs, in Richtung ökofeministische Utopie. Dabei setzt sie vor allem auf selbst konstruierte und reparierbare Werkzeuge, wie das Lenkrad und die Armprothese. Gerade letztere wurde teilweise kontrovers, teilweise enthusiastisch aufgenommen, da Charlize Theron als nicht-körperbehinderte Schauspielerin eine einarmige Kriegerin spielt (vgl. Smith). Allerdings bleibt zu vermerken, dass die Genese ihrer Beeinträchtigung, die kompensatorische Entwicklung ihrer handwerklichen Fähigkeiten und ihrer enormen Resilienz erst im Prequel *Furiosa* genauer erklärt werden. Entscheidend ist, dass die körperlich versehrte Furiosa in keinem Moment vor dem Einsatz physischer Gewalt

---

5 Die *whiteness* des Petro-Patriarchats wird in *Fury Road* hyperbolisch noch dadurch betont, dass Immortan Joe und seine Anhänger ihre Körper mit grellweißer Farbe bemalen und sich – in einer wunderbar ironischen Geste – den Mund mit einem spezifischen Spray verchromen, analog zur Verchromung eines Autos, um damit noch mehr Virilität und Entschlossenheit auszudrücken.

zurückschreckt, sondern diese als notwendiges Mittel in ihrem Krieg gegen die Repression durch das Petro-Patriarchat versteht und zu nutzen weiß. Dass sie sich derart selbstverständlich und effizient in der Welt der Motoren und Patriarchen bewegt, ist sicherlich auch eine werkinterne, an die Fans der Kultfilmreihe gerichtete Referenz: auch Furiosa donnert nahezu die gesamte Laufzeit des Films hindurch in ihrem monströsen Fahrzeug durch die Wüste, was als visuelle Hommage an die *Mad Max*-Filmreihe und ihre Öl-, Auto- und machtversessenen Figuren verstanden werden kann, zugleich aber eine markante Subversion darstellt: zwar brettert Furiosa in der gewohnten apologetisch wirkenden Auto-Ästhetik die eponyme und genreeigene „Road" entlang, sie schlägt aber von Vornherein – ihren Gegner im Rückspiegel entschlossen fixierend (*Fury Road* 11:45–12:09) – eine neue und eigene Fahrtrichtung ein, bringt die Ökokrieger:in auf den Plan und damit die Filmreihe auf neues Terrain.

Furiosas Handlungen deute ich erstens als *kriegerisch*, da sie als Vertreterin der unterdrückten Frauen und der unter chronischem Wassermangel leidenden Bevölkerung agiert. Furiosa führt insofern einen typischen „Befreiungskrieg" (Schubert und Klein) oder auch „Antiregime-Krieg", da es ihr um den „Sturz der Regierenden" geht und sie für „die Veränderung des politischen Systems und der Gesellschaftsordnung" (BpB) kämpft. Ich interpretiere die Figur zweitens als *ökokriegerisch*, da ihre Handlungen auf der ökofeministischen Prämisse basieren, nach der die rücksichtslose Ausbeutung der Frau strukturell mit der Ausbeutung natürlicher Ressourcen korreliert (vgl. Griffin, Gaard, Plumwood, Warren). Konsequenterweise verfolgt Furiosa das Ziel, die sexuelle Versklavung der Frauen abzuschaffen die, neben dem Zwang zur Reproduktion, auch als Rohstofflieferantinnen für Muttermilch ausgebeutet werden. In einer verstörenden Sequenz ist zu sehen, wie die Brüste zahlreicher Frauen an Melkautomaten angeschlossen sind und ihnen, gegen ihren Willen, Muttermilch in großen Mengen abgepumpt wird (vgl. *Fury Road* 12:39–13:03). Diese an Massentierhaltung erinnernden Bilder, in der die industrielle Gewinnung von Muttermilch als überlebenswichtigem Rohstoff gezeigt wird, fungiert als Sinnbild für die ökofeministische Kritik an der Korrelation von patriarchaler Gewalt, Ressourcenabbau und rücksichtslosem Extraktivismus. Furiosa initiiert die Befreiung der zur Ressource degradierten Frauen und setzt sich für eine ökologische, faire und nachhaltige Gesellschaftsordnung ein, weshalb sie als prototypische Ökokrieger:in gelten kann. Sie ist autark, durchsetzungsstark, handwerklich geschickt und führt einen ökofeministisch motivierten Befreiungskrieg an, der zu einer konvivialen Erneuerung der Gesellschaft führen soll.

III

In der dystopischen Graphic Novel *Endzeit* von Olivia Vieweg dominieren zwar ebenfalls Destruktion, Gewalt und blutiger Kampf, allerdings vollzieht sich die Handlung hier nicht in einer postapokalyptischen Wüste, sondern in einem von Zombies dominierten Deutschland. Weimar wird, gleich im ersten Panel, qua Blocktext als „geschützte Stadt" (*Endzeit* 2018, 5) eingeführt und in der anschließenden *aspect-to-aspect*-Sequenz[6] das berühmte Goethe und Schiller-Denkmal als Sammelstelle für Wasserkanister etabliert, versehen mit dem schriftlichen Hinweis „Bitte nicht hamstern, wir haben wieder genug Wasser 😉" (*Endzeit* 2018, 6). Mit diesem Incipit demonstriert die Comiczeichnerin und Autorin ihren humorvollen Umgang mit den gängigen Genrekonventionen: Nicht New York City, sondern ‚Weimar City' wird hier als eine der letzten Bastionen der Menschheit eingeführt und nicht die Freiheitsstatue, sondern das Denkmal der Weimarer Klassik wird gezeigt, ein ironischer Kommentar in Bezug auf die zahlreichen US-amerikanischen Zombie-Erzählungen und visuellen Codes des Genres, abschließend unterstrichen durch das Zwinker-Emoji. Doch diese ironisch-heitere Exposition wird bereits in der nächsten Sequenz durchbrochen, in der Stacheldrahtzaun und blutverschmierte Gartenwerkzeuge, namentlich Kreuzhacken und eine Mistgabel, zu sehen sind (Abb. 2).

Die Leser:innen werden sodann sukzessive mit der dystopischen Diegese vertraut gemacht, wobei sie zunächst ins Innere einer Psychiatrie geführt werden, wo sie die Protagonistin Vivi kennenlernen, eine ängstliche und von der Abteilungsleiterin psychisch missbrauchte junge Frau, die scheinbar an Wahnzuständen leidet. Auch hier findet sich eine bedeutungsvolle visuelle Referenz auf die klassische deutsche Literatur, wenn in einer *action-to-action*-Sequenz zu sehen ist, wie Vivi nachts auf einem dunklen Flur ein leuchtend gelbes Reclam-Heftchen findet, dessen Titel zwar schwarz übermalt ist, das aber dennoch als Georg Büchners *Woyzeck* dechiffriert werden kann (*Endzeit* 2018, 20). Dass Vivi ausgerechnet dieses Drama an diesem Ort in die Hände fällt, enthüllt einmal mehr, dass die Figur sich offenbar in einer Missbrauchssituation, ähnlich der des Soldaten Franz Woyzeck befindet. Zumal die Leser:innen bereits wissen, dass die Klinikleiterin Vivi eigenmächtig Medikamente verabreicht und sie zugleich mit in der postapokalyptischen Welt kostbaren Seltenheiten, wie etwa Erdbeeren, gefügig zu ma-

---

6 Bei dieser Art von Sequenzgestaltung geht es oft um die Evokation von Stimmungen an spezifischen Orten und die Panels der Sequenz zeigen einzelne Details desselben Gegenstandes oder Settings; Abel und Klein erläutern die Sequenz wie folgt: "aspect-to-aspect: von Gesichtspunkt zu Gesichtspunkt, unterschiedliche Ansichten/Aspekte *eines* Ortes, *einer* Stimmung etc. werden gezeigt" (Abel und Klein 85; Hervorhebung im Original).

Abb. 2: Stacheldrahtzaun rund um Weimar und blutiges Werkzeug, *Endzeit* 2018, S. 7.

chen versucht. Kurz darauf wird Vivis Antagonistin Eva vorgestellt, die der unbeholfenen und furchtsamen Vivi zeigt, was es heißt, „Arbeiten am Schutzzaun" (*Endzeit* 2018, 28) zu verrichten. In einer großformatig angelegten *action-to-action*-Sequenz reißt Eva Vivi eine Feile aus der Hand und stößt diese ins Auge eines Zombies, nur um direkt hinterher ein Beil zu ergreifen und damit den Arm einer jungen Helferin abzutrennen, die gerade gebissen wurde (*Endzeit* 2018, 48–53). Diese gewaltvolle Sequenz kulminiert, als die Zaun-Aufseherin Eva eine Pistole in die Hand drückt und sie an die bedingungslosen „Regeln der Stadt" (*Endzeit* 2018, 56) erinnert, woraufhin die Tötung der bereits armamputierten jungen Frau erfolgt, was bezeichnenderweise nicht visualisiert, sondern allein durch das Soundwort „Blamm" (*Endzeit* 2018, 57), in weißem Lettering auf grellrotem Hintergrund, jäh vermittelt wird. Eine Verkettung von Umständen führt im Anschluss daran dazu, dass Vivi und Eva sich in einer Zwangsgemeinschaft wiederfinden und beide versuchen, von Weimar nach Jena zu gelangen, wo angeblich an einem Heilmittel gegen die von den Zombies übertragene Infektion gearbeitet wird. Während dieses Roadtrips erfahren die Leser:innen vereinzelte Details über die Apokalypse und die Biografien der Figuren, wobei das zentrale Trauma Vivis, die immer wieder von Visionen geplagt wird, vorerst ein ungeklärtes Spannungselement bleibt. Der Ton zwischen den ungleichen Frauen wird allmählich freundlicher und Eva stellt während einer längeren Dialogsequenz lakonisch fest, dass man eigentlich noch Glück gehabt habe, mit dieser Form der Apokalypse, woraufhin sie der irritierten Vivi erklärt: „Naja, immerhin sind nicht die Toten aus den Gräbern gestiegen. Das wäre für Weimar nicht gut ausgegangen", schließlich lägen „oben in den Bergen um Buchenwald" die „armen Seelen" (*Endzeit* 2018, 98). Kurze reflexive Passagen wie diese zeigen, dass *Endzeit* mehr ist als eine schlichte Zombie-Dystopie. Nicht nur die Weimarer Klassik, auch die NS-Konzentrationslager gehören zu Deutschland, und die Figuren in *Endzeit* sind sich dieser Historie nur allzu bewusst. In einem farblich auffällig warm gezeichneten ganzseitigen Panel sind kurz darauf zwei Giraffen zu sehen, die plötzlich an den beiden durch die deutsche Provinz streifenden Frauen vorbeilaufen (*Endzeit* 2018, 128), woraufhin Eva erstaunt feststellt, dass die großen Tiere wohl aus dem Erfurter Zoo stammen müssten und es erstaunlich sei, dass sie nach zwei Jahren Apokalypse noch am Leben seien. Diese Digression verdeutlicht einmal mehr, dass in *Endzeit* nicht nur kritische Perspektiven auf das kulturgeschichtliche Gedächtnis geworfen werden, sondern auch auf den spezifischen Überlebensdiskurs im Anthropozän (Freiburg und Bayer 25–27), allerdings fehlen bis zu dieser Stelle explizite Angaben zur genauen Ursache der massenhaften Infektion. Die Begegnung mit den beiden Giraffen fungiert jedoch als wichtiger Marker innerhalb der Beziehung der beiden Figuren, da Eva und Vivi nunmehr in der Lage sind, aufeinander und auf ihre Umwelt zu reagieren. Konfrontiert mit dem ungewöhnlichen Anblick einer anderen Art, scheinen die beiden Figuren jene von Donna Haraway als zentral erachtete „ability to respond" (vgl. Kerner 149) erstmals als Haltung zu entdecken, die sich als Alternative zum bekannten egoistischen, gewissermaßen ‚zombiehaften' Überleben-im-Alleingang anbietet. Entsprechend platziert ist auch die einzige dezidiert ökofeministische Aussage im Text, denn Eva räsoniert noch in derselben Nacht: „Ich glaube, die Erde ist 'ne kluge alte Frau …", „… und die Menschen haben ihr zu lange keine Miete gezahlt", „Und das da draußen …", „… das ist jetzt die Räumungsklage" (*Endzeit* 2018, 135).

Doch nach dem versöhnlichen Moment mit den Giraffen wird die eben erst erlernte Fähigkeit, wieder mit Optimismus und Empathie auf die Umwelt zu blicken, erneut auf die Probe gestellt und es gelingt Vivi nicht, Eva aus einer lebensbedrohlichen Lage zu retten. Aus Wut über Vivis Handlungsohnmacht verlässt Eva sie, woraufhin Vivi, die das erste Mal auf sich gestellt ist, in einen eigenartigen Garten gelangt, der als „Kompensations-Heterotopie" (Foucault 20) innerhalb der postapokalyptischen Welt lesbar ist. Dort wachsen nie gesehene Blumen – was mit der vorangegangenen ökofeministischen Reflexion Evas verbunden wird, wenn Vivi sich fragt „habt ihr etwa gewartet, bis die Menschen weg sind?" (*Endzeit 2018*,172) – Marienkäfer surren durch die Luft und auf einem Gartentischchen stehen frisch eingeschenkter Kaffee und Kuchen. Überwältigt von dieser Idylle gibt sich Vivi den Versuchungen hin, wird aber kurz darauf ein weiteres Mal von ihren traumatischen Erinnerungen eingeholt und zugleich von einem Zombie angefallen. Ihre Rettung erfolgt diesmal durch das beherzte Eingreifen einer neuen Figur, die Vivi mit einer Mistgabel zur Hilfe kommt, zunächst nur im Profil zu sehen ist und einige Panels darauf als hybride Gestalt mit Gartenhut portraitiert wird. Die eine Gesichtshälfte dieser ominösen Retter:in ist von Pflanzen überwuchert, Augen- und Mundpartie gleicht denen der Zombies, die andere Gesichtshälfte ist unversehrt und menschlich (Abb. 3).

Abb. 3: Die hybride Figur der Gärtner:in, *Endzeit* 2018, S. 181.

Die schematisch visualisierte Janusgesichtigkeit dieser Gärtner:in wird durch ihre Aussagen in den folgenden Panels noch zusätzlich verkompliziert. Sie ist keineswegs ‚halb Mensch, halb Zombie', sondern ‚mehr als Menschlich' und stellt etwas Neues, Hybrides dar. Sie distanziert sich klar von der rein menschlichen Lebenswelt („ich will keine Menschen mehr um mich", *Endzeit* 2018, 183) und interagiert innerhalb ihres spezifischen Habitats auf neue Weise mit Natur und Technik. So enthüllen die nächsten Panels, dass die namenlose Gestalt in einem Gewächshaus offenbar biochemische Experimente mit Pflanzen durchführt – gezeigt werden Reagenzgläser, Petrischalen, in denen es wuchert, Tabletten-Blister und Spritzen (*Endzeit* 2018, 187) – und dabei offenbar auch mit psychedelischen Wirkstoffen experimentiert. Denn um die unter ihren Erinnerungen leidende Vivi zu beruhigen, verabreicht sie dieser – wie zu Beginn bereits die manipulative Klinikleiterin – eine Erdbeere, die nun allerdings zum religiösen und ökokritischen Symbol überhöht wird. So erklärt die Gärtner:in zunächst „Die Früchte dieses Gartens lassen dich alles vergessen" (*Endzeit* 2018, 196) – was innerhalb eines paradiesisch gezeichneten Gartens offensichtlich die Umkehrung der göttlichen Erkenntnis darstellt – um diese schöpfungsgeschichtliche Referenz sodann mit einer evolutionsgeschichtlichen zu konterkarieren, wenn sie der sedierten Vivi ins Ohr flüstert: „Ich verrate Dir ein Geheimnis ... die Dinosaurier sind auch nicht ausgestorben. Sie sind noch unter uns. Vielleicht werden wir keine Herrscher mehr sein ... aber immer noch Teil dieses wunderschönen Gartens" (*Endzeit* 2018, 198–199). Nach dieser Affirmation der Evolutionstheorie mutiert die ominöse Gärtner:in ein weiteres Mal in eine unerwartete Richtung. Denn als Vivi entdeckt, dass diese ihre Weggefährtin Eva lebendig begraben hat, konstatiert die Gärtner:in emotionslos: „Aus der wird nichts, die hat einen schlechten Charakter" (*Endzeit* 2018, 211). Sie willigt ein, Eva gehen zu lassen, aber nur, wenn Vivi dafür bei ihr bleibt, woraufhin sich Eva vehement mit der Mistgabel für Vivi einsetzt und die Gärtner:in schließlich beide ziehen lässt, nicht, ohne ihnen noch eine Harke mitzugeben (*Endzeit* 2018, 218–219).

Die Gartensequenz stellt in *Endzeit* den Wendepunkt der Handlung dar und bleibt trotz der expliziten intertextuellen und symbolischen Referenzen mehrdeutig. Einerseits gibt es eindeutige Bezüge auf den Garten Eden, den Apfel vom Baum der Erkenntnis – der hier zu einer ‚Frucht des Vergessens' invertiert wird – und eine verführerische Figur, die zugleich Mensch, Zombie und Pflanze zu sein scheint. Andererseits ist diese Figur merkwürdig emotionslos und brutal gegenüber Eva, die sie als „Abfall" (*Endzeit* 2018, 212) bezeichnet und sich damit als Vertreterin der künstlichen Selektion bzw. als Eugeniker:in zu erkennen gibt, die in ihrem Garten nur die ‚guten' und ‚besonders wertvollen' Pflanzen züchten will. Die hybride Gärtner:in changiert damit zwischen Religionskritik, Darwinismus, Ökofeminismus, Posthumanismus sowie Euthanasie und verweigert sich einer eindeutigen Lesart. Während Vieweg in der ersten, wesentlich kürzeren Fassung ihrer Graphic Novel[7] der Gärtner:in noch ein Motiv gab und sie als Wissenschaftlerin darstellte, die vor der Zombie-Katastrophe am Max-Planck-Institut beschäftigt und an der Entwicklung eines Grippe-Impfstoffs beteiligt war (vgl. *Endzeit* 2012, 49–51), ist die Figur in der zweiten Fassung deutlich ambivalenter. Sie er-

---

7 Mit dieser ursprünglichen Fassung von *Endzeit* machte Vieweg 2012 ihr Diplom; danach nahm sie an der Drehbuchwerkstatt München teil, wo sie die erste Fassung zu einem Drehbuch ausarbeitete, das von Carolina Hellsgård verfilmt wurde (vgl. Hellsgård 2018).

scheint als Ökokrieger:in mit unklarer Intention, als hybride Schwellenfigur, die zwischen Leben und Tod, Außen- und Innenraum sowie zwischen Natur und Kultur steht. Der von ihr als geschütztes Habitat verteidigte Garten ist ein Ort der Rekreation inmitten ökologischer Destruktion und sozialem Chaos und zugleich Forum posthumanistischer und sozialdarwinistischer Ideen. So spricht sie davon, dass die Menschen in Zukunft nicht mehr die „Herrscher" wären, aber noch immer in diesem „wundervollen Garten" leben könnten, womit die Metapher der Erde als irdischem Paradiesgarten zwar erhalten bleibt, den Menschen aber auch eine neue, unterlegene Rolle darin zugeordnet wird. Die Visualisierungen in dieser Sequenz, die sich gegenseitig überwuchernde und überlagernde Sphären in psychedelisch wirkendem Lila, Gelb und Rosa zeigen und menschliche Körper, die von Pflanzenstrukturen durchdrungen werden (vgl. Abb. 3), bekräftigen damit gegenwärtige Positionen des symbiotischen Posthumanismus (vgl. Karpouzou und Zampaki) sowie des materiellen Ökofeminismus, der jegliche Form des Speziezismus ablehnt und von der globalen Interdependenz aller Arten ausgeht (vgl. Alaimo; Barad; Bennett; Grewe-Volpp). Ganz im Sinne der Anthropozän-Kritik räumt die Gärtner:in den Menschen allenfalls noch die Rolle als Relikt einer einstmals dominanten Spezies ein, die ihrer Ansicht nach, analog zu den Dinosauriern, durchaus fortbestehen könne, nur eben in keiner dominanten Position mehr.

Bezeichnend ist schlussendlich, dass Vivi und Eva *gemeinsam* jene Garten-Heterotopie samt widersprüchlicher Hüter:in verlassen, um solidarisch und offen für neue Beziehungsformen gen Jena weiterzuziehen. Auch diese beiden Figuren sind am Ende der Erzählung zu Hybriden mutiert, denen Äste und Blumen aus dem Körper ranken (*Endzeit* 2018, 279) und die – als pointierte Haraway-Hommage – am Ende der Handlung einen zutraulichen Hund als Weggefährten (vgl. Haraway 2016a) annehmen, um sich in dieser neuen Interspezies-Gemeinschaft den Herausforderungen der Apokalypse zu stellen. Im Gegensatz zur ambivalenten Gärtner:innenfigur sind Vivi und Eva am Schluss der Graphic Novel damit eindeutig als Ökokrieger:innen erkennbar, die sich in ihren jeweils überlagernden Zugehörigkeiten anerkennen – an ihren Körpern sind zombie-, pflanzen- und menschentypische Merkmale zu erkennen – und kämpferisch-optimistisch in die Zukunft blicken.

IV

Bevor Viewegs graphische Erzählung mit Frauke Bergers *Grün* kontrastiert wird, sei eine systematische Einordnung der Werkzeuge, mit denen die bis hierhin diskutierten Ökokrieger:innen operieren, vorgeschlagen. Wie gut sich dafür die Theorie der *Selbstbegrenzung* nach Ivan Illich eignet, lässt sich an der zweigesichtigen Gärtner:in veranschaulichen. Vor der Katastrophe war diese Figur eine Wissenschaftlerin, die medizinische Forschung zu Impfstoffen durchführte; nach der Zombie-Apokalypse greift sie zu einfachem Gartengerät, das in seiner Handhabung und in seiner Konsequenz zum Set jener „tools for conviviality" (Illich 1973) gehört, die Illich bereits in den 70er Jahren als Voraussetzung für jede Form von zukunftsfähiger Gesellschaft beschrieben hat:

> Werkzeuge sind den gesellschaftlichen Beziehungen intrinsisch. Zwischen dem Einzelnen und der Gesellschaft besteht durch die Werkzeuge eine Beziehung; entweder weil er sie beherrscht, oder weil er von ihnen beherrscht wird. [..] Werkzeuge sind dann konvivial, wenn sie jedem, der sie benutzt, die bestmögliche Gelegenheit bietet [*sic*], die Umwelt mit den Ergebnissen seiner Visionen zu bereichern. (Illich 2014, 41)

Werkzeuge sollen nach Illich also so beschaffen sein, dass sie ein möglichst großes Maß an Autonomie ermöglichen und insgesamt einer konvivialen Form von Gesellschaft dienlich sind, d. h. einer Form des Zusammenlebens, die auf Rücksichtnahme und Selbstbegrenzung basiert. In einer konvivialen Gesellschaft soll es entsprechend jedem möglich sein, maximal autonom „mit Werkzeugen umzugehen, die in so geringem Maße wie möglich anderen unterstünden" (Illich 2014, 41). Illichs durchaus kontrovers rezipierte Position gegenüber technologischen Entwicklungen besagt, dass technologischer Fortschritt dann abzulehnen sei, wenn dieser dazu führe, dass Werkzeuge nicht mehr eigenständig genutzt und in ihrer Funktionalität durchdrungen werden könnten. Illich argumentiert deshalb für eine generelle Veränderung der „Tiefenstruktur von Werkzeugen" und postuliert, dass wir nicht länger Werkzeuge anstreben dürften, die uns „Arbeit abnehmen", sondern solche, mit denen wir „selbst arbeiten können" (Illich 2014, 27). In Illichs Ausführungen dient – ironischerweise – ausgerechnet das Münztelefon als Beispiel für ein konviviales Werkzeug; eine Idee, die angesichts des Smartphones als unserem ubiquitären und potenten digitalen Alltagswerkzeug der Gegenwart freilich überrascht: „Wer etwas Kleingeld hat, kann anrufen, wen er will. […] Das Telefon gestattet es jedem, einer Person seiner Wahl zu sagen, was er will; er kann Geschäfte machen, von Liebe sprechen oder einen Streit vom Zaun brechen" (Illich 2014, 43). Verständlicher wird Illichs Argumentation, wenn er erläutert, dass sich vor allen Dingen die meisten „Handwerkzeuge" für den konvivialen Gebrauch geradezu anböten, dass aber der Zugang auch zu diesen „vorsätzlich beschränkt" werden könne, etwa wenn „einfache Zangen und Schraubenzieher nicht mehr dazu taugen, moderne Autos zu reparieren" (ebd.). Hier wird der Bezug zur Gegenwart und dem Smartphone als unserem meistgenutzten ‚Handwerkzeug', schnell erkennbar, sind wir doch in aller Regel nicht selbst in der

Lage, dieses in seinen Affordanzen undurchsichtige und komplexe Gerät zu reparieren bzw. wird eine einfache, autonome Reparatur durch die Nutzer:innen bekanntlich oft durch das spezifische Design im Sinne Illichs „vorsätzlich verhindert". Aber auch ohne Illichs extreme Deutung zu teilen, nach der nicht länger die Maschinen uns, sondern die Menschen den Maschinen dienten – diese Diagnose stammt wohlbemerkt aus dem Jahr 1973, als weder Smartphone noch KI als Werkzeuge existierten – ist sein Begriff von Konvivialität sehr produktiv, steht er doch für „den autonomen und schöpferischen zwischenmenschlichen Umgang von Menschen mit ihrer Umwelt" (Illich 2014, 28). Um genau diesen Umgang, so meine These, geht es in *Fury Road*, *Endzeit* und *Grün*.

Furiosa hat ihre Armprothese selbst konstruiert, ebenso wie ihr Lenkrad, das ein simples mechanisches Werkzeug ist, mit dem sie indes so „autonom und schöpferisch" umzugehen vermag, dass sie das gesamte politische System verändert und damit eine konviviale Gesellschaftsordnung ermöglicht, was in der letzten Filmszene durch die faire Verteilung des zuvor monopolisierten Wassers angedeutet wird. Die ambivalente Ökokrieger:in in *Endzeit* betrieb vor der Katastrophe jene Art von medizinischer Forschung, die Illich besonders kritisiert, da sie nicht länger dem Zweck diene, Menschen zu heilen, sondern „selbst neue Krankheiten" verursache (Illich 2014, 16). Diese polarisierende Haltung gegenüber medizinischer Forschung trifft für die erzählte Welt von *Endzeit* durchaus zu, da hier die Forschung an Grippe-Impfstoffen zur Zombie-Katastrophe geführt hat – freilich ein zentraler Topos des Zombie-Narrativs, der dazu dient, den Menschen und sein Fortschrittsbestreben als eigentliche *causa* für die Zerstörung der Welt darzustellen.[8] Konsequenterweise setzt die Ökokrieger:in deshalb jetzt wieder auf einfachste Handwerkzeuge – Gießkanne, Mistgabel, Rechen, Harke – und bestellt damit den ‚neuen Garten'. Die Figur bleibt indes, wie oben erörtert wurde, in Teilen jener prä-apokalyptischen, anti-konvivialen Ordnung verhaftet, was sich darin zeigt, dass sie trotz allem weiterhin biotechnologische Experimente durchführt, Vivi als Testobjekt für sich manipuliert und infizierte Menschen wie Eva für lebensunwürdig erachtet. Sie steht damit an einer „Wasserscheide" (Illich 2014, 16–26): eine Gesichtshälfte der Figur repräsentiert eine neue, posthumane und zugleich konviviale Art des gesellschaftlichen Zusammenlebens, die andere symbolisiert den alten, egoistischen, fortschrittsgläubigen, letztlich aber todbringenden Lebensmodus. Im Gegensatz dazu setzen Vivi und Eva zum Schluss gänzlich auf konviviale Werkzeuge: Sie wehren sich ausschließlich mit einfachstem

---

8 In *I am Legend* von 2007 etwa ist es die Forschung an einem Krebsheilmittel, in *28 Days Later* aus dem Jahr 2002 das Experimentieren mit Schimpansen und in *Resident Evil*, auch von 2002, die geheime Entwicklung eines Virus, das tote Zellen reanimieren soll; in allen Settings führt die medizinisch-biologische Forschung zu einer weltweiten Zombie-Katastrophe.

Gerät gegen die Aggressoren und verkörpern zugleich eine Versöhnung von Natur und Kultur. Sie versuchen, „die Umwelt mit den Ergebnissen" ihrer „Visionen zu bereichern" (Illich 2014, 41), wobei die Vision vorsieht, rücksichtsvoll und solidarisch mit allen Spezies zu leben, trotz überall lauernder Lebensgefahr. Die blutige Spitzhake aus der ersten Sequenz (vgl. Abb. 2) hat sich somit vom rein defensiven Mordwerkzeug zu einem konvivialen Werkzeug entwickelt, das die zu hybriden Ökokrieger:innen verwachsenen Gefährtinnen Vivi und Eva nun vereint.

V

Auch in Frauke Bergers zweibändiger Graphic Novel *Grün*[9] wird eine postapokalyptische Gesellschaft imaginiert, allerdings eine extraterrestrische, sodass sich diese Erzählung der typischen Science-Fiction zuordnen lässt, während *Fury Road* und *Endzeit* eher in den Bereich der Speculative Fiction gehören (vgl. Oziewicz). *Grün* ist ein visuell eindrückliches und rezeptionsästhetisch anspruchsvolles Werk, das sich der gewohnten Lesart von Comics entzieht. Die *closure*[10] ist von Beginn an sehr schwierig, die Sequenzen erscheinen stark fragmentiert und bereits die ersten Panels irritieren. Es ist unklar, an welchem Ort die Handlung einsetzt, was für Wesen zu sehen sind, aus wessen Perspektive erzählt wird und was genau passiert. Yvonne Müller konstatiert, dass *Grün* mit diesem konfusen Stil jene von Haraway geforderte Cyborg-Sprache realisiere, nach der „noise", „pollution" und „fusion" (vgl. Haraway 1991) den Phallogozentrismus ablösen sollen. Diese drei Prinzipien würden hier zwar „bild-sprachlich" durch die „gezeigte Ambivalenz, Unklarheit und Selbstreflexivität" dargestellt, blieben aber dennoch „eher unbegreiflich" (Müller 16). Die Handlung von *Grün* spielt auf dem Planeten Han, dessen Ressourcen beinahe gänzlich abgebaut wurden, sodass der Rest des Planeten einem abgenagten Apfel ähnelt (*Grün I* 9). Han wird von diversen Spezies bewohnt, die die Leser:innen erst nach längerer Lektüre verschiedenen Habitaten zuordnen können. In der ersten Sequenz spricht eine Figur, deren Kopf an einen Fisch mit geöffnetem Maul und einen Hasen mit Schlappohren zugleich denken lässt (vgl. *Grün I* 4), davon, dass „der Wald seit der Seuche gefährlicher" geworden sei und es ist von „Scheiben" (*Grün I* 4) die Rede, die offenbar ein Wäh-

---

9 Im Folgenden zitiert mit *Grün I* und *Grün II*.
10 „Closure (wörtl. ‚Schließung', im Dt. häufig ‚Induktion' oder auch ‚Inferenz'): Leistung des Lesers, aus den einzelnen Panels des Comics eine zusammenhängende Geschichte zu konstruieren, also gewissermaßen die Lücken zwischen den Panels zu schließen" (Abel und Klein 316).

rungssystem darstellen, aber es bleibt völlig unklar, wer diese Figuren sind und in welchem Setting sie sich befinden. Im Hintergrund der einzelnen Panels sind Röhren und Leitersysteme zu erkennen und die braun-beige Farbgebung lässt an einen unterirdischen Gang denken, aber erst als ‚herausgezoomt' wird und der Handlungsort in einem Panel als Ganzes zu sehen ist, wird deutlich, dass es in der Welt der eben gesehenen Figuren nur noch wenig Lebensraum gibt. Die meisten Flächen sind Sumpf- oder Wüstenland, durch das, „Relikte des hochtechnologischen Zeitalters" umherwandern, die als „Archen" bezeichnet werden. Diese „Archen" sind wie enorme weiße Roboterhunde mit Menschensiedlungen auf dem Rücken dargestellt (*Grün I* 8–9). Die Analogie zur vom Klimawandel und Ressourcenabbau bedrohten Erde ist damit zwar von Beginn an deutlich, zugleich aber werden typische Zuschreibungen unterlaufen, da Grün jene Farbe ist, die wir mit Nachhaltigkeit und ökologischer Verantwortung assoziieren und ebendiese Farbe wird hier zum ‚Planetenkiller'.

Nach der verwirrenden Einleitung folgt Kapitel I, „Der Wüstenring", in dem die Hauptfigur Lis eingeführt wird, wobei zunächst, ebenso wie bei der Einführung von Furiosa, nur Ausschnitte ihres Körpers zu sehen sind, bevor das Gesicht und die Figur in ihrer ganzen Erscheinung preisgegeben werden (vgl. *Grün I* 12–13). Sofort fällt die ungewöhnliche Ästhetik der Figur auf: Sie trägt weißes Haar, eine Schutzbrille, die mit einem Nackenschutz verbunden ist, von der Brust an abwärts hängt ein Banner mit einem Emblem, ihre Unterarme und Handgelenke werden von rot-weißen Protektoren geschützt, sie trägt Stutzen und läuft barfuß, in der Hand trägt sie einen weißen dicken Ast und auf dem Rücken einen großen Rucksack, aus dem diverse Matten und Stoffe ragen. Im Vergleich zu Furiosa, Vivi oder Eva ist das uneindeutige Geschlecht dieser Ökokrieger:in besonders auffällig; sie ist explizit geschlechtsneutral gezeichnet, das einzig spezifisch feminin zu lesendes Attribut ist eine Art Bustier, das sie trägt. Diese non-binäre Ästhetik wird im weiteren Verlauf noch verstärkt, etwa, wenn Lis ohne ihre Schutzkleidung zu sehen ist. Auch dann erinnert die Figur durch ihre Tätowierungen und ihr rabiates Auftreten allenfalls an klischeehafte Inszenierungen indigener Krieger:innen, aber ihre geschlechtliche Identität bleibt offen. Die Handlung von *Grün* gibt vor, dass sich Lis, aufgrund eines nur angedeuteten fatalen Fehlverhaltens in der Vergangenheit, auf eine typische Quest, oder auch: Held:innenreise, begibt, um dabei nach dem Ursprung der Seuche zu suchen. Zur Seite tritt ihr dabei ein Hybrid namens Lun, als anthropomorphe Zusammensetzung diverser Teile gezeichnet und mit der narrativen Funktion eines heiteren Picaros ausgestattet (vgl. *Grün I* 34–35). Die Beziehung dieser beiden Figuren lässt sich, wie die von Vivi und Eva, zunächst als reine Zwangsgemeinschaft verstehen, aber auch Lis und Lun entwickeln sukzessive die Fähigkeit, sich gegenseitig zu unterstützen. Während ihrer Reise durch verschiedene Habitate lernen sie, zunehmend rücksichtsvoller aufeinander zu reagieren und legen insbesondere ihren zu Beginn intensiv gegeneinander ausgespielten Speziezismus allmählich ab. Auch den kreativ visualisierten Bewohner:innen der verschiedenen Habitate begegnen Lis und Lun von Mal zu Mal weniger misstrauisch und schaffen es letztlich auch nur mit deren Unterstützung, ihre Rettungsmission erfolgreich durchzuführen. Am Schluss kennen sie den „name of the game", sie wissen, es geht darum, „miteinander zu werden" (vgl. Kerner 151) und den geteilten Lebensraum vor der Zerstörung zu bewahren. Diese neue, unbedingte Kollaboration jenseits einseitiger Zugehörigkeit wird im letzten Panel des ersten Bandes besonders hervorgehoben (Abb. 4).

Lis ist hier mit zahlreichen konvivialen Werkzeugen ausgestattet, die für die Planetenrettungsmission benötigt werden. Neben dem markanten Holzstab und der Schutzbrille trägt sie nun auch einen speziellen Pflanzenkragen, der als Infektionsschutz vor der grünen Seuche fungiert (vgl. *Grün I* 48), eine Leiter sowie diverse Tragetaschen und Beutel. Mit Letzteren scheint implizit Ursula Le Guins feministische Erzähltheorie aufgerufen (vgl. *The carrier bag of fiction* 168), was allerdings am Schluss des zweiten Bandes ironisch konterkariert wird, wenn Lis zum finalen Befreiungsschlag gegen die grüne Seuche ausholt und dazu eine riesige Axt aus einer ihrer Taschen hervorzieht (vgl. *Grün II* 59), die sie als „Spezialwerkzeug" (*Grün II* 61) bezeichnet.[11] Auffällig ist zudem, wie Christina Becher herausgearbeitet hat, dass in *Grün* sehr viel vegetabile – also von Pflanzen verursachte – Gewalt inszeniert wird. Die Rezipient:innen haben es deshalb gerade nicht mit einer „passiven, duldenden Natur zu tun, sondern mit sich schnell fortbewegenden Ausläufern einer alles Leben vertilgenden pflanzlichen Mutation" (Becher 70), sodass Lis' gewaltige Axt, die sie am Schluss gegen die vermeintliche ‚Wurzel allen Übels' auf dem Planeten Han richtet, die Leser:innen neuerlich in ihrer Bewertung der ambigen Figuren und ihrer Werkzeuge herausfordert. Neben der kriegerisch dreinblickenden Lis steht im Abschlusspanel von Band 1 die deutlich kleinere Figur Lun, wobei das Ensemble an das ikonisch ungleiche Paar von Don Quijote und Sancho Panza denken lässt.[12] Lun ist als Mensch-Pflanzen-Hybrid mit der leitmotivischen Holzmaske erkennbar und benötigt außer dieser keinerlei Ausrüstung, da sie als Hybrid bereits maximal anpassungsfähig ist.

---

[11] In Ursula Le Guins vielrezipierter Theorie geht sie davon aus, dass am Anfang von Erzählkultur und produktivem Miteinander gerade nicht die dem Mann zugeordnete Waffe stand, sondern der der Frau zugeordnete Behälter bzw. die Tasche. Dass Lis also ausgerechnet eine Axt aus ihrem mysteriösen, die ganze Zeit über mitgeführten Behälter zieht, lässt sich als ein weiteres Vexierspiel mit geschlechtercodierten Werkzeugen und Werten lesen.

[12] Vgl. hierzu etwa die analoge Anordnung der Bronzefiguren am Denkmal für Cervantes in Madrid.

Abb. 4: Ganzseitiges Portrait-Panel von Lis und Lun, *Grün* I, S. 56.

Die Handlung dieser äußerst kreativen und herausfordernden graphischen Erzählung ist zu komplex, um sie hier in Gänze wiedergeben zu können; nur so viel sei erläutert: Lis und Lun werden am Ende von Band I versklavt und in die „Tiefgärten" geschickt. Dort angekommen, begegnet Lis dem „Ältesten", einem grünen, vielarmigen Wesen, das die Tiefgärten beherrscht. Dieser führt Lis in einen Raum, in dem die „Seuchenträger" (*Grün I* 49) an den Wänden hängen, lauter kleine, abgestorbene Hybride, die der „Älteste" als seine „Kinder" bezeichnet, die durch Lis' Schuld verloren seien. Bevor er Lis aus Rache dafür erwürgen kann, interveniert Lun und verkündet, sie hätte das „nötige Werkzeug" (*Grün I* 52), um eine Holzmaske zu bauen, mittels derer die Hybriden genesen würden. In einer *moment-to-moment*-Sequenz wird dann gezeigt, wie einer der Pflanzenhybride dank der Maske von Lun wieder zum Leben erwacht (*Grün I* 53). Auf die einzelnen Stationen der Quest in Band II kann hier nicht im Detail eingegangen werden, zentral ist indes, dass auch Lis in der fortgesetzten Erzählung eine Verwandlung vollzieht, analog zu jener, die Vivi und Eva durchleben. Auch sie ist zum Schluss nicht mehr ‚nur' eine genderfluide, souverän auftretende Ökokrieger:in, die ihr konviviales Werkzeug für ein solidarisches Miteinander einsetzt, sondern sie agiert als selbstlose, bis in alle Ewigkeit wartende Hüter:in des „erschöpften Planeten" (*Grün II* 68).

Grün lässt sich insgesamt als narrativ-ästhetisches Novum deuten, dessen Errungenschaft darin liegt, die spezifische Entwicklungsfähigkeit des Comics in Bezug auf die Darstellbarkeit ökologischer Veränderungen eindrücklich zu belegen. Meine Argumentation schließt dabei an Yvonne Müller an, die ihre Lektüre von *Grün* zum Anlass nimmt, den Comic als literarische Gattung zu definieren, die alle „Bedingungen von Haraways Cyborg-Literatur" erfülle (Müller 26), womit Müller meint, dass im Comic alle zur Sprache kämen, auch diejenigen, die sich nicht verbal artikulieren könnten (wie etwa Pflanzen); außerdem würden im Comic Welten und Beziehungen visualisiert, die wir für gewöhnlich dualistischer und normierter imaginierten. Die Lektüre von *Grün* gestaltet sich im Vergleich zur linear erzählten *Endzeit* deutlich schwieriger, auch wenn sich die Erzählungen in vielerlei Hinsicht strukturell ähneln. Im Zentrum steht jeweils ein Figurenpaar mit semantisch und intertextuell aufgeladenen Namen – *Vivi* bedeutet die Lebendige, mit *Eva* wird der Sündenfall aufgerufen, *Lis* und *Lun* sind dezidiert geschlechtsneutrale Namen, die in ihrer symbiotischen Beziehung nicht nur an Don Quijote und Sancho Panza, sondern auch an Yin und Yan erinnern. Die ungleichen Paare begegnen sich zunächst mit gegenseitiger Ablehnung, treffen im Laufe der Handlung auf diverse unbekannte Kreaturen, meistern, wie es die Quest erfordert, zahlreiche Hindernisse und sind am Schluss nicht nur körperlich stark transformiert, sondern haben auch einen neuen Umgang mit dem verfügbaren Werkzeug erlernt. In beiden Erzählungen geht es zudem um die allmähliche Auflösung der Dichotomie von Natur und Kultur. Dazu sei abschließend noch auf ein Panel aus *Grün* verwiesen, das in seiner Ikonographie an die zu Beginn erörterte Filmsequenz aus *Fury Road* erinnert. Auf dem doppelseitigen Panel ist ein von Palisaden umzäunter Ort im sogenannten Wüstenring des Planeten dargestellt, an

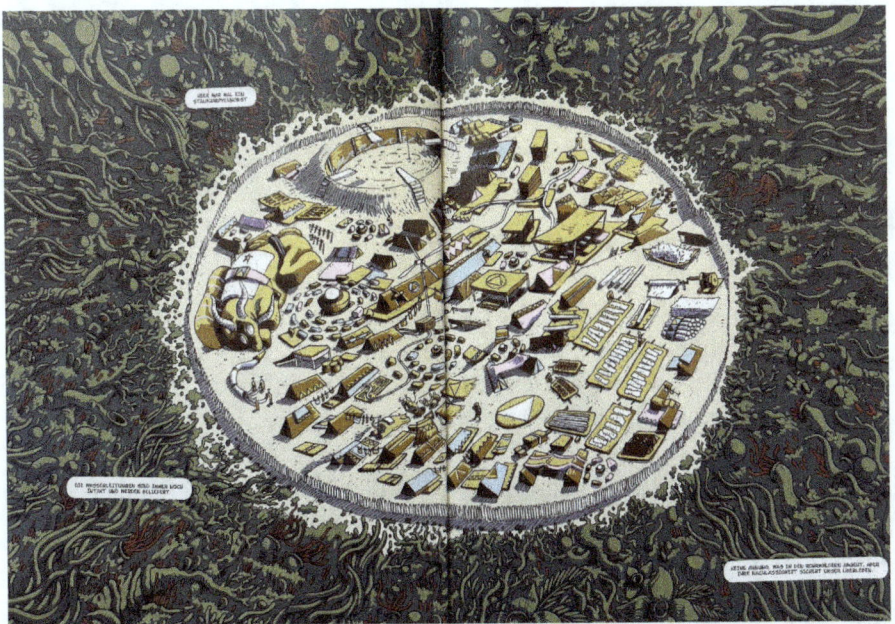

Abb. 5: Doppelseitiges Panel mit Zellstruktur, *Grün I*, S. 18–19.

den sich Lis zu Beginn der Handlung auf ihrer Flucht vor der grünen Seuche retten kann (Abb. 5).

Im Zentrum des Panels befindet sich eine widerständige, der Seuche trotzende und das Leben schützende ‚Zelle' in der, mitochondrienartig, Menschen, Nutztiere und Werkzeuge abgebildet sind. Darum herum bewegen sich, dominant, invasiv und bedrohlich wirkende Strukturen, die die grüne Seuche repräsentieren. Das Panel greift damit visuell die mikroskopische Aufnahme einer Eizelle auf, die von Tausenden Spermien umringt ist. Diese binäre Bildsprache, die kulturell-ökofeministische Essentialismen zu transportieren scheint, nach der ‚das Weibliche' schützt, wärmt und Leben spendet, während ‚das Männliche' aggressiv ist, bedroht und zerstört, verändert sich jedoch bereits im Laufe des ersten Bandes. „Die zu Anfang des ersten Bandes bildlich etablierte Trennung von menschlicher und nicht-menschlicher Sphäre wird im Verlauf der Diegese mehrfach durch Bilder der Durchmischung, Durchdringung und Kollaboration aufgehoben" (Müller 12). Auch in *Grün* wird damit letztlich eine Hybridisierung getrennter Sphären affirmiert und die Ökokrieger:innen Lis und Lun setzen, wie Furiosa, Vivi und Eva, ihr Leben ein, um dichotome Annahmen über das Verhältnis zwischen Natur und Kultur, Wissenschaft und Spiritismus, Schöpfungsgeschichte und Evolutionslehre, Männlichem und Weiblichem, Materiellem und Immateriellem, zu überwinden, weil das Überleben aller Spezies letztlich davon abhängt.

VI

Im direkten Vergleich von *Endzeit* und *Grün* fällt nicht nur auf, dass die Figuren mit konvivialen Werkezeugen ausgestattet sind, sondern auch, dass der Garten innerhalb der Diegese ein wichtiges Werkzeug darstellt. Sowohl die rauschhaft lila-gelb gezeichnete Idylle in *Endzeit* als auch die ‚verseuchten' Tiefgärten in *Grün* sind Habitate jeweils besonderer Schwellenfiguren, die konfrontiert werden müssen, um die konviviale Erneuerung der gemeinsamen Lebenswelt bewerkstelligen zu können. Zwar erscheint der Garten in beiden Graphic Novels als ein Ort der Liminalität und fungiert als Kompensations-Heterotopie, er wird aber bei Vieweg und Berger darüber hinaus auch zum Aushandlungsort ökofeministischer Anliegen. Der *hortus*, in der europäischen Literaturgeschichte ein topischer Ort männlich-diviner Schöpfung und narrativer Selbstreflexion (vgl. Sennefelder), wird hier dergestalt transformiert, dass er als *hybridus* einer ökofeministisch inspirierten Revolte erscheint. Zudem hat der Vergleich ergeben, dass die Inszenierung der Ökokrieger:innen auf ökofeministischen Parametern basiert. Furiosa ist eine idealtypische Cyborg, die „eintaucht" in „Formen des Wissens und der Praxis, die für die meisten Frauen unangenehm sind" (Haraway 2017, 296) und sowohl Vivi und Eva als auch Lis und Lun gelingt es, wie von Haraway gefordert, sich als „verwandt" zu begreifen. Gerade *Grün* kreist immer wieder um die Frage, wie diese Verwandtschaft („kinship") genau aussehen kann, wie sie gestaltet, begrenzt und gelebt werden soll, damit ein „artenübergeifendes Aufblühen" (vgl. Haraway 2016b, 17) möglich wird. *Endzeit* und *Grün* affirmieren schließlich beide das Credo, das nur diejenigen überlebensfähig sind, denen es gelingt, jenseits starrer Freund-Feind-Muster zu handeln und die sich offen zeigen für eine neu zu erlernende „Responsabilität" (Hoppe, zitiert nach Kerner 149)[13] gegenüber unbekannten, hybriden und zunächst befremdlichen Lebensformen, „gleichgültig, ob das Gegenüber ein Hund oder ein Baum, die Familie, ein Fluss oder ein Ökosystem ist" (Kerner 149). Neben Haraway und Daggett als theoretischen Referenzen lassen *Fury Road* und die beiden Graphic Novels aber auch wei-

---

[13] Der Begriff der „Responsabilität" stammt, Charlotte Kerner zufolge, von der „Soziologin und Haraway-Expertin" Katharina Hoppe; da Kerner in ihren Quellenangaben als Nachweis für den Begriff lediglich „Gespräch der Autorin mit K. Hoppe im Mai 2023" (Kerner 224) angibt, wird hier die entsprechende Seitenangabe aus Kerners Buch zitiert.

tere Auseinandersetzungen mit dem ökokritischen Diskurs der Gegenwart erkennen. Neben Anspielungen auf die Gaia-Hypothese in *Endzeit* lässt sich etwa die als „Ökosystem auf vier Beinen" (vgl. Kerner 127) dargestellte „Arche" in *Grün* als graphische Umsetzung von Lynn Margulis' These dekodieren, nach der wir „Symbionten auf einem symbiontischen Planeten" seien (vgl. Kerner 128).

Im Besonderen hat der hier vorgenommene medienkomparatistische Blick zeigen können, dass die Ökokrieger:innen nicht nur figurative Übersetzungen ökofeministischer Überzeugungen repräsentieren, sondern veritable Krieger:innen sind, die mit speziellem Werkzeug operieren. Furiosa bekämpft, einarmig und souverän, das Petro-Patriarchat und führt einen Befreiungskrieg; Vivi und Eva kämpfen gegen eine durch medizinische Forschung hervorgebrachte Zombie-Epidemie und führen einen Verteidigungskrieg, ebenso wie Lis und Lun, die gegen eine ominöse grüne Seuche antreten. Die Ökokrieger:innen zeichnen sich alle durch eine uneindeutige und mit heteronormativen Geschlechterrollen brechende Geschlechtsidentität aus, wobei die Figur Lun in *Grün* als posthumaner Mensch-Pflanzen-Hybrid am innovativsten visualisiert ist. Das Gesicht dieser schelmischen Begleiter:innenfigur bleibt hinter einer Holzmaske verborgen, der Körper ist amorph, instabil und zugleich materiell flexibel und lässt sich als „postanthropozentrische" Figur begreifen, die sowohl „Artenhierarchie" als auch „anthropozentrischen Exzeptionalismus" als obsolete Prinzipien entlarvt (Braidotti 217–218). Die Erzählungen sind dabei, wie etwa während der Diskussion der Garten-Sequenz in *Endzeit* deutlich wurde, keineswegs ausschließlich optimistisch in Bezug auf posthumane Entwicklungen. Insbesondere in der Figur der Gärtner:in kommt die nach wie vor ambivalente Beziehung zwischen transhumanistischen Ansätzen des *human enhancement*[14] (vgl. Bostrom) und der von Ivan Illich kritisierten, unreflektierten Technologieeuphorie zum Ausdruck.

Abschließend sei nochmals betont, dass ich die Ökokrieger:innen als Beispiele einer gerade im Entstehen begriffenen figurenästhetischen Wende begreife, bei der auf bekannte Topoi und Ideen des Ökofeminismus und Posthumanismus rekurriert wird, diese aber durch auffällig retrograde Werkzeuge ergänzt werden. Im Einzelnen wurden hier Armprothese, Lenkrad, Harke, Mistgabel, Holzstab, Axt oder Holzmaske besprochen und die Bedeutung der Gärten und der Gefährt:innen reflektiert. Zusammenfassend ist zu konstatieren, dass die Ökokrieger:in-

---

14 *Human enhancement* ist ein Begriff aus der Bioethik und meint die Verbesserung und Weiterentwicklung der Funktionen des menschlichen Körpers durch Technologie, wie etwa aktuell durch den Einsatz hochentwickelter Prothesen oder konzentrationssteigernder Substanzen. Der Begriff zielt aber auch auf die zugehörigen Visionen von Optimierung und Auslagerung ab, etwa durch so genanntes „genome editing" oder durch die komplette Digitalisierung des menschlichen Bewusstseins (vgl. Dickel).

nen als Figuren mit einer spannenden neuen Ästhetik und großem ökokritischen Potential gelten können, die sich für eine konviviale Vision von Gesellschaft einsetzen.

Literaturverzeichnis

Abel, Julia und Christian Klein, Hg. *Comics und Graphic Novels. Eine Einführung*. Metzler, 2016.

Alaimo, Stacy. „Trans-corporal feminism and the ethical space of nature". *Material Feminisms*. Hg. von Stacy Alaimo und Susan Hekman. Indiana UP, 2008. S. 237–264.

Alien. Regie von Ridley Scott. UK, USA 1979. 117 Minuten.

Barad, Karen. „Posthumanist Performativity. Toward an Understanding of How Matter Comes to Matter". *Material Feminisms*. Hg. von Stacy Alaimo und Susan Hekman. Indiana UP, 2008. S. 120–154.

Becher, Christina. „Nach dem Kollaps. Pflanzliches Aufbegehren in Frauke Bergers *Grün*". *Closure. Kieler e-Journal für Comicforschung* 7 (2020): S. 66–89. closure.uni-kiel.de/closure7/becher. 30.11.2020.

Bennett, Jane. *Vibrant Matter. A Political Ecology of Things*. Duke UP, 2010.

Berger, Frauke. *Grün*. Bd. 1, Splitter, 2018.

Berger, Frauke. *Grün*. Bd. 2, Splitter, 2019.

BpB, Glossar. „Kriege und Konflikte. Kriegstypen". *Bundeszentrale für politische Bildung*, bpb.de/themen/kriege-konflikte/dossier-kriege-konflikte/504298/kriegstypen/. 11. Februar 2025.

Bostrom, Nick. *Die Zukunft der Menschheit. Aufsätze*. Suhrkamp, 2018.

Braidotti, Rosi. „Posthumanes Wissen". *Navigationen. Zeitschrift für Medien- und Kulturwissenschaften. Multispecies Communities* 21.1 (2021): S. 217–241.

Daggett, Cara New. „Petro-masculinity. Fossil Fuels and Authoritarian Desire". *Journal of International Studies* 47.1 (2018): S. 25–44.

Daggett, Cara New. *Petromaskulinität. Fossile Energieträger und autoritäres Begehren*. 2. Aufl., Matthes & Seitz, 2023.

Dickel, Sascha. „Der Neue Mensch – ein (technik)utopisches Upgrade. Der Traum vom Human Enhancement". *APuZ* 9. September 2016. bpb.de/shop/zeitschriften/apuz/233464/der-neue-mensch-ein-technik-utopisches-upgrade/. 25. April 2025.

Elsberg, Marc. *°C-Celsius*. Blanvalet, 2023.

Endzeit. Regie von Carolina Hellsgård. Grown Up Films, Zweites Deutsches Fernsehen (ZDF), ARTE GEIE, Deutschland, 2018. 90 Minuten.

Fallwickl, Mareike. *Die Wut, die bleibt*. Rowohlt, 2022.

Foucault, Michel. *Die Heterotopien. Der utopische Körper. Zwei Radiovorträge*. Suhrkamp, 2005.

Freiburg, Rudolf und Gerd Bayer, Hg. „Survival. An Introductory Essay". *The Ethics of Survival in Contemporary Literature and Culture*. Springer Nature, 2021. S. 1–45.

Furiosa. A Mad Max Saga. Regie von George Miller. Netflix, Australien, 2024. 148 Minuten.

Gaard, Greta. *Ecofeminism. Women, Animals, Nature*. Temple UP, 1993.

Grewe-Volpp, Christa. „Ökofeminismus und Material Turn". *Ecocriticism. Eine Einführung*. Hg. von Gabriele Dürbeck und Urte Stobbe. Böhlau, 2015. S. 44–56.

Griffin, Susan. *Woman and Nature. The Roaring Inside Her*. Harper & Row, 1978.

Grusin, Richard. „Introduction. Anthropocene Feminism. An Experiment in Collaborative Theorizing". *Anthropocene feminism.* Hg. von Richard Grusin. Minnesota UP, 2017. S. VII–XIX.
Haraway, Donna. *Simians, Cyborgs, and Women. The Reinvention of Nature.* Routledge, 1991.
Haraway, Donna. *Das Manifest für Gefährten. Wenn Spezies sich begegnen – Hunde, Menschen und signifikante Andersartigkeit.* Merve, 2016a.
Haraway, Donna. *Staying with the Trouble. Making kin in the Chthulucene.* Duke, 2016b.
Haraway, Donna. *Monströse Versprechen. Die Gender- und Technologie-Essays.* Argument, 2017.
Henkel, Lea. „Lass raus". *Fluter,* fluter.de/weibliche-wut. 26. November 2024.
I am Legend. Regie von Francis Lawrence. USA 2007. 100 Minuten.
Illich, Ivan. *Tools for Conviviality.* Harper & Row, 1973.
Illich, Ivan. *Selbstbegrenzung. Eine politische Kritik der Technik.* 3. Aufl., C.H. Beck, 2014.
Kac-Vergne, Marianne. „Sidelining Women in Contemporary Science-Fiction Film". *Miranda. Revue Pluridisciplinaire du Monde Anglophone* 12 (2016): S. 1–17.
Kerner, Charlotte. *We are volcanoes. Die Öko-Visionärinnen Rachel Carson, Lynn Margulis, Donna Haraway.* Westend, 2024.
Karpouzou, Peggy und Nikoleta Zampaki, Hg. *Symbiotic Posthumanist Ecologies in Western Literature, Philosophy and Art.* Peter Lang, 2023.
Le Guin, Ursula. „The Carrier Bag Theory of Fiction". *Dancing at the Edge of the World. Thoughts on words, women, places.* Hg. Von Ursula Le Guin. New York, 1989. S.165–170
Maciejewski, Christina Caroline Heide. *Die globale Umweltkrise im deutschsprachigen Ökothriller. Wissenspopularisierung, Unterhaltung, kritische Funktion.* 2020. Universität Vechta, PhD Diss., voado.uni-vechta.de/bitstream/handle/21.11106/320/Dissertation%20Christina%20Maciejewski.pdf?sequence=2&isAllowed=y. 19. Februar 2025.
Mad Max. Fury Road. Regie von George Miller. Netflix, USA, Australien, 2015. 120 Minuten.
Müller, Yvonne. *Erzählen nach dem Menschen. Frauke Bergers posthumaner Comic ‚Grün'.* Wehrhan, 2024.
Oziewicz, Marek. „Speculative Fiction". *Oxford research encyclopedia of literature,* oxfordre.com/literature/display/10.1093/acrefore/9780190201098.001.0001/acrefore-9780190201098-e-78.15. Februar 2025.
Plumwood, Val. *Feminism and the Mastery of Nature.* Routledge, 1993.
Rauschenberger, Pia. „Die Wut der Frauen". *Deutschlandfunk Kultur,* deutschlandfunkkultur.de/genderforschung-die-wut-der-frauen-100.html. 15. Februar 2025.
Reglińska-Jemioł, Anna. „Victim-Warriors and Restorers. Heroines in the Post-Apocalyptic World of Mad Max: Fury Road". *Text Matters. A Journal of Literature, Theory and Culture* 11.11 (2021): S. 106–118.
Resident Evil. Regie von Paul W.S. Anderson. Deutschland, UK 2002. 100 Minuten.
Schätzing, Frank. *Der Schwarm.* Fischer, 2005.
Schneider-Özbek, Katrin. „Frau rettet Welt? Ontologisierung des Weiblichen im Ökothriller". *Technik und Gender. Technikzukünfte als geschlechtlich codierte Ordnungen in Literatur und Film.* Hg. von Marie-Hélène Adam und Katrin Schneider-Özbek. KIT Scientific Publishing, 2016. S. 151–172.
Schneider-Özbek, Katrin. „Der Ökothriller. Zur Genese eines neuen Genres an der Schnittstelle von Thriller und ökologischem Narrativ". *Ökologische Genres. Naturästhetik, Umweltethik, Wissenspoetik.* Hg. von Evi Zemanek. Vanderhoeck & Ruprecht, 2018. S. 229–246.
Schubert, Klaus und Martina Klein. *Das Politiklexikon.* 7. aktual. u. erw. Aufl., Dietz, 2020. Zitiert nach: bpb.de/kurz-knapp/lexika/politiklexikon/17756/krieg/. 11. Februar 2025.
Sennefelder, Anna Karina. *Rückzugsorte des Erzählens. Muße als Modus autobiographischer Selbstreflexion.* Mohr Siebeck, 2018.

Smith, Sue. „What is Disability Studies to Make of Fetal Amputee and Cosplayer Laura Vaughn and Her Emulation of Female Warrior, Imperator Furiosa of *Mad Max: Fury Road*?". *Journal of Literary & Cultural Disability Studies* 14.4 (2020): S. 487–491.
Sweeney-Baird, Christina. *The End of Men*. G.P. Putnam's Sons, 2021.
The Terminator. Regie von James Cameron. USA, 1984. 107 Minuten.
28 Days Later. Regie von Danny Boyle. UK, 2002.113 Minuten.
Vieweg, Olivia. *Endzeit*. Carlsen, 2018.
Vieweg, Olivia. *Endzeit*. Schwarzer Turm, 2012.
Warren, Karen. *Ecofeminism. Women, Culture, Nature*. Indiana UP, 1997.

Kalina Kupczyńska
Autorinnenschaft im Comic – das Selbstbild als Autorin bei Marie Marcks und Birgit Weyhe

Abstract: Der Gegenstand des Beitrags ist *Autorinnenschaft* in den Comics von Marie Marcks und Birgit Weyhe. Mit *Autorinnenschaft* wird ein Begriff vorgeschlagen, der sich auf Formen der weiblichen und queeren Autorschaft bezieht. Ausgehend von den bestehenden Studien zur Autorschaft, die bisher ausschließlich männlichen Comic-Künstlern gewidmet wurden, werden Topoi der *Autorinnenschaft* untersucht. Das Ziel der Analyse ist, anhand der grafischen Selbstdarstellungen der Illustratorin und Karikaturistin Marie Marcks (1922–2014) und der Comic-Autorin Birgit Weyhe (*1969) eine historische Entwicklungslinie der *Autorinnenschaft* im deutschen Comic vorzuschlagen.

Das Vorwort des 2010 erschienenen Buches *Graphic Women. Life Narrative & Contemporary Comics* von Hillary L. Chute beginnt mit einer Auflistung von „women creating significant narrative graphic work" (Chute 1). Chute, deren Buch als wegweisend und produktiv für die Comicforschung zu grafischen Narrativen von Frauen breit rezipiert wurde, legitimierte mit der Aufzählung ihr Forschungsfeld – eine Geste, die fünfzehn Jahre später verblüffen mag. Comics und Graphic Novels von Frauen erscheinen 2025 als ein selbstverständlicher Gegenstand der internationalen Forschung, was sich zum einen in der auf dem Markt vorhandenen Anzahl der Werke von Comic-Autorinnen, und zum anderen in den Publikationen niederschlägt, die ebendiese Werke wissenschaftlich thematisieren.[1] Zugleich lässt sich in der internationalen Comicwissenschaft eine Ausdifferenzierung des Forschungsfeldes beobachten – die Repräsentation von ‚Frauen' wurde durch die Perspektive auf ‚Gender' bzw. ‚Gender/Queer' abgelöst.[2] Die Comic-Forschung folgte damit der Entwicklung in vielen Bereichen der Geisteswissenschaften – eine intersektionale Sicht auf Repräsentationen von Individuen und Menschengruppen feiert Erfolge (vgl. Beckmann u. a.; Losleben und Musubika), nicht zuletzt aufgrund ihrer interdisziplinären Anschlussfä-

---

[1] Explizit zu Comics von Frauen für Frauen und über Frauen, vgl. etwa Kuczyńska; Lightman; Bajac-Carter; Gilmore; Fägersten et al.; Bauer et al.; Aarons; Welker.
[2] Vgl. u. a. Sina; Eckhoff-Heindl und Sina; Aldama; Gundermann; de Dauw; Lobnig et al.

ථ Open Access. © 2025 bei den Autorinnen und Autoren, publiziert von De Gruyter. [cc) BY-NC-ND] Dieses Werk ist lizenziert unter der Creative Commons Namensnennung - Nicht-kommerziell - Keine Bearbeitungen 4.0 International Lizenz.
https://doi.org/10.1515/9783112218631-007

higkeit sowie der „herrschaftskritische[n] Herangehensweise" (Gouma und Dorer 183).

Chutes Legitimationsbedürfnis wird außerdem nachvollziehbar, wenn man den Blick auf die wissenschaftliche Auseinandersetzung mit der Comic-Autorschaft richtet – auch hier fällt eine Fokussierung auf Comic-Autoren und damit ein Desiderat auf: Analysen von (Selbst)Repräsentationen der Künstlerinnen sind in den einschlägigen Studien kaum auffindbar. Die Fokussierung auf Comic-Autoren lässt sich mit der langanhaltenden Dominanz von Männern in der Comicbranche erklären (vgl. Chute 1), was das Image des Comics als „a guy's medium" (Sinclair 4; Chute 20) nachhaltig prägte. Wie soziologische Untersuchungen zu Lebens- und Arbeitsverhältnissen in der Comicbranche suggerieren, ist der Trend keinesfalls überwunden: „comics seem to entrench instead of repudiate a very traditional mainstream creatorship – speaking of the comics industry as a field with equal opportunities would be perverse" (Brandl und Moore 28). So ist der Erfolg in der Comicwelt damit verbunden, „to pass as [...] a heterosexual, white, able-bodied, cismale raising no children in the home" (ebd.). Wie diese Situation mit der Autorschaft und ihrer Inszenierung im Comic zusammenhängt, zeigt die Studie zu US-amerikanischen Comic-Autoren von Daniel Stein, aus der hervorgeht, dass „Selbstporträts und Selbstinszenierungen von Comic-Autoren [...] im theatralen Raum der amerikanischen Populärkultur" (Stein 233) eine lange Tradition haben und bis in die Anfänge der Comicgeschichte zurückreichen. Stein belegt an einigen Beispielen, dass es „ein[en] Topos im Zeichenrepertoire von Comic-Autoren gibt, der [...] auf eine gesteigerte Selbstreflexivität sowie auf ein verstärktes Gattungsbewusstsein hindeutet" (ebd.). Steins Untersuchung zieht ausschließlich Comic-*Autoren* in Betracht, seine Beispiele sind u. a. Art Spiegelman und Robert Crumb, d. h. die Vertreter der *Comix-Underground*-Szene;[3] der Blick wird zudem punktuell auch auf die Superhelden-Comics gerichtet.

Steins Befunde sind für die hier zu verfolgenden Fragestellungen insofern wegweisend, als sie eine historische Entwicklung aufzeigen, die zur Etablierung einer Tradition in der Selbstinszenierung von Comic-Autoren beigetragen hat. Im Anschluss an Stein wird im Folgenden diskutiert, ob sich in den Comics von zwei deutschsprachigen Comic-Autorinnen Topoi der Selbstdarstellung benennen lassen und wenn ja, welche, und wie diese Selbstdarstellung kontextualisiert wird. Der Fokus liegt also auf der Inszenierung von Autorinnenschaft – diese wird vor

---

3 Als *Comix-Underground* wird eine am Ende der 1960er und Anfang der 1970er Jahre aktive Gruppe von Comic-Künstler:innen bezeichnet, die Comics unabhängig vom Mainstream zeichneten und in eigens gegründeten, meistens kurzlebigen Magazinen herausgaben.

dem Hintergrund der bestehenden Arbeiten zur Autorschaft im Comic kritisch analysiert.

‚Autorinnenschaft' ist eine aus der Genderform für ‚Autorschaft' abgeleitete Neubildung, die ich als Bezeichnung für weibliche, queere und nicht gendernormative Autorschaft nutze. Der Begriff soll zum einen einer *Sichtbarmachung* von Comic-Autorschaft von Frauen, queeren und nicht-heteronormativen Personen und zum anderen der *Repräsentation* diverser Formen der Autorschaft im Comic dienen. Der Begriff ‚Autorinnenschaft' zielt somit auf das Erfassen feministisch geprägter Haltungen innerhalb der internationalen Comicszene und auf Inklusion einer wachsenden Gruppe von Comic-Künstler:innen, die sich jenseits der männlich kodierten und heteronormativen Repräsentationsmodi positionieren.

Wie die Entwicklung innerhalb der deutschen Comicszene seit 2000 zeigt, wird Comic-Autorschaft auch als politisches Engagement für marginalisierte Gesellschaftsgruppen verstanden und eingesetzt. Als eine wichtige Zäsur innerhalb dieser Entwicklungstendenz kann die Gründung der Comic-Gewerkschaft im Jahr 2022 genannt werden – sie zeigt ein Bedürfnis nach organisierter gemeinschaftlicher Zusammenarbeit zum Zweck der Repräsentation der Comic-Schaffenden.[4] Auf die Gründung folgte die Veröffentlichung der Studie *Harte Fakten, große Aufgaben: Die Arbeitsrealität Comicschaffender im deutschsprachigen Raum*, wo „demografische Faktoren" gesammelt und ausgewertet wurden, „um eine intersektionale Analyse zu ermöglichen" (Becker et al., Vorbemerkung). Im Vorwort der Studie wird auf zwei Aspekte in der „akademischen Beschäftigung mit Comics" (ebd. 5) aufmerksam gemacht: auf die Abkehr von „textzentrierter, philologischer oder hermeneutischer Betrachtung von ‚Werken'" zugunsten einer „Untersuchung von Comic-*Kontexten*" (ebd. 5; Herv. i. Orig.) und auf die steigende Relevanz von „Fragen der gesellschaftlichen Teilhabe, der politischen und sozialen Machtgefällen (sic)" in Bezug auf „tatsächliche Entstehungsbedingungen von Comics" (ebd. 6).

Vor dem Hintergrund dieser Entwicklungen in der deutschsprachigen Comicproduktion und Comicforschung bekommt die Frage nach spezifischer Gestaltung der ‚Autorinnenschaft' eine besondere Brisanz, denn zu den bereits etablierten Ansätzen (etwa im Bereich der Narratologie und Comic-Autobiografie; vgl. El Refaie 53) kommt eine soziohistorische Perspektive hinzu. Eine solche Verbindung von Herangehensweisen ist insofern produktiv, als sie, wie ich im Folgenden an

---

4 Vgl. das Manifest der Comic Gewerkschaft vom 1. September 2022, zugänglich auf der Website comicgewerkschaft.org. 24. März 2025.

zwei Beispielen ausführe, als Leitfaden der Veränderungen innerhalb der Comicbranche seit den 1980er Jahren fungieren kann.⁵

Marie Marcks (1922–2014) und Birgit Weyhe (*1969) gehören zwei unterschiedlichen Generationen deutscher Zeichnerinnen an. Anhand ihrer künstlerischen Biografien sowie ihrer Inszenierungen von Autorschaft lassen sich die Formen und Etappen der gesellschaftlichen Anerkennung von *Autorinnen* verfolgen. Marcks' autobiografische Aufzeichnungen, auf die ich im Folgenden eingehe, haben aus der Sicht der Forschung zur weiblichen Autorschaft und zur Comic-Autobiografie einen Seltenheitswert – sie dokumentieren eine frühe Phase der Reflexion über die gesellschaftliche Position einer freien Illustratorin. Wenn man bedenkt, dass Marcks' Schaffensphase in die 1950er und 1960er fällt, mag das Vorfinden derselben Themen – allen voran die Bedeutung des eigenen Arbeitszimmers – in den fünfzig Jahre später entstandenen Comics von Birgit Weyhe überraschen. So ergibt sich mein Fokus auf das Werk dieser Autorinnen aus der auffälligen Ähnlichkeit der Topoi der Autorinnenschaft in ihren grafischen Arbeiten und damit aus einem Interesse für die Transformation der Darstellung von Autorinnenschaft innerhalb der deutschen Comicgeschichte. Zugleich verfolge ich die Absicht, künstlerische Arbeiten wichtiger und in der Forschung wenig beachteter Zeichnerinnen wie Marcks im Rahmen des brisanten Diskurses der Autorschaft zu re-kontextualisieren.

I

Der Fall der Zeichnerin und Illustratorin Marie Marcks (1922–2014) markiert einen wichtigen Punkt in der Geschichte der Comic-Autorinnenschaft. Zum einen ist die Comic-Autorschaft zum Zeitpunkt der künstlerischen Aktivität von Marcks noch nicht als Beruf ausdifferenziert, daher auch die gängige Benennung als ‚Illustratorin' bzw. ‚Karikaturistin' (vgl. Fahrenberg; Kronthaler). Zum anderen gibt es gute Gründe dafür, Marcks aufgrund ihres Gesamtwerks, das kaum längere Narrationen umfasst, als Illustratorin und Karikaturistin zu bezeichnen. Eine Ausnahme bilden zwei Bände ihrer Autobiografie, beide untertitelt als „Autobiographische Aufzeichnungen": *Marie, es brennt!* (1984) und *Schwarz-weiss und bunt* (1989), auf die ich im Folgenden Bezug nehme. Marcks' Autobiografie verbindet in formaler Hinsicht die Merkmale des Comics und der Bildgeschichte – Marcks

---

5 Bei den ausgewählten Beispielen handelt es sich um Comics, in denen die jeweilige Autorin die beiden Ebenen – Text und Bild – selbst gestaltet hat, daher werde ich die Aspekte der geteilten bzw. kollaborativen Autorinnenschaft nicht berücksichtigen.

arbeitet ohne Panel-Layouts, verwendet Sprechblasen und stellt Bild und Text auf einer Seite auf unterschiedliche Art und Weise zusammen. Die Textpassagen dominieren, Zeichnungen dienen sowohl als Illustration als auch als integraler Teil der Erzählung.

Die Bedeutung der Arbeiten von Marcks für die Geschichte der Comic-Autorinnenschaft liegt in erster Linie in der Möglichkeit der Nachverfolgung der einzelnen Etappen einer weiblichen Biografie im Bereich der Text-und-Bild-Kunst. Marcks erzählt in *Schwarz-weiss und bunt* von ihrer Arbeit als Zeichnerin von Anfang der 1950er bis Mitte der 1960er Jahre; das Buch endet kurz vor dem Anfang der Studentenrevolte 1968. Sie gibt Einblick in mentalitätsgeschichtliche Entwicklungen dieser Zeit und hält zugleich das fest, was Ingo Berensmeyer für Literatur diagnostiziert:

> In modernity, under the "imperative of permanent innovation" (Reckwitz 2012, 11), the self-description of the artist becomes "a large part of the [artist's] job" (McGurl 2009, 48), something to be performed inside as well as outside the text, in interviews, public readings, and later on dedicated author websites and social media platforms that present curated author images. (Berensmeyer 49)

Große Teile von Marcks' „autobiographischen Aufzeichnungen" gelten der Thematisierung der Arbeit einer freischaffenden Zeichnerin und der Bemühung, sich innerhalb der männlich dominierten Job- und Auftragslandschaft zu positionieren. Zu betonen ist Marcks Stellung als Pionierin – andere Zeichnerinnen und Karikaturistinnen der 1960er und 1970er Jahre, die meistens in einem Atemzug mit Marcks genannt werden – Franziska Becker (*1949) und Claire Bretécher (1940–2020) – waren deutlich jünger. Marcks habe sich im Alleingang „mit ihren seit den sechziger Jahren in der *Süddeutschen Zeitung* und *Die Zeit* veröffentlichten politischen Karikaturen eine Ausnahmestellung auf diesem ansonsten von Männern dominierten Feld erobert" (Vetter-Liebenow o.S.).

Die Bandbreite der Auftragsjobs, die Marcks im Lauf der 1950er und 1960er Jahre übernimmt, reicht von Plakatentwürfen für einen amerikanischen Soldatenklub in Heidelberg über Gestaltung von Messeständen, Schaufenstern, und Einladungskarten bis hin zur Beschriftung der Türen an der Wirtschaftshochschule in Mannheim. In Marcks eigenen Worten: „Ich nahm an Aufträgen an, was ich nur kriegen konnte: Hier ein Plakat, dort eine Illustration, nochmal ein Mosaik an einem Schulneubau, und mal ein Wandbild" (*Schwarz-weiss* 19).

Ein solches Statement kann man in Biografien vieler Zeichner:innen nicht nur aus dieser Zeit finden (siehe etwa Spiegelman) – prekäre Beschäftigung vor allem am Anfang der künstlerischen Laufbahn war und ist ein Teil der Lebensrealität vieler Comic-Künstler:innen. An Marcks' Bekenntnis ist allerdings ungewöhnlich, dass sie diese Erfahrung in ihr Autorinnenbild integriert, neben ihrem

Selbstbild als Mutter und Ehefrau. Die instabilen Arbeitsbedingungen sind mit der familiären Situation eng verbunden – die Geburt jedes Kindes (insgesamt fünf) wird entsprechend vermerkt und bedeutet eine Pause und eine Einschränkung im Arbeitsleben. Anfang der 1950er Jahre quittiert Marcks den gesicherten Posten für einen US-amerikanischen Soldatenklub, um der achtjährigen Tochter das Los eines „Schlüsselkindes" (*Schwarz-weiss* 3) zu ersparen. 1956, als ihr Mann in Yale eine Fellowship antritt, bleibt sie erst einmal allein zurück, worüber sie rückblickend schreibt: „Eigentlich weiß ich nicht, wie ich den ganzen Kram geschafft habe mit Kindern, Schule, Haushalt, Aufträgen, unendlicher Korrespondenz [...]" (*Schwarz-weiss* 33). Nachdem sie ihrem Mann in die USA folgt und das Arbeitsangebot des Malers Josef Albers, eines Freundes ihres Vaters, an der School of Arts ablehnt – und zwar aus „Angst vor seinen vielen Vierecken[6] und 3 Kindern zu Hause" (*Schwarz-weiss* 36) – geht sie auf Arbeitssuche. Da erfolgt erst einmal eine harte Konfrontation mit dem *American Dream*: „Ich fuhr in den 76. Stock rauf und wieder runter, oder in den 122. Stock, Zimmer 2003 und wieder runter und rauf und runter. [...] Viele freundliche Art-Direktorinnen wiesen mich an viele andere Verlage weiter" (*Schwarz-weiss* 40). Unvermeidlich wird auch das Thema der männlichen Konkurrenz angesprochen: „Viele von ihnen fragten mich, ob ich this nice young European Artist Tomi Ungerer kenne, er sei eben dagewesen und habe hier hübsche Arbeiten hinterlassen ... " (*Schwarz-weiss* 42).

Marcks' Position als Zeichnerin ist von dem allgemeinen Status der Frauen im Zeichner-Gewerbe dieser Zeit in vielerlei Hinsicht beeinflusst, die Ablehnung ihrer Arbeiten in den US-amerikanischen Verlagen ist nur eines der Beispiele. Andere von ihr geschilderte Situationen deuten auf Minderwertigkeitsgefühle sowie das Fehlen eines verlässlichen Netzwerks hin. Auf der Weltausstellung in Brüssel 1958 beobachtet Marcks den US-amerikanischen Cartoonisten Saul Steinberg bei der Arbeit und verzeichnet: „Ach, wie kümmerlich und doof ist dagegen mein Zeug!" (*Schwarz-weiss* 64). Wenn sie für ihre Arbeit an der Mitgestaltung des deutschen Pavillons in Brüssel eine Rechnung ausstellen soll, ruft sie ratlos einen Kollegen in Berlin an – sie muss sich dann zwar *Mansplaining* gefallen lassen, aber ein guter Rat ist auch dabei. Illustrationen, die sie als Auftragsarbeiten für einen Heidelberger Filmclub entwarf, kommentiert sie im Nachhinein selbstkritisch mit dem Satz: „Mein feministisches Bewußtsein war allerdings damals noch vollkommen unterentwickelt!" (*Schwarz-weiss* 83). Die Einladungskarten etwa – die Marcks in ihre Aufzeichnungen miteinbezieht – stellen Frauen „in ihrer aus männlicher Perspektive konstruierten, erotisierten Weiblichkeit" (Beuel,

---

[6] Josef Albers ist vor allem für seine quadratischen Bilder bekannt, in denen er das Zusammenwirken diverser Farben analysierte.

et al. 94) dar, was den Mustern der „kommerziellen Bildsprache der Fünfziger" (ebd.) folgt. Tatsächlich ergibt sich aus den häufigen Einsprengseln aus Marcks' Tagebüchern, dass ihr Aufbegehren gegen die vorgesehenen Frauenrollen erst spät einsetzt – und zwar als das gesellige Leben des als Akademiker tätigen Mannes zunimmt und die Haushaltspflichten hauptsächlich von ihr als Ehefrau bestritten werden müssen. Ein kurzer, hastiger Eintrag aus dem Jahr 1964 veranschaulicht den Druck, dem Marcks ausgesetzt war: „6.6. Matthias mit Clique Twist-Party. Irrsinnstag, Kinderbetrieb. Vergebl. Versuch zu arbeiten" (*Schwarzweiss* 91). Marcks, die in einer liberalen Künstlerfamilie aufwuchs, rebellierte als Jugendliche bzw. junge Erwachsene zwar gegen Autoritätspersonen, etwa gegen ihren Büro-Chef in der Flugzeugmotorenfabrik, in der sie zur Kriegszeit als technische Zeichnerin arbeiten musste,[7] doch handelte sich dabei aber kaum um Protest aus einem frauenemanzipatorischen Bewusstsein heraus.

Marcks' Selbstdarstellung als Zeichnerin fällt dementsprechend ambivalent aus, sie bestätigt das literaturwissenschaftliche Urteil, demzufolge „[d]ie Kopplung von Autorschaft und Weiblichkeit ein prekäres, vielfach auch paradoxes Verhältnis bezeichnet" (Künzel 17). In *Schwarz-weiss und bunt* wechseln sich zwei Darstellungen ab, mit denen die Künstlerin sich be-zeichnet: Man sieht sie erstens im Arbeitskittel, mit Malutensilien, bei der Arbeit oder bei Gesprächen über Aufträge (Abb. 1), und zweitens ebenfalls am Arbeiten, allerdings im privaten, häuslichen Umfeld (Abb. 2).

Abb. 1: Selbstdarstellung bei Verhandlung mit Auftraggebern (*Schwarz-weiss* 20).

---

7 Diese Episode findet sich im ersten Band der „autobiographischen Aufzeichnungen", siehe Marcks 1984.

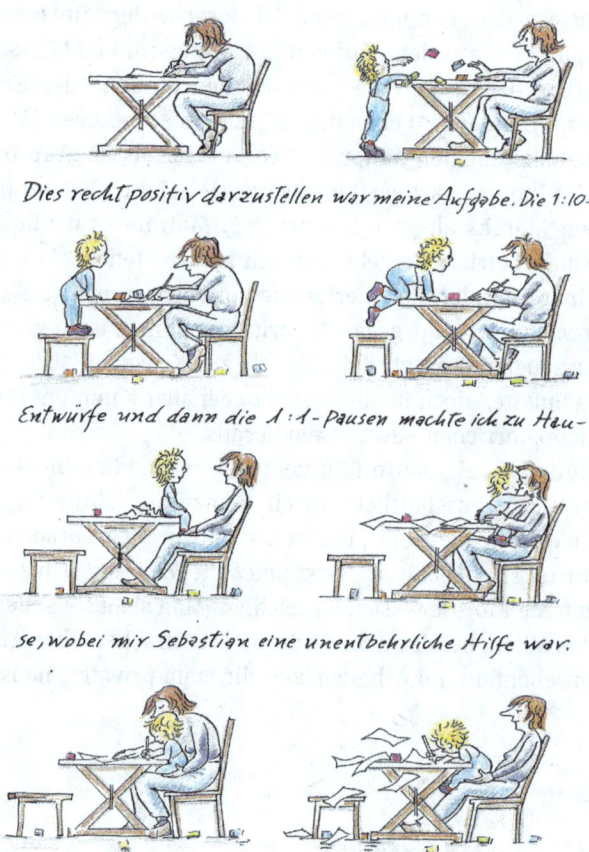

Abb. 2: Arbeit und Mutterschaft (*Schwarz-weiss* 61).

Das Selbstbild ist in seinem Äußeren genderneutral. Marcks verzichtet auf jegliche Attribute der Weiblichkeit, die sie sonst in ihren grafischen Arbeiten anwendet – und zugleich ist es von ihrem Selbstbild als Mutter nicht abgekoppelt, im Gegenteil. Die Anfertigung der Tafeln für die Weltausstellung in Brüssel, erfolgt „mit Hilfe" des kleinen Sebastian – allein die Szenerie mit dem großen Arbeitstisch und dem kleinen Maltisch für den Sohn demonstriert die (notwendige) Einbeziehung der Kinder in den Arbeitsalltag. Das erste Selbstbild (Abb. 1), das sich in einigen Variationen im Buch wiederfindet, veranschaulicht vor allem eins: Das Agieren in einem männerdominierten Milieu, das in den 1950ern für Frauen *nicht* vorgesehen war. Dem setzt Marcks ein Selbstbild gegenüber, das sie jenseits jeglicher Genderklischees als souveräne Handwerkerin und Macherin, sozusagen als eine *poeta faber*,[8] zeigt.

Das zweite Selbstbild (Abb. 2) kombiniert den Topos der (männlichen) Selbstrepräsentation am Arbeitstisch mit der zeitkonformen gendertypischen Darstellung bei Durchführung der Haushaltspflichten. Wenn man nach Thierry Groensteen den Tisch des/der Comicschaffenden als „l'attribut qui résume un lieu (l'atelier), une profession, une activité, un sacerdoce" (das Attribut, das einen Ort (das Atelier), einen Beruf, eine Tätigkeit, ein heiliges Amt zusammenfasst) (Groensteen 2013a) deutet, wird der intendierte Kontrast deutlich – nicht nur fehlt bei Marcks der übliche Hintergrund des Künstlerateliers, auch von einer ‚heiligen Schaffensstätte' kann kaum die Rede sein. Marcks ruft den Topos auf, um ihn zu modifizieren – so wird ein kooperativer, geteilter, inklusiver Raum erzeugt, in dem Kreativität zwischen dem kleinen und dem großen Tisch entsteht. Der Seitenlayout – acht ungerahmte aufeinanderfolgende Sequenzen – ist insofern auffällig, als man eine solche Seitenkomposition im Buch nur noch einmal findet, und auch da wird Marcks mit ihren Kindern dargestellt. Die zeitliche Dehnung der Szene, erreicht durch die Seitenkomposition, ist ein Signal für die Rezeption: die Lesenden sollen bei dieser einfachen und an sich stummen Szene verweilen, erst dadurch entfaltet sich ihre Bedeutung. Die Zeit kommt so als die wertvollste Ressource sowohl für Zeichnerin als auch Mutter zum Ausdruck; an einer weiteren Stelle notiert Marcks:

> Natürlich war ich, wie alle Mütter, die Kinder in diesem Alter haben, ständig müde. Die nicht enden-wollende Arbeit mit kleinen Kindern wird aber reich belohnt und ich bin froh, daß ich diese Glücksmomente seinerzeit aufgeschrieben habe, sonst wären sie wohl im Meer des Vergessens versunken. (*Schwarz-weiss* 93)

Den Selbstbildern von Marcks ist anzumerken, dass mit ihnen in gewisser Weise Neuland betreten wird, denn auf eine genealogische Traditionslinie der weiblichen Comic-Autorschaft konnte die Zeichnerin kaum zurückgreifen. Marcks selbst erzeugt hier zum ersten Mal *Autorinnenschaft*, was erstens in der Selbstdarstellung als Handwerkerin und zweitens in der Kontrastierung des Topos „le créateur [...] devant sa table à dessin" (der Schöpfer [...] vor seinem Zeichentisch) (Groensteen 2013a) und der qua Mutterrolle erreichten inklusiven Schaffenssituation zum Vorschein kommt. Was Nancy K. Miller als Antwort auf Roland Barthes' Text *Der Tod des Autors* konstatiert, nämlich dass „das weibliche Subjekt [...] dezentriert, ‚ohne Ursprung', nicht institutionalisiert (war)", und daher „die Beziehung

---

[8] „Das Fachwissen, das Handwerk sowie der korrekte Gebrauch von Regeln sind die Grundlage für die Arbeit des *poeta faber* [...]" (Karnatz 36).

der Frau zu Integrität und Textualität, zu Begehren und Autorität strukturell wichtige Unterschiede zu jener universellen Position (des schreibenden Selbst; K.K.)" (255) aufzeigt, lässt sich ohne weiteres auf die Selbstbilder von Marcks beziehen. Die Beziehung zur Autorschaft muss erst geübt werden, ist allerdings nur bedingt autonom, da sie stets in Beziehung zum Umfeld (Kinder, Ehemann, Auftraggeber) steht. So entsteht Autorinnenschaft aus einem kommunikativen Prozess, dessen Ergebnis weniger eine Selbstbehauptung als eine Lebenspraxis ist.

Wichtiger als eine „sich immer neu erzeugende, nicht tot zu kriegende performative Funktion, Geste und künstlerisch-theatralische Inszenierung" (Wagner-Egelhaaf 211) ist hier der Probelauf einer Selbstdarstellung als Autorin, bei dem Autorschaft vor allem als eine zu verhandelnde Praxis wahrgenommen wird. Damit entstehen Grundmuster einer Autorinnenschaft, deren zentrale Merkmale Offenheit und Prozessualität sind.

Der Fall Marie Marcks markiert in der deutschen Comic-Geschichte einen Punkt, an dem sich nicht nur Autorinnenschaft, sondern auch der unabhängige Comic zu formen beginnt. Wie Brett Sterling nachweist, etablierte sich in Deutschland erst im Lauf der 1980er Jahre eine Reihe kleiner Verlage, „die Comics nach ihrem Geschmack aussuchen und an ein [...] Publikum bringen konnten" (Sterling 362). Mit Gründung des Comic-Magazins *Strapazin* (1984) wurde eine Plattform für „alternative Comics aus der ganzen Welt" erschaffen, wo „am Anfang auch deutschsprachige Künstler*innen vertreten waren" (Sterling 363).

Die Dynamik in der deutschsprachigen Comiclandschaft seit den 1980ern macht die Verschränkung der Entwicklungen des Mediums und der Autorschaft deutlich: „As the comics medium comes into its own, not only does authorship of a comic become all the more difficult to determine but the issue of comic authorship itself becomes all the more pressing" (Mag Uidhir 48). Mit der allmählichen Unabhängigkeit von Großverlagen und vom *Mainstream*-Geschmack entstand ein Raum, in dem ‚Comic-Autor' als Berufsbezeichnung geltend gemacht werden konnte und sollte: ‚Comic-Autor' war nun die Instanz, die für die Gesamtheit der ästhetischen Entscheidungen im Zusammenhang mit einem Werk zuständig war.

II

Während Marie Marcks in ihrem autobiografischen Comic optisch kaum von anderen Figuren zu unterscheiden war, setzt Birgit Weyhe auf bewährte Mittel der Erkennbarkeit – sie zeichnet ihre Avatarin-Figur stets in einer gestreiften Bluse und einer schwarzen Weste (vgl. Kraenzle 222).⁹ Ob dahinter eine (selbstironische) Referenz auf Selbstmarkierungen von Jean-Christophe Menu (gestreifte Bluse) und Art Spiegelman (schwarze Weste) steckt, lässt sich hier nicht entscheiden; die Geste selbst verortet die Autorin in einer Entwicklungsetappe von Autorinnenschaft, in der eine Selbstpositionierung innerhalb des Comicbetriebs in den Comics selbst stattfindet. Weyhes erste Comic-Narrationen in Buchlänge erscheinen in der Zeit der Etablierung des Comics „auf den Literaturseiten" der „meinungsführenden überregionalen Zeitungen" in Deutschland (Ditschke 270) und der „Verbreitung des Labels ‚Graphic Novel'" (ebd. 276); der Avant Verlag, der ihre Comics seit 2011 veröffentlicht, brachte schon 2009 Ulli Lusts Debüt heraus, „ein(en) Meilenstein [...] für den deutschsprachigen, um nicht zu sagen für den modernen feministischen Comic überhaupt" (Hartmann). In ihrer dritten Graphic Novel *Im Himmel ist Jahrmarkt* von 2013 zeichnete Weyhe ihre Avatarin in einem Setting, das seitdem als ihr Erkennungszeichen gilt: Sie sitzt in gestreifter Bluse und schwarzer Weste am Schreibtisch, mit dem Rücken zum Betrachter, in die Arbeit vertieft. Diese Konstellation ist in Weyhes Arbeiten oft anzutreffen – man bekommt sie in der Entrücktheit zu sehen, in der der Schaffensprozess sich vollzieht. Symbolisch zeigt sich darin die Ambiguität der Dokumentaristin: Die Rückenfigur ist zugleich ab- und anwesend, und bekommt so einen „ephemeren [...] Charakter" (Kirsten 110). Im Deutungsrepertoire der Rückenfiguren in der Kunst- wie auch Filmgeschichte finden sich solche Semantisierungen wie „Scham/Trauer" und „Nachdenklichkeit"; ebenso wird Rückenfiguren „ein großes enigmatisches Potenzial attestiert" (ebd. 107) sowie das Bergen einer „Bildspannung" (ebd. 121). Diese Bildspannung ergibt sich zum einen aus dem Bruch mit dem Prinzip der Frontalität, das für die dokumentarischen Comics von Weyhe grundsätzlich gilt, und zum anderen aus dem Bruch mit der tradierten Art und Weise der (männlichen) Selbstdarstellung im Comic.

Das Prinzip der Frontalität ist dem Genre des dokumentarischen Comics geschuldet – die Autorin, bemüht um Objektivität ihrer Perspektive, stellt die Protagonist:innen ihrer Recherchen meistens *en face* dar; so erfasst sie diese im Modus der Aussage, die sich direkt an die Betrachtenden richtet. In denjenigen Comics, in denen der „interaktive Modus" (Lefèvre 39) dominiert, d. h. wo die Lesenden „eine vermittelte Repräsentation" (ebd.) der Interaktion zwischen der Zeichnerin und ihren Figuren erhalten, wendet sich auch Weyhes Avatarin direkt an die Leser:innenschaft, damit diese die Gespräche quasi mitverfolgen kann (vgl. Weyhe 2022; Weyhe 2016). Diese Art der Selbstdarstellung wurde von Schmid

---

9 Für offizielle Zwecke, etwa gegenüber solchen Institutionen wie dem Goethe Institut, stellt sich Birgit Weyhe folgendermaßen dar: goethe.de/ins/fr/de/kul/li/lit/cad/21535088.html (26.11.2024).

gedeutet als eine „authenticating strategy that testifies to the veracity of the material presented"; zugleich positioniere sich Weyhe damit auch als „cultural mediator" (Schmid 109). Auch Weyhes Ästhetik und deren Vermengung von visuellen Stilen und (Bild)Sprachen, darunter auch Stereotypen, trägt zu dieser Positionierung bei (vgl. Kraenzle 229).

Indem Weyhe als Rückenfigur am Schreibtisch zu sehen ist, schafft die Autorin eine Antithese zur Offenheit der Gesprächssituation und markiert den Bereich der Gestaltung des gesammelten Materials, der dem Blick der Betrachtenden entzogen wird. Die Rückenfigur verweist so auf eine Trennung der einzelnen Arbeitsbereiche – aber offensichtlich auch auf die Selbstreflexion, die die Sicht der Anderen auf ihre Arbeit betrifft. In *Im Himmel ist Jahrmarkt* wird die Autorin als Rückenfigur von ihren zwei Töchtern gesehen und angesprochen, deren Rufe sie wegen ihrer Kopfhörer nicht hört. Zu der Reflexion über die Arbeitsgestaltung kommt somit auch eine Reflexion über die Perspektive der Nächsten hinzu, wodurch die private, familiäre Ebene in die Thematisierung der Autorinnenschaft miteinbezogen wird.

Der Bruch mit der tradierten Selbstdarstellung der Comic-Autoren lässt sich zum einen an der Verweigerung des Einblicks in den Schaffensprozess, d. h., der Entrückung der Schreibszene beobachten, was mit der Selbstdarstellung qua Übertreibung etwa bei Robert Crumb und Art Spiegelman stark kontrastiert. Die von „Überzeichnung und Verfremdung" (Kupczyńska 377) geprägten Selbstdarstellungen der *Underground*-Comickünstler, die in den ersten Comic-Autobiografien Anfang der 1970er Jahre oft anzutreffen waren, zielten vor allem auf eine *Exponierung* des Schaffensaktes. Dieser vollzog sich am für die Lesenden gut sichtbaren Reißbrett oder Schreibtisch, und stilisierte den Künstler als einen mit dem Stoff bzw. der Form Ringenden (Spiegelman) bzw. als einen der sein Schaffen als Lustquelle und zugleich Ort der Befriedigung der Libido behandelt (Crumb). Auf dem Cover der Comic-Anthologie *Breakdowns* von 1977 schluckt Spiegelman schwarze Tinte; im Kurzcomic *Die 17 Gesichter des R. Crumb* steht Crumbs Avatar onanierend am Schreibtisch mit „einem säuischen Comic von Crumb" in der Hand, und erklärt den Lesenden: „Hier bin ich im Studio, bei meiner „harten" Arbeit!" (Crumb).

Auch im französischen Comic dieser Zeit finden sich, etwa bei Jean Giraud, vereinzelte Beispiele des „image archétypale du dessinateur à sa table" (archetypischen Bildes des Zeichners an seinem Tisch) (Groensteen 2013a); Groensteen zufolge war es das neue Genre des autobiografischen Comics, das die Modi und die

Ziele der Selbstrepräsentation grundlegend veränderte.[10] Allerdings muss angemerkt werden, dass Groensteen sich ausschließlich auf Selbstdarstellungen von Comic-Autoren bezieht, was die Frage aufwirft, inwiefern das Genre der Autobiografie auch für die Autorinnenschaft eine dermaßen revolutionäre Wirkung hatte.

In Weyhes autobiografischem Erstlingswerk *Ich weiss* (2008) über ihre Kindheit in Uganda wird der Prozess der Arbeit an der autobiografischen Narration nicht thematisiert, erst die späteren dokumentarischen Comics wie *Im Himmel ist Jahrmarkt* und *Madgermanes* brachten die Ebene der Selbstdarstellung als Autorin, und damit auch die Selbstreflexion, ins Spiel. In den Comics der Autorinnen aus Weyhes Umfeld aus der Zeit des Studiums an der Hamburger Hochschule für Angewandte Künste – darunter nennt sie Anke Feuchtenberger, Barbara Yelin, Line Hoven, Marijpol, Jul Gordon (Courth 70) – kommt die Thematisierung der Autorinnenschaft selten zum Ausdruck. Und wenn das Selbstbild einer Autorin auftaucht – wie es etwa bei Anke Feuchtenberger der Fall ist, wenn ihre Avatarin im charakteristischen schwarz-weiß gepunkteten Kopftuch sich erkennbar macht – geschieht es nicht im Modus der Exponierung des Schaffens, sondern vielmehr als Begleitung, Beobachtung oder versteckte Steuerung des Erzählprozesses. Für die dokumentarischen Comics von Yelin über die Holocaust-Überlebende Emmie Arbel[11] gilt ebenfalls, dass die Zeichnerin in Panels als Zuhörerin und Gesprächspartnerin zu sehen ist; niemals taucht sie allein auf. Für solche ausgewiesenen Comic-Autobiografinnen wie Ulli Lust und Dominique Goblet gehört die Selbstdarstellung als Zeichnerin nicht notwendigerweise zur autobiografischen Narration; die Ebene des Schaffensprozesses wird nur *en passant* gezeigt.[12] Als vorläufiger Befund kann somit festgehalten werden, dass das autobiografische Genre für die Autorinnenschaft nicht dieselbe verändernde Wirkkraft hatte wie für die (männliche) Autorschaft. Zugleich zeigt das Beispiel der dokumentarischen Comics von Weyhe und Yelin einen genrespezifischen Umgang mit Autorinnenschaft, der auf die Bedeutung der begleitenden Präsenz der Autorin (Yelin) sowie auf die Trennung der Arbeitsbereiche Recherche und Gestaltung verweist (Weyhe).

Bei Weyhe findet sich ebenfalls eine Art der Selbstdarstellung, die Groensteen als zweiten Topos der Autorschaft bezeichnet, nämlich „l'auteur entouré de ses personnages" (der Autor umgeben von seinen Figuren) (Groensteen 2013a). Für

---

10 „Les modalités de l'autoreprésentation et la visée même du geste autoreprésentatif ont été bouleversées par l'essor spectaculaire, au cours des deux dernières décennies, de la bande dessinée autobiographique" (Die Modalitäten der Selbstdarstellung und das eigentliche Ziel der selbstdarstellenden Geste wurden durch den spektakulären Aufschwung der autobiografischen Comics in den letzten beiden Jahrzehnten erschüttert) (Groensteen 2013a).
11 Vgl. dazu Yelin 2022; Yelin 2023.
12 S. Goblet; Lust.

die Anthologie SPRING mit dem Schwerpunkt ‚Arbeit' zeichnete die Autorin Kurzcomics, in denen sich zwei emanzipatorische Statements manifestieren. In *Arbeit. Ein eigenes Arbeitszimmer. Frei nach einem Essay von Virginia Woolf*[13] zeigt Weyhe zunächst ihren Arbeitsplatz, und nimmt ihn als einen Ausgangspunkt für ein Selbstgespräch über ihre Arbeit. Nicht nur sieht man *en detail* das Arbeitszimmer, die Zeichnungsutensilien (Abb. 3), und die Avatarin *en face* am Schreibtisch, sondern bekommt auch einen Einblick in die Sicht Anderer – der Tochter, zufälliger Personen – darauf, was Gegenstand ihrer beruflichen Beschäftigung ist.

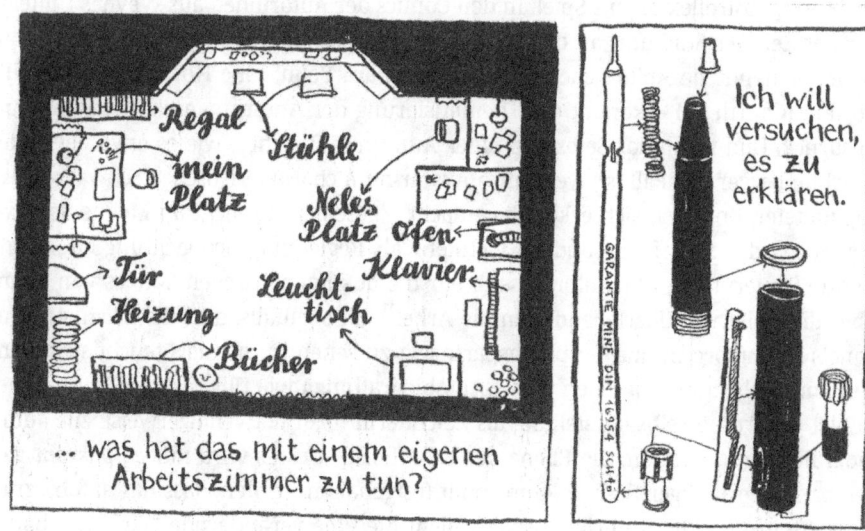

Abb. 3: Eigener Arbeitsraum (*Arbeit* 39).

Im Selbstgespräch kommen auch Weyhes Figuren zu Wort – ein krokodilartiges Wesen und ein dicker Vogel. Sie sprechen darüber, was sie als Comicfiguren können und was ihr Status in der durchgenormten Arbeitswelt ist: „In unserer Gesellschaft scheint Kunst nicht als Arbeit zu zählen. / Manchmal ist sie schwer zu verstehen. / Sie läßt sich nicht kategorisieren. / Sie ist nicht genormt. / Aber alle kennen sich damit aus" (*Arbeit* 44). Das Bedürfnis nach einem eigenen Arbeitszimmer ergibt sich aus ebendieser „Einstellung weiter Teile unserer Gesellschaft" (*Arbeit* 46) zur Comic-Kunst, d. h. aus der fehlenden Wertschätzung der Tradition der grafischen Erzählung. „Wir brauchen alle ein eigenes Arbeitszimmer" (*Arbeit* 48), heißt das Fazit. Begründet wird es mit dem Bedürfnis nach Raum, um „von-

---

13 Im Folgenden mit *Arbeit* abgekürzt.

einander zu lernen", „Dinge ausprobieren zu können", „Fehler zu machen", aber auch, „weil es Orte geben muss, die von ökonomischen Motiven abgekoppelt sind" (*Arbeit* 47). Ein „rein praktischer Grund" (*Arbeit* 46) ist auch dabei, mit einem Panel, in dem Weyhes Tochter aus Versehen ein Tintenfass umkippt.

Auch in einem anderen Comic aus der fünfzehnten Ausgabe von SPRING mit dem Titel *Meine Arbeit* sieht man Weyhes Avatarin mit ihren Figuren – diesmal beanspruchen diese ein noch stärker ausgeprägtes Mitspracherecht für sich, bestehen darauf, die Autorin bei ihrem Spaziergang zum Hamburger Hafen zu begleiten, wo sie ihre Gedanken zum Thema ‚meine Arbeit' sammeln möchte. Im Hafen entrollt sich vor den Augen der Figuren und der Lesenden die koloniale Vergangenheit der Stadt und die weiterhin bestehenden kolonialen Praktiken des „Land Grabbing" (*Meine Arbeit* 123). Weyhes Avatarin schlüpft in die Rolle des *poeta doctus*; so wird der Spaziergang zu einer Führung durch die Geschichte der Arbeit unter dem Zeichen kapitalistischer Unterdrückung der (kolonialen wie heimischen) Arbeitskräfte. Eine Kakaobohne äußert sich empört: „Eigentlich sollte man dieses System (der Kindersklaverei auf Kakaoplantagen, K.K.) boykottieren und nur zertifizierte Produkte konsumieren" (*Meine Arbeit* 122). Jeder Vorschlag der Figuren – im Hafen Kaffee oder Kakao zu trinken, die Fähre zu nehmen – führt zu einer Narration über Arbeitsbedingungen und Ausbeutung, das bedeutet „große Profite für die Händler hier"/ „Und miese Bedingungen für die Arbeiter in den Produktionsländern" (*Meine Arbeit* 121). Dies bleibt nicht ohne Folgen für das marktwirtschaftliche Selbstbewusstsein der Figuren, die am Ende eigene Forderungen zur Verbesserung der Arbeitsverhältnisse erheben, darunter „längere Pausen", „mehr Perspektive" „Vielfarbigkeit", und „mehr Humor" (*Meine Arbeit* 129). Daraufhin wird die Ebene der Diegese abrupt verlassen; die Avatarin zeigt sich deutlich irritiert vor den schwarz übermalten Postulaten (Abb. 4). Auf der letzten Seite des Comics sitzt Weyhes Avatarin wie gewohnt mit dem Rücken zu den Betrachtenden am Schreibtisch (Abb. 5).

Der Topos des Comic-Autors, der von seinen Figuren „umringt oder bedrängt" (Stein 233) wird, ist in der Comicgeschichte bestens etabliert – Daniel Stein führt Beispiele u. a. von George Herriman, Chester Gould und Art Spiegelman an. Aus seiner Sicht deutet diese Art von Selbstdarstellung „auf eine gesteigerte Selbstreflexivität sowie ein verstärktes Gattungsbewusstsein hin" (Stein 233). Laut Stein werden etwa in Herrimans Selbstdarstellungen „die Autormodelle des *poeta vates* (der Autor, der nicht auf die Inspiration der Götter, sondern auf Ideen seiner Figuren wartet) und des *poeta faber* (der Autor als Handwerker, der aus dem kompetenten Umgang zeichnerische Objekte schafft), karikiert" (Stein 222).

Im Fall von Weyhe scheint jedoch ein anderer Aspekt wichtiger zu sein, den Stein wie folgt beschreibt: „die Figuren ‚leben' in der Vorstellung des Autors, sie sind ein Teil von ihm, werden durch sein künstlerisches Talent animiert und kön-

Abb. 4: ‚Streik' der Figuren (*Meine Arbeit* 129).

nen sogar Autorität über ihre fiktionalen Geschichten einfordern" (Stein 224). Weyhes Figuren bekommen noch mehr Funktionen – im Comic über die Geschichte des Hamburger Hafens ‚spielen' sie die Leser:innenschaft, denn sie sind die ersten Adressat:innen der Erzählung über die Ausbeutung. Indem sie ihre Meinung über Weyhes Kolonialismuskritik äußern – „Mit Dir macht es wirklich gar keinen Spaß, einen Ausflug zu unternehmen" (*Meine Arbeit* 128) – performen sie zugleich die selbstkritische Wahrnehmung der Autorin. Sie entscheiden über die Narration, indem sie diese offen als ‚unlustig' unterbrechen, bringen damit also auch die Genealogie des Mediums ins Spiel, d. h. die „humorvolle Intention', die der Begriff Comic konnotiert" (Frahm 348), und welche ihm in der Hierarchie der Künste ursprünglich eine minderwertige Stellung oder gar „position du cancre" (das Image eines Dummkopfs; Groensteen 2013b), einbrachte. Außerdem wird auch hier miteinander gesprochen. Das dialogische Moment zwischen der Avatarin und den Figuren wird damit als ein Merkmal von Weyhes Herangehensweise aufgezeigt. Nicht zuletzt manifestiert sich in Weyhes Arbeit-Comics das von Stein thematisierte „verstärkte Gattungsbewusstsein" – die Kommunikation und

Abb. 5: Am Schreibtisch, mit dem Rücken zum Betrachter (*Meine Arbeit* 130).

Konfrontation zwischen der Avatarin und den Figuren zeigen das Spezifische des dokumentarischen Modus von Weyhe, bei dem die Repräsentation der Befragten und der Befragenden stets vor den Augen der Betrachtenden ausgehandelt wird.[14]

III

Im Comic *Arbeit. Ein eigenes Arbeitszimmer* kündigt die Avatarin von Birgit Weyhe auf der vorletzten Seite an: „Dieses Thema hat einen fatalen Nachteil. / Es

---

[14] Dieses Merkmal, das auf die erhöhte Sensibilität gegenüber den Modi der Repräsentation hindeutet, ist in Weyhes Graphic Novel *Rude Girl* (2021), dessen Gegenstand die Lebensgeschichte der afroamerikanischen Germanistikprofessorin Priscilla Layne ist, besonders stark ausgeprägt.

wird hier kein allgemeingültiges Fazit geben" (*Arbeit* 47). Sie schließt mit dem an Virginia Woolf angelehnten Statement über die Wichtigkeit des eigenen Arbeitszimmers, also mit einer Forderung die, und dies ist bezeichnend, in keiner der mir bekannten Selbstdarstellungen von Comic-Autoren vorkommt. Implizit veranschaulicht die Fokussierung auf den Arbeitsplatz, wie selbstverständlich der Topos des Zeichners in seinem Atelier und an seinem Arbeitsplatz sowohl in der erwähnten Forschung zur Comic-Autorschaft als auch in den dort vorkommenden Beispielen erscheint. Greift Weyhe das Thema mit dem Wissen auf, dass Marcks, die zu ihren „absoluten Vorbildern"[15] zählt, gerade dieses eigene Arbeitszimmer entbehren musste? Und wenn ja, ist es als symptomatisch zu betrachten, dass sie als Referenztext Woolfs Essay und nicht etwa die Autobiografie von Marcks nennt?

„Mit Autorschaft werden nicht nur Innovation und Authentizität verknüpft, sondern auch Autorität" (Wenk 23). Mit Autorinnenschaft ist eine Verflechtung von Positionen und ermächtigenden Gesten verbunden, die Autorität als verhandelbar setzt, so wie sie auch die Autorinnenstellung in einem dialogischen Miteinander thematisiert. Daher wird auch der zweite Topos der Comic-Autorschaft – der Zeichner umgeben von seinen Figuren – bei Birgit Weyhe als eine Form von Kommunikation dargestellt, die über die Selbstinszenierung hinausgeht und Modi der eigenen Verfahrensweise miteinbezieht und reflektiert. Dass auch die eigene Autorität keineswegs eine einfache Haltung ist, zeigt die irritierte Reaktion der Avatarin auf den ‚Streik' der Figuren in Abb. 4 – diese betrifft ja nicht nur das Verhalten eigener Geschöpfe, sondern die gesamte Situation, in der sich die Autorin-Avatarin mit Gewalt durchsetzen muss. *Meine Arbeit* zeigt noch einmal: „Die Kritik der Autorschaft ist [...] Teil einer umfassenden Kritik an Autoritäten" (Fleig 223), davon ist die eigene Autorität nicht ausgenommen. Anders als in den von Stein angeführten Beispielen kann bei Marcks genauso wenig wie bei Weyhe eine ausgeprägte karikierende Haltung gegenüber den tradierten Autormodellen – *poeta vates, poeta doctus, poeta faber* – beobachtet werden. Es mag an dem liegen, was Miller für die weibliche Autorschaft diagnostizierte: „Historisch gesehen steht Identität für Frau nicht in jenem Verhältnis zu Ursprung, Institution und Produktion, das für die männliche Identität typisch ist. Deshalb fühlten sie sich (als Kollektiv) [...] noch nie durch *zu viel* Selbst, Ego, Cogito usw. belastet" (255; herv. i. O.). Der Bezug zur tradiert männlichen Comic-Autorschaft ist kaum präsent. Vielmehr sind die Selbstbilder von einer Präsenz nahestehender Personen, und zwar explizit Kindern, mitgetragen; bei Weyhe kommen die eigens erfundenen Figuren hinzu. So macht sich in dem Raum der eigenen Kreation so

---

15 So Birgit Weyhe in einer privaten Korrespondenz mit der Autorin am 15. November 2024.

etwas wie eine ‚zweite Stimme' bzw. ein ‚zweiter Blick' bemerkbar, die/der neben der „double dose of the author's voice, through both the linguistic and visual channels" (Bredehoft 106) das Werk mitgestalten. Diese kommunikative Eigenschaft der Selbstbilder von Marie Marcks und Birgit Weyhe markiert einen gemeinsamen Moment in der Selbstdarstellung der Autorinnen und kann zugleich als eine Kontinuität in der Entwicklungsgeschichte von Autorinnenschaft im deutschsprachigen Comic bezeichnet werden.

Literaturverzeichnis

Aarons, Victoria. *Memory Spaces. Visualizing Identity in Jewish Women's Graphic Narrative*. Wayne State UP, 2023.

Aldama, Frederick Luis, Hg. *The Routledge Companion to Gender & Sexuality in Comic Book Studies*. Routledge, 2020.

Bajac-Carter, Maja, Hg. *Heroines of comic books and literature. Portrayals in comic books and literature*. Rowman & Littlefield, 2014.

Bauer, Heike, Andrea Greenbaum und Sarah Lightman, Hg. *Jewish Women in Comics. Bodies and Borders*. Syracuse UP, 2023.

Becker, Romain, Nino Bulling und Sheree Domingo. „Harte Fakten, große Aufgaben. Die Arbeitsrealität Comicschaffender im deutschsprachigen Raum". Hg. von der Comic-Gewerkschaft und der Gesellschaft für Comicforschung. 29. November 2024. https://www.comicgesellschaft.de/gewerkschaftsstudie/ (11.11.2024).

Beckmann, Anna, et al., Hg. *Comics und Intersektionalität*. De Gruyter, 2024.

Berensmeyer, Ingo. *Author Fictions. Narrative Representations of Literary Authorship since 1800*. De Gruyter, 2023.

Beuel, Hanna, Gregor Nikolaus Matti und Sönke Parpart. „Blaustrumpf statt Feinstrumpf? Liebesgeschichten, Geschlechter- und Blickordnungen in der Constanze 1950/51". *Faszinosum 1950er Jahre. Literatur, Medien und Kultur der jungen Bundesrepublik*. Hg. von Jasmin Assadsolimani. Transcript, 2024. S. 87–106.

Brandl, Katharina und Anne Elizabeth Moore. "Bound to fail. Living and working conditions in the comics industry". *Closure. Kieler e-Journal für Comicforschung* 5 (2018): S. 5–30. 23. Oktober 2024.

Bredehoft, Thomas A. "Style, Voice, and Authorship in Harvey Pekar's (Auto) (Bio)Graphical Comics". *College Literature Visual Literature* 38.3 (Summer 2011): S. 97–110.

Chute, Hillary L. *Graphic Women. Life Narrative & Contemporary Comics*. Columbia UP, 2010.

Comic Gewerkschaft. „Manifest der Comic Gewerkschaft vom 1. September 2022 ". comicgewerkschaft.org/manifest. 24. März 2025.

Courth, Tillmann. „Die Frau mit dem goldenen Händchen. Interview mit Birgit Weyhe". *Comixene. Fachmagazin Comic + Cartoon* 127 (2018): S. 66–71.

Crumb, Robert. „Die 17 Gesichter des Robert Crumb". *Die 17 Gesichter des Robert Crumb*. (Urspr. in: „XYZ Comics" 1972). Übers. von Harry Rowohlt, Zweitausendeins, 1975. o. S.

de Dauw, Esther, Hg. *Hot Pants and Spandex Suits. Gender Representation in American Superhero Comic Books*. Rutgers UP, 2021.

Ditschke, Stephan. „Comics als Literatur. Zur Etablierung des Comics im deutschsprachigen Feuilleton seit 2003." *Comics. Zur Geschichte und Theorie eines popkulturellen Mediums*. Hg. von Stephan Ditschke, Katharina Kroucheva und Daniel Stein. Transcript, 2009. S. 265–280.

Eckhoff-Heindl, Nina und Veronique Sina, Hg. *Spaces Between – Gender, Diversity and Identity in Comics*. Springer, 2020.

El Refaie, Elisabeth. *Autobiographical Comics. Life Writing in Pictures*. UP of Mississippi, 2012.

Fahrenberg, WP., Hg. *Meister der komischen Kunst. Marie Marcks*. Antje Kunstmann, 2011.

Fägersten, Kristy Beers, et al., Hg. *Comic Art and Feminism in the Baltic Sea Region. Transnational Perspectives*. Routledge, 2021.

Fleig, Anne. „Weibliche Autorschaft nach dem Gender Turn. ‚Frau' und ‚Ich' in essayistischen Texten von Juli Zeh und Antje Ravic Strubel". *Die Zukunft von Gender. Begriff und Zeitdiagnose*. Hg. von Anne Fleig. Campus, 2015. S. 220–240.

Frahm, Ole. „Comics". *Komik. Ein interdisziplinäres Handbuch*. Hg. von Uwe Wirth. Metzler, 2017. S. 339–349.

Gilmore, Leigh und Elizabeth Marshall. *Witnessing Girlhood. Toward an Intersectional Tradition of Life Writing*. Fordham UP, 2019.

Goblet, Dominique. *Faire semblant c'est mentir*. L'Association, 2007.

Gouma, Assimina und Johanna Dorer. „Intersektionalität. Methodologische und methodische Herausforderung für die feministische Medienforschung". *Handbuch Medien und Geschlecht. Perspektiven und Befunde der feministischen Kommunikations- und Medienforschung*. Hg. von Johanna Dorer et al. Springer Fachmedien, 2023. S. 183–197.

Groensteen, Thierry. „Autoreprésentation". *neuviemart2.0. dictionnaire*, April 2013a, citebd.org/neuvieme-art/autorepresentation. 18. November 2024.

Groensteen, Thierry. „Parodie". *neuviemart2.0. dictionnaire*, Januar 2013b. citebd.org/neuvieme-art/parodie. 29. November 2024.

Gundermann, Christine, Hg. *Zwischenräume. Geschlecht und Diversität in Comics*. Bachmann, 2021.

Hartmann, Andreas. „Besuch beim Comic-Verleger Johann Ulrich. Selber machen, was er lesen wollte". *Taz*, 4. März 2023.

Karnatz, Ella Margaretha. *Autorschaft, Genres und digitale Medien*. Transcript, 2023.

Kirsten, Guido. „Zur Rückenfigur im Spielfilm". *Montage AV* 20.2 (2011): S. 104–124.

Kraenzle, Christina. "Risking Representation: Abstraction, Affect, and the Documentary Mode in Birgit Weyhe's *Madgermanes*". *Seminar. A Journal of Germanic Studies* 56.3–4 (2020): S. 212–234.

Kronthaler, Helmut und Stiftung Illustration, Hg. *Lexikon der Illustration im deutschsprachigen Raum seit 1945*. edition text + kritik, 2009.

Kuczyńska, Kinga, Hg. *Polski komiks kobiecy*. [Polnischer Frauencomic] Timof i cisi wspólnicy, 2012.

Künzel, Christine. „Einleitung". *Autorinszenierungen. Autorschaft und literarisches Werk im Kontext der Medien*. Hg. von Christine Künzel und Jörg Schönert. Königshausen & Neumann, 2007. S. 9–23.

Kupczyńska, Kalina. „Autobiografie, confessional writing und Graphic Memoir". *Autobiografie intermedial. Fallstudien zur Literatur und zum Comic*. Hg. von Kalina Kupczyńska und Jadwiga Kita-Huber. Aisthesis, 2019. S. 373–390.

Lefèvre, Pascal. „Die Modi dokumentarischer Comics". *Die dokumentarischen Comics. Reportage und Biografie*. Hg. von Dietrich Grünewald. Bachmann, 2013. S. 31–49.

Lightman, Sarah, Hg. *Graphic Details. Jewish Women's Confessional Comics in Essays and Interviews*. McFarland, 2014.

Lobnig, Naomi, Marina Rauchenbacher und Katharina Serles, Hg. *Comics Studies x Gender Studies. Schnittmengen von Forschung, Lehre und Praxis – Intersections of Research, Teaching, and Practice*. De Gruyter [erscheint 2025].

Losleben, Lisa Katrin und Sarah Musubika. *Intersectionality*. Routledge, 2023.

Lust, Ulli. *Wie ich versuchte, ein guter Mensch zu sein*. Avant, 2017.

Mag Uidhir, Christy. "Comics and Collective Authorship". *The Art of Comics. A Philosophical Approach*. Hg. von Roy T. Cook und Aaron Meskin. Wiley-Blackwell, 2012. S. 47–67.

Marcks, Marie. *Marie, es brennt! Autobiographische Aufzeichnungen I*. Frauenbuch Verlag – Weissmann Verlag, 1984, o.S.

Marcks, Marie. *Schwarz-weiss und bunt. Autobiographische Aufzeichnungen II*. Frauenbuch Verlag – Weissmann Verlag, 1989, o.S. [Seitenzahlen im Text in eckigen Klammern]

Meyer, Christina und Lukas Wilde. „Zum Geleit. Aus Sicht der Comicforschung". *Harte Fakten, große Aufgaben. Die Arbeitsrealität Comicschaffender im deutschsprachigen Raum*. Hg. von Romain Becker, Nino Bulling und Sheree Domingo. Oktober 2024. 11. November 2024.

Mitchell, Adrielle. "Comics and Authorship". *The Routledge Companion to Comics*. Hg. von Frank Bramlett, Roy T. Cook und Aaron Meskin. Routledge, 2016. S. 239–247.

Miller, Nancy K. „Wechseln wir das Thema/Subjekt. Die Autorschaft, das Schreiben und der Leser". Übers. von Bettina Raaf. *Texte zur Theorie der Autorschaft*. Hg. von Fotis Jannidis, et al. Reclam, 2000. S. 252–278.

Schmid, Johannes. „Framing and Translation in Birgit Weyhe's *Madgermanes* ". *Situated in Translations. Cultural Communities and Media Practices*. Hg. von Michaela Ott und Thomas Weber. Transcript, 2019. S. 107–117.

Sina, Véronique. *Comic – Film – Gender. Zur (Re-)Medialisierung von Geschlecht im Comicfilm*. Transcript, 2016.

Sinclair, Carla. „Introduction". *From Girls to Grrrlz*. Hg. von Trina Robbins. Chronicle Books, 1999. S. 4.

Spiegelman, Art. *MetaMaus*. Übers. von Andreas Heckmann. Fischer, 2012.

Stein, Daniel. „Was ist ein Comic-Autor? Autorinszenierung in autobiografischen Comics und Selbstporträts". *Comics. Zur Geschichte und Theorie eines popkulturellen Mediums*. Hg. von Stephan Ditschke, Katharina Kroucheva und Daniel Stein. Transcript, 2009. S. 201–237.

Sterling, Brett. „Jenseits des Mainstreams. Zur Entwicklung der deutschsprachigen Comic-Produktion und ihrer avantgardistischen Strömungen seit 1980". *Studien zur Geschichte des Comics*. Hg. von Bernd Dolle-Weinkauff und Dietrich Grünewald. Bachmann, 2022. S. 359–382.

Vetter-Liebenow, Gisela. „Dazu muss man einfach geboren sein ... ". *Franziska Becker*. Edition Wilhelm-Busch-Museum Hannover, Madsack, 2008. o.S.

Wagner-Egelhaaf, Martina. „Auf der Intensivstation. Oder: Die Automaschine. Zu John von Düffels *Missing Müller (Müllermaschine) (1997)*". *Was ist ein Künstler? Das Subjekt der modernen Kunst*. Hg. von Martin Hellmold et al. Fink, 2003. S. 195–211.

Welker, James. *Transfiguring Women in Late Twentieth Century Japan. Feminists, Lesbians, and Girls' Comics Artists and Fans*. U of Hawaii P, 2024.

Wenk, Silke. „Mythen von Autorschaft und Weiblichkeit". *Mythen von Autorschaft und Weiblichkeit im 20. Jahrhundert*. Hg. von Kathrin Hoffmann-Curtius und Silke Wenk. Jonas Verlag, 1997. S. 12–29.

Weyhe, Birgit. *Ich weiss*. Avant, 2017.

Weyhe, Birgit. *Ich weiss*. Mami, 2009.

Weyhe, Birgit. *Im Himmel ist Jahrmarkt*. Avant, 2013.

Weyhe, Birgit. *Madgermanes*. Avant, 2016.

Weyhe, Birgit. „Arbeit. Ein eigenes Arbeitszimmer. Frei nach einem Essay von Virginia Woolf". *SPRING* 15 (2018): S. 39–48.

Weyhe, Birgit. „Meine Arbeit." *SPRING* 15 (2018): S. 117–130.
Weyhe, Birgit. *Rude Girl*. Avant, 2022.
Yelin, Barbara. "Aber ich lebe". *Aber ich lebe. Vier Kinder überleben den Holocaust*. Hg. von Charlotte Schallie. Bundeszentrale für politische Bildung, 2022. S. 9–46.
Yelin, Barbara. *Emmie Arbel. Die Farbe der Erinnerung*. Reprodukt, 2023.

Lynn Marie Kutch
Gender, Race, and the Silenced Asian Other in Olivia Vieweg's *Huck Finn: Die Graphic Novel*

Abstract: Olivia Vieweg's 2013 *Huck Finn: Die Graphic Novel* sets itself apart from other adaptations of Mark Twain's classic text by replacing the Black enslaved person Jim with Jin, a young Asian female sex worker. A reconceptualization involving a trafficked minoritized female character raises questions not only about authorial and narrative choices in rendering cultural Otherness and gendered oppression, but also about the efficacy of the graphic novel's social message, especially given the marginalized character's lack of authentic self-representation. With a focus on the prominence of Asian stereotypes that paradoxically render Jin more invisible, this study investigates the graphic novel's appraisal of racial and sexual patterns as concerns the historically present yet voiceless Asian woman in German culture.

Olivia Vieweg's *Huck Finn: Die Graphic Novel* (2013) reimagines Mark Twain's *Adventures of Huckleberry Finn* (1884) through a striking narrative shift: it replaces Jim, the enslaved Black man, with Jin, a young Asian female sex worker. This adaptation raises critical questions about representation, marginalization, and the portrayal of cultural Otherness, particularly in the context of German society, where Asian women have been historically marginalized. While Twain's novel has long been typecast as a middle and high school schoolbook in the United States and other English-speaking countries, its layered appeal extends beyond young readers. Toni Morrison has described a text "that had given so much pleasure to young readers [yet] was also complicated territory for sophisticated scholars" (2). Vieweg's adaptation capitalizes on this stratification, blending a manga-influenced aesthetic with mature themes such as parental neglect, child abuse, and human trafficking. By doing so, her graphic novel challenges conventional perceptions of both Twain's work and commonly perceived boundaries of the graphic novel medium itself. *Huck Finn* thus invites critical engagement with issues of race, gender, and agency in contemporary comics storytelling.

In the decade since *Huck Finn*'s publication, monumental global cultural shifts, such as the #MeToo movement and anti-racist protests of 2020, have reinvigorated the discussion of social justice themes embedded in Twain's original novel. These powerful civic movements have inspired new topical retellings that seek to redress not only the unjust suppression of Jim's voice, but also the erasure, or at least the devaluing, of the female perspective (see Everett; Walker and Kwame Anderson; and Time). A social atmosphere of vigorous, culturally sensitive dialogues draws renewed critical attention to Vieweg's now more than ten-year-old adaptation, whose content not only revives the "decades-long debate about racial representation" central to Twain criticism (Valkeakari 29) but also substantiates Morrison's characterization of youthful amusement inhabiting complicated adult territory. On the surface, Vieweg's unruly teenage Huck shares the slangy linguistic features and a reckless sense of adventure with his 140-year-old predecessor. On an analytical level, the motivation for this reimagined Huck's rebellious actions and the arc of his development similarly beg to be dissected, as Twain scholars have done for decades. From scrutinizing the protagonist's moral character and his capacity for sympathy (Clarke 492), to recognizing Huck's fundamental innocence in a corrupt world (Ciocia 197), time-traversing trends in Twain scholarship converge in the plea to take "seriously the voice of a child, a teenager" (Levy 57). *Huck Finn* set in 2013 in Halle an der Saale, increases the magnitude of matters of morality, lost innocence, and the cherished youth voice with the creation of Jin. Its doubling to two children's voices, as well as the gender recasting of the original enslaved major character, would seem to certify *Huck Finn* as a rebellious and socially transformative text. A reconceptualization involving a trafficked minoritized female character, however, necessarily raises questions about authorial and narrative choices in rendering cultural Otherness and gendered oppression, especially given the marginalized character's lack of self-representation.

Vieweg's ostensibly daring narrative move problematically exhibits two devices that German translators of Twain's text have frequently deployed: difference and deficit. Although the more than 30 translations into German have consistently resisted branding Jim as cognitively and linguistically deficient, "this does not mean that those difference-generating strategies cannot carry stigma" (Berthele 608). In other words, adapters' and translators' efforts to deemphasize shortcomings amid original textual markers of difference and deficit do not render these adaptations and translations immune to critical appraisal. The current analysis approaches *Huck Finn* with these distinctions in mind, where "difference" refers to Asian cultural and female gender markers outside the mainstream identity that Huck's narrative prominence generates; and "deficit" indicates Jin's coping with trauma in the shadow of Huck's development or even completely out of sight. Regarding the two interlocking visual and textual levels aids in determining to what degree the Othered Jin approaches Huck's privilege of agency and movement. First, Jin's illustrated story of difference, notably not without visual reinforcement of Asian stereotypes, suggests her affixed positioning as an exoticized female character on the outside of white German dominant culture and in the margins of a traditionally "fiercely masculine" story (Kidd 53). Second, *Huck Finn*'s narrative choices emphasize Jin's tangential relationship to the central plot that prioritizes Huck's privileged position and agency to be active, rebellious, and most importantly seen. With a focus on the visible prominence of Asian stereotypes that paradoxically render Jin more invisible, examining a select series of splash pages reveals ways that *Huck Finn* imparts patterns of racial and sexual subordination as concerns the historically present yet invisibilized Asian woman in German culture.

Critical attention to Othering is not new in the context of evaluating and examining *Adventures of Huckleberry Finn* adaptations and translations, which by virtue of the source material also treat themes of marginalization and representation. The nearly 25 *Huck Finn* graphic novel versions,[1] published in a variety of Asian and European languages, appear, much unlike Vieweg's, more as illustrated versions than innovative adaptations because of their close adherence to Twain's original plot. Like Vieweg's, however, this international survey of *Huck Finn* graphic novels appears uniformly geared toward youth audiences, as evidenced by cover art, choice of publisher, and marketing techniques. Beyond these general and perhaps predictable observations, many of the illustrated versions of *Huck Finn* adaptations also elicit questions about graphic representations of race by authors of privilege. Comics scholars have suggested various approaches to reading stereotypical features and coloration that often engender one-dimensional characterizations. For example, Michael D. Harris's discussion of trends in Black American comics offers a useful framework for evaluating artists' traditionally stereotypical portrayals, which ultimately rely "on the visual in the sense that the visible body must be used by those in power to represent non-visual realities that differentiate insiders from outsiders" (Harris 2). Jim is an enslaved person in the late 1800s American Deep South; and a graphic depiction that physically distinguishes him from white characters reflects this disparity. Although this quality of mirroring reality is true, artistic decisions concerning this "visible body" can result in, as Qiana Whitted explains in her evaluation of Blackness in comics, an "excluded presence to be seen, not to see" (83). Additionally, and of particular relevance to *Huck Finn* adaptations, specific time periods also generate stereotyped images, as Jeet Heer contextualizes in his afterword to *Black Comics: Politics of Race and Representation*: "the affinity of comics for caricatures meant that the early comic strips took the existing racism of society and gave it vicious and viru-

---

1 These include manga versions such as Crystal S. Chan, Kuma Chan, and Jeannie Lee's *Adventures of Huckleberry Finn* (2017), Spanish-language versions such as Thomas M. Rattliff, Penko Gelev, Maria Patricia Esguerra's *Las aventuras de Huckleberry Finn* (2016), as well as Hindi (Roland Mann and Naresh Kumar, 2010) and Tamil versions (Pai, 1988).

lent life" (Heer 253). Thus, adaptations that remain true to Twain's original story necessarily mirror his perception and rendering of societal realities of slavery and discrimination and, by association, link to decades-old criticism of Twain's flawed interpretation of racial conditions (Valkeakari 29–31). Vieweg's narrative transplantation to present-day Eastern Germany untethers her version from the original historical context and allows *Huck Finn* to construct its own systems and patterns for examination and reflection of Twain's themes. However, the textual and temporal distancing does not shield Vieweg's graphic novel from prevalent Twain criticisms of an attempted yet incomplete assessment of racism and participation in negative racial stereotyping.

Despite similarities to Twain's original and to other existing graphic adaptations, Vieweg's text departs from the original by presenting a pared-down version with far fewer characters and less developed ancillary plot lines than the original supplies. This narrative reduction allows the societal patterns that Vieweg's text highlights and references, and that Jin navigates, to emerge that much more clearly. The main players are Huck, Jin, Maik (Jin's trafficker), the widow who provides for Huck, Huck's father, and members of two families involved in a decades-old feud. More detailed plot elements accompany the closer analysis below, but, in general, the story follows a simple trajectory. Corresponding to Twain's characterization, Huck's burning sense of adventure drives him to leave the widow's home, to briefly take up residence with his abusive, alcoholic father, and then to devise and carry out a plan to fake his own death. With the fortuitous find of a raft, he sets out on his own until he is reunited on a stormy night with Jin, who has managed to escape her trafficker, Maik. After a head-on accident with a cruise ship completely decimates the raft, the two wash ashore and are taken in by one of the feuding families. After sexist and discriminatory treatment by the family's patriarch, Jin sets out on her own while Huck's morbid fascination with the psychopathic Benny compels him to stay behind. Benny's concerning criminal behavior eventually proves even too much for Huck's sensibilities and shortly thereafter, he and Jin are together again on the river. The story ends with Jin's ostensible liberation, which Huck, as the dominant yet decidedly still immature teen, insensitively encourages her to embrace: "Mann, du bist frei! Hallo? Freu dich mal!" (*Huck Finn* 137). On the latter part of her journey, she exhibited signs of independence and maturity; but this final impression of Jin's being "freed" by the consummate symbol of "boy culture" illustrates notions of racial and gender markers existing outside of the mainstream (difference). These designations ultimately lead her to experience personal growth and trauma recovery somewhere off the printed page (deficit).

In the entire field of *Huck Finn* adaptations, Vieweg is the first to my knowledge to install a female character into the classic role of Jim. In an interview, the author explains her conceptualization and shares that it was immediately clear that she would develop "die Asiatin Jin" to replace the enslaved person Jim (MDR 2.32–2.44). The pithy comment about Jin's origin story evokes questions about representation, the influence of historically and culturally ensconced social systems, and even the author's social justice-oriented motivations. On the one hand, viewing the graphic novel through these critical lenses draws parallels to the branch of Twain criticism that views the Huck-Jim relationship as reflecting a "muddled terrain of good intentions, confusion, wavering, and inconsistency" influenced by the author's worldview (Valkeakari 29). On the other hand, attempting to diagnose implied ethical relationships of authors to their work often lacks pertinence or productiveness, as Leonard Rifas contends:

> To move past moralizing questions about a cartoonist's intentions or individual responsibility (which ordinarily remain both unanswerable and irrelevant to practical antiracist work), it helps to refocus on the larger patterns of cooperation that allow these picture-stories to come into existence and be circulated. (29)

General notions about contract theory, and contributions from two of its prominent contemporary voices, can assist in delineating some elements of "larger patterns of cooperation" identified by Rifas. Rudimentary aspects of Robert Mills's seminal work *The Racial Contract* (1997) offer a useful scaffold for understanding entrenched Eurocentric notions of race. Mills examines a firm and accepted system of white domination over non-white people, which results in "an exploitation contract that creates global European economic domination and national white racial privilege" (31). In *The Sexual Contract* (1988), which predated and inspired Mills's work, Carol Pateman historicizes a gendered facet of contract theory that has legitimized subordination of women, "For Hobbes, all women become servants as wives in the natural state and thus are excluded from the original pact that forms civil society" (50). Pertinent to Vieweg's adaptation centralizing a sex worker, marriage and prostitution are key institutions that underpin Pateman's understanding of the servitude and exclusion necessary for the sexual contract. In terms of Vieweg's "picture story," to recall Rifas's terminology above, the visual aspect under closer consideration is the system of splash panels, i.e., full-page panels that individually function as notable breaks in the otherwise linear and continuous narrative strands. Specifically, these panels call attention to the stark contrasts between the journey of maturation the privileged white male Huck undergoes and the exploited and invisible non-white female Jin.

Theorizing the functionality and effect of splash pages or splash panels has a long history in comics studies. Scott McCloud, in his foundational *Understanding Comics: The Invisible Art* (1994), discusses ways that splashes either slow down or speed up a narrative, in either case signifying an important moment or narrative shift (102). Charles Hatfield, in *Alternative Comics: An Emerging Literature* (2005), details the power of splash panels as "scene-setting images" that influence how the comic marks the synchronism of its storylines (54). Indeed, the notion of a narrative interruption suspending the rhythmic flow of images and even reducing the "forward momentum of the text" unites much of comics scholarship about splash pages (Postema 33). *Huck Finn*'s splash pages not only operate as significant moments for eliciting readers' emotional responses and interpretations, but also as "resets" or breaks that temporarily task readers with evaluating respective characters' evolution and progress toward maturity and personal growth. These splashes, which according to Duncan et al. "celebrate the prowess and graces of a character," will indicate stark disparities between the two characters in matters of aptitude and gracefulness (110). For Huck's character, the splashes indicate pauses in his developmental journey toward moral maturation, but not major setbacks. For Jin, on the other hand, the elements and composition of the splashes only serve to reinforce her ornamental and passive nature, as well as her inability to match Huck's repeatedly reinforced forward momentum and bold visibility.

In contemporary German culture, Asian women and girls experiencing the opposite of inclusion and visibility find voice in Hami Nguyen's 2023 appeal for an end to anti-Asian racism in Germany. In her *Das Ende der Unsichtbarkeit*, the author uses the terms "unsichtbar" and "ausgeklammert" to describe the lives of those in her community of Vietnamese immigrants in Germany (H. Nguyen 11). These are labels that relate to the aforementioned organizing principles of difference and deficit respectively; the close readings of the splash panel "resets" reaffirm these descriptors for Jin. In the following, I consider six splash pages that occur at pivotal points in the narrative and that, corresponding to elements of comics theory on splash pages, relay complete, self-contained stories. I then briefly contextualize the Asian stereotyping perpetuated in those panels from historical, German-language pop culture, and sociological perspectives. Additionally, I discuss the traditional significance and narrative function of stereotypes and stereotypical images in the field of comics studies, while also interrogating these explanations and considering ideological conflicts between agency and lack of agency that stereotyping in comics could evoke.

In Vieweg's graphic novel, Jin's exclusion and marginalization emerge as early as the first narrative sequence at a time when Huck is also shown struggling with feeling "ausgeklammert." The perceived equality, or even superior maturity of Jin vis-à-vis Huck given her life experiences as a sex worker, proves deceiving when the graphic novel presents two dissimilar stories of inequitable youthful development. *Huck Finn*'s establishing shots reveal a system in which white males, even if juvenile, dominate the scene in the small German city of Halle an der Saale. In Huck's case, however, the conduct of his friends and a veiled discussion of larger social circumstances that determine family politics deliver the initial impression of his friend group's victimizing and excluding him. For example, Huck cannot be fully accepted into the boys' *Bande* because he lacks biological family members to use as collateral in the case of Huck's disloyalty to the gang (*Huck Finn* 10). Visual cues in a three-quarter page display the dichotomy of Huck's characterization and establish a baseline against which to measure Huck's personal development: excluded, yet also confident, and ultimately assertive.

Appearing in close-up as the main figure in the panel, Huck impresses the reader as a rebellious and undaunted young man. He rolls a cigarette, smokes, and leisurely relaxes next to a case of beer on a rooftop with his friends (*Huck Finn* 8). However, in the context of the requirement to kill family members, the boys' mention of Huck's father noticeably triggers Huck. Motion lines, part of a common comics syntax, suggest quivering, and exaggeratedly wide eyes indicate a deep sense of spiraling fear (*Huck Finn* 10). The boys' remarks about the widow with whom he lives sharpen the focus on this ambivalent nature of Huck's character early in the story. Despite his cocky response "Ach, bei der bleib' ich eh nicht mehr lange," the final panel of the prologue once again indicates this initial display of vulnerability as he processes the gang's family member requirement (*Huck Finn* 10). Although Huck faces hardships and experiences exclusion typical within a peer group, visual cues in the opening sequence nonetheless make it clear that this story is his to tell. Even if it could be argued that Jin's painful backstory renders her more mature than Huck, she often appears one-dimensional and ornamental in the absence of a continuous storyline or backstory, which would imbue her with the consistent and visible agency and confidence of her male counterpart. The last panel in the opening sequence emphasizes the complexities of Huck's character, presenting a zoomed-out view with Huck appearing much smaller against the backdrop, yet self-assured with his long stride away from the group and into his own adventure.

Before we move into the closer reading of Splash Page One, which I have named "The Morning After" for ease of identification, some narrative contextualization of this pivotal moment is necessary. Huck and Jin's initial interaction precedes the first selected splash page, which will establish the stereotypical representation of Jin as subordinate and lacking self-determination in an unjust social system. Before the first splash, or narrative reset, Jin tries to assert herself while Huck's behavior substantiates his (yet-to-be-developed) individual empowerment that he unwittingly, yet automatically, enjoys as a member of the dominant society. Confidence acquired from the opening scenes continues to embolden him as he wanders around the city, contemplating his next move. As Huck impudently urinates on a wall, Jin enters the scene and admonishes him: "das kannst du doch nicht einfach machen," to which he replies in a demeaning and sexist manner:

"Also von einer Schlampe lass ich mir nix sagen" (*Huck Finn* 16). This exchange not only typifies the initial dynamic of their relationship but also spotlights how inherited patterns of dominance filter down into individual relationships, even among teenagers. This lead-up narrative establishes a sharp contrast to the first splash page that will immediately dissolve any trace of assertiveness on Jin's part. Vieweg's clothing choices for Jin have arguably already begun to diminish any indication of self-determination: she is shown in a highly sexualized way wearing only a camisole and underpants. In addition to the wardrobe's visual shorthand that emphasizes her criminalized sexuality, the panel composition reinforces her lack of societal power.

Further visual cues reaffirm Huck and Maik's guaranteed male access to agency. For example, as Huck reacts to Jin's admonishment, the reader sees his full face head on, while hers narrowly occupies the right side of the frame; and only the back of her head, her hair, and a camisole strap are visible as she attempts to assert herself (*Huck Finn* 16). A larger, overarching system of exploitation, one that objectifies and removes self-determination, becomes clear as Maik brutally interrupts any momentary trace of Jin's self-confidence and drags her away by her hair (*Huck Finn* 17). As opposed to *Huck Finn*'s dedication of narrative space to Huck's history of trauma, this is one of the few instances where the graphic novel explicitly portrays Jin's abuse. This deficit of expression reflects a condition that can apply across cultures, where "ethnic and racial others [live] in an economy of narrative scarcity" and where abundant and complex white representation abounds (V.T. Nguyen 203). A parallel scene to the one mentioned above in which Huck strides confidently away from his group of friends features Jin in about the same visual size as Huck in the frame (*Huck Finn* 17). However, her head pulled forward with her hair in Maik's grasp and her body bent at an unnatural angle indicate physical pain and societally enforced submission and visually proclaim the lack of decision-making power over her next destination.

In many ways, Huck's as-yet-ambiguous characterization is consistent with Twain's focus in the original on Huck's process of developing a sense of ethics in the role of "a fundamentally moral and innocent figure in a corrupt world" (Ciocia 197). Also similar to the original, Vieweg's graphic novel depicts Huck's process of moral maturation as complex, in contrast to his marginalized counterpart's one-dimensionality. Although Huck technically belongs to the white majority, he is still a teen who lacks life experience. A careful reading of one particular panel that precedes "The Morning After" conveys Huck's deficit of experience and his underdeveloped maturity at this point. Huck's face appears in full close-up, indicating prominence, but the trafficker's brutality has clearly had a visible negative effect on Huck, as seen by his fearful eyes and a black crest in the background behind him. Fittingly for this reading, McCloud identifies the comics narrative feature of panel background as a "valuable tool for indicating invisible ideas [that affect] our reading of inner states" (132). As in the original, incident after incident tests Huck's moral character and calls into question expectations and limitations that affect the "inner state" of this adolescent rebel. Interpretations of Twain's original point to the implausibility of Huck's ignorance to the vileness of slavery, "it is hard to believe, given when and where [Twain's Huck] grew up, that he could be unaware that there is an alternative moral perspective, which has it that slavery is immoral" (Clarke 492). Likewise, it would seem just as inconceivable to conclude that Vieweg's Huck has no sense of the impropriety of Jin's exploitation. Any discussion of Huck's maturation in moral matters, whether he immediately succeeds in that moment or not, still strongly suggests that Huck has the luxury of agency, while Jin remains in a stereotypical and ornamental role, still lacking individual empowerment.

We will now turn to the close reading of Splash Page One "The Morning After" (Fig. 1), the "reset" aspect of which causes readers to temporarily retreat from the narrative action to inventory the characters' developmental trajectories and examine the implied social structures that furnish each character with disparate, inequitable experiences. As the encounter in this first splash evidences, Huck's complete freedom of movement and free will sharply contrast Jin's restrictions. Huck, having stayed up all night chasing adventure, encounters Jin returning in the early morning from a "customer's" house. The splash prominently features Jin in the foreground, once again showing the exaggeration and magnification of stereotypes that define her and do not allow for a differentiated reading or understanding of this marginalized person. Bruises frame her eyes, and she hugs her clothing to her chest. Paradoxically, despite the invisibility and hiddenness of her personal character development, implied stereotypes of Asian sex workers and exoticized women occupy a disproportionately prominent space on this single page. Jin's wardrobe and her blank gaze intensify the focus on her portrayal between "thingness and personhood," one derived from a "vast and tenacious history of Oriental female objectification, refracted through the lenses of commodity, sexual fetishism," as Anne Anlin Cheng chronicles in her study about ornamentalism and the "yellow woman" (419). Although Cheng writes generally about Asian femininity in Western contexts, a "vast and tenacious history" can also be regarded in the context of German history.

In this case, former East German economic reality blends with pop culture to establish assumptions of the "Asian woman" that in turn, consciously or subconsciously, influenced the creation of Jin's character. When Berna Gueneli maintains that cinematic and pop media portrayals of Japanese women have resulted in three versions of feminizations, "[a]estheticized artificialization/reification, eroticization, and infantilization," (326) she could just as well be referring to Jin's

Fig. 1: Jin returns home (*Huck Finn* 23).

characterization. In the panel, Jin's gaze is directed beyond the left side of the page. By contrast, the reader clearly sees Huck's wide eyes gazing at her. With actions again marked by ambiguity, graphic cues convey his consternation with a speech bubble, empty except for three dots, floating high in the air above his head. Jin's exposed body and bruised face disclose the trauma of invisibility for Asian women and the related limitations of "linguistic symbols and narrative structures" to describe suffering "rejected by history" that "cannot be seen, known, or explained" (Siyi 59). Consistent with the tradition of denying a non-white character narrative space, this will be the last readers see of Jin for a while.

Depictions of Huck's experience with and boldly depicted audacious renunciation of parental abuse lead up to the second splash page, which I have labeled "The Raft." Exerting his autonomy, Huck leaves the widow's home in search of his father. This carefree period of independence is short-lived, however, as his inebriated father grows violent. Bold and oversized sound words punctuate the brutal sequence and offer an additional sensory layer to represent the fear that Huck experiences, or, as Petersen labels it, "different degrees of sound presence" (587).

After a disturbing occurrence, conveyed by a visually striking panel in which his father hallucinates seeing snakes, Huck wields his self-determination and asserts: "Eins war klar, noch mal würde ich das nicht mitmachen" (*Huck Finn* 31). Although he has been victimized, Vieweg's version of Huck, much like Twain's source character, affords him the power and cunning intellect to devise and carry out a scheme to fake his own death.

As emphasis for the next step in his developmental transition, the next splash page features a broad horizon and a raft floating up to him as he stands on the riverbank (*Huck Finn* 37). Components of this image are consistent with Thierry Groensteen's description of splashes as "favoring wide open spaces and emphasizing decors and atmospheres" (45). The composition of "The Raft" also supports Duncan's observations that, while the splash depicts a "single instant of time," "the larger the panel, the longer the time span depicted in it" (68). This full-page composition invites the reader to see Huck "behind the scenes" of his protracted process of maturation, making significant, if scary, developmental progress. Jin's story and trauma, however, remain out of sight (*Huck Finn* 40–42). The splash features the limited tone coloration – muted browns, oranges, sienna, and sepia – that characterizes the entirety of *Huck Finn*. The splash also accentuates the prominent nature imagery that creates the foundation and acts as a recognizable *leitmotif* for most of the splash panels. Just as the one-page panels perform separate functions for Huck and Jin, the nature aspects serve a different function for each as well. Narrative and visual elements intimate Huck's agency while nature images for Jin underscore her portrayal as a passive ornament. In the splash, readers see Huck from the back, standing on the banks of the river. His eyes are not visible, but the composition nonetheless indicates a straight line from his gaze to the raft, one that highlights his socially affirmed power of boldly renouncing authority. Subsequent scenes where they appear together on the raft make Huck and Jin seem like equals in this developmental journey. Visual and narrative evidence from other moments in the text, however, continues to overwhelmingly support the idea that any attempted development or gesture toward autonomy is only read alongside Huck's actualized development and inside limited and firmly formed social structures, repeatedly negating any gains for Jin.

The analysis of a pair of splash pages, consisting of what I have named "The Fish," and "On the Raft," requires some context. Scenes leading up to these two splash pages underscore the above-mentioned repudiation of progress for Jin. Having returned from his fact-finding mission with Maik, Huck sails away with Jin on the raft, but visual details that emphasize her exclusion, her life in the shadows, and her blending into her environment, and thus into the natural background, prevail over any narrative indications of equal status or ability. As opposed to Huck's development, which should theoretically and ideally peak in moral growth and heightened self-awareness, Jin's tendency, consistent with trends for Asian youth in Western countries, bends toward a self-awareness "of [her] marginalization and invisibility" and the necessity to develop skills for negotiating place (Mistry and Kiyama 584). Paradoxically, any active awareness is only of her exclusion as she continues to occupy an ornamental function and placement on the perimeter of the narrative action. When Huck takes initiative and an active role in spotting a rowboat containing two of Maik's cronies, Jin, still hidden, blends into the surrounding natural elements behind a tree. She is only able to act as a curious commentator on her counterpart's bold actions with the question: "was treibt er da?!" (*Huck Finn* 63). The page composition and her question inscribe Huck as the agent who has the power to act. Yet, at this point, the ambiguity and thus complexity of his character, manifests itself again.

As readers of Twain's original had over a century before, *Huck Finn*'s readers witness Huck working toward moral maturity. Vieweg's Huck, along with his source character, is involved in the debate about being "uncompromised in their critique of society [and] the extent to which they are ideologically implicated with the status quo" (Ciocia 205). Huck's internal dilemma is clearly expressed when he says: "Vielleicht sollte ich denen Jin einfach ausliefern . . . das könnte mir 'ne Menge Ärger ersparen. Und ich könnte meine eigene Flucht fortsetzen" (*Huck Finn* 59). His subsequent maneuvers verify his role as the active white savior who can display evolving intellectual and strategic skillfulness because he succeeds in sending Maik's men away. Jin, on the other hand, still behind the tree, now appears even smaller with the branches and leaves overwhelming the frame (*Huck Finn* 64). While this scene offers readers a look inside Huck's line of thinking, visual aspects make it clear that Jin's "thinking" is limited to taking on the role of background scenery for Huck's maturation process.

With this contextual information in mind, we can proceed to the analysis of "The Fish" and "On the Raft." Repeated insights into Huck's moral dilemma, and views of Jin as nothing more than a natural ornament, have preceded the splash page pair that once again resets, interrupts, and allows the reader to take inventory of the characters' contrasting developmental tracks. Despite his decision to do the right thing and his success in getting Maik's people to move on, Huck once again considers the morality of his actions and weighs potential gain against the amount of unnecessary trouble Jin has caused him: "Na ja, ich hab beschlosssen . . . dass ich mir keinen Kopf mehr machen werde, was das, Richtige' ist . . . Von nun an werde ich nur noch das tun, was gerade am bequemsten ist. So sieht's aus" (*Huck Finn* 65). "The Fish," another purely nature-oriented splash page, which is bright orange and features a fish catching a fly as its focal point, interrupts Huck's doubts about the right moral decision. Because it is a single panel, lacks transition to other panels, and interrupts a sequence, it can, as McCloud theorizes, "produce a sense of timelessness" because the "panel offers no clues as to its duration" (102). "On the Raft" appears directly opposite the fish page and beckons the reader to take a textual inventory of Huck and Jin's personal development and respective prominence or invisibility as told through the plot lines outside of this panel (Fig. 2). This time, darker browns and black offset the pale orange and add depth of feeling to the scene, while also supplying a sort of foreboding foreshadowing (*Huck Finn* 67). In a recurring pattern, a birds-eye view of the two characters as small figures side by side on the raft delivers the deceptive message that the two teens have become equals. That might be a valid interpretation if we were to disregard the speech bubbles also present on the splash page. The pair reclines on the raft with identical body language and physical size, but their brief exchange about Jin's supreme trust in Huck underscores the dissimilar social statuses and degrees of autonomy (*Huck Finn* 67). Huck has the authority to promise action and Jin can merely trust in that authoritative promise.

Fig. 2: Huck and Jin on the raft to Hamburg (*Huck Finn* 67).

The visual shock of the next splash under consideration here, titled "The Crash," might call to mind Groensteen's discussion of disruptive "oversized panels," as he calls splash pages, which "break up the rhythm of the layout, creating a small visual surprise" (45). The "surprise" in this case is quite significant rather than "small," however, as a giant cruise ship approaches the tiny raft (*Huck Finn* 70). The graphic novel signifies the urgency of the situation with Vieweg's signature oversized and exaggerated sound words, which as Petersen suggests, "represent sensations at the speed they would be activated in the narrative" (578). Although readers know that Huck and Jin have jointly embarked on the journey and now experience this accident together, Jin is noticeably absent from the page. Instead, readers only see Huck's wide-eyed shocked reaction and a view from behind of his cowering body as the ship threatens his life. Only in the subsequent pages do readers see the pair's mutual reaction to the catastrophe. Jin's re-entry into the scene could suggest progress on her path to identity, which represents the universal "need to seek agency so they can work toward liberation," or "dismantling structures and doctrines which reinforce subordination" (Kim 115). As the two continue on the river with the goal of escaping the local reach of Maik and his cronies and arriving in Hamburg far away from Halle, Jin seems to make strides toward her liberation right alongside Huck. External factors, however, will work to preempt any immediate advancement on that journey, which propels the two of them, but especially Jin, back into established oppressive structures. The ensuing narrative storyline "between the splashes" shows Jin sinking further into those established structures because of overt sexism and stereotyping. The hope would be that the graphic narrative ultimately lifts Jin out of these structures, but that emancipation will elude her.

After Huck and Jin wash ashore, the Schäfers, one of the town's feuding families, rescue them. Huck takes the lead in fabricating the story that has brought them to Hamburg, while Jin fades into the background of skepticism and cautiousness. The prominent Asian stereotypes of sexualization and submissive femininity, as seen by her host's overtones of sexual assault, cause Jin's subsequent literal invisibility, or extended leave of absence from the text's main action. Any opportunity for the graphic novel to assess her gender-related trauma and to allow Jin to complete steps toward resolution disappear along with her. By contrast, readers continue to accompany Huck on his moral journey. For another lengthy section, where the story deepens Huck's characterization and moral development, Jin is essentially written out of the story, once again denied a narrative voice and thus representation in her own story.

The final splash page in the series is "Jin in the Water," which I argue carries the greatest potential for readers to construe and evaluate Jin's involvement, or lack thereof, in her own self-development and autonomy. Jin appears prominently on the page, which suggests that she is still part of the story, but with prescribed limitations (*Huck Finn*, Fig. 3). She appears knee-deep in a body of water, supporting herself with a large stick, and gazing into the distance (*Huck Finn* 103). Before and after this splash interrupts the narrative flow, Huck has actively continued with his adventure. The page composition as well as Jin's placement and posing in it only reinforce her merely decorative function. Jin's rendering as a passive subject corresponds to Cheng's "ornamental personhood of Asiatic femininity" (428). The splash page's portrait-like character, however, evokes a further association with comics syntax. Postema has characterized splash panels, which she labels "single panel pages" as "individual works of art rather than parts of a sequence" (32). Similarly, Duncan also alludes to this role of splashes as pieces of art "[that] operate as pin-ups that show off the artist and talent" (110). Jin as the clear subject amidst nature images adorning this single panel of art relates on a thematic level to art exhibits such as those found in museums memorializing World War II-era comfort women,[2] another historical aspect of female Asian identity that supplements images and perceptions discussed elsewhere in this article. Displaying politically determined and gender-influenced trauma, the exhibits aim to highlight the women's long paths to identity formation (Siyi 56–57). Theoretically, *Huck Finn*'s purpose and impact could reflect that of the museums: that is, the establishment of "equality and human rights through the awareness of history and culture in pursuit of the concepts of justice and peace" (Siyi 58). Through its narrative and visual choices, *Huck Finn* does indeed raise awareness, and could draw attention to human rights, but it does not succeed at constructing even a scant impression of equality.

One conclusion that has emerged from the reading and interpretation of Jin's character thus far is that she stands out because of her perceived foreignness and stereotypical portrayal. Yet, in a contradictory way, she remains largely invisible to the reader for the same reasons. In her personal identity work, H. Nguyen reaches similar conclusions and indirectly comments on the paradoxical invisibility that results from the prominence of Othering and stereotyping. H. Nguyen's firsthand observations about racial power dynamics resemble those that restrain and restrict Jin. Like *Huck Finn*'s female character, German society defines the Asian woman externally, eliminates her from the conversation, and does not empower her. H. Nguyen reports feelings of being "von Außenstehenden und von Nicht-Betroffenen markiert und gelesen," and "nicht selbstverständlich mitgedacht oder mitgemeint," even in the context of the theoretically more inclusive

---

2 Examples of these museums include the *Women's Active Museum on War and Peace* in Tokyo, Japan, and *The War and Women's Human Rights Museum* in Seoul, Korea.

Fig. 3: Jin alone in the water (*Huck Finn* 103).

label *Person mit Migrationshintergrund* (H. Nguyen 19, 21). Although *Huck Finn* does highlight moments where Jin appears to have the upper hand, or at least a capable helping hand, her consistent exclusion from mainstream society and inclusion in nature scenes reminds readers that Jin's story remains frustratingly incomplete. Additionally, that she is not "mitgedacht" or "mitgemeint" becomes clear when Jin rejoins Huck only after he has experienced vital milestones of personal and moral maturation on his developmental journey. As seen throughout the narrative, Huck's adventure is made visible, which results in heightened intellectual curiosity, privilege to embark on an adventure, escape his traumatic environment, and experience moral development and maturation. Jin's traumatic experiences, on the other hand, remain largely invisible, as evidenced concretely by the number of pages where she is missing, and thus excluded, from the narrative. Consequently, readers do not see any degree of moral development or self-determination in Jin's character, contrary to what Huck enjoys, confirming that this remained his story all along. The graphic novel's final page bookends the prologue, as Huck calls his friend Tom to inform him that he is bringing a "Lady" along to be a part of the *Bande*. Here, Huck again exhibits his confident long stride, head tipped back with orange smoke floating up from a cigarette, while Jin follows behind, eyes fixed on her presumed hero (*Huck Finn* 142).

As this close reading of textual and visual attributes in *Huck Finn* has shown, Vieweg's reconceptualization of the enslaved Jim as Jin relies heavily on Asian female stereotyping and Othering. Thematizing discrimination typifies any iteration of Twain's *Adventures of Huckleberry Finn*, but the specific racially defined roles differ by geographic location, time period, and minority group referenced. Vieweg's *Huck Finn* presents Jin's current station as traditionally prescribed and subordinate. Grace Ji-Sun Kim elucidates in her study on the suffering of Asian immigrants in the United States, "an Asian woman who has been displaced to a Western cultural setting evokes desires for an exotic Otherness" (114). Jin's physical appearance corroborates this condition of Othered exoticism and could have cultural roots in the former East Germany's steady and consistent propagandization of officially warmly welcomed Vietnamese comrades. Descriptors from several official GDR government publications like "delicate," "petite," and "pretty" find visual expression in Jin (Mann 82–84). Other cultural phenomena speak to ongoing and firmly anchored biased attitudes against Asian women. The website thaifrau.de (still active in 2025) offers a portal for German men, "repulsed by women's lib" to "look beyond their borders" for "exotic" and "childlike" women with a "simple nature" and "naive femininity" (Berger 362). Referencing this information here is, of course, not intended to suggest a straight line between East German propaganda or Asian dating sites and the derivation of Jin's character. Instead, this contextualization suggests a prevalent commonness of these signifiers that allow them easy entry into the composite characterization of a young Asian female sex worker in modern-day Germany.

In addition to the aspects related to the former East Germany, a number of firmly rooted perceptions about female Asian identity in German pop culture originated years before economic demands brought tens of thousands of guestworkers to the GDR in the 1960s. Specifically, German cinematic impulses of the twentieth century have arguably contributed to the perpetuation and continuing tradition of Asian stereotypes in Germany that reach back centuries. Gueneli, in her study on the fetishization of Japanese femininities in Weimar-era film, investigates the origins dating back as early as the seventeenth century of the image of Japanese women as licensed sex workers, with broader circulation of "remarkably one-dimensional" images by the nineteenth century (Gueneli 327). In addition to the fact that Jin operates in the sex work milieu, the graphic novel's visual portrayal of her also displays this one dimensionality. Zach Ramon Fitzpatrick extends the timeline of stereotypically sexualized Asian women, and with it the intensified persistence of female Asian stereotypes, to the mid-twentieth century with his analysis of the film *Bis zum Ende aller Tage* (1961). While this film, according to Fitzpatrick, is the first to focus on immigration and prejudice against Asian immigrants, it also relies on the "stereotypical cinematic blueprint to this day" of the "relationship between a white man and an Asian woman involved in sex work" (27). As the brief reference to contract theory above indicates, establishing a moral hierarchy requires a tacit agreement that one group exploits another group; and the exoticized Asian female has operated in various contexts as the permanently exploited.

The narrative vacuum where Jin's story resides for much of the text could also correspond to sociological aspects of German dominant culture and its historical treatment of non-dominant communities. Exploring this ostracism in the context of what he labels an ambivalent relationship between Germany and its immigrants, Dutch sociologist Ruud Koopmans provocatively asserts that "exclusion [by the dominant group] is tied to the concept of national identity" (643). He identifies uniquely German barriers for incorporating minority communities into the mainstream culture, maintaining that, unlike in other European countries that have adjusted legislation to keep pace with changing demographics, "Germany's ethno-cultural conception of citizenship and nationhood stands in the way of inclusion" (Koopman 627). When German citizenship is defined along ethnic lines, permanent labels and exclusionary language develop, resulting in a phenomenon for which sociologist Sandra Bucerius indicts mainstream culture, having "denied its immigrants an 'official sense of belonging'" (40). Not surprisingly and of interest to the current analysis of *Huck Finn* that trains the spotlight on two teenage voices, politics of exclusion take root early, as Moffitt et al. declare in their article about underrepresented minority youth in the secondary school system, "Who is marginalized and who is afforded opportunity is often delineated along lines of class and race" (832). Perhaps less straightforward than this finding, however, is the set of factors that contribute to a covert understanding of race in Germany. In other words, rhetoric and assigned labels have real world implications for members of marginalized groups: "the use of alternate terms to designate the perceived Other, including *Ausländer* (foreigner), immigrant or the more recently created *Menschen mit Migrationshintergrund* (people with migration background) have become racialized, meaning their primary referents are people of color" (Moffitt 832). Though *Huck Finn* does not explicitly use these terms or ethnic labels (other than some slurs by the villainous characters) to achieve the clear delineation between the two young characters, the visual choices – and even or especially excluded images – strongly suggest Jin's marginalization.

Whether Vieweg as a German reader of Twain's original explored similar aspects of her own culture, such as gendered and ethnic Othering as well as racial exploitation, and correspondingly reshaped the original's thematic and historical frameworks (Berthele 589), is unclear and even "unanswerable" and "irrelevant" (Rifas 29). What becomes clear upon closer examination, however, is that *Huck Finn*'s overall conceptualization of the "die Asiatin Jin" reinforces aspects of social and historical discriminatory practices. This perpetuation compels the reader to draw connections to specific origins and forms of cultural Otherness as regards Asian identity in Germany. Introducing or imagining an alternative dynamic, such as centralizing Jin and her liberation story, or at least presenting her narrative parallel to Huck's, remains absent. Rather than Jin's moments of presence in the text, her extended omission and resulting invisibility provide the strongest evidence for the claims of her consistent marginalization and ultimate lack of autonomy. Jonathan Bignell, in a discussion of media semiotics, explains this interaction between visible and invisible significance, "Every sign present has meaning by virtue of the other signs which have been excluded and are not present in the text" (14). Applying this to *Huck Finn,* the selected splash pages gain in significance at the expense of excluded images: Jin's story is lost to the main narrative that privileges Huck's. With attention to comics mechanics, Duncan et al. elucidate both the process and the result of both the image selection and exclusion process. One method is paradigmatic choice, which refers to the author's curation of illustrations "that could have made sense or communicated nearly the same meaning at the same point in the panel" (Duncan et al. 62–63). Even if an alternative conceptualization of the text were to retain the reductive visual devices that indicate "exploited Asian woman," other authorial choices, such as granting the two characters equal "screen time" and emphasizing Jin's hard-won independence by highlighting her singular voice at the end, could have invited readers to extract meaning contained in the necessarily two-dimensional and caricatured drawings.

Considering the role that clichéd depictions and generalizations have traditionally played in comics production offers an entry point for determining the balance between stereotype as an "essential tool in the language of graphic storytelling," and the expectation of the artist to "recognize its impact on social judgment," to cite Will Eisner's 2013 addendum to his oft-quoted assertions about stereotypes in comics (Eisner 2013, 3–4). Years before offering this more balanced and nuanced view, Eisner had characterized stereotypes and oversimplification as an "accursed necessity of comics storytelling," inherent in the form itself, which necessitated "the simplification of images into repeatable symbols" or stereotypes (Eisner 1996, 17). Indeed, past adaptations of *Adventures of Huckleberry Finn* bear out the stubborn persistence of Eisner's "accursed necessity." If comics readers are looking for racial stereotypes in Huck Finn adaptations, whether in *Illustrated Classics* of decades past, or updated manga versions from well into the 2000s, they can certainly find them. And it could surely be argued in those cases as well as that of *Huck Finn*, that those oversimplified images efficiently communicate shorthand messages that otherwise require disproportionately lengthy visual and verbal exposition.

Rifas, for his part, does not renounce the use of "repeatable symbols" or stereotypes. Instead, he proposes accounting for and indexing their use, for example with qualifiers such as "satiric, ironic, parodic, or even idiotic" (Rifas 35). By doing so, he contends, the critical reader can dissolve the focus on "suspect imagery" and instead listen "for the 'conversations' that a comic participates in" (Rifas 35). Vieweg has, at the very least, with her arguably "satiric" and even "parodic" display of racial stereotypes, joined in the concurrent conversations of traditional criticism of Mark Twain's work. At the same time, she has updated critical discussions of racial and sexual politics that the original evokes. In his critical confrontation with Eisner's views on stereotypes, Andrew J. Kunka discusses the difficulties of "disentangling" problematic images and assessing the "limitations of imagination and empathy for both readers and a [comics] creator" (74). Part of this work of unraveling involves viewing caricature alongside character, that is to say the way a character is drawn over how it is written (Kunka 68). The question becomes one of formula: does character or caricature carry the heavier weight? As regards *Huck Finn*, racist stereotypes (caricature) play a superior role in illuminating Jin's struggle with and possible power to overcome racism and discrimination (character).

Yet, this alignment with elements of original Twain criticism – particularly Twain's attention to his audience and their expectations in matters of caricature and character – complicates the question further. Narrative and graphic magnification of Asian stereotypes as a method for raising awareness or generating sympathy with a minoritized group might seem an effective method. Dramatists like Mihyang Amy Ginther, however, in her directives for actors with racialized identities, confounds that logical jump. She views the cultivated exoticism, for example as displayed in *Huck Finn*, as a misplaced tool to generate sympathy. Instead, she advocates for a "dramaturgy of deprivation" that exists in opposition to one of empathy for marginalized characters and that can counterproductively leave "white audiences feeling passively satisfied" (Ginther 1). This indicator of white contentment recalls Sidonie Smith's address to the "privileged, safe subject" whose "reading rehearses a form of rescue of the other through the invitation to empathetic identification and outrage" (64). Likewise, Ginther advocates for withholding a gratifying happy ending, and for resisting the temptation to fill in "gaps and provide closure where there is none" (2). Historical and sociological evidence, as well as contemporary testimonials about Asian identity, support the idea that closure has not been achieved for members of those communities because they do not own their stories. This raises a further related question about why *Huck*

Finn would attempt to deliver this closure. Whether as a result of societal truths and structures, author's intention, or publisher's expectations and limitations, the graphic novel displays an approved and comfortable version of a story that presumably would like to draw attention to the important social issue of human trafficking through a highly developed character, but whose unexamined use of caricature obstructs that aim.

When Toni Morrison characterizes Twain's original as "sardonic, photographic" and "persuasively aural," she could just as easily be talking about a graphic novel adaptation; and she could be speaking the comics language of the gutter in her assertion that the "major feats lie in the silences" (Morrison 154). In Jin's case, her sexualization and exoticization, which force her out to the margins, lie between the disruptive splashes. With an eye on the critical aptitude for influencing rebel teenage narratives and their modernized adaptations, Ciocia advocates for capitalizing "on the subversive potential of disaffected teenage narrators, where compelling vernacular voices, and their distinctive positions as outsiders are powerful tools for social critique" (196). But, as we have seen, one teenage narrator stands much further outside than the other. In addition to the white-crowd-pleasing happy ending, *Huck Finn*'s visual and narrative cultivation of firmly rooted patterns of Asian identity, societally normalized oppression, fetishization, exoticism, and invisibility have ultimately, and seemingly contradictorily, resulted in a perpetuation of ensconced structures that limit a deeper understanding of marginalized communities. Any critical discussion of these social conditions cannot succeed because Jin, the character whose experiences should ideally shed light on the social ill of sex trafficking, was not able to find her voice.

Works Cited

Berger, K. "The Thai Wife: Medicine for German Men Damaged by Women's Libbers?" *Germany in Transit: Nation and Migration, 1955–2005*, edited by Deniz Göktürk et al., U of California P, 2007, pp. 362–365.

Berthele, Raphael. "Translating African-American Vernacular English into German: The Problem of 'Jim' in Mark Twain's Huckleberry Finn." *Journal of Sociolinguistics*, vol. 4, no. 4, Nov. 2000, pp. 588–613.

Bignell, Jonathan. *Media Semiotics: An Introduction*. Manchester UP, 1997.

Bucerius, Sandra M. *Unwanted: Muslim Immigrants, Dignity, and Drug Dealing*. Oxford UP, 2014.

Chan, Crystal S., et al. *Adventures of Huckleberry Finn*. Manga Classics, Inc., 2017.

Cheng, Anne Anlin. "Ornamentalism: A Feminist Theory for the Yellow Woman." *Critical Inquiry*, vol. 44, no. 3, Apr. 2018, pp. 415–446.

Ciocia, Stefania. "'The World Loves an Underdog,' or the Continuing Appeal of the Adolescent Rebel Narrative: A Comparative Reading of *Vernon God Little*, *The Catcher in the Rye* and *Huckleberry Finn*." *Children's Literature in Education*, vol. 49, no. 2, June 2018, pp. 196–215.

Clarke, Steve. "Huckleberry Finn's Conscience: Reckoning with the Evasion." *The Journal of Ethics: An International Philosophical Review*, vol. 24, no. 4, Dec. 2020, pp. 485–508.

Duncan, Randy, Matthew J. Smith, and Paul Levitz. *The Power of Comics and Graphic Novels: Culture, Form, and Content*. Bloomsbury Academics, 2023.

Eisner, Will. *Fagin the Jew*. Dark Horse Comics, 2013.

Eisner, Will. *Graphic Storytelling and Visual Narrative*. Poorhouse, 1996.

Everett, Percival. *James*. Doubleday, 2024.

Fitzpatrick, Zach Ramon. "The World(s) of Anna Suh: Race, Migration, and Ornamentalism in *Bis zum Ende aller Tage* (*Until the End of Days*, 1961)." *East Asian German Cinema*, edited by Joanne Miyang Cho, Routledge, 2021, pp. 146–175.

Ginther, Mihyang Amy. "Dramaturgy of Deprivation 었다,: An Invitation to Re-Imagine Ways We Depict Asian American and Adopted Narratives of Trauma." *Journal of American Drama & Theatre*, vol. 34, no. 2, Spring 2022, pp. 1–8.

Groensteen, Thierry. *Comics and Narration*. Translated by Ann Miller, UP Mississippi, 2011.

Gueneli, Berna. "Art, Artifice, and Eroticized Infantilization: Imagining Japanese Femininities in the Weimar Republic in Fritz Lang's *Harakiri* (1919) and Kapitän Mertens's '*Kio, Die Lasterhafte Kirschblüte*' (1924)." *German Quarterly*, vol. 96, no. 3, June 2023, pp. 326–43.

Harris, Michael D. *Colored Pictures: Race and Visual Representation*. U of North Carolina P, 2003.

Hatfield, Charles. *Alternative Comics: An Emerging Literature*. UP of Mississippi, 2005.

Heer, Jeet. "Afterword." *Black Comics: Politics of Race and Representation*, edited by Sheena C. Howard and Ronald L. Jackson II, Bloomsbury, 2013, pp. 251–256.

Kidd, Kenneth B. *Making American Boys: Boyology and the Feral Tale*. U of Minnesota P, 2004.

Kim, Grace Ji-Sun. "INVISIBILITY." *Journal of Feminist Studies in Religion*, vol. 39, no. 2, Sept. 2023, pp. 111–115.

Koopmans, Ruud. "Germany and Its Immigrants: An Ambivalent Relationship." *Journal of Ethnic and Migration Studies*, vol. 25, no. 4, 1999, pp. 627–647.

Kunka, Andrew J. "How Else Could I Have Created a Black Boy in That Era?" *Desegregating Comics: Debating Blackness in the Golden Age of American Comics*, edited by Quina Whitted, Rutgers UP, 2023, pp. 61–76.

Levy, Andrew. "The Boy Murderers: What Mark Twain and Huckleberry Finn Really Teach." *The Missouri Review*, vol. 32, no. 2, 2009, pp. 42–58.

Mann, Roland, et al. *The Adventures of Huckleberry Finn*. Campfire, 2010.

Mann, Siegfried. "How Do Foreign Workers Live in the GDR?" *Germany in Transit: Nation and Migration, 1955–2005*, edited by Deniz Göktürk et al., U of California P, 2007, pp. 82–84.

McCloud, Scott. *Understanding Comics: The Invisible Art*. HarperPerennial, 1994.

MDR Thüringen Journal. "Comiczeichnerin Olivia Vieweg über 'Huckleberry Finn.'" *YouTube*, uploaded by MediaContainer, youtube.com/watch?v=DuFS6OkLzpo. 4 Aug. 2013.

Mills, Charles W. *The Racial Contract*. Cornell UP, 1997.

Mistry, Jayanthi and Fuko Kiyama. "Navigating Marginalization and Invisibility as Asian Americans in the U.S." *American Psychologist*, vol. 76, no. 4, May 2021, pp. 582–595.

Moffitt, Ursula, et al. "We Don't Do That in Germany! A Critical Race Theory Examination of Turkish Heritage Young Adults' School Experiences." *Ethnicities*, vol. 19, no. 5, 2019, pp. 830–857.

Morrison, Toni. Introduction. *The Oxford Mark Twain*, edited by Shelley Fisher Fishkin, Oxford UP, 1996, pp. 1–8.

Nguyen, Hami. *Das Ende der Unsichtbarkeit*. Ullstein, 2023.

Nguyen, Viet Thanh. *Nothing Ever Dies: Vietnam and the Memory of War*. Harvard UP, 2016.

தழுவி எழுதியவர்: நானெர்லி ஃபார் ; சித்திரம்: பிரான்ஸிஸ்கோ ரெடொண்டோ, et al. ஹக்கிள்பரி ஃபின் [Huckleberry Finn. Adapted by: Naunerle Farr; Illustration: Francisco Redanto, et al.] Edited by Dinesh V. Pai, Paikō Kiḷāciks, 1988.

Pai, Dinesh V. et al. *Huckleberry Finn*. Cochin, 1988.

Pateman, Carol. *The Sexual Contract: 30th Anniversary Edition*. Stanford UP, 2018.

Petersen, Robert S. "The Acoustics of Manga: Narrative Erotics and the Visual Presence of Sound." *International Journal of Comic Art*, vol. 9, no. 1, Apr. 2007, pp. 578–590.

Postema, Barbara. *Narrative Structure in Comics: Making Sense of Fragments*. RIT Press, 2013.

Ratliff, Thomas M. and Mark Twain. *Las Aventuras de Huckleberry Finn*. Translated by María Patricia Esguerra, Illustrated by Penko Gelev, Primera edición, Panamericana Editorial, 2016.

Rifas, Leonard. "Race and Comix." *Multicultural Comics: From Zap to Blue Beetle*, edited by Frederick Luis Aldama and Leonard Rifas, U of Texas P, 2010, pp. 27–38.

Siyi, Wang. "Memorials and Memory: The Curation and Interpretation of Trauma Narratives—using the Examples of Exhibitions on the Theme of 'Comfort Women' in East Asian Society." *Chinese Studies in History*, vol. 53, no. 1, Jan. 2020, pp. 56–71.

Smith, Sidonie and Julie Watson. *Life Writing in the Long Run*. Maize Books, 2016.

Time, Mark. *Black Lives Matter Too, Two: The Death of Huckleberry Finn*. John/Zavaz, 2020.

Twain, Mark. *Adventures of Huckleberry Finn*. Edited by Shelley Fisher Fishkin, introduction by Toni Morrison, Oxford UP, 1996.

Valkeakari, Tuire. "Huck, Twain, and the Freedman's Shackles: Struggling with *Huckleberry Finn* Today." *Atlantis (0210–6124)*, vol. 28, no. 2, Dec. 2006, pp. 29–43.

Vieweg, Olivia. *Huck Finn: Die Graphic Novel*. Suhrkamp, 2013.

Walker, David F., and Marcus Kwame Anderson. *Big Jim and the White Boy*. Penguin Random House, 2024.

Whitted, Qiana. "'And the Negro Thinks in Hieroglyphics': Comics, Visual Metonymy, and the Spectacle of Blackness." *Journal of Graphic Novels and Comics*, vol. 5, no. 1, 2014, pp. 79–100.

Andreas Stuhlmann
Anke Feuchtenberger's Graphic Novel *Genossin Kuckuck* as Palimpsest: History, Memory, Violence, and Transformation

Abstract: Anke Feuchtenberger's autofictional graphic novel *Genossin Kuckuck* (2023) draws on personal memories and accounts from her family and is set in the fictional village of Pritschitanow spanning from the end of World War II to the present. Following an introduction to the author's work and its relationship to the feminist comic avant-garde, the article examines *Genossin Kuckuck* and shows that it is constructed as a multilayered, polyphonic palimpsest of stories about violence, injustice, and resilience across three generations of women. Uncovering the palimpsest structure of *Genossin Kuckuck* allows us to understand the complex and protracted composition of the book. The various story arcs and episodes connected by themes and leitmotifs are both following and parodying the compositional technique of the great modernist novel. As such, Feuchtenberger succeeds in creating a testament to the feminist comic avant-garde that has been reinvigorating the artform since the 1990s.

I

The publication of Anke Feuchtenberger's latest graphic novel *Genossin Kuckuck – ein deutsches Tier im deutschen Wald* by Reprodukt in September 2023 marked both a significant milestone in her oeuvre and a rebirth of a feminist comic avant-garde.[1] In the spirit of this avant-garde, Feuchtenberger has always challenged her audience, her peers, and herself with a process of aesthetic transformation and formal evolution. In the 1990s, as art critic Peter Schjeldahl has noted, graphic novels as an avant-garde art form were "to many in their teens and twenties what poetry once was" (Schjeldahl 162). Comics, as Schjeldahl asserted, were once formally simple, easily consumable entertainment, while avant-gardes "are always cults of difficulty" (Schjeldahl 162). If "difficult" is used here as a cipher for "experimental" or "challenging" – to differentiate these comics from those released by mainstream

---

[1] Rights to an English translation under the working title *Comrade Cuckoo* have been procured by Lucas Adams for New York Review Comics, who also published a translation of Feuchtenberger and Katrin de Vries' *Die Hure h* as *W the Whore*. Cf. Feuchtenberger and de Vries 2023.

ə Open Access. © 2025 the author(s), published by De Gruyter. [cc) BY-NC-ND] This work is licensed under the Creative Commons Attribution-NonCommercial-NoDerivatives 4.0 International License.
https://doi.org/10.1515/9783112218631-009

publishing houses – then it fits the description of many graphic novels within this avant-garde. Rather than a "cult" the respective artists form a global culture composed of a network of synchronic and diachronic, as well as national and international relationships. Indeed, if the term avant-garde implies a form of challenge or rebellion against the old order, then this revolt is both overtly political and at the same time directed at renewing and reinventing the artform. Informed not just by other comics or literary texts, as Christian Gasser has observed, but also by TV, advertising, pop music, video clip aesthetics, video games and computer graphics, the various narrative styles employed by these avant-garde comic artists are shaped by collage, fragmentation, parody, discontinuity and repetition (Gasser 10). As varied as these styles are, they playfully embrace convention just as much as provocation, they oppose closure, distance, artistic autonomy, and the apolitical nature of representation (Hutcheon 27 et passim). German comic culture is also overtly political – Gasser speaks of its "unverblümten, manchmal agitatorischen Charakter" (Gasser 11). It keeps an ambivalent, somewhat antagonistic stance to "bourgeois" culture and is often deeply feminist – as exemplified in Feuchtenberger's work.

Now regularly referred to as its "grande dame,"[2] Feuchtenberger has been a dominant figure of German language comic culture and the European comic avant-garde for over three decades. She began her career in East Berlin in 1988 at the *Produktionsgenossenschaft des Handwerks* (*PGH*) "Glühende Zukunft." In the period following German reunification, she designed political posters and playbills for theater productions, drew illustrations for a feminist magazine, published her first strips and albums, and broke into the front row of comic artists with a short story in the comic magazine *Strapazin*'s 1993 special issue on Berlin.[3] In the early 1990s, *Strapazin* was a platform for a young, international comic avant-garde, while Berlin functioned as the focal point of a budding German comic culture. This new culture brought together artists from West Germany, such as Hendrik Dorgathen, Martin tom Dieck, and Markus Huber, who were rooted in a particular "Western" comic tradition, and also from East Germany such as Feuchtenberger, Atak, or Henning Wagenbreth, who brought with them a completely different set of artistic, visual, and narrative influences.[4] Feuchtenberger quickly became a driv-

---

[2] As seen, for example, on the homepage of the Goethe Institute: goethe.de/ins/lv/de/kul/sup/com/20477753.html?forceDesktop=1. Last accessed May 14, 2025.

[3] Biz Nijdam covered Feuchtenberger's early work in her PhD thesis (Nijdam 2017); a recent overview of the various aspects of Feuchtenberger's oeuvre and career can be found in Stuhlmann and Frahm.

[4] In their interview with Feuchtenberger, Giordana Piccinini, Alessio Trabacchini, and Emilio Varrà ask her extensively about her influences as a young artist growing up in the GDR, i.e., removed from "Western" comic culture (Piccinini, Trabacchini, and Varrà).

ing force within this new culture and in 1999, she was featured in the groundbreaking exhibition "Mutanten" as one of just two female artists alongside eleven male colleagues from Germany and Switzerland.[5] Based on the strength of her publications in *Strapazin*, Feuchtenberger was invited to present her work at the 1996 Angoulême International Comics Festival where she forged relations with other avant-garde artists including Canadian Julie Doucet, Belgian Dominique Goblet and Israelis Rutu Modan and Yirmi Pinkus. In 2025, she returned to Angoulême once more, when *La Camarade Coucou*, the French translation of *Genossin Kuckuck*, was nominated for the festival's major award.

Since 1997 she has held a position as professor of drawing at Hamburg's University of Applied Sciences (Hochschule für Angewandte Wissenschaften Hamburg/HAW). Together with her HAW-colleague and fellow *Strapazin*-contributor Stefano Ricci, Feuchtenberger founded her own publishing company, MamiVerlag, in 2007. In 2017, Feuchtenberger was invited to contribute a poster for an exhibition at the *Bundestag* on women's voting rights, and in 2018 she created a monumental altar for a museum of sacral art in Münster

II

Genossin Kuckuck, with its octavo format, its 438 pages divided into forty-one chapters and a coda, its variety of media from charcoal to red and black ink, graphite and pencil, its black-and-gold cover design, and its golden edge-coloring, has the appearance of a volume of sacred scripture. Its subject matter is memory, in many different forms, both individual and collective, and it is an exploration of the collective subconscious, as much as it is a love letter to Western Pomerania – where Feuchtenberger grew up and lives to this day – its people, its complex history, and its natural world. "Es ist alles absolut wahr und es ist alles erfunden," Feuchtenberger told interviewer Marina Knoben in March 2024 (Knoben). Feuchtenberger displays the fragmented nature and the uncertain truth-claims of memories by combining a variety of narrative approaches. The extensive autofictional work includes both fantastical and realistic elements.[6]

---

5 Burkhard Müller wrote an early portrayal of Feuchtenberger for the catalogue of the "Mutanten" exhibition (99–108).
6 Glowing reviews for *Genossin Kuckuck* in many of the noteworthy German feuilletons (see Hoffmann; Koopmann; Stillich) led to a nomination for the prestigious *Preis der Leipziger Buchmesse* 2024 in the general fiction category. This nomination was the first for a comic. In 2023, Birgit Weyhe, a former student of Feuchtenberger's, but long since a master graphic storyteller in her own right, was nominated for *Rude Girl* in the non-fiction category.

Overall, the multiple storylines of *Genossin Kuckuck* are told in a non-linear way and punctuated by surreal, dreamlike, or mythical episodes. The book opens with a pact for life being made by best friends Kerstin and Effi, two teenagers growing up in the fictional village of Pritschitanow in the north-eastern corner of the German Democratic Republic in the 1960s.

But soon, their friendship is tested and their lives torn apart by forces beyond their control. The family backgrounds of both girls are problematic: Kerstin Grund grows up with only her older brother Jochen and her grandmother. The siblings' parents are largely absent, as they are "Helden im Dienste des Sozialismus. Sie sind nicht tot, aber weg" (*Genossin Kuckuck* 16). The siblings and grandmother live in the tiny old village school building where Kerstin's grandmother is also the headmistress and Russian teacher. Effi Mettel, on the other hand, lives with both her parents: her mother Rosi, whom Kerstin idolizes, and her father, hobby hunter Helmuth "Waidgenosse" Mettel. Mother Rosi, however, harbors terrible secrets. The cast of main characters is completed by Frank Sternemann and Torsten Greiff, Kerstin's brother's two teenage friends. After the boys steal a pig's head from the local boneyard, they are institutionalized and brutally forced to fit the mold of the New Socialist Man.[7] The turmoil of the "Wende" years does not offer a chance to heal broken relationships but rather exacerbates the harm and the pain experienced earlier. Decades later, the enormous pigsty of the Socialist farmer's collective has been demolished and Rosi Mettel has built a home for senior citizens on its foundation. This is where Kerstin finds her grandmother, when she, like Frank and Torsten, returns to the village. Yet, while Kerstin seeks to reconnect with her grandmother, the men return to uncover who committed them to the institution for wayward teenagers and to exact revenge. Taken together, the storylines resemble a puzzle of violence and abuse, of pain and trauma, of lies and deceit.

As this article will illustrate, *Genossin Kuckuck* – the working title was "Ein deutsches Tier im deutschen Wald" – is the result of a complex and long process of artistic transformation: Between 2009 and 2023 Feuchtenberger wrote and drew dozens of separate story arcs for the storyworld of this project, creating eventually the largest graphic novel in her oeuvre.[8] By the time *Genossin Kuckuck* was published in 2023, more than fifteen years had passed since Feuchtenberger's last graphic novel, the final installment of *Die Hure h* from 2007. As such, then, in size as well as in artistic ambition, *Genossin Kuckuck* was nothing short of an artistic rebirth.

---

7 See the concept the New Socialist or Soviet Man (Mensch) as described, for instance, in Herschel and Edith Alt, *The New Soviet Man. His Upbringing and Character Development.*

8 Some themes and motifs can be traced back even further to her album *wehwehweh.supertraene.de* and to various stories included in the collection *Die Spaziergängerin*.

The final version of the title of the book, "Genossin Kuckuck," came to her late in the process in 2023, as she told Katrin Gottschalk of *die tageszeitung*, inspired by the intertext "Cuckoo Madame," a song by Robert Wyatt (Gottschalk). Wyatt's song personifies the cuckoo, a bird which lays its eggs in another's nest to have their chicks raised by the other bird. The mystery of such a *Kuckuckskind* lies at the center of Feuchtenberger's book.

To understand Feuchtenberger's aesthetic and narrative project in this work, we will uncover the palimpsest-like intertextual structure of *Genossin Kuckuck* as the fundamental principle of the complex and protracted composition of the graphic novel. The various story arcs and episodes are connected by themes and leitmotifs which are simultaneously aligned with and parodying the composition technique of the great modernist novel. For our analysis of the intricacies of the storyworld presented, it will be helpful to focus on central leitmotifs such as the slugs, the "grano blu," the ducks, the dress that is never finished, the lost photos and the empty paintings.

The palimpsest structure and the leitmotifs are evidence of the role transformation plays in shaping the whole project. *Genossin Kuckuck* is not only the result of a process of artistic transformation, but transformation is also a central principle of the storyworld of "Ein deutsches Tier im deutschen Wald." Drawing on memories as an ever fluid, transient material, the graphic novel's storyworld is in constant flux, i.e., in a constant process of passing and becoming that affects all aspects of this world – from historical events to characters and their bodies and the natural world surrounding them. The book feels less like a finished product and more like a series of snapshots of a project in flux. Feuchtenberger breaks down the barriers between different states of awareness, different modes of perception, and different states of being. The surreal that is a hallmark of many avant-garde movements and was a dominant feature in Feuchtenberger's earlier works such as *Somnambule* (1998) or *Die Hure h* (1996–2007), is here employed in a more constrained manner: Several episodes from the biographical and historical story arcs are mirrored in dreamlike, surreal scenes. Feuchtenberger creates a densely woven net of leitmotifs that provides readers with clues on how to navigate the fragmented memories and connects the 'realist' and 'surrealist' story arcs. Feuchtenberger's comics call into question images which we would otherwise readily accept as representations of 'reality.' In a self-reflexive mode, her images examine their own mode of production and the way they create (hi)story as they point to the medium's conditions and potentialities (Engelmann 11). The constant flux of the storyworld is also underscored by the non-linear storyline. In arranging the various layers of the story, Feuchtenberger does not let herself be restrained by a chronological timeline of events but follows patterns of association which might trigger memories. The discontinuity is paired with repetition.

Repetition is of course not specific to Feuchtenberger's comic art but a typical feature of the medium.[9] Feuchtenberger repeats scenes by separating cause and effect of an event in the story, or by showing us the same event from different perspectives. For instance, various stories within the storyworld of "Ein deutsches Tier im deutschen Wald" deal with pain and suffering passed on from generation to generation through the memory of transgenerational trauma. Yet resilience comes from the transformative forces of nature, and life's eternal cyclicality always returns balance to the world.[10] Before readers even enter the storyworld, Feuchtenberger establishes that she does not believe – in spite of her engagement with history and especially with historical violence against women – that she ought to tell history 'the way it really was'; she revokes the promise of closure that is so essential to sequential graphic narratives (Frahm 32), refusing to point to a message or identifiable meaning, instead stressing her subjective viewpoint and her perspective as a feminist.

Turning our attention to Feuchtenberger's creation of *Genossin Kuckuck*, it is important to note that she worked as usual without drafts or a storyboard. Citing Heinrich von Kleist's idea of the "allmähliche Verfertigung der Gedanken beim Reden" ("on the gradual production of thoughts while speaking") as one of her guiding principles, she experiments with various styles, various drawing materials and various forms of storytelling. As a result, story arcs and episodes within the project vary significantly in technique, style, and mode. Most notable is the constant alternation between the more fluid narrative style of episodes drawn in ink and the more static, still life-like charcoal images that are darkly evocative and brimming with an enclosed energy that give the final book its rhythm. By both stressing the fragmentary nature of memory and rejecting the conventions of the traditional novel, Feuchtenberger embraces a parodistic approach to the form and reveals rather than hides the bricolage character of the book.[11] She uses an unreliable narrator and creates a polyphonic narrative (Allen 14) that gives voice to many diverse characters. The different voices are hence never fully har-

---

9 As Jens Balzer has noted, a comic is built on repetition and variation. As a comic repeats a panel over and over while varying it, even the smallest graphic changes imply semantic changes (Balzer 176). Balzer and Martin tom Dieck have shown this in their graphic novel *Salut, Deleuze!* where the crossing of the river Styx plays out over and over again in variation.
10 Feuchtenberger has created narratives of those cycles of eternal transformation in other works, such as her adaptation of the story of the "Skeleton Woman" and the sexual violence against women she encoded into the majestic serenity of the Münster altar (Skelettfrau; Nijdam and Stuhlmann; Stuhlmann).
11 It would be interesting to compare *Genossin Kuckuck* with Dominique Goblet's *Faire semblant c'est mentir* (2007) and explore the obvious similarities in style, approach, and topic.

monious, and sometimes even offer competing truth claims. Across the storyworld, Feuchtenberger employs female focalization (Kupczyńska). As in her other works, most characters in this case are female, including the narrator, Kerstin, Effi, Rosi, the grandmother, the *Königin* Vontjanze and the dog, the Anatiden and the "Große Frau." The male characters include the Russian soldiers, Effe Erre/Jochen, and the father, "Waidgenosse" Metell. The latter all attempt to dominate the world through violence, while the women are more attuned to nature and its hidden powers. Yet in a world dominated by patriarchal power structures, women are inevitably both victims, accomplices, and sometimes even perpetrators of (physical and emotional) violence.

With regard to the sequencing of panels in a comic, Frahm reminds us, that it is the act of reading that places them into a "chrono-logical' order and not the appearance on the page where all panels are simultaneously present. Each new panel gives us a new image, its contents a new recombination of text and graphic elements which mimic and alter the previous image. Hence, following Linda Hutcheon, Frahm does not see the relation between panels as one of mimesis, but of parody (Frahm 37; Hutcheon 101). Hutcheon understands parody as performing a dual role within postmodern avant-garde literature: It informs a self-conscious, self-contradictory, self-undermining stance and is also present in a set of narrative features such as ironic quotation, pastiche, appropriation, or intertextuality (Hutcheon 1, 93 et passim). The same is true for Feuchtenberger's portrayal of her central characters. She constantly alters their appearance with every new variation of telling the story. With this fragmented, or "de-constructed" identity of her characters (Beckmann et al. 177), she rejects not only the notion of a single, unified personal identity but also the idea of an "essence" behind the visual and textual signifiers. The body that in a comic is always a parody, always fragmented, always present in multiple variations on the same page and never a stabile entity (Klar 224), is pushed to the extremes of a constant transformation in *Genossin Kuckuck.*

In the final analysis, Feuchtenberger calls into question the categories of "human" and "nonhuman," while examining the practices through which these boundaries are stabilized and destabilized (Barad 808; Rauchenbacher). To her, all creatures are equal. She subverts our accepted hierarchy of the natural world and removes humans from our presumed position of domination.[12] For instance, she draws humans with bear or raven heads and includes talking ducks and royal slugs. With the storyworld of *Genossin Kuckuck* in constant flux and metamorphosis, she is fascinated by states of being "in-between," by mushrooms that

---

[12] With Barad, Marina Rauchenbacher calls Feuchtenberger's approach "posthumanist." Cf. Rauchenbacher 14.

are neither animal nor plant, or by plasma that is neither solid, liquid, nor gas. A central image of the whole project that Feuchtenberger introduces early on is the slug. In the exposition, as Kerstin and Effi seal their pact for life, Effi calls Kerstin "die schönste Schneckenprinzessin" (*Genossin Kuckuck* 9, Fig. 1). "Schnecke," "Schneck," or "Schneckchen" are commonly used as terms of endearment in German (Grimm col. 1213). However, when Effi spends time with the boys at the bus stop, Kerstin becomes jealous and finds her "schleimig" (*Genossin Kuckuck* 97). Slugs are a hermaphrodite or intersexual species and some change their sex a few times during their life cycle and can be read as a sexually charged metaphor. As a slug invasion infests Pritschitanow, slugs representing oppressed or unregulated sexual desires appear all over the book.

III

As the remainder of this article will illustrate, the graphic novel *Genossin Kuckuck* exhibits its genesis as an assemblage, a vast intertextual network of visual, linguistic, textual, and cultural precursor texts and references, resembling a truly polyphonic intertextual cosmos (Allen 22, 29–30). Put differently, with its layers of memory and layers of the memories of its production, it can be read as a palimpsest.

As a metaphor for a text with various multilayered and previously produced texts, a palimpsest is employed as a narratological tool as well as in different models of intertexuality (Dillon 11; Allen 98–100). Palimpsests, understood both literally and metaphorically, give us access to different historical layers of a text and hence can concurrently contain multiple meanings. Exploring the palimpsest structure of Feuchtenberger's *Genossin Kuckuck*, we can begin at the material level. In an interview with Giordana Piccinini, Alessio Trabacchini, und Emilio Varrà, Feuchtenberger described her process working with charcoal:

> Das Zeichnen mit Kohle zum Beispiel ist sehr sinnlich. Es ist wie Staub. Es erzeugt sofort einen Raum, Licht. Ich kann korrigieren, bis die Zeichnung erscheint, die schon vorher auf dem Papier war, zumindest scheint mir das so. Da ich viel korrigiere, waren unter manchen Zeichnungen schon andere, und das gefällt mir, sogar die Haut hat eine Transparenz, mit vielen Schichten. Du siehst nicht, was darunter ist, aber du fühlst etwas Komplexes. (Piccinini, Trabacchini, and Varrà 75)

Since Feuchtenberger never works with drafts, each individual drawing already resembles a palimpsest, as it contains the traces of previous versions. Furthermore, the fragmented, bricolage structure of the narrative indicates the palimpsest-like structure of the book as a whole. To explore its composition, I will look

Fig. 1: Anke Feuchtenberger, *Genossin Kuckuck*, p. 9.[13]

---

13 I am immensely grateful to Alexandra Rügler and Dirk Rehm at Reprodukt, Berlin, for their generous help with the illustrations.

at several episodes from the storyworld of "Ein Deutsches Tier im deutschen Wald" that Feuchtenberger extracted from the project for other publications between 2011 and 2014 and later re-integrated into the final book *Genossin Kuckuck*, namely (1) *grano blue*, a folio comic album from 2011 that contains four scenes, (2) the short story "Effi redet Blech" published in *Orang* in 2013, (3) "Die Königin Vontjanze," a small pamphlet to accompany an exhibition, and (4) a cycle of drawings Feuchtenberger contributed to a new edition of Kleist's *Marquise von O . . .*, also published in 2014. A review of these four intertexts will show how Feuchtenberger constructed the final book, *Genossin Kuckuck*, out of existing material and how she employs themes and leitmotifs, carefully crafting and structuring her storyworld.

(1) One previously published work that stems from the story world of "Ein deutsches Tier" and is later integrated in *Genossin Kuckuck* is the thirty-two-page folio-size album *grano blu* published by Canicola in Bologna in 2011. The album features four different scenes from the storyworld of "Ein deutsches Tier im deutschen Wald," all of them linked to the mysterious "grano blu," blue beads that themselves are connected to the supernatural, spiritual or surreal narrative level of the project.

The first scene, drawn in simple ink, focuses on the relationship between Kerstin and her brother Effe Erre, later renamed Jochen. Effe Erre is drawn as a tall, athletic man with a hairy body and a completely bald head. The caption to his vignette at the frontispiece reads "Der große alte Effe Erre, schön wie eine geschälte Lärche, lebt nun enthaltsam. Er ist stark, bewältigt das allein" (*grano blu* 1). It is unclear whether "enthaltsam" here means "celibate" or "temperate" and whether it refers to his previous sexual promiscuity or his drug consumption. The episode juxtaposes Effe Erre's hard physical work on a farm with Kerstin's mysterious transformation when she multiplies as she steps into the village pond.

The second episode from *grano blu*, seven splash pages in charcoal with small text boxes above and below the drawings, begins with three images. We see an empty hallway, a telephone on a wall, and a line of telephone poles along a country road with wind turbines in the background, locating the episode in the present. The next four panels feature a group of three young women in identical outfits, part dress, part uniform, and part habit (Fig. 2). From the text, we learn that an emergency call has summoned them from 'the home' to rescue the survivors of the village's summer party by the river. Dried up and bloated, people have turned into grey, sluggish, amorphous blobs after the consumption of the mysterious substance "grano blu."

FÜR ZWEI VON UNS WAR ES DAS ERSTE MAL. DIE ÄLTESTE ALLERDINGS WUSSTE, WAS ZU TUN WAR.

Fig. 2: Anke Feuchtenberger, *Genossin Kuckuck*, p. 88.

The third and last section of *grano blu* consists of twenty-three pages with four panels per spread, in a similar, but more elaborate and intricate ink than the first. The story alternates between two episodes: (a) A letter Effi wrote to Kerstin from a mysterious home for girls, and (b) Effe Erre's war on slugs in his yard. In her letter, Effi tells Kerstin about her reluctant adaptation to life at 'the home.' Shifting the focalization, the letter is written from the perspective of a somewhat precocious girl who does not fully understand where she is, why she is being punished, and what is happening with her. The girls, including Effi, are depicted here as little children, a portrayal that is at odds with earlier depictions of Effi as a teenager, and with her covertly sexually-charged activities. Even though Feuchtenberger changes Effi's body into that of a child, there is no return for her to a state of innocence given what has been done to her through violence, drugs and indoctrination. Effi tells Kerstin about the preparations for the grand annual ceremony to be held down by the river. The girls practice "innere Einkehr" (*grano blu* 21) by lying on their backs with their legs pushed upwards and spread and also engage in "Plasma singen" (*grano blu* 23), an intimate physical dialogue in which the two girls spew a bubbly substance.[14] When on good behavior, the girls are allowed to play in the garden where they devour the lavishly growing butterbur and sometimes find "Körnchen (. . .) von einem wunderbaren Blau" (*grano blu* 22). Whatever the mysterious mission of the 'home' may be, it appears that the girls' chubby children's bodies are slowly transforming into slugs.

In the alternating fourth scene, as an invasion of slugs plagues the village's gardeners, Effe Erre, otherwise reformed and sober, resorts to drastic measures. Since burning them does not defeat the slugs, a neighbor recommends blue fertilizer, but to Effe Erre's disgust, the slugs killed by the chemical are just greedily eaten up by their sisters who just keep on multiplying. Changing into a beautifully crocheted dress made by the "Irish students" at the "convent" for Kerstin (*grano blu* 28), Effe Erre eventually shows off his feminine side and turns to use ducks as a natural defense against the slugs.

When Feuchtenberger adapted *grano blu* for *Genossin Kuckuck*, she turned the four scenes recounted above into five chapters of the novel. In chapter two, after being bullied by Effi, Kerstin runs into the woods and dives into the pond, summoning the mythological "Große Frau" with her cuckoo-call (*Genossin Kuckuck* 22). In chapter seven, Jochen tosses his sister into the pond while she attempts to release slug eggs because she had tried to strong-arm him into taking the blame for a teapot which she accidentally broke. But instead of crying for help, Kerstin just quietly and majestically floats away (*Genossin Kuckuck* 76).

Chapter 9 of *Genossin Kuckuck* features the seven charcoal splash pages mentioned above and we now recognize the hallway and the phone from the home that Rosi built after German reunification. The chapter also now identifies the three uniformed women as "Anatiden" – anatidae being the biological family of ducks who take care of the poisoned, sluggish villagers. Chapter 11 includes Effe Erre's war on the slugs and is entitled "Arioniden" (meaning "Slugs"). In Chapter 12, "Das Kleid," Feuchtenberger made one change of note: The dress which in *grano blue* was crocheted by Irish students is now the one Kerstin's grandmother had worked on but never finished while waiting for Kerstin's return (*Genossin*

---

14 The texture of plasma also refers to Kerstin's observation of Effi becoming "schleimig" whenever she spends time with the boys.

Kuckuck 112–113). The dress, just as in Homer's *Odyssey*, becomes a powerful, multilayered metaphor not just for Effe Erre/Jochen's transformation, but for the fabric of a kinship that has complicated patterns of belonging and appropriation, of care, kindness, hope and faith woven into it.

(2) As mentioned above, another earlier work that Feuchtenberger integrated into *Genossin Kuckuck* is a twenty-page story entitled "Effi redet Blech," which appeared in the comic magazine *Orang* in January 2013. Here, Feuchtenberger tells the story of Kerstin and Effi's eventual falling out. Effi Mettel is "schon entwickelt" ("Blech" 44) and the physical changes of their bodies, both equally desired and feared, open up a rift between the girls. Effi, who hates to be groped by her father's Russian hunting friends, now prefers to spend time with the boys at the bus stop, especially with Kerstin's brother Effe Erre.[15] Since Kerstin does not understand what Effi both is trying to and avoiding to tell her, Kerstin perceives Effi as talking nonsense, "[sie] redet Blech," as the expression goes. Metal appears in the story not only in the wordplay that makes up Effi's name. A brass keychain made in socialist Poland for export to both East and West lands first in Effe Erre's hands and is passed on to Effi, eventually becoming a key piece of evidence for Effi's sexual abuse, just like the brass of the medals on the chests of the Russian visitors and the trinkets they bring as presents. Even though the story is told retrospectively, the narrative focalization is once again close to Kerstin's naive perspective as a child. As a result, readers must piece together the story just as she does. Soon afterwards, Effi becomes "träge und abwesend" ("Blech" 57), which alerts Kerstin's grandmother, a stalwart comrade and champion of German-Russian friendship, to prompt Effi to confide in her. Soon after the confidential talk, Effi disappears. The entire story "Effi redet Blech" was included in *Genossin Kuckuck* with only minor adjustments as its fifteenth chapter. The episode shows Feuchtenberger on the one hand as a master comic short storyteller, but it is also a key sequence of the graphic novel as it unlocks the secrets surrounding the end of Kerstin's and Effi's friendship and alludes to why and how Effi was sent away.

(3) A third previously published work included in *Genossin Kuckuck* is the short story *Die Königin Vontjanze* from 2014[16] which features 18 large charcoal drawings in a hyperrealist style similar to the charcoal series in *grano blu*. The images

---

[15] The theme of sexual abuse runs through the whole book; women (and also men) of different generations are subjected to such abuse, but Feuchtenberger never addresses it explicitly.

[16] This was Feuchtenberger's contribution to the 2014 exhibition "MUMMY" that opened the Hamburg Comic Festival. Feuchtenberger and Stefano Ricci had invited five other comic artists, Anton Engel, Jul Gordon, Magdalena Kaszuba, Gosia Machon, and Birgit Weyhe, to contribute to a show that explored the possibilities of narrative, figurative, and poetic drawing. The works

appear to include autobiographical aspects as we seem to recognize tokens of Feuchtenberger's personal life in the countryside in Western Pomerania: an old country house, a dog, and the portrait of a small child. These images are contrasted with scenes of wildlife, more precisely of spiders and slugs – and it is one particularly noble slug, the regal "Königin Vontjanze," that becomes the main protagonist. We follow her slow, somewhat laborious journey from the butterbur plantation by the river across the sun-soaked stone slabs of the village's old parade square. "Sie wiegt anmutig grüßend ihr Köpfchen hin und her" (*Vontjanze* 4), as if the slug were taking a royal salute. Her body glistens majestically, especially when she slides over the "verkohlten Klümpchen (. . .) der letzten Verbrennung" (*Vontjanze* 3, see Fig. 3). As the focus of the narrator zooms in on the slug, we enter a world of strange beauty. Feuchtenberger fills the whole page with the animal's round, soft, and otherworldly body; it appears gigantic and simultaneously repulsive and gorgeous (see Fig. 3). Eight pages later, we see the broken body of a dead slug. The text box above it reads: "Effe Erre, angesichts der Schönheit [of the royal slug, A.S.], bittet um Vergebung für das gestrige Massaker" (*Vontjanze* 11). Only readers of *grano blu* will be able to decode the reference to Effe Erre's failed attempt of massacring the slugs by using fire and poison. But here, Effe Erre never enters the picture. Instead, the dog, as the human's companion and part of both the human and the natural world, stands in for him and seems to mimic Effe Erre's suspicious gaze as it intently watches the royal slug (*Vontjanze* 12).[17] Then, as if to fulfill an unspoken command from its master, the dog suddenly lunges forward and, with one quick bite, kills the innocent, helpless beauty (*Vontjanze* 16), before it spits it out (17). The short story "Königin Vontjanze" also functions as an introduction to the story arc of surreal episodes in the novel in which we enter the world of slugs, mushrooms and constant metamorphosis that mirrors and complements the main protagonists.

(4) We now turn to a series of drawings Feuchtenberger created in 2013 for a new illustrated edition of three of Heinrich von Kleist's most prominent novellas, including *Die Marquise von O . . .*, for which she was commissioned by Büchergilde Gutenberg. The intent was to contrast the familiar stories with contemporary, distinctly different visual representations. Feuchtenberger includes these drawings about Kleists's novella in the coda ("Nachtrag") of *Genossin Kuckuck* which is the section of the book in which the themes of violence, history, patriarchy, and

---

were documented in seven small brochures published by Ricci's and Feuchtenberger's MamiVerlag, among them "Die Königin Vontjanze."

17 Lena Winkel has written an insightful piece on the central role dogs play in Feuchtenberger's work. Cf. Winkel.

Fig. 3: Anke Feuchtenberger, *Genossin Kuckuck*, pp. 226–227.

transgenerational trauma are most poignant. Kleist had been a long-time but always problematic artistic dialogue partner for Feuchtenberger, notwithstanding the fact that she had also wrestled with the multiple ways in which (patriarchal) power and (male) violence shape and damage bodies, minds, and souls through discursive practices in his works. "Seit Jahren," Feuchtenberger states in her introduction,[18] "tauchen in meinen Bildern Links zu Kleist auf" ("Anmerkungen" 1). Feuchtenberger chose to include ten large scale charcoal drawings which very clearly tell their own story within a 'silent' graphic narrative, a comic without words (Lamothe) interspersed into Kleist's novella. Neither the time period in which Feuchtenberger sets her story nor her cast of characters reference Kleist's novella. Some images are realistically drawn, and they seem to depict a German village in the mid-1940s. We see a woman with paperwork at a table, men in a rubble-filled street with their hands raised above their heads, two grieving women covering their mouths, and two infants in a crib. The surreal here is present in images of a Russian soldier riding down a flight of stairs as a winged demon on a four-legged cock; or in an image of a couple in front of a collapsed building who are joined by an injured man wrapped in bandages from head to toe like a mummy.

---

[18] Feuchtenberger, „Anmerkungen zur Arbeit an der *Marquise von O . . . .*" (2014). Hereafter referred to as "Anmerkungen."

While Feuchtenberger sympathizes with Kleist as the victim of a brutal Prussian military education[19] she also cites the callous distich he published in *Phöbus* in April 1808 that shows Kleist was aware that he used sexual violence as a bait for readers' attention.[20] Feuchtenberger questions Kleist's empathy with the victim here, not despite, but because of his own traumatic experience as a child: While Kleist might have been "ohnmächtig," or powerless, at the hands of his training officers, he mocks the "Ohnmacht," the shocked fainting, of a female reader faced with the violence he portrays. Feuchtenberger hence decides to contrast the text of Kleist's novella with images of stories revolving around the post-war situation in East Germany in 1945, in particular the violence during and after Nazi Germany's liberation committed by the Russian army. Drawing on accounts by her mother and grandmother, she "verlegte (. . .) das Geschehen der *Marquise von O* . . . in diese Zeit" ("Anmerkungen" 1). Using the verb "verlegen," which in German can also mean "to misplace," Feuchtenberger never situates her story exclusively in one particular time and place but rather takes the liberty to leap "in großen Sprüngen" ("Anmerkungen" 2) back and forth between different times and places. Both in Kleist's novella and in her own family's stories she detected suppressed, unarticulated feelings, "Gefühle des Zorns über die Ungerechtigkeit" and the desire for "heimliche Rache" ("Anmerkungen" 2) locked away with these memories. Feuchtenberger worries what this trauma might have meant for the children born into this brutality: "Ich glaube, beim Lesen der Erzählung und beim Zeichnen permanent das wütende Schweigen der Frauen aus der Generation meiner Großmutter zu hören. Das glückliche Ende ist nur eine papierne Oberfläche über dem unterirdischen Brodeln. Wie immer bei Kleist" ("Anmerkungen" 2).[21]

When she eventually included her "illustrations" of Kleist's novella in *Genossin Kuckuck*, the images appear in sequence and become hence readable as a graphic story. Placing this story of violence against women in the post-WWII period at the end of the book, as a "Nachtrag," Feuchtenberger adds a special emphasis to it, as if handing her readers a key to a deeper understanding of the en-

---

[19] This can be seen in the following quote: "Spätestens als 14-Jähriger muss Kleist erzieherische Gewalt durch die preußische Kadettenanstalt ohnmächtig erlebt haben" ("Anmerkungen" 1).
[20] "Dieser Roman ist nicht für dich, meine Tochter. In Ohnmacht! Schamlose Posse! Sie hielt, weiß ich, die Augen bloß zu" (Kleist 62).
[21] Feuchtenberger's illustrations of Kleist's novella also echo a very different work of art of hers, namely an altar, which she created for the *Museum des Landschaftsverbandes Westfalen-Lippe* in Münster in 2018. The museum had invited her to design and build a response to one of its most famous pieces, the massive winged altar by the so-called Schöppinger Master (around 1470). Accepting the commission, Feuchtenberger was adamant to shift the focus of her piece to a female sensibility and perspective, placing the plight of women, especially sexual violence and rape during wartime, at the center of her work.

tire graphic novel. The introductory text to the "Nachtrag" suggests that the images that follow are to be read as a collection of artwork, "selbst gemalt" (*Genossin Kuckuck* 433) by Rosi, the mother, who hung them in the hallway of the retirement home she built. As readers, we have already 'seen' them before, when in Chapter 4 Frank Sternemann and Torsten Greiff are visiting the home.[22] Yet, when Torsten pauses in the hallway to study them, the frames on the wall are blank (*Genossin Kuckuck* 41). This picture gallery thereby echoes another lost archive in the book, namely a photo album that Kerstin's grandmother kept for her and that Torsten and Frank steal and eventually destroy when they visit the retirement home looking for clues as to why they were institutionalized as teenagers. Here, in the coda, Rosi gives Kerstin a tour of her art, and the texts Feuchtenberger adds in the gutters between the panels provide Rosi's commentary. Thus, the images become a gallery of Rosi's memories and help both Kerstin and the readers understand Rosi better as a traumatized and conflicted character. She claims that the first image of the woman at work at the table which readers of Kleist's novella might have interpreted as a depiction of the *Marquise von O . . .* , is rather a self-portrait of her, Rosi, as a young woman. In the third panel with the image of the cock-rider, Rosi comments: "Wir Frauen hatten uns alle im Keller versteckt. Danach durften wir 40 Jahre nicht darüber reden. Die Russen waren ja unsere Befreier" (*Genossin Kuckuck* 434). This is a literal echo of an earlier panel that had originally appeared in the story "Effi redet Blech": We see two women facing each other as one paints a smear of coal dust on the other's face to make her less attractive to Russian soldiers looking to rape girls and women.[23] The text above and below the panel reads (in Kerstin's voice): "Zu der Geschichte von den Mädchen, denen die Röcke über dem Kopf zusammengebunden waren, gehören auch mit Ruß beschmierte Gesichter und schwarz gefärbte Zähne. / Die Großmutter sagt, dass es sie selbst nicht erwischt hat. Und überhaupt seien die Russen doch unsere Freunde" (*Genossin Kuckuck* 143). Like Kleist's text, both Feuchtenberger's words and her images are elliptical. The few sentences, just like the image, leave out the actual traumatic event of the rape.

Both in Kleist's as well as in Feuchtenberger's story, Russian soldiers are the perpetrators, and the rape they committed is neither addressed nor brought to jus-

---

22 The two men's last names are an explicit reference to Kleist's life. The two physicians *Kreisphysikus* Dr. Sternemann and *Chirurgus forensis* Greif performed the autopsies of Heinrich von Kleist and Henriette Vogel in December 1811 (Cf. Minde-Pouet 51–53).
23 The image from "Eiffi redet Blech" in turn echoes a similar one in an earlier short story by Feuchtenberger entitled "Alte Rose," reprinted in *Die Spaziergängerin* on page 21 – which shows many similarities to scenes from *Genossin Kuckuck* and might also provide a clue to how Rosie received her name.

Fig. 4a: Anke Feuchtenberger, Heinrich von Kleist, *Die Marquise von O . . .*, p. 186.

tice (Dutoit). Rosi's words here echo Feuchtenberger's reference to the "wütendes Schweigen" of her own grandmother's generation. The caption to the panel showing the two women silently covering their mouths in pain reads accordingly: "Wir hatten es ja selbst erlebt, oder mit angesehen" (*Genossin Kuckuck* 435).

Allowing the coda to establish its own rhythm, Feuchtenberger changes the sequence and the size of the images from those in her Kleist story. One major change occurs midway through the sequence when she replaces one image with another. The sixth image of her Kleist story shows three characters at a table. One the left side, the image shows an older man in a three-piece suit, turning his head to the left and looking up to a younger woman. Opposite them we see an older woman with braided hair, but without a body, her hands floating above the table with a torn string of pearls in front of her (see Fig. 4a). In *Genossin Kuckuck*, however, the woman in the scene on the right has a full human body but the head of a raven, wears a black dress, and has a large egg in front of her (see Fig. 4b). The latter image evokes the concept of the proverbial *Rabenmutter*, a term used in German to describe a supposedly callous, cruel, or 'unnatural' mother. In an interview, Feuchtenberger pointed to her own more lenient view of a "Rabenmutter" as opposed to a "Kuckucksmutter" who, at least in the world of birds, acts far more cruelly by refusing to raise her chicks herself (Gottschalk). In the caption to this panel, Rosi states that she did not want any children. Yet when the newly founded German Democratic Republic urged woman to help secure the future of Socialism, she relented and had a child. As a possible witness, if not a victim herself of rape and violence committed by Russian soldiers, Rosi passes down her trauma to her

Fig. 4b: Anke Feuchtenberger, *Genossin Kuckuck*, p. 436.

daughter Effi who herself becomes a victim of sexual assault. Just like in Kleist's story, Rosi has Effi sent away to a "home" to avoid shaming the family. In *Genossin Kuckuck*, Feuchtenberger deletes the last two images of her Kleist story, so that the final image of the "Nachtrag" is the one of the two infants in the crib. The caption reads: "In der Wochenkrippe haben sie dich und Effi immer zusammen spielen lassen. Ihr wart viel draussen" (*Genossin Kuckuck* 438). Here, too, the happy ending is just "papierne Oberfläche über dem unterirdischen Brodeln" ("Anmerkungen" 2), as Feuchtenberger stated in her above comment on Kleist.

IV

To conclude, uncovering the palimpsest-like structure of *Genossin Kuckuck* allows us to understand the complex and protracted composition of the book. The various story arcs and episodes connected by themes and leitmotifs are both aligned with and parodying the compositional technique of the great modernist novel. As this article has shown, the project of *Genossin Kuckuck* is both rooted in and connected with a complex network of previous texts in Feuchtenberger's oeuvre. Not only does the book transcend the vast majority of contemporary German graphic novels in scope and ambition, it also occupies a singular place within the German contemporary literary landscape and proves that the feminist avant-garde of the 1990s continues to energize the genre of the comic.

Works Cited

Allen, Graham, *Intertextuality*. Routledge, 2000.

Alt, Herschel and Edith Alt. *The New Soviet Man. His Upbringing and Character Development*. Bookman, 1964.

Goethe Institut. "Anke Feuchtenberger: Surreale Bilderwelten." *Goethe Institut*, goethe.de/ins/lv/de/kul/sup/com/20477753.html?forceDesktop=1. 15 May 2025.

Balzer, Jens. "Differenz und Wiederholung: Von Tintin zu den Oubapoten," *Schreibheft: Zeitschrift für Literatur*, no. 51, 1998, pp. 175–177.

Barad, Karen. "Posthumanist Performativity: Toward an Understanding of How Matter Comes to Matter." *Signs*, vol. 28, no. 3, 2003, pp. 801–831.

Beckmann, Anna, et al. "de_konstruierte Identität. Aushandlungen von gender in der *Hure h* von Anke Feuchtenberger und Kathrin (sic!) de Vries." *Comics an der Grenze: Sub/Versionen von Form und Inhalt*, edited by Matthias Harbeck, Linda-Rabea Heyden, and Marie Schröer, Bachmann, 2017, pp. 165–178.

Dillon, Sarah. *The Palimpsest: Literature, Criticism, Theory*. Bloomsbury Academic, 2007.

Dutoit, Thomas. "Rape, Crypt, Fantasm: Kleist's Marquise of O . . . ." *Mosaic*, vol. 27, no. 3, 1994, pp. 45–64.

Engelmann, Jonas. *Gerahmter Diskurs – Gesellschaftsbilder im Independent-Comic*. Ventil, 2013.

Erll, Astrid. *Memory in Culture*. Palgrave Macmillan, 2011.

Feuchtenberger, Anke, and Katrin de Vries. *Die Hure h*. Jochen Enterprises, 1996,

Feuchtenberger, Anke, and Katrin de Vries. *Die Hure h zieht ihre Bahne*n. Edition Moderne, 2003.

Feuchtenberger, Anke. *Die Skelettfrau. Nach einem Märchen der Inuit*. Büchergilde Gutenberg, 2002.

Feuchtenberger, Anke, and Katrin de Vries. *Die Hure h wirf den Handschuh*. Reprodukt, 2007.

Feuchtenberger, Anke. *wehwehweh.superträne.de*. MamiVerlag, 2008.

Feuchtenberger, Anke. *grano blu*. Canicola, 2011.

Feuchtenberger, Anke. *Die Spaziergängerin*, Reprodukt, 2012.

Feuchtenberger, Anke. "Alte Rose." *Die Spaziergängerin*, Reprodukt, 2012, pp. 17–25.

Feuchtenberger, Anke. "Effi redet Blech." *Orang*, no. 10, ed. Sascha Hommer, 2013, pp. 38–57.

Feuchtenberger, Anke. *Die Königin Vontjanze*. MUMMY Series, no. 5, MamiVerlag, 2014.

Feuchtenberger, Anke. "Anmerkungen zur Arbeit an der *Marquise von O* . . . ." *Michael Kohlhaas. Die Marquise von O . . . Der Findling*. By Heinrich von Kleist, illustrated by *Johannes Grützke, Anke Feuchtenberger, and Martin Grobecker*, Büchergilde Gutenberg, 2014.

Feuchtenberger, Anke, and Katrin de Vries. *Die Hure h*. (complete edition) Reprodukt, 2022.

Feuchtenberger, Anke, and Katrin de Vries. *W the Whore*. Translated by Mark Nevins. New York Review Books, 2023.

Feuchtenberger, Anke (as Feuchtenbergerowa). *Genossin Kuckuck*. Reprodukt, 2023.

Feuchtenberger, Anke. *Camarade Coucou*. Translated by Monique Rival. Futuropolis, 2024.

Frahm, Ole. *Die Sprache des Comics*. Philo Fine Arts, 2010.

Gasser, Christian. "Mutantenkosmos. Von Mickey Mouse zu Explomaus." *Mutanten: Die deutschsprachige Comic-Avantgarde der 90er Jahre*, edited by Christian Gasser, Hatje Cantz, 1999, pp. 5–18.

Gordon, Jul, Brigitte Helbling, Magdalena Kaszuba, and Birgit Weyhe, editors. *Tandem – in Class with Anke Feuchtenberger*. MamiVerlag, 2023.

Gottschalk, Katrin. "Zeichnen ist immer auch Staunen." *taz*, taz.de/Illustratorin-Anke-Feuchtenberger/!5998015/. 29 March 2024.

Heers, Andre. "Lebende Schrift: Anke Feuchtenbergers Typographie." *Die Königin Vontjanze: Kleiner Atlas zum Werk von Anke Feuchtenberger*, edited by Andreas Stuhlmann and Ole Frahm, textem, 2023, pp. 79–80.

Helbling, Brigitte. *"Orang X: Heavy Metal* – Aufhören, wenn's am Schönsten ist." *ComicLitMag*, 3 April 2013, culturmag.de/litmag/orang-x-heavy-metal/68904, 25 November 2024.

Hoffmann, Jule. "Menschen und Tiere im Sozialismus." *Deutschlandfunk Kultur*, Studio 9, 20 September 2023, https://bilder.deutschlandfunk.de/4c/c9/a3/f3/4cc9a3f3-fb08-441d-badf-08df7bcec34f/anke-feuchtenberger-genossin-kuckuck-ein-deutsches-tier-im-deutschen-wald-100.pdf. 6 December 2024.

Hutcheon, Linda. *The Politics of Postmodernism*. Routledge, 1989.

Klar, Elisabeth. "Wir sind alle Superhelden! Über die Eigenart des Körpers im Comic – und über die Lust an ihm." *Theorien des Comics: Ein Reader*, edited by Barbara Eder, Elisabeth Klar, and Ramón Reichert, Transcript, 2011, pp. 219–236.

Kleist, Heinrich von. *Der Dichter über sein Werk*, edited by Helmut Sembdner, 2nd ed., Wissenschaftliche Buchgesellschaft, 1996.

Knoben, Martina. "Das geht auf die Knochen. Die Comickünstlerin Anke Feuchtenberger im Porträt." *Süddeutsche Zeitung*, 19 March 2024.

Koopmann, Jan-Paul. "Graphic Novel *Genossin-Kuckuck*: Traum und Trauma." *taz*, 28 September 2023.

Kupczyńska, Kalina. "Gendern Comics, wenn sie erzählen? Über einige Aspekte der Gender-Narratologie und ihre Anwendung in der Comic-Analyse." *Bild ist Text ist Bild: Narration und Ästhetik in der Graphic Novel*, edited by Susanne Hochreiter and Ursula Klingenböck, Transcript, 2014, pp. 213–232.

Lamothe, John. "Speaking Silently." *Studies in Popular Culture*, vol. 41, no. 2, 2019, pp. 69–94.

Minde-Pouet, Georg. *Kleists letzte Stunden. Teil 1: Das Akten-Material*. Weidmann, 1925.

Müller, Burkhard. "Das Erwachen des Mond-Dämons." *Mutanten: Die deutschsprachige Comic-Avantgarde der 90er Jahre*, edited by Christian Gasser, Hatje Cantz, 1999, pp. 99–108.

Nijdam, Elisabeth. *Drawing for me means communication: Anke Feuchtenberger and German Art Comics after 1989*. 2017. University of Michigan, PhD Thesis, deepblue.lib.umich.edu/handle/2027.42/140838. 6 December 2024.

Nijdam, Elisabeth and Andreas Stuhlmann. "Anke Feuchtenberger's *Die Skelettfrau* (2002): Between Indigenous Storytelling, Cultural Appropriation, and Comics Translation." *Die Königin Vontjanze: Kleiner Atlas zum Werk von Anke Feuchtenberger*, edited by Andreas Stuhlmann and Ole Frahm, textem, 2023, pp. 137–150.

Piccinini, Giordana, Alessio Trabacchini, and Emilio Varrà. "Neue Formen der Schönheit: Ein Interview mit Anke Feuchtenberger." *Die Königin Vontjanze: Kleiner Atlas zum Werk von Anke Feuchtenberger*, edited by Andreas Stuhlmann and Ole Frahm, textem, 2023, pp. 59–77.

Rauchenbacher, Marina. "Comics – posthuman, queer-end, um_un-ordnend." *Genealogy+Critique*, vol. 8, no. 1, 2022, pp. 1–27.

Schjeldahl, Peter. "Words and Pictures: Graphic Novels Come of Age." *The New Yorker*, 17 October 2005, pp. 162–168.

"Schneckchen." *Deutsches Wörterbuch von Jacob Grimm und Wilhelm Grimm*, vol. 15, col. 1213, *Wörterbuchnetz*, Trier Center for Digital Humanities, version 01/23, woerterbuchnetz.de/DWB. 6 December 2024.

Sternburg, Judith von. "Anke Feuchtenberger: *Genossin Kuckuck* – Auf der Spur von Schneckchen." *Frankfurter Rundschau*, 15 March 2024.

Stillich, Sven. "Hinter der Angst leuchtet die Freiheit." *Die Zeit*, 28 September 2023.

Stuhlmann, Andreas. "Ein Triptychon von Tracht und Bleiche: Anke Feuchtenbergers Altar als Intervention für das Leben." *Die Königin Vontjanze: Kleiner Atlas zum Werk von Anke Feuchtenberger*, edited by Andreas Stuhlmann and Ole Frahm, textem, 2023, pp. 157–172.

Stuhlmann, Andreas and Ole Frahm. *Die Königin Vontjanze: Kleiner Atlas zum Werk von Anke Feuchtenberger*. textem, 2023.

tom Dieck, Martin and Jens Balzer. *Salut, Deleuze!* Arrache Cœur, 1997.

Winkel, Lena. "Hunde höflich zeichnen. Reflexiver Anthropomorphismus im Werk von Anke Feuchtenberger." *Die Königin Vontjanze: Kleiner Atlas zum Werk von Anke Feuchtenberger*, edited by Andreas Stuhlmann and Ole Frahm, textem, 2023, pp. 173–183.

II **Einzelanalysen/Individual Analyses**

Katrin Sieg
"Theater of Ir/reconciliation: Empathy and Anger in Decolonial Theater"

Abstract: This article examines the play *Hereroland* (2019–2023), in which German and Namibian performers jointly wrestled with German colonial violence and tackled questions of postcolonial reconciliation, reparations, and repair. *Hereroland* demonstrates that theater can function as both the agent and the site of decolonization, revealing the ways in which the colonial past is negotiated and the decolonial future imagined collectively. The play's two iterations illuminate distinctive approaches to inviting audiences into political allyship in Germany and Namibia. Immersive techniques serve to emotionally involve spectators in both versions, but the tone shifts from empathy with Ovaherero demands for reparations in the Hamburg production, to anger about stalled decolonization in the Namibian version. I ask about the reasons and the consequences of that shift and argue that the play's insistence on holding open a space of irreconciliation is a rare, yet all the more important and instructive instance in decolonial theater.

The Joint Declaration by the Federal Republic of Germany and the Republic of Namibia of 2021, which had been negotiated over six years by representatives of the German and Namibian governments, specifies the terms of a public apology and compensation payments for the killing of an estimated 80% of Ovahereros and 50% of Namas between 1904 and 1908 in what was then the colony of German-Southwest Africa. In 2015, the German government had first recognized this event as a genocide. Once published, the Declaration was immediately criticized by stakeholders in both countries. Behind the mask of shared dialogue and mutual agreement, observers critical of Germany detected not only arrogance but also "a soft version of denialism" (Melber 169), which admitted to genocide but separated an apology from reparations, precluding true reconciliation. Purportedly including all affected parties, the negotiations excluded traditional Ovaherero and Nama leaders, foregoing the opportunity to foster public reckoning and

---

Note: I wish to express my gratitude to Gernot Grünewald, Jörg Pohl, Lizette Kavari, and Gift Uzera, who spoke to me about both iterations of *Hereroland*. Thank you to the Thalia Theater for making recordings and other materials available. I deeply appreciate Barbara Mennel and Lauren van der Rede for reading and commenting on early versions of this article, as well as the two anonymous reviewers. I also wish to express my regret that due to the vagaries of international financial transactions, I was unable to obtain permission to publish photos of the Namibian production.

∂ Open Access. © 2025 the author(s), published by De Gruyter. [cc) BY-NC-ND] This work is licensed under the Creative Commons Attribution-NonCommercial-NoDerivatives 4.0 International License.
https://doi.org/10.1515/9783112218631-010

community healing, while prioritizing German interests and perpetuating asymmetric power relations. Those intergovernmental negotiations were denounced for their lack of transparency and the exclusion of civil society groups in both countries (van Wyck 2021; Zimmerer 2024a). The secretive, exclusionary procedure aimed at a settlement of damages that limits future obligations. Due to civil society pressure the Namibian government reopened negotiations and a modified draft of the Joint Declaration was published in July 2024. While it made some improvements, the lack of inclusion and transparency was not rectified (Zimmerer 2024a).[1] The Joint Declaration contradicts the colonial memory culture that has tentatively emerged in both countries in recent years.

Things appear to be afoot in Germany as far as recognizing colonial wrongdoing is concerned.[2] Over the past decade, the efforts of museums to repatriate human remains and colonial artifacts have generated much scholarly and public attention. They have started to challenge postcolonial scholars' earlier accusation of "colonial amnesia" (El-Tayeb; Kößler). However, museums are not the only cultural institutions now keen to facilitate a critical reckoning with Germany's colonial past. In particular, plays and performances offer new opportunities for Germans and people from the former colonies to jointly confront a painful history. This article examines the play *Hereroland*, a coproduction of Thalia Theater, Hamburg, and the National Theater of Namibia, Windhoek, which premiered in Hamburg in January 2020, as an alternative forum for negotiating postcolonial relations. It is, to my knowledge, one of the first critical, full-length theatrical representations of the colonial genocide presented on the German stage, and the first to be performed in both Germany and Namibia.[3]

---

1 For instance, the offending phrase "from today's perspective" was removed from the affirmation that a genocide had taken place. Payments are now couched as "atonement" rather than development funds and increased by an unspecified amount, with a portion to be paid upfront.

2 In particular, the decade-long controversy surrounding the monumental Humboldt Forum in central Berlin, which opened in 2021 and houses part of the Ethnology Museum's collection of non-European material culture, put questions of colonial-era hoarding, the Berlin Republic's relations to the Global South in an era of increasing inequality and mass migration, and what Germany owes those it has plundered front and center. For a short survey of the evolving colonial memory culture in Germany, see Rogers.

3 In 2019, the documentary play *Herero_Nama*, whose cast included a Herero and Nama activist, premiered at Schauspiel Köln, under the direction of Turkish-German artist Nuran David Calis. Outside Germany, there are several significant artworks created by a South African artist, a South African director, and an African American playwright, respectively, that tackle the subject: William Kentridge's installation *Black Box/Chambre Noire* (2005) and the controversial performance installation *Exhibit_B* by white South African artist Brett Bailey (2010) were both shown in Germany. U.S. playwright Jackie Sibblies Drury's *We are Proud to Present a Presentation of the Herero of Namibia, formerly German Southwestafrica, Between the Years 1884–1915* (2012) was not.

My contention is that *Hereroland* is a tremendously rich and thought-provoking experiment in rehearsing decolonial justice. I draw on Doris Kolesch's reflections on immersive theater to illuminate how the joint ensemble's use of immersive techniques facilitated encounters with geographically or socially distant others imaginatively and corporeally, and how it allowed spectators to grasp decolonial relations as messily multiperspectival and multidirectional. Immersive techniques are key to addressing German audiences as "implicated" (Michael Rothberg) in colonial and neocolonial relations, while allowing them to realize decolonial agency and allyship. And I discern a specifically decolonial form of the "theater of anger" conceptualized by Olivia Landry in another context. It impresses on spectators the urgency of transforming entrenched injustices, while it also emphatically resists too-quick solutions that promise reconciliation in the sense of settling damages and achieving closure. This theater of *irreconciliation* furiously insists on holding open space for feminist, cross-racial, and intergenerational critiques of deferred decolonization. It centers Ovaherero perspectives but aspires to broad civic debate about what genuine decolonization might mean as a collective project. While the two strategies of immersive theater and the decolonial "theater of anger" complement each other in many ways, I ask whether the power differences shaping international coproductions make them equally viable.

Hereroland's wrestling with decolonial repair has broad implications for European publics. It amplifies civic and cultural endeavors to grapple with the damages wrought by European arrogance and white supremacy, which structure the relations between the Global North and South. Europeans have been shielded from calls for redress, because national histories and national maps long insinuated fictions of sovereignty that denied shared violent histories along with continued economic and political dependencies. The story of one production I tell below is based on attending *Hereroland* in Hamburg, viewing recordings of the Hamburg and Windhoek versions, and conducting interviews with directors and three cast members. It has implications for the many cases in which the victims of colonial violence are geographically distant from their former oppressors, and often struggle against their own postcolonial nations' discrimination of ethnic minorities – another legacy of the colonial era. My research hopes to contribute to wider debates about theater as a site where decolonizing political imaginations are brought to bear on domestic as well as international relations, and where decolonial solidarity can be practiced.

I

The wealthy northern port city of Hamburg is home to a sizable Black community, and local decolonial and antiracist activist organizations had long thematized the involvement of Hamburg's wealthy merchants and ship owners in colonial trade, conducted decolonial city walks and harbor tours, and promoted a critical approach to colonial monuments. In 2014, the Hamburg senate announced its intent to study and commemorate the city's colonial involvement and critically contextualize urban manifestations of the colonial past.[4] It funded a research center at the University of Hamburg, which was tasked to examine Hamburg's "(post-)colonial legacy."[5] In addition, the senate inaugurated a series of public roundtables (2017–2024). In 2018, senator of culture Carsten Brosda met with a delegation of Ovahereros and Namas and apologized for the city's colonial involvement and the suffering of their ancestors. The artistic director of the Thalia Theater, Joachim Lux, sought to contribute to these broad civic efforts and hired independent director Gernot Grünewald to create a play on the topic of Hamburg's colonial history. The project was co-financed by the TURN fund, a German cultural program that from 2012 to 2021 supported German-African cultural cooperations.[6]

Grünewald was not only known for his productions of devised documentary plays,[7] but for his familiarity with the Namibian theater scene.[8] Ndjavera had long been involved in political theater. Before Namibian independence in 1990, he had been active in the Black groups that toured the country and were described variously as popular, agitprop, and community theater drawing on the ideas of Bertolt Brecht and Augusto Boal. This political theater was aligned with

---

[4] Transcripts of the roundtables and a strategy paper are archived by the *Projektstelle für die Dekolonisierung Hamburgs*.
[5] Led by Jürgen Zimmerer, the research center examines the connections and aftereffects of colonialism in Hamburg, Germany and the former colonies, resulting in the publication of an app as well as the book *Hamburg: Tor zur kolonialen Welt* (*Hamburg: Gateway to the Colonial World*, 2021). For more information see geschichte.uni-hamburg.de/arbeitsbereiche/globalgeschichte/forschung/forschungsstelle-hamburgs-postkoloniales-erbe.html.
[6] Under the terms of the fund, German institutions or organizations could apply for matching funding to cooperate with an African partner who was not required to contribute financially.
[7] Theater scholar Rosemary Parsons defines devised theater as "the process of creative collaboration by a group of performers to generate and assemble a performance through improvisation, discussion and rehearsal, inclusive of the resultant production" (Parsons 8).
[8] In *Oshi-Deutsch* (2016), a coproduction of the Theater Osnabrück with the National Theater of Namibia, Grünewald and his Namibian co-director Sandy Rudd traced the lives of some of the 430 Namibian children who were raised in the German Democratic Republic and abruptly returned to Namibia after the country became independent and the GDR ceased to exist in the same year.

the South West African National Union and South West Africa People's Organization (SWAPO) liberation movements and sought to inform and mobilize rural and disenfranchised populations about topical issues (Olivier-Sampson 172–174). In 2016, Ndjavera had devised a play that linked the Ovaherero genocide with contemporary problems, which had been produced by the National Theater of Namibia. Ndjavera decided to incorporate parts of that project into the play about the presence of the colonial past he would co-direct with Grünewald. While the two divided up responsibilities – Ndjavera directed a new iteration of his play set in the center of the stage, Grünewald devised a number of documentary "stations" that were dispersed throughout the immersive theater space – all ensemble members collaborated on both components of *Hereroland*.

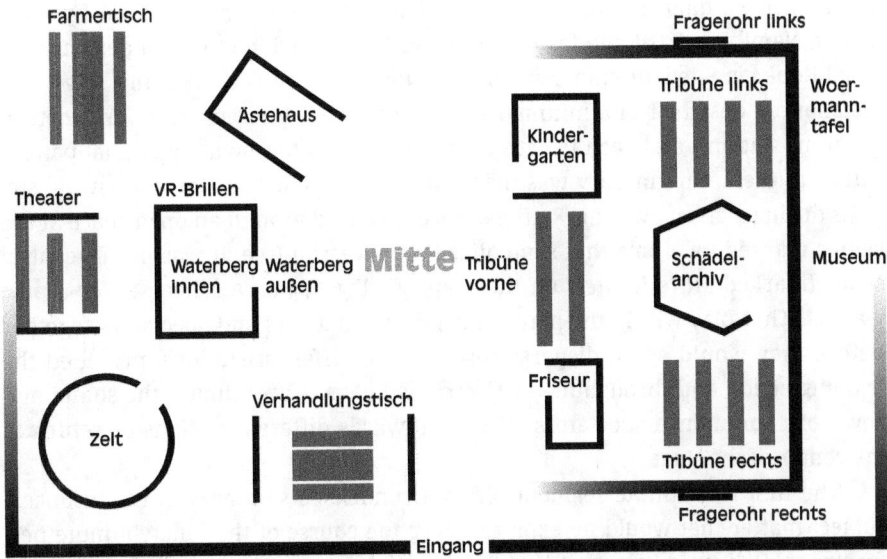

Fig. 1: map of stage. Farmertisch=Farmer's Table. Verhandlungstisch=Negotiation Table. Waterberg Innen/Aussen=Waterberg Interior/Exterior. VR-Brillen=VR glasses. Friseur=Hairdresser. Tribüne links/rechts=Risers left/right. Fragerohr links/rechts=Question Tube left/right. Zelt=Tent. Ästehaus=Twig house. Mitte=Center. With permission by Thalia Theater.

The play's two components – the play-within-the-play and the stations – employ distinct methods to inform and emotionally involve Hamburg spectators, in order to foster empathy with the Ovaherero cause of demanding recognition and reparations. The former, which takes the form of a trial to ascertain German historical guilt and legal liability, traces the failure of Ovahereros to obtain justice either within a system of international law, or within an apparatus of theatrical representation wedded to Enlightenment conceptions of knowledge and reasoning. Its Boalian dramaturgy, in which performers reflect on the political conditions of social action, serves to question why both the law and the theater actively prevent the Ovaherero from establishing their full humanity. By inviting Germans to witness and empathize with Ovaherero suffering, the play-within-the-play urges them towards political allyship, and towards exerting pressure on their own government while it negotiated decolonial repair. The stations complement that endeavor by proffering evidence of the historical crime. Techniques typical of immersive theater not only promote corporeal proximity and emotional openness to the plight of Ovahereros but also push audience members to resist (neo-) colonial white supremacy.

Hereroland brought together an ensemble of six white German and five Ovaherero actors, dancers, and musicians. The costumes were designed by well-known Namibian artist and fashion designer Cynthia Schimming. Set designer Michael Köpke created an immersive installation that occupied the entire stage. The installation, designed in a minimalist, modular style, offered space for nineteen different stations, and each ticketholder was sent on her own, individual path to fifteen of them. No itinerary was the same, and no audience member saw all stations during a given evening. Stations were arranged around an open space at the center marked by a pole that symbolized an ancestral tree. It was in this central space (marked *Mitte [center]* on the map, see Fig. 1) that a rehearsal for a play was set. That play-within-the-play, which drew all actors and spectators together before they would again disperse towards the different stations, provided the framing action and throughline of *Hereroland*. Every five minutes the sound of a cow horn summoned spectators to move towards different stations or return to the center of the stage.

The first five-minute segment offers a condensed summary of the historical subject matter that would be explored over the course of the ninety-minute performance. Delivered in a matter-of-fact tone by the company standing in a circle facing outwards towards audience members, the actors chronicle the uprising against German settlers' appropriation of land and physical abuse of Ovahereros (*Hereroland* Videorecording of Hamburg performance). They relate the battle at Waterberg, which concluded with German troops chasing Herero men, women, and children into the arid Omaheke desert, where many perished. They narrate the internment of survivors in concentration camps, where more died of hard labor. And they sum up the lasting consequences of the genocide by naming the confiscation of "nearly all of Herero land," which was sold to German settlers, as the cause of extreme inequality in today's Namibia, where "wealth, land and privilege [are] concentrated among white German-speaking descendants of settlers" (*Hereroland* Videorecording of Hamburg performance). Subsequent segments set up the situation of a trial, which investigates the genocide to determine German guilt, and pits witnesses for the prosecution against the statements of the defense counsel representing the German government. The opening indictments echo those made in a lawsuit in the United States that[9] was dismissed in 2019 because the judge found no grounds for jurisdiction. The stage trial ends with an invitation to audience members to reflect on just solutions in small group discussions with performers.

While the ensemble is initially united by a friendly camaraderie and the shared purpose to give the Ovaherero cause a public hearing, subtle differences between German and Namibian cast members become increasingly evident. These differences are attached to divergent theatrical styles and methods of truth seeking. At the same time, the technique of stepping in and out of theatrical roles, drawn from Bertolt Brecht and Augusto Boal, serves to brake the mounting momentum driving towards failure and investigate its structural causes. The divergence of Ovahereros and Germans becomes evident when the prosecutor calls as the main witness a character introduced as Fluksman Vleermuis, a trickster figure who compares himself to Till Eulenspiegel, Nasruddin, and Harlequin from European popular cultural history. He speaks in sly, punning rhymes and wears a Harlequin costume. When forced into a dream state induced by being bound with ropes to the pole/ancestral tree (see Fig. 2),

Fig. 2: Fluksman Vleermuis aka Tree Spirit (Otja Henock Kambaekua), *Hereroland*. Thalia Theater (January 2020). Coproduction with National Theatre Namibia. Photograph by Armin Smailovic.

---

9 The lawsuit objected to the exclusion of Herero and Nama representatives from the intergovernmental negotiations and asked for direct reparations to descendants. The suit was brought under the Alien Tort Statute, a 1789 law that is often invoked in human rights cases.

Vleermuis is able to connect to previous generations of ancestors and "see" racist acts in German-Southwest Africa as well as in Berlin.

The company's action of binding the trickster, with a certain sadistic glee and against his protests, prompts his clairvoyant witnessing of an Ovaherero *sangoma* (witch doctor) being strung up on the tree, having his skull sawn open, brain measured, and body dismembered and castrated by gabbing, beer-guzzling German doctors. In the second testimony, Vleermuis takes off his harlequin costume and reveals himself as a Tree Spirit, wearing precolonial Herero attire (leather apron, necklace, and skull cap). In that second testimony, the Tree Spirit describes a similar scene, now located in Berlin. He sees German doctors dissect the bodies of Ovaherero participants in a *Völkerschau* who are taken to a concentration camp near Berlin, where their skulls are measured and their brains weighed. The play underscores scientific racism as a felt experience shared by colonized subjects and those targeted by the Nazi state. The testimony scenes impress on viewers the horrific sensation of finding oneself violated, dehumanized, and declared inferior by an ostensibly rational, scientific apparatus, and allowed to be tortured and killed with impunity. The witness testimony conveys that this nightmarish feeling was experienced by Ovahereros both in the colony and the metropole, where a group of them participated in an exhibition of people from the German colonies in 1896. The two scenes follow a dream logic by amalgamating settler aggression and racial science in the colonies with metropolitan entertainment, Nazi punitive practices, and Nazi medical experiments. The testimony scenes home in on the discourse of scientific racism as the underlying crime that made the colonial genocide possible and later climaxed in the Holocaust.

The production's focus on racial science exposes discrepancies between the moral and material conclusions Germans have drawn from the racialization of Jews in the Nazi racial state, and their lack of response to the racist treatment of colonized Africans. Whereas the extermination of European Jews has been recognized as central to modern German identity and cosmopolitan ethics (Levy and Sznaider), the genocide of Ovahereros and Namas has not catalyzed a comparable reckoning or obligation to make reparations. This discrepancy has struck many Ovahereros as a sign of ongoing racial discrimination. After the publication of the Joint Agreement, Ovaherero Paramount chief Vekuii Rukoro accused Germany of being willing to negotiate with the Jewish Claims Conference on behalf of Jews everywhere, agreeing to pay $90 billion in compensation for the Holocaust, but not with Hereros and Namas, "because they were white Europeans, and we are Black Africans" (Rukoro quoted in Rogers). To wit, the Federal Republic of Germany in its response to the 2017 Herero lawsuit invoked the legal principle of "intertemporality," which bars the retroactive application of the term *genocide* (coined in 1948 by the jurist Rafael Lemkin), in order to limit liability for the genocide perpetrated by German colonial troops in 1904 (Melber 169; Hackmack 4). In effect, this principle bars contemporary Ovahereros from holding Germans responsible for the genocide. It leaves intact colonial-era views of colonial subjects as savage insurgents, rather than scrutinize these views through human rights norms codified after World War II, which purport to be universal. In the play-within-the-play, the German defense counsel and trial observers, too, regard the methods by which Ovahereros seek to establish historical truth as confirmation of their irrationality. In response to the Tree Spirit's testimony, the German defense counsel and some German trial observers scoff at and cast doubt on its veracity. The rational language of the law cannot accommodate the time-and-space-bending powers of the ancient being of which the Tree Spirit is an avatar. According to the defense counsel, it's all "hocus-pocus" (*Hereroland* Textbuch 17), not admissible in court.

The production frames its opposition to the law's narrow rules of truth-finding in theatrical terms. By taking the appearance of a trickster and invoking the names of clown, Nasruddin, and Harlequin, the Tree Spirit calls on European theatrical traditions that put greater stock on the sly wisdom and bodily agility of sassy subalterns than Enlightenment drama and its rational, bourgeois protagonists. Ndjavera and his Ovaherero cast members thus appeal to sidelined forms of knowledge archived in forms of physical comedy. However, the play exposes the risks of such an appeal, as the occult forces invoked by the Tree Spirit cannot unsettle the rationalism marshalled by the trial format. Finding himself laughed at, he entirely loses his composure and hurls accusations against Germans who have done nothing but "kill, and kill, and kill" (*Hereroland* Textbuch 17). An Ovaherero woman tries to intervene on his behalf: "Listen Germans, listen good: to the language inside of dreaming, of seeing, when he starts unfolding our myths!" (*Hereroland* Textbuch 17), but she too is yelled down in the tumult. Like the comic *Hanswurst* who was chased off the stage in the eighteenth century, allowing German national theater to constitute itself as enlightened, so the outraged Tree Spirit is ridiculed and shut up as the rationalist stage cannot tolerate his dire revelations (see Fig. 3).[10] He does not go without a fight, though (Fig. 3), asking questions in turn, and demanding explanations for the ideological precepts of German colonial rule:

> Like some explanation of 'the master race must rule?', like 'the Kaffirs caused the war?' – like, 'we the Germans came to protect, to preach the gospel, to hand out bibles in exchange for Lebensraum' [. . .] like, we too stupid to survive; like hang them high, like send them into the desert, like they stupid; they lazy; they don't deserve to live; I saw you! In the dark – what you did; everything – I saw. (*Hereroland* Textbuch 17)

---

[10] This scene also resonates with highly emotional moments during the Truth and Reconciliation hearings in South Africa, when the public performance of abject suffering, thought to bring about social healing, reenacted a powerlessness that was not relieved by the justice system (Cole).

"We brought light to a dark continent," the defense counsel retorts (*Hereroland* Textbuch 17), insinuating that past events should be judged by their historical rationale, not by contemporary ethical or legal norms.

Fig. 3: Confrontation Tree Spirit (Otja Henock Kambaekua) vs. German defense counsel (Jörg Pohl). In background: Herero spectator (Glenn-nora Tjipura, left), and Prosecutor (Lizette Kavera, right). *Hereroland*, Thalia Theater (January 2020). Coproduction with National Theatre Namibia. Photograph by Armin Smailovic.

At this moment, two antagonistic lineages of performance confront each other, a dominant one wedded to the upholding of social order (and proper comportment in the court), and a marginalized one based on arcane rites that grant access to higher truths.[11] Contrite, the Ovaherero prosecutor promises to uphold "emotional discipline" (*Hereroland* Textbuch 17) and submits evidence in the eminently neoliberal genre of the PowerPoint presentation replete with a bullet point list of perpetrators and their deeds, whereupon the judge thanks them for their "reconciliatory conclusion" (*Hereroland* Textbuch 19). Cementing this shift in power between the opposing parties, the defense counsel's presentation confirms that a genocide took place but raises so many practical hurdles to implementing a fair process of repair – how to console the living for the loss of their loved ones? How to return all the human remains that are unidentifiable? How to redistribute land

---

11 See theater scholar Sue-Ellen Case's tracing of the gradual and incomplete ostracization of esoteric and occult performance practices and traditions from European theater, which as an institution put itself in the service of modern governmentality and a specific notion of science.

without creating economic chaos and racial strife? – that it seems futile to even attempt it. Why not just extend an apology but defer reparations indefinitely? The Tree Spirit's outburst and the defense counsel's equivocating ultimately collapse the power constellation on stage with that in the political sphere. The play-within-the-play thereby brilliantly illuminates the alignment of theatrical forms with hegemonic notions of epistemology and law. What started out as a shared endeavor between Germans and Ovahereros to devise an alternative to intergovernmental negotiations ends up with an ensemble split along national and racial lines, and German cast members parroting the political discourse. This dramaturgy powerfully articulates the actually existing predicament and urges spectators to become involved in contemplating just solutions in the concluding discussion.

Even as conciliation is framed as submission to the dominant order in the above scene, the play-within-the-play holds out hope for the eventual redemption of Ovaherero suffering and for a reconciliation between the German people, the German minority in Namibia, and Ovahereros that centers on repairing the latter's enduring dispossession. It ends with Ovahereros plaintively laying claim to the land now owned by German-speaking descendants of settlers, before the play concludes with inviting spectators into group discussions about decolonial justice. The poetic image of the bound Tree Spirit in agony undeniably resonates with the Christian image of crucifixion. Christian tropes of suffering endow both Ovaherero anguish, and performers' willingness to subject themselves to cruelty and ridicule on stage, with deeper spiritual meaning. Christian iconography heroizes the group's suffering and urges spectators to honor its protracted battle against science and the law. Jurist Judith Hackmack, an expert in transitional justice and critic of the Joint Declaration, secularizes this conviction when she writes that "it is well known that truth-telling from the perspective of the survivors, as well as commemoration, can have a reparative and healing effect. They can also contribute toward (re)establishing the agency of survivors that was lost as a result of the international crimes" (Hackmack 5). Whether understood through the lens of Christian or secular understandings of testifying, the dramatization of Ovahereros' pain predicates reconciliation on repair.

The play-within-the-play brings into view larger questions about the legal system's capacity to accommodate radically divergent ways of knowing and methods for establishing truth. Science is both thematized as a discourse of racist terror deployed against a colonized population and revealed as the discursive foundation on which the trial, with its rules of verifiable evidence, is based. To challenge science's alliance with the state, Ovaherero plaintiffs draw on arcane, subaltern traditions within the European cultural archive. However, these are incapable of unsettling the framework of international law, which had historically categorized Ovahereros as primitive subjects to be disciplined by force rather than German citizens and rights-bearers. By drawing attention to the disparity between Jews, whose racialization by the Nazis post-war Germans recognized as an act of barbarism and agreed to repair, and Ovahereros, who, German lawyers argue, should be treated according to colonial-era legal doctrines, the play-within-the-play calls for a comparative understanding of racial science, and for the decolonization of official antiracism in Germany.

The stations, in turn, offer the evidence of an unmastered colonial past that the witness's testimony fails to furnish. They were based on material that Grünewald and the Thalia cast members had collected in Hamburg and during their research trip through Namibia. Distributed throughout the theater space, the stations were devised in a documentary style that was no less emotionally affecting than the central drama. They immerse spectators in intimate settings that foster physical closeness to descendants of genocide survivors and put them in one-on-one encounters with performers. Multimedia screens and virtual reality glasses transport spectators to the sites of genocide, and scenes that require them to interact with performers break down the traditional division between actor and spectator. On the one hand, these techniques typical of immersive theater promote corporeal and emotional openness to the Ovaherero cause and push spectators towards an actively supportive stance. On the other hand, these techniques bring them uncomfortably close to blatantly racist situations and figures, provoking active resistance to white supremacy. Immersion heightens audience members' awareness of their own social positioning vis-à-vis scenes of suffering and chauvinism. It thereby leaves room for agency, for the possibility of changing neocolonial relations rather than being determined by them.

German theater scholar Doris Kolesch argues that immersion does not equal complete absorption, but is characterized by the interruption of, and reflection on, theatrical or mediatized illusion, and by the tension between merging with and emerging from a theatrical or mediatized situation. Seeking to elaborate the critical potential of immersive formats, she identifies specifically their capacity to "raise awareness of the specificity of a given point of view, to inaugurate a critical relation to representation" (Kolesch 65). She attributes these to the deconstruction of the kind of elevated vantage point and a/the rationalist, ostensibly neutral gaze at the world that had been dominant since the Enlightenment and was expressed in key cultural technologies that historically constructed what Mary Louise Pratt punningly called "imperial eyes" in the title of her eponymous book. The troubling partiality of such a relationship between subject and world has been problematized from various perspectives, including feminist and postcolonial ones, over the last decades. As the stark binaries of self and other gave way to multi-perspectivity, situated knowledge, and affective, empathic relations, so our current immersive technologies promise to grasp the contemporary condition of feeling both planetary linkages and profoundly emotional enmeshments to unprecedented degrees. Kolesch's contentions illuminate why immersive theater techniques can lend themselves to decolonizing projects.

In *Hereroland*'s immersive stations spectators hear about colonial rape in the intimate spaces of a woman's bedroom and a hairdresser's tiny salon; physical proximity to the woman and interaction with the hairdresser potentially heighten spectators' receptivity to sensitive, painful stories and allow them to grasp kinesthetically and emotionally how the genocide reshaped social relations into the present. Only a single audience member at a time squeezes into the tiny hairdresser's stall and takes a seat on the chair, while the hairdresser draws her into a conversation about hair, identity, and family genealogy. One spectator, a grandmother, told me that she was profoundly shaken by a performer's revelation, while he gently touched her shoulders and hair, that his grandfather was the result of his great-grandmother's rape by a German colonial soldier.

At other times, closeness to performers provokes disidentification with colonial whiteness. In the cramped space of a private museum, where a tour guide narrates the history of Namibia from a settler perspective (see Fig. 4), one of the Hamburg actors portrays a contemporary German-speaking Namibian guide who holds forth about the local swimming pool going to seed after the end of Apartheid. The close quarters make his aggressive tapping of photos on the museum walls more intimidating and repulsive. And at the station "Colonial Theater," a bourgeois woman on the colonial lecture circuit, dressed in a Victorian-era white lace dress, tries to recruit German women to join the settlement project as farmers' wives and thus prevent racial mixing. Two female audience members played along with the lecturer's rousing call that women are needed for the colony, and let the performer grab and lift their hands. While one smiled, perhaps trying to please the performer, the other cringed. Did she dislike becoming a co-performer, or did she object to being conscripted into colonial white femininity? These performances of white supremacy and colonial nostalgia offer object lessons in how *not* to relate to the past and to people of color in a multiracial democracy. They provoke repulsion against these figures and sentiments. By encouraging audience members to become co-performers in such scenes, the stations allow them to experience themselves as "implicated subjects" in postcolonial relations, to cite Michael Rothberg's term for "positions aligned with power and privilege without being themselves direct agents of harm; they contribute to, inhabit, inherit, or benefit from regimes of domination but do not originate or control such regimes" (Rothberg 1). That position allows them not only to actively witness postcolonial suffering, but also reflect on ways in which patterns of perception, behavior, and feeling may potentially be transformed.

Fig. 4: Guide (Jörg Pohl) at Station Museum. *Hereroland*, Thalia Theater (January 2020). Coproduction with National Theatre Namibia. Photograph by Armin Smailovic.

While in 2020, many Germans knew little if anything about colonial history, the stations drive home the point that historically, Hamburg citizens had been colonial enthusiasts who avidly followed events in the colony, including the Herero genocide. For instance, one station reenacts the graveside eulogy for Hamburg merchant Adolph Woermann, the owner of a shipping line, politician, and colonial profiteer for whom two streets and a square in Hamburg were then still named (the streets have been renamed in the meantime). The eulogy thus underscores the veneration of Woermann, whose ships transported the troops that carried out the Herero genocide, among Hamburg's elite. Being addressed as fellow mourners, audience members become co-performers in this scene and are encouraged to reflect on their implication as beneficiaries of Hamburg's international trade.

The stations also point towards active decolonial struggles. At the station "Postcolonial Hamburg," a young woman presents a slide show that documents activists' efforts to topple or recontextualize colonial monuments and rename streets and buildings honoring colonial merchants and military men in the city. Her presentation conveys the frustrations of activists at the difficulty of decolonizing endeavors and the indifference of politicians and ordinary people alike. At the station "Schädelarchiv" (Skulls Archive), a professor of medicine recounts his efforts to research the provenance of Ovaherero skulls in his institute's holdings, and chronicles the many bureaucratic obstacles to restituting these human remains. Together, these stations alert Hamburg audiences to a range of individuals and initiatives that have tried to make a difference but have, so far, failed to do so in any significant way. The collaboration of Ovaherero and German cast members in *Hereroland* acknowledges racialized power differences between them. At the same time, the Boalian dramaturgy and immersive format of the stations offer opportunities for actively "unlearning imperialism" (Ariella Azoulay). They promote an emotional, embodied engagement that urged audiences to take up the critique of white supremacy and practice decolonial allyship beyond the theater.

The Ovaherero cast under David Ndjavera was highly motivated to tell their side of the story, alert Germans to their government's bad faith negotiations, and urge them to consider what postcolonial justice and international solidarity might mean as a broad social project. While *Hereroland* aimed to open the secret negotiations to public scrutiny and advocated for wide civil engagement, it remained wedded to the idea of reconciliation, and even framed Ovaherero suffering through Christian tropes of redemption and forgiveness. The deaths of Ndjavera in 2021 and Schimming in 2022 would open a path to a much different telling of the story of genocide, and a different conception of allyship.

II

When the coronavirus pandemic shuttered theaters and drastically cut down international travel soon after *Hereroland's* successful run in Hamburg, the cast and crew had to defer their plans to take the show to Namibia. With every new wave of infection, touring plans had to be postponed, and tragically, Ndjavera died of Covid in 2021. Later that year, Joachim Lux, the artistic director of the Thalia Theater decided to scrap the set and cancel the show in Namibia for good. Ovaherero ensemble members took to social media to protest his unilateral decision and Lux reconsidered. Under the direction of Ovaherero cast member Lizette Kavari, the ensemble decided to recreate the play from scratch, which several participants described as a welcome opportunity to recreate it under much changed conditions. Whereas all Ovaherero actors continued their participation in this new iteration of the play, which I will call *Hereroland 2*, only two of the German actors did, leading to a centering of Ovaherero experiences in the performance. The stations were reconceived as virtual portals with the help of digital technologies: seventeen different scenes were filmed with a 360-degree-camera in Hamburg and across Namibia. Audience members could scan QR codes displayed on the perimeter of the respective performance space with their cell phones and insert them in cheap cardboard viewers the company had brought from Germany. The sponsorship of a large Namibian phone service provider made it possible to bring extra cell phones and portable wifi stations even to small towns and villages. The lack of a bulky, intricate set freed the production to tour even to remote locations in Namibia with only a few props and costumes that fit on the back of a truck. The new version was performed in the capital of Windhoek, Swakopmund (a predominantly German town), and Okakarara and Otjinene (where many Ovaherero live) in June 2023. One of the Windhoek performances was livestreamed to audiences in the Thalia Theater, creating a unique opportunity for Namibians and Germans to debate reparative justice across a large geographical distance.

Lux's willingness to listen to Ovaherero protests might have been due to the heightened sensitivity to anti-racist critiques at that particular historical moment. The killing of African American George Floyd by a Minneapolis police officer in 2020 had rekindled the Black Lives Matter movement, which focused public attention to police violence and structural racist discrimination worldwide. In Namibia, Black Lives Matter added fuel to the Rhodes Must Fall movement that had spread out from South African universities in 2015 and sought to decolonize not just cityscapes, but an education system that reproduced racial and class inequalities. It also intersected with land reform efforts aiming to rectify colonial land theft. Ovaherero are keen to assume stewardship of land and are frustrated that descendants of German settlers make up 2% of the Namibian population but own 70% of arable land. In addition, calls for racial justice buoyed social protests directed against the extraordinarily high rates of sexual and gender-based violence in Namibia, which scholars and activists attribute to high degrees of militarized violence during colonialism, Apartheid, and the liberation struggle. Young Namibians regard the fight for sexual rights and freedom, and for the decriminalization of LGBTQ identities in the 2020s, as efforts to remove misogynist, homophobic, and transphobic structures and ideologies that had been imposed under colonialism. In short, public protests and social media campaigns bundled widespread discontents with the stalled decolonization for which young Namibians held the aging SWAPO leadership responsible that had been in power for over a generation. It is against this backdrop that the Ovaherero performers, most of them in their mid-to-late twenties, created *Hereroland 2*.

As this younger generation stepped up to tell the story of the colonial genocide and stalled decolonization, they did so with unmistakable anger. The Ovaherero performers decided to dispense with Ndjavera's play and instead created a series of thematically linked scenes, some of which are set during German colonialism, others in contemporary times. Performers remain present as themselves to different degrees even when they depict historical characters, mythical figures, and social types. The scenes, which do not follow a conventional plot, show colonial invasion, destruction, and the interruption of traditions, as well as the yearning for cultural renewal and social justice today. In the last scene, ensemble members discuss how to envision the future and invite audience members into the conversation.

As the political critique of the play became sharper, the production replaced Ndjavera's conciliatory intercultural universalism with an Ovaherero-centric aesthetic. A considerable part of the dialogue is in Otjiherero, although code switching to English, Namibia's official language, allows non-Otjiherero speakers to follow the gist of a given scene. The playing space is anchored by an actual tree and demarcated by a simple chalk circle drawn on the floor, around which spectators are seated. The minimalist set and costumes bolster the indigenization of the world of the play. From the tree's leafy crown dangle ritual implements, a furry water flask, and a human skull. Blankets, cooking implements, and a large calabash set out around the tree evoke a traditional Ovaherero home.[12] The Tree Spirit is now freed from the Harlequin costume. The costumes of male and female performers, too, index traditional precolonial and postcolonial Ovaherero attire. Two of the men and one woman appear in leather aprons, chunky necklaces, and headdresses, while Kavari wears a red dress with voluminous skirt and tight bodice along with the emblematic "cow-horned" headdress, the kind of dress worn by older or married Ovaherero women on festive occasions today, recalling the historic centrality of cattle to Ovaherero culture. Ovaherero praise poems and rituals like the spitting of water on the earth are performed several times during the play. The resulting performance is not only visibly and audibly indigenized, but also more confrontational than the first version. This greater assertiveness is especially palpable in scenes that use graphic imagery to convey the story of the genocide.

The ensemble draws on long-established and more recently emerging tropes to underscore the depth of German cruelty and Ovaherero suffering. Early in the

---

12 Mukaiwa includes one production photo that provides a glimpse of the production aesthetic.

play, an Ovaherero poet composes a song about the arrival of German colonial troops, when a *Schutztruppen* soldier tosses a severed head into the lap of an Ovaherero woman played by Glenn-nora Tjipura, which she proceeds to scrape, retching and keening. She is forced to clean the skull of flesh before it is shipped to German institutes of racial science. While she scrapes, an Ovaherero man in jeans and a suit jacket, both torn and bloody, stumbles onto the stage. His anguished, then angry monologue combines a report on the genocide with reflections on how cultural loss, effected by Christianization, compounded literal killing and material dispossession. The characters' poem and monologues loop and layer temporally disjointed moments, from the German military invasion, the plight of survivors in the Shark Island concentration camp, and a present characterized by coerced assimilation, into a grievous montage. In a later scene, an Ovaherero man, his legs shackled, shuffles across the stage, led by German soldiers. Both scenes activate iconic depictions of the Ovaherero and Nama genocide circulating in Germany and Namibia.[13]

The two scenes compress the colonial genocide into iconographies of extreme brutality that are a far cry from the narrative descriptions of torture in the prior version. They also reinterpret the Christian mission (a source of succor in the original *Hereroland*) as part of cultural genocide. It was as if the ensemble had decided to dispense with mollification and insisted that audiences face the cruel extent of colonial and postcolonial violence. Importantly, the depiction of victimization is yoked to expressions of deep anger. As she scrapes, the Ovaherero woman speaks of the "murderous rage in [her] eyes" even as she is forced to "continue with the task at hand" (*Hereroland 2* Videorecording of Windhoek performance). She finishes her narrative of being raped by German soldiers by cursing the "Bloody bastards!!" The Tree Spirit witnesses Germans "trying to wipe my people off the face of the earth as they killed, [. . .] and killed more and killed and killed, and killed, and killed, and killed" (*Hereroland 2* Videorecording of Windhoek performance). As he punctuates his exclamation with clenched fists and jaws, he vows "never to forget the injustice, the killing, the grabbing of land and

---

[13] The image of nine emaciated and shackled Herero men who had surrendered to German troops, first published in a coffee table book in 1907 (Arthur Koppel Aktiengesellschaft), initially functioned as a visual trophy of Germans' military victory over "insolent barbarians" (Zeller 319), but Hereros began appropriating this depiction of their suffering in the 1990s, when Ovaherero organizations began calling for an apology and reparations (Förster 306). By contrast, the iconicity of the Herero woman holding a skull is more recent and constituted the first time that Hereros appropriated a trope from the critical discourse on German colonialism that has circulated across a range of popular media internationally. It draws its power from the debates surrounding human remains and their restitution from German museums and research institutes, which have captured public attention since the first repatriation of skulls to Namibia in 2011.

voices of women and children crying for mercy" (*Hereroland 2* Videorecording of Windhoek performance). In the last scene before the concluding discussion, an Ovaherero woman played by Lizette Kavari excoriates Germans for grabbing Ovahereros' land, for conscripting them to back-breaking labor in the effort to turn land into plantations, for squeezing them onto communal land (the equivalent of reservations), and for forcing genocide survivors into exile. Leaning forward and spitting out her final indictment, she accuses them of committing mass rape and turning women into little more than pets for breeding. Performers respond with unmistakable physical anger to specific injustices, set out the oppressive long-term effects of colonial violence, and channel rage into protest and revolutionary fervor. Their monologues confront the audience in physically aggressive direct address. They aim to rouse spectators with verbal provocations and kinetic energy. These scenes communicate the debilitating experience of being persistently denied justice. By asking spectators to endure and take up performers' wrath, these performances of anger put spectators under duress, and thereby open up the possibility of imagining different futures. These are all hallmarks of what Olivia Landry calls the "Theatre of Anger," a type of theater whose description she grounds in the postmigrant theater she observed in Berlin during the first two decades of this century. Just as the postmigrant theater of anger in Germany refuses integration into an unjust, racist system, its decolonial manifestation in *Hereroland 2* refuses reconciliation to the postcolonial status quo. The decolonial theater of anger calls out both enduring white supremacy and the accommodations to it that national and tribal leaders have made. Accordingly, I call it a theater of "irreconciliation." It taps into the radical decolonial movements that have emerged in Namibia over the last decade and amplifies them.

Landry notes that anger has been viewed as a negative, unproductive, even destructive affect within philosophical traditions from the Stoics to contemporary thinkers like Martha Nussbaum and Carolin Emcke (Landry 24), and in European theatrical traditions that, since the Enlightenment, have advocated for the stage as a moral institution dedicated to a pedagogy of tempering passions (Landry 29). However, anger has also been recognized as an important impulse to social justice movements. Aristotle thought of anger as a justified and necessary response to patent injustice, ennobled by being felt and acted upon in defense of others. It is a key impulse for bringing into being a just society. In more recent times, Landry points to Black feminists from Audre Lorde and bell hooks to Sarah Ahmed, who have found anger to be a source of clarity, power, and creativity. Drawing on their ideas, Landry sets out to "recuperate anger as a powerful tool against social injustice, a source of strength, and a catalyst for change" (Landry 25). Against a dominant culture that negates self-worth and that reads angry Black people as irascible and their anger as unattributed, she praises anger for its refusal of victimhood and finds it revelatory of grievances that have not been listened to or redressed (Landry 32). Anger, Landry posits, is relational, requiring attentive listening, and it is performative in that, as Marilyn Frye contends, intense emotions are speech acts that can only succeed if they are taken up and carried forward by those who witness them (Frye 88). Landry underscores that the theater of anger is political theater, which shares with Brecht's epic theater the refusal of catharsis and insistence on confronting audiences with the causes of oppression, pressing them to become involved in removing those causes and changing society (Landry 38). At the same time, the body's corporeal presence, affects, and emotions, inherited from performance art since the 1960s, provide a vital charge whose importance Brecht only recognized in his late work (Landry 38).

The "raging monologues" presented in *Hereroland 2* are key to the theater of anger: they pierce the fourth wall and open up channels of kinesthetic transmission that demand to be taken up by spectators. The arrangement of spectators around the circular playing space, where they can watch both the performers and audience members on the other side of the circle, fosters the audience's confrontation with the causes of trauma and enduring oppression. In one scene, performers even invite spectators to enter the circle to closely observe a dance that reenacts an Ovaherero prophet's surrender to German colonial troops, who then shoot him. When the company performed *Hereroland 2* in Otjinene, several men from the community even joined the dance spontaneously, overcoming the separation of stage and auditorium.

Hereroland 2's emphasis on anger demonstrates how profoundly the conditions for decolonial work had changed since the elder generation of Namibian artists first conceived the play a mere three years prior. Whereas Ndjavera (born in 1969) and Schimming (born 1953) were socialized under Apartheid, five of the six Namibian performers were born after independence and were trained in majority-Black institutions that promoted pride in Black struggles against racist colonial and Apartheid systems; only musician Ben Kandukira was born before 1990. Bell hooks's thoughts about the anger of Black people in the United States are also pertinent to postcolonial, post-Apartheid Namibia: "To perpetuate and maintain white supremacy, white folks have colonized Black Americans, and a part of that colonizing process has been teaching us to repress our rage, to never make them the targets of any anger we feel about racism" (hooks 14). She adds that "[m]ost black people internalize this message well" (hooks 14). Similarly, performers highlight how parents and grandparents had to keep their anger bottled up, evoked so devastatingly by Tjipura's speech as she scrapes the skull. Now the younger generation refuses to hide their rage any longer.

The targets of anger in *Hereroland 2* are not only the German government for bungling the Joint Declaration, and the German-speaking minority in Namibia, but also the Namibian government, and even traditional Ovaherero leaders. The blunt enumeration of historical violence challenges the SWAPO government's official national narrative of anticolonial resistance. Embodied at the Independence Museum in Windhoek and at official memorials such as Heroes' Acre (Wilson 68–71), that narrative subsumes Ovaherero suffering and uprising under the story of national resistance and liberation. By contrast, the play aims to have the specificity of Ovaherero suffering during and since the colonial genocide recognized in the Namibian public sphere. Finally, performers satirize traditional Ovaherero leaders' authoritarianism and patriarchal comportment, aligning the production with feminist calls for equality in the Namibian public sphere.

The reconceived virtual stations, some of them newly created for *Hereroland 2* and filmed on location, echo the critique of stalled decolonization. A number of them criticize the continued symbolic domination of Namibian cityscapes by settler colonial perspectives. In addition, they problematize the economic domination of German-speaking farmers in Namibian agriculture and tourism and call for the decolonization of these sectors through land reform. At the same time, they acknowledge that climate change threatens the land's ability to sustain agriculture. However, in contrast to the central live performance, which is characterized by intense corporeal and verbal expressions of anger, the stations provide analyses of the causes of anger that are emotionally understated. They require a high degree of viewers' emotional involvement and completion. For instance, the station "City Walk Swakopmund" (like "Museum" and "Cemetery") features sites and institutions that embody settler history, and virtually places spectators in close aural proximity to an off-screen German-speaking guide who offers nostalgic, revisionist glosses on the town's history, as well as disparaging comments about graffiti applied to a large, centrally located monument to fallen *Schutztruppen* soldiers, which Ovahereros want to see removed. Rather than perform anger, this station and similar ones incite this very rage. The narrators strike an affable, confidential tone, seemingly imagining that they share a story with like-minded white visitors. Listeners are exposed to an unvarnished glimpse of white supremacy; those who refuse interpellation into this presumed camaraderie are all the more jolted into a decolonial critique. While the virtual surrounds appear placid, visiting them may well leave viewers seething.

Finally, the play directs a good part of its anger towards both contemporary Ovaherero culture and its political leadership. In a raging monologue, an Ovaherero woman (Kavari) bitterly deplores the youth's forgetting of their ancestor's sacrifices and abandoning of "the tradition that governs a Herero person, their homestead and identity" (*Hereroland 2* Videorecording of Windhoek performance). Both Tjiipura and Kavari note that mass rape was part of colonial warfare, and Kavari deplores the degradation of women, which persisted through

Apartheid and after independence, as a feature of the "present [Herero] civilization" and its "loss of a compass" (*Hereroland 2* Videorecording of Windhoek performance). The women's wrath resonates with the decades-long struggles against the high rates of sexual and gender-based violence, including femicide, in independent Namibia (Edwards-Jauch).[14] Namibian sociologist Lucy Edwards-Jauch argues that "colonial history and traditional forms of African patriarchy converge to justify women's subordination, gender inequality and different dimensions of violence against women" (Edwards-Jauch 56). A notion of decolonization that seeks to counter these patriarchal, militarized structures by reverting to precolonial African cultural norms does not sufficiently take into account the existence of patriarchal and homophobic traditions that predate colonization. Mushaandja and Edwards-Jauch, among others, thus call for a progressive, feminist, and queer remaking of Africanness.[15] *Hereroland 2*'s centering of women in the troping of historical violence, and of rape as a key dimension of colonial subjugation, amplifies the focus on sexual and gender-based violence within decolonial discourses in Namibia. Moreover, the young women's wearing of traditional Ovaherero dresses in performance, usually reserved for older, married women, signals the ensemble's simultaneous embracing and reimagining of precolonial traditions. By amplifying the feminist critique of coloniality, *Hereroland 2* positions women within longer histories of patriarchal violence, and situates them in proximity to feminist movements that intersect with decolonial struggles for land rights, fair distribution of resources, and racial justice.

The concluding discussion scene skewers Ovaherero traditional leaders for their autocratic and paternalistic ways. In that scene, Kandukira as the only older actor takes on the role of moderator and invites first the performers and then the audience to participate. Dressed in the kind of uniform worn by traditional leaders at official parades and commemorative events, he struts about the stage, proclaims himself "paramount chief," asks to be addressed by that title, and notes that he will shut up anyone who speaks out against him. He scoffs at the notion of a chief listening to his subjects, but sighs that such are the rules of democracy. Several of the Namibian performers buck at his rules of decorum. Their impatience with him frames the production as a challenge to traditional authority and

---

14 Protests against gender-based violence culminated in the #SlutShameWalk of 2019 and the #ShutItAllDown protests of young feminist and queer activists in 2020, but are situated within a longer history of student anticolonial and civil rights activism in Namibia. See Van Wyk 2022; Becker 2020; Becker 2010.

15 See Mushaandja. By contrast, scholars like Heike Becker (2007) doubt the existence of precolonial patriarchy in Namibia, and artist-activist Hildegard Titus argues that precolonial queer histories were eclipsed by colonialism and the Christian mission.

hierarchical structures and a plea for democratizing access to deliberation and decision-making. One performer comments that neither the SWAPO government nor Ovaherero traditional leaders could be trusted to make responsible decisions about the reparations that might soon flow from Germany. He argues that traditional leaders are fighting amongst themselves, rendering prospects dim that they are capable of making wise choices about the common good. The only half-satirical final scene raises larger questions about how Ovahereros might address and heal historical, intergenerational trauma, and calls for fresh ideas about reparations that go beyond returning land to Ovahereros and Ovahereros to the land: "Should we even have money? Or should we have scholarships? Should we have infrastructure?" asks Otja Kambaekua (*Hereroland 2* Videorecording of Windhoek performance). The concluding discussion clarifies the broadening meanings of decolonization in contemporary Namibia: besides the overcoming of colonial and Apartheid racisms, the production envisions cultural renewal that does not merely revive precolonial African traditions but aims to create a genuinely democratic culture grounded in civic participation and gender equality.

Germans play relatively marginal roles in the angry theater of irreconciliation. The two German actors who participated in *Hereroland 2* took on the parts of a *Schutztruppen* soldier and a composite of missionary and merchant, respectively. Their costumes certify them as belonging to the core personnel of the colonial project; yet on stage they play only supporting roles as silent executioners of the genocide.[16] Actor Jörg Pohl, who had played a number of prominent characters in *Hereroland* and portrayed the colonial soldier in *Hereroland 2*, characterized his work on the latter as an act of solidarity with his Ovaherero colleagues, subordinating his actorly ego to the project of bolstering their historical and political claims. In the discussion at the end of the play, for which he took off his costume and make-up, he stressed that he is here mostly to listen, not to talk, and that Germans must learn more about this shared past and take responsibility for it. He relates a story about the presence of Namibian copper in a famous Hamburg church as an example of becoming more conscious about the city's colonial involvement (Gramlich). Framing listening and learning, theatrical research and collaboration, as allyship, also led the German actors to distinguish themselves more visibly from the theatrical roles they played. Strikingly, the two actors chose to wear white make-up with dark circles around the eyes, lending them the ghostly appearance of skulls. "Whiteface" underlines the deadliness of colonial

---

16 Mathias Häussler has argued that among the settler population, traveling merchants, known for their treacherous behavior, were among the most hated by indigenous Namibians; he regards settlers as key to the escalation of genocidal violence.

whiteness but also serves to hold it at a distance. On the one hand, the actors expose white masculinity as a social construction whose historically specific cruelty should be held up for inspection. On the other, whiteface underscores the categorical difference of the performers from these toxic social types. Through their striking make up and costumes, the performers marked their own position as supporters of the Ovaherero cause.

The confrontational directness of *Hereroland 2* thrilled some spectators, affirmed (if not exactly comforted) others, but affronted some who saw their settler ancestors incriminated. A glowing review in the daily newspaper *The Namibian* indicates that the urbane, international audience in the capital Windhoek was gripped by the performance (Mukaiwa), although Grünewald also remembered some German-speaking Namibians walking out during the skull-scraping scene without waiting how this historical experience would be contextualized in the course of the play.[17] In the coastal resort town of Swakopmund, where German speakers predominate, the play was presented in a school auditorium to scant audiences. Three performers remember them as reticent and cold, while Grünewald commended the descendants of German settlers for showing up at all. By contrast, the performances in the small town of Okakarara and the remote village of Otjinene were warmly received. Spectators were highly engaged: they sang along, wept, cajoled and encouraged, and even entered the playing space to join West Uarije in a dance. The varied reception suggests that *Hereroland 2* worked as an affirmation of Ovaherero struggles, fanning their dedication to wrestling with decolonial justice, and of their yearning for unity. It shows that German-speaking Namibians are divided about listening to Ovaherero perspectives; perhaps the anguish and anger they witnessed pushed some of them into recognizing past and present pain and injustice, and taking up the social, economic, and political obligations flowing from that recognition.

III

The two iterations of *Hereroland*, one promoting empathy with Ovahereros, the other anger at incomplete decolonization, offer equally valid strategies of decolonial performance. Both reject the Joint Declaration's attempt to settle damages and draw a line under the past. The Hamburg version co-directed by Ndjavera strove for a notion of reconciliation that emphasized the need for broad social dialogue within and between both countries and underscored the Ovaherero

---

[17] Conversation with Gernot Grünewald, October 1, 2024.

quest for material reparations as crucial for any reconciliation between Ovahereros, German-speaking Namibians, and Germans. The production's use of immersive techniques forged both planetary linkages and emotional enmeshments, to facilitate decolonial allyship and reflect on indebtedness and obligation. The Namibian version echoed the insistence on material reparations. But it also vehemently called out the accommodations that different groups in independent Namibia, including Ovaherero traditional authorities, have made in the postcolonial bargain to secure social peace at the cost of reckoning with colonial injustices and the legacies of Apartheid. The decolonial theater of anger rejects any reconciliation that accepts or takes for granted the postcolonial status quo, instead holding open a space where decolonial justice must first be imagined and debated before any concrete plans for reparations and repair can be implemented. These different accentuations became especially clear with regard to land: whereas the earlier version suggests that justice hinges on restoring ownership of the land to Ovahereros, the later version evinced skepticism at restoring precolonial conditions, and envisioned alternatives to resuming cattle herding. The feminist critique of sexual and gender-based violence historically and in the present, moreover, propelled a simultaneous reclaiming and remaking of Africanness as a source of cultural and spiritual resurgence.

Arguably, the decolonial theater of anger might have impressed on German audiences as well the fury and impatience Ovahereros feel about Germans' century-long denial of the Herero and Nama genocide, waffling about reparations, and one-sided official antiracism. The shift from empathy to anger raises the question whether there's more at stake than simply adapting to different locations and political constellations. Is the emphasis on empathy, reconciliation, and forgiveness in the Hamburg version also a function of international power dynamics? Would an angry stance in Hamburg have affronted audiences, turning them off support for the decolonial cause at a time when that support was already tenuous? A theater of empathy might be merely a euphemism for coddling German audiences. Would a decolonial theater of anger that hinged after all on an invitation, simply have led to being disinvited? Hamburg audiences could witness the decolonial theater of anger only during a single performance, when they were connected via livestream to the stage in Windhoek. The responses of two (very appreciative) German spectators, who stepped up to the microphone during the concluding discussion, are not sufficient to judge how *Hereroland 2* might have fared in Germany. The very unique circumstances under which a theater of anger could burst forth in Namibia also highlights the fact that its emergence in postmigrant Berlin theater rests at least in some part on the security that its angry subjects cannot, as German citizens, be disinvited, evicted, or deported (at least for now), even when they are persistently construed as Others. This is a luxury unavailable to citizens of the Global South whose international mobility is contingent on the goodwill of the Foreign Office, which issues their visas. As the political climate is turning against decolonial confrontations, a decolonial *international* theater of anger might simply not be feasible in the foreseeable future.

What are the prospects for continuing the decolonization of official Namibian memory culture? In recent years, cultural funding for international projects has increasingly supported bringing Namibian artists to Germany to do research, sometimes in colonial archives, take up longer residencies, and to show their work, outside of the constraints of cooperation. Cultural institutes even, on occasion, initiate South-South exchanges among artists from former German colonies on the African continent. These developments are particularly important given that several of the Namibian artists I spoke to have experienced indifference, disrespect, and even physical danger in the theatrical "contact zone" (Pratt; Haakh). *Hereroland* and *Hereroland 2* are highly instructive as examples of ethical international collaboration. In the emergent "colonial cultural industry" described to me by the director of the *Goethe Institut* in Windhoek, in which German artists and organizations cast about for Hereros (sometimes Namas) to authenticate colonial fictions couched as "collaborative" endeavors, international grants have allowed German partners to shape how anticolonial and decolonial critique is performed to German and African publics. As Nora Haakh has argued in another context, only repeated exposures to the German arts infrastructure enables foreign artists to navigate "conditional invitations" and structural inequality in the postcolonial contact zone (Haakh 263). The wrapping up of the TURN fund in 2021 eliminated an important source of support for cultural cooperation between German and African artists just when decolonial projects picked up steam. The funding cuts to the arts enacted in 2024 further limit opportunities for foreign artists to present their work in Germany or collaborate with colleagues there (Philipp). Without German grants, it will be more difficult for Namibian artists to realize decolonial work that could shape debates in the Namibian public sphere.

The collapsing support for international collaboration and cultural diplomacy signals that governmental support for decolonial projects is flagging in Germany. Hopes that the shift towards a decolonial German memory politics would be institutionalized by the coalition government of social democratic, green, and liberal parties that came to power in December 2021,[18] were disappointed. The critical commemoration of colonialism, proposed by then-Minister of Culture Claudia Roth in June 2024, was scuttled and is no longer included in the federal framework for memory politics, which remains focused on Nazi atrocities and the so-

---

[18] The coalition collapsed in November 2024, triggering federal elections in February 2025.

cialist past; historian Jürgen Zimmerer publicly criticized the Minister for demoting victims of colonialism to second class status (Zimmerer 2024b). The network "Decolonial Memory Culture in the City," which ran in Berlin from 2018 to 2024, seeded a plethora of cultural endeavors, and boosted decolonial cultural expertise, has concluded its work. Funding for the postcolonial research center in Hamburg was not renewed. The right-wing party *Alternative für Deutschland*, which gained the second largest share of votes in the federal elections of 2025, opposes decolonial memorialization, restitution, and reparations. Despite these structural obstacles, I argue that cultural institutions and projects have an important role to play in negotiating the colonial past even in the absence of official, political support, or indeed because of it.

Works Cited

Arthur Koppel Aktiengesellschaft. *Zur Erinnerung an den Bau der Otavi Bahn 1903–1906: Unseren Freunden gewidmet*. Selbstverlag, 1907.

Azoulay, Ariella Aisha. *Potential History: Unlearning Imperialism*. Verso, 2019.

Becker, Heike. "A Concise History of Gender, 'Tradition,' and the State in Namibia." *State, Society and Democracy: A Reader in Namibian Politics*, edited by Christiaan Keulder, Macmillan Education Namibia, 2010, pp. 171–199.

Becker, Heike. "Gender, Making Tradition: A Historical Perspective on Gender in Namibia." *Unravelling Taboos: Gender and Sexuality in Namibia*, edited by Suzanne LaFont and Dianne Hubbard, Legal Assistance Centre, 2007, pp. 99–128.

Becker, Heike. "#ShutItAllDownNamibia: Young Namibians are Hitting the Streets Against Gender-Based Violence and Colonial Legacies." *Rosa Luxemburg Stiftung News*, Rosalux.de/en/news/id/43225/shutitalldownnamibia. 27 October 2020.

Case, Sue-Ellen. *Performing Science and the Virtual*. Routledge, 2006.

Cole, Catherine M. *Performing South Africa's Truth Commission: Stages of Transition*. Indiana UP, 2009.

Edwards-Jauch, Lucy. "Gender-based violence and masculinity in Namibia: A structuralist framing of the debate." *Journal for Studies in Social Sciences*, vol. 5, no. 1, 2016, pp. 49–62.

El-Tayeb, Fatima. *European Others: Queering Ethnicity in Postnational Europe*. U of Minnesota P, 2011.

Federal Republic of Germany and the Republic of Namibia. "Joint Declaration: United in Remembrance of our Colonial Past, United in our Will to Reconcile, United in our Vision of the Future." parliament.na/wp-content/uploads/2021/09/Joint-Declaration-Document-Genocide-rt.pdf 5 May 2021.

Förster, Larissa. *Postkoloniale Erinnerungslandschaften: Wie Deutsche und Herero in Namibia des Kriegs von 1904 gedenken*. Campus, 2010.

Forschungsstelle Hamburgs (post-)koloniales Erbe. *Universität Hamburg*, geschichte.uni-hamburg.de/arbeitsbereiche/globalgeschichte/forschung/forschungsstelle-hamburgs-postkoloniales-erbe.html. 21 May 2025.

Frye, Marilyn. *The Politics of Reality: Essays in Feminist Theory*. The Crossing P, 1983.

Gramlich, Noam. *Zur Kolonialität von Kupfer: Eine situierte Mediengeologie der Mine in Tsumeb*. Campus, 2024.

Haakh, Nora Marianne. *Layla and Majnun in der Contact Zone: Übertragungen aus dem Arabischen ins Deutsche im Bereich des zeitgenössischen Theaters*. 2019. Freie Universität Berlin, PhD Thesis.
Hackmack, Judith. "Repairing the Irreparable? Tackling the long-term Effects of German Colonialism in Germany & Namibia." *European Center for Constitutional and Human Rights Policy Paper*, October 2022, pp. 1–8.
Häussler, Matthias. *Der Genozid an den Herero: Krieg, Emotion und extreme Gewalt in Deutsch-Südwestafrika*. Velbrück, 2018.
Hereroland Textbuch. Unpublished script of Hamburg production. Thalia Theater, 2020.
Hereroland. Videorecording of Hamburg performance. 19 January 2020.
Hereroland 2. Videorecording of Windhoek performance. 29 June 2023.
hooks, bell. *Killing Rage: Ending Racism*. Henry Holt & Co., 1995.
Kößler, Reinhart. *Namibia and Germany: Negotiating the Past*. Westfälisches Dampfboot, 2015.
Kolesch, Doris. "Vom Reiz des Immersiven: Überlegungen zu einer Virulenten Konfiguration der Gegenwart." *Paragrana*, vol. 26, no. 2, 2017, pp. 57–66.
Landry, Olivia. *The Theatre of Anger: Radical Transnational Performance in Contemporary Berlin*. U of Toronto P, 2021.
Levy, Daniel, and Natan Sznaider. "Memory Unbound: The Holocaust and the Formation of Cosmopolitan Memory." *European Journal of Social Theory*, vol. 5, no. 1, 2002, pp. 87–106.
Melber, Henning. *The Long Shadow of German Colonialism: Amnesia, Denialism and Revisionism*. Hurts & Co., 2024.
Mukaiwa, Martha. "'Hereroland' is an Ambitious Examination of 1904 Genocide." *The Namibian*. namibian.com.na/hereroland-is-an-ambitious-examination-of-1904-genocide/. 8 July 2023.
Mushaandja, Nashilongweshipwe. "Critical Visualities & Spatialities: Protest, Performance, Publicness and Praxis." *Namibian Journal of Social Justice*, vol. 1, 2021, pp. 192–201.
Olivier-Sampson, Laurinda. "Representing Namibian Drama (1985–2000): Frederick Philander." *Writing Namibia: Literature in Transition*, edited by Sarala Krishnamurthy and Helen Vale, U of Namibia P, 2018, pp. 172–182.
Parsons, Rosemary. *Group Devised Theatre. A Theoretical and Practical Examination of Devising Processes*. Lambert Academic Publishing, 2010.
Philipp, Elena. "Verlässlich war gestern." *Der Freitag*, 9 January 2025, p. 22.
Pratt, Mary Louise. *Imperial Eyes: Travel Writing and Transculturation*. Routledge, 1992.
Projektstelle für die Dekolonisierung Hamburgs. *Freie und Hansestadt Hamburg*, hamburg.de/politik-und-verwaltung/behoerden/behoerde-fuer-kultur-und-medien/themen/koloniales-erbe/team-dekololonisation-110440. 21 May 2025.
Rogers, Thomas. "The Long Shadow of German Colonialism." *The New York Review of Books*, 9 March 2023, p. 40.
Rothberg, Michael. *The Implicated Subject: Beyond Victims and Perpetrators*. Stanford UP, 2019.
Titus, Hildegard. "Decolonising Namibia's Queer History." *The Namibian*. namibian.com.na/decolonising-namibias-queer-history/. 26 May 2023.
Van Wyk, Bayron. *'Anything about us, without us, is against us': An Ethnography of the Genocide Reparations and Decolonial Movements in Namibia*. 2022. University of the Western Cape, MA Thesis.
Van Wyk, Bayron. "Apology and Reparations: Reflections on the Genocide Reparations Agreement between Germany and Namibia." *Rosa Luxemburg Stiftung*, Rosalux.de/en/news/id/45028/apology-and-reparations. 21 September 2021.
Wilson, Paul. "Remembering the Herero-Nama Genocide in Namibia." *African Arts*, vol. 56, no. 1, 2023, pp. 62–81.

Zeller, Joachim. "'Images of the South West African War': Reflections of the 1904–1907 Colonial War in Contemporary Photo Reportage and Book Illustration." *Hues between Black and White: Historical Photography from Colonial Namibia 1860s to 1915*, edited by Wolfram Hartmann, Out of Africa Publishers, 2004, pp. 309–323.

Zimmerer, Jürgen. "Hinterzimmerdeal mit Namibia wirft neue Fragen auf: Zum Streit um die Anerkennung des Genozids an den Herero und Nama." *Universität Hamburg*, Kolonialismus. blogs.uni-hamburg.de/2024/07/03/pressekomumentation-hinterzimmererdeal-mit-namibia-wirft-neue-fragen-auf-zum-streit-um-die-anerkennung-des-genozids-an-den-herero-und-nama-zuerst-erschienen-bei-africa-table/. 3 July 2024a.

Zimmerer, Jürgen. "Koloniales Erbe Deutschlands: Sind Opfer außerhalb Europas Opfer zweiter Klasse?" *Tagesspiegel*, Tagesspiegel.de/kultur/koloniales-erbe-sind-deutsche-opfer-ausserhalb-europeas-opfer-zweiter-klasse-12092588.html. 2 August 2024b.

Caroline Schaumann
Haarbüschel, *Pausbacke*, and *Fledermaus*: Christopher Kloeble's Recasting of the Schlagintweit Expedition in *Das Museum der Welt* (2020)

Abstract: In *Das Museum der Welt* (2020), Christopher Kloeble presents a fictionalized recasting of the 1854–1857 expedition by the three Bavarian Schlagintweit brothers to India, the Himalayan Mountain range, and parts of Central Asia. Complementing recent rewritings of expeditions in colonial times (Kehlmann, Hamann, Trojanow), Kloeble, too, seeks approaches and writing strategies that undermine the hierarchies of traditional travelogues. Kloeble portrays the Schlagintweit expedition from the vantage point of a fictional young Indian travel companion, a trickster and rogue hero in the picaresque tradition who undermines the dominant power relations. This shift in perspective and genre allows for several interventions: it avoids a heroic glorification of the Schlagintweits and decenters the European gaze, highlighting the importance and agency of so-called historical minor characters such as translators, assistants, and guides. Drawing on the subversive potential of mimicry (Bhabha), this essay suggests that Kloeble's *picaro* depicts the Schlagintweits' mission with wit and irony, exposing the utterly irrational elements of enlightenment science in the colonies and offering a pointed critique of Western discovery and exploration.

I

Upon the recommendation of Alexander von Humboldt, in 1854 the British East India Company invited the brothers Hermann, Adolph, and Robert Schlagintweit to an exploration of India, the Himalayan Mountain range, and parts of Central Asia, with some expenses funded by the Prussian King Friedrich Wilhelm IV. The British Empire was primarily interested in the prospective practical applications of their research, such as the expanse of forests for building materials, agricultural lands for the cultivation of tobacco, coffee, tea, and spices, as well as coal and mineral deposits. The modest Prussian support was more concerned with a geographical investigation of the Himalayan region mirroring the comprehensive and comparative aims of Humboldt's own research. The Schlagintweit brothers spent the following three years (1854–1857) in India and high Asia in varying groups of regional guides, translators, and assistants, exploring topographies, glaciers, vegetation, and cultural sites.

As the Schlagintweit journey itself became the subject of critical reevaluation in the twentieth and twenty-first centuries, it also invited experimental forms of writing. In *Das Museum der Welt* (2020, translated into English as *The Museum of the World* [2022]), Christopher Kloeble presents a fictionalized view of the expedition from the perspective of a young Indian travel companion. Kloeble depicts the Schlagintweits' mission with wit and irony, similar to Daniel Kehlmann's *Die Vermessung der Welt* (2005) – the fictional biographical account of Carl Friedrich Gauß and Alexander von Humboldt – especially with respect to the latter's journey to South and Central America 1799–1804. Like Kehlmann, Kloeble portrays the nineteenth-century German protagonists in a distant, laconic, and humorous if not satirical tone, though without resorting to the frequent indirect speech that characterized Kehlmann's novel. Both authors point to the utterly irrational elements of Western science in the wake of the enlightenment, specifically as it concerns Germans' scientific expeditions to colonized lands. If the unadorned style in both novels functions as a distancing device that prevents adulation or heroic embellishment, Kloeble goes a step further by denying the explorers their own rendering of the voyage and by refraining from an omniscient narrator to convey the events. Instead, Kloeble portrays the expedition from the vantage point of a fictional Indian adolescent boy. Through this shift, Kloeble not only avoids a heroic glorification of the Schlagintweits but decenters the European gaze altogether, pointing to the gaps in the documented historical tradition.

Kloeble's novel continues the efforts of contemporary German-language writers to critically illuminate and reevaluate historical expeditions of colonial times. Aside from the aforementioned *Die Vermessung der Welt*, Christof Hamann in his novel *Usambara* (2007) retells the story of Mount Kilimanjaro's first European ascent in 1889 by the German geographer Hans Meyer and the Austrian mountaineer Ludwig Purtscheller, mediated by several interlocutors and fictional travel companions. In *Bis ans Ende der Meere* (2009), Lukas Hartmann revisits James Cook's Third Pacific Voyage (1776–1779) through the eyes of its young draftsman, the novel's main character John Webber. Multiple shifts of perspective also inform Ilija Trojanow's *Der Weltensammler* (2006) fictionalizing the life and obsessive travels of Richard Francis Burton, a multilingual British colonial officer. Trojanow juxtaposes Burton's point of view with the (fictional) reports of guides and servants he encounters in British India, Mecca, and East Africa. Finally, the Austrian writer Raoul Schrott, in his meticulously researched *Eine Geschichte des Windes oder: Von dem deutschen Kanonier der erstmals die Welt umrundete und dann ein zweites und ein drittes Mal* (2019), adopts the perspective and baroque folksy voice of Hannes from Aachen who (presumably) accompanied Ferdinand

Magellan as an unpaid gunner on his circumnavigation of the world and returned as one of only eighteen survivors.

In his incisive analysis of literary rewritings of expeditions in colonial times, Hansjörg Bay credits Hamann and Trojanow with an inventive narrative structure that aptly conveys colonial entanglements while also cautioning against a "kolonialen Wiederholungszwang" (Bay 2012, 130). Specifically, Bay contends that the literary recastings he analyzes feed into our continued fascination with so-called Western discovery but run the risk of reinscribing local inhabitants in lower profile or cliched patterns. Kloeble, too, focuses on European exploration, but the novel's peculiar narrative perspective, its complex cast of characters, episodic plot, and use of humor and satire encourage a much-needed questioning of the Schlagintweit expedition's hierarchies, priorities, and recording methods. Kloeble focalizes the narrative through the perspective of a historical minor character through a multilingual boy who acts as a translator to the Bavarian Schlagintweit brothers. But as readers learn over the course of the novel, the narrator's perspective is more complicated than it first seems. As the illegitimate son of a Hanoverian soldier and an Indian mother who died in childbirth, the fictional main character and narrator Bartholomäus was placed in a Bombay orphanage and grew up under the tutelage of a Bavarian missionary, Father Fuchs (also a fictional character). In this way, Bartholomäus carries the double legacy of colonizer and colonized, literally embodying the transcultural negotiations in the contact zones of colonization that Homi K. Bhabha outlined in his concept of hybridity.

To Bhabha, cultural identities emerging in such a Third Space carry transformative capacity, as also exemplified in his essay "Of Mimicry and Man: The Ambivalence of Colonial Discourse" (1984). When the colonized are forced to assimilate and imitate colonial powers, the mimicry of colonizer culture (via language and cultural practices) begins to blur the difference between colonized and colonizer, which, as Bhabha suggests, produces an ambivalence that lays bare the disingenuousness of the colonial mission and threatens its claim to superiority. In this way, mimicry is both a subservient survival strategy and functions as a form of resistance that destabilizes the colonial system. In Kloeble's novel, mimicry indeed becomes a tool of subversion when Bartholomäus passes through both India's privileged and poor spaces, outsmarting German explorers and British governors alike. Conversely, Bartholomäus' transformative power to assimilate highlights the Schlagintweits' clumsy and failed attempts to adapt to India's cultures, resulting in their utter dependence on translators, guides, and other expedition members.[1] If Bhabha

---

[1] Hansjörg Bay (2009) offers a useful critical juxtaposition of Bhabha's mimicry and colonizers' assimilation (117–122).

emphasized intercultural contact and interdependence over a clearly demarcated opposition of colonizer and colonized, he was at times criticized for downplaying the imbalance of colonial power relations.

Gayatri Chakravorty Spivak has precisely highlighted the power dynamics of colonial representation. By outlining the potential and tendency for misrepresentation and exclusion, Spivak offers a pointed critique of appropriation when hegemonic groups speak for marginalized groups (Spivak 1988). Indeed, this poses a dilemma for Western authors to either reinscribe a European perspective of exploration or adopt a (presumptuous) perspective of the colonized that is neither familiar nor much documented in prevailing historical records.[2] Kloeble fashions as narrator an orphaned Indian boy, an outsider between colonizer and colonized but bestowed with power and influence far greater than historical realities permit. To be sure, this fictionalized mediation does not change the hierarchical and asymmetrical structures of the colonial discourse, and it cannot speak for the subaltern or imbue the dispossessed with more agency. Rather, I suggest, the interventions of Kloeble's idealized narrator that readers can readily expose as wishful thinking help illuminate the complex, tenuous, and uneven configurations of European exploration while pointing to significant gaps in historical documentation. By harkening back to the tradition of the picaresque genre, the narration follows Gregor Schuhen's genre definition: "der *picaro* reist umher, er ist permanenter Gewalt ausgesetzt, er betrügt, er taktiert, er macht Späße, er dient, er erzählt" (Schuhen 17). In this way, *Das Museum der Welt* disrupts our expectations of exploration narratives, allowing for the laws of probability to be stretched. To Michaela Holdenried, inverted strategies of representation help create critical distance to established discourses: "Gerade weil sie sich nicht das 'Recht auf Repräsentation' anmaßen, erweisen sich derlei literarische Formen als glaubwürdiger in der Darstellung fremdkultureller Alterität als andere" (Holdenried 296). In *Das Museum der Welt* it is precisely the quixotic literary form that lays bare the tensions between absent and existing documentation and the pressing need for imagination.

II

Along their historic 1854–1857 journey, the Schlagintweits produced maps, drawings, photographs, and descriptions of landscapes, the flora and fauna, and provided studies on geology and meteorology along with (often discriminatory) observations of peoples and civilizations. They also compiled a vast collection of

---

2 See also Bay 2009, 134.

plant specimen, rocks, and cultural artifacts. As the brothers, with the help of guides, translators, and porters, climbed mountains, surveyed the land, documented its cultures, and amassed artifacts, they adhered to a *Weltanschauung* indebted to enlightenment and European liberalism rooted in deep-seated beliefs of Western superiority. Their vast measurements and comparative perspectives followed Humboldt's approach; yet in contrast to their mentor they did not seek to elucidate the interactions of ecological and cultural forces and did not question the colonial paradigm nor voice political or environmental critiques as Humboldt did (see Schaumann 2017 and 2024).

While the brothers largely slipped into obscurity, a biographical sketch in the ideologically colored *Helden der Berge* (published in 1935, then in revised form in 1970) by the influential South Tyrolean Alpinist, writer, actor and film director Luis Trenker glorified them as heroic mountaineers embarking on larger-than-life adventures on the "dark" subcontinent:

> Das ist das seltsame Schicksal der drei Brüder Schlagintweit! Alles haben sie auf das eine Ziel gesetzt: Himalaya! Ihr Geld, ihre Gesundheit, ihre Existenz, ihr Leben; denn sie waren Deutsche und machten die Sache gründlich. Dafür wurden sie aber auch gründlich vergessen. [. . .] der Winkel zwischen Indien, China und Turkestan war damals noch ziemlich unbekannt, und die Asienkarte wies hier einen hellen, weißen Fleck auf, der besagte, daß hier alles noch finster und dunkel sei. Aber gerade dieser Fleck war es, der den Brüdern Schlagintweit keine Ruhe ließ. (*Helden der Berge* 83)[3]

If Trenker posthumously attempted to recuperate the German mission in colonial India, a special exhibit at the Alpines Museum in Munich in 2015, followed by historian Moritz von Brescius's study *German Science in the Age of Empire: Enterprise, Opportunity, and the Schlagintweit Brothers* (2018), brought the brothers and their ambitious and ambiguous journey to renewed attention eight decades later, highlighting the Schlagintweits' often questionable research methods, their precarious funding, and the role of their travel companions. Rudi Palla's 2019 biographical account, *In Schnee und Eis: Die Himalaja Expedition der Brüder Schlagintweit*, followed suit, seeking to correct the hero worship:

> Hermann, Adolph und Robert waren gewiss nicht die heroischen Reisenden, die in unerschlossenen Gebieten, inmitten einer unbändigen Natur geforscht hatten, als die sie in verschiedenen patriotischen Publikationen verherrlicht wurden. (*In Schnee und Eis* 185)

Nevertheless, the book's main thrust follows Trenker in depicting the brothers as indefatigable mountaineers willing to risk their lives to conquer Himalayan

---

[3] Luis Trenker, "Die drei Himalajabrüder: Adolf, Hermann und Robert Schlagintweit," *Helden der Berge* (83), hereafter referred to as *Helden*.

heights and gain scientific insights. In this way, the back cover claims, the Schlagintweits advance

> tief hinein in den Himalaja, um dort wissenschaftliche Daten zu erheben, die höchsten Pässe der Welt zu erklimmen – und um Ruhm zu erlangen setzen sie sogar ihr Leben aufs Spiel. Und wurden dennoch von der Nachwelt vergessen. (*Schnee* n.p.)

Despite outwardly rejecting Trenker's glorification, Palla's book reiterates many of Trenker's views, such as the emphasis on the brothers' sacrifice, their risking of life and limb, their mountaineering achievements in unknown territories, and their perceived missing recognition.

With his novel, Kloeble takes a decidedly different approach, choosing fictional interventions to counter both the glorification of the Schlagintweit brothers as heroes and the dearth of historical records. After detailing the best-known achievements of the brothers in a short preamble, Kloeble concludes: "They would never have been able to achieve all this without the help of numerous people who accompanied them. One of them was an orphan boy from Bombay" (n.p.).[4] The fictional intervention continues with three quotes about the Schlagintweits that preface the novel, one from a letter by Alexander von Humboldt, one from a novel by Jules Verne, and a fictional quote by Kloeble's protagonist Bartholomäus: "I wish the Schlagintweits had never come to India" (n.p.). This bold – and sometimes criticized[5] – move lends the power of speech to someone who usually would not have had a public voice, an orphan between the ages of 12 and 15 years of age over the course of the novel and a figure loosely based on a composite of several historical travel companions of the expedition. By adding a fictional quote to the historical documents, Kloeble suggests that we will have to imagine the histories of those not privileged enough to be preserved in official records or documents. And by placing Bartholomäus' words next to the well-known praise by Humboldt and Verne, Kloeble invites readers to question the expedition's overall value. When Bartholomäus utters the same wish later in the novel (*Museum* 142), he calls attention to issues of exploitation and violence in the wake of colonial exploration, exposing and highlighting the discrimination and injustices stemming from the Schlagintweit expedition.

As an uncannily bright yet ill-mannered child, Bartholomäus witnesses the Schlagintweit exploration and the entire world of adults differently from them. Not being motivated by adult drives pertaining to power, wealth, and sex, Bartho-

---

4 Christopher Kloeble, *Das Museum der Welt*. Translated into English by Rekha Kamath Rajan as *The Museum of the World*, hereafter referred to as *Museum*.
5 See Miryam Schellbach's scathing review in the *Frankfurter Allgemeine Zeitung*, which, however, contains several errors in its description of the book.

lomäus remains unencumbered to freely describe and evaluate political plots, drug trades, and amorous innuendos. He is also privy to encounters and conversations precisely because he is not seen as an adult. In this aspect, the novel bears some resemblance with Günter Grass' *Die Blechtrommel* (1959). Bartholomäus has a much-expanded view because he observes the world from below, from a frog's-eye view, so to speak. While Bartholomäus may not have sufficient background knowledge to explain the motives, tactical moves, and competing goals of the various expedition members and other protagonists, as a brown and presumedly naïve child he remains "invisible" (*Museum* 137) in the world of white influential adults and is given considerably more leeway. Over the course of the novel, Bartholomäus becomes a protégé with privilege and access and is entrusted with confidential information from several rivaling protagonists.

Das Museum der Welt comprises a coming-of-age story, depicting Bartholomäus' development through travels and encounters, in which the narrator observes love, lust, and violence in personal relationships as well as political plots for power and control. As Paul Michael Lützeler pointed out in his review in the *Tagesspiegel*, the novel depicts Bartholomäus' growth like a *Bildungsroman* through insights, mishaps, opportunities, coincidences, disillusionment, and learning processes. Yet I propose that *Das Museum der Welt*, with its trickster protagonist who stumbles into adventures, deceives his superiors, and survives calamities, resembles even more a picaresque novel, a genre which permits Kloeble to critically probe the expedition and its goals.

Juxtaposing the *Bildungsroman* and the picaresque novel, Maren Lickhardt concludes: "Der pikareske Weg ist kein progressiver und oftmals idealisierter Bildungsweg. Die zyklische Struktur schließt innerhalb der erlebten Handlung eine lineare Progression, einen Fortschritt oder Aufstieg aus" (Lickhardt 193). In the tradition of the picaresque, the various destinations along Bartholomäus' journey become sites of trial and error but do not build up in continuous progression. Lickhardt sees a renewed rise of the picaresque in the twentieth and twenty-first centuries, since it emphasizes "Unterwegssein und unzuverlässiges Erzählen, ein[en] unvorhersehbare[n] Weg und ein[en] uneindeutige[n] Bericht" (Lickhardt 192). Indeed, the genre proves exceedingly suitable to capture the unforeseen and unintended, productive and destructive aspects of European exploration. By assuming a voice that is at once appealing and unreliable, Kloeble highlights both the central importance of low-status travel companions and their regrettable absence in historical documentation. Another important aspect of the picaresque genre is its capacity for delivering a political critique. Pertaining to his own novel of colonial exploitation *Eine Geschichte des Windes*, Raoul Schrott explains:

> Umso reizvoller war es, diese Expeditionen einmal nicht aus der Heldenperspektive der hohen Herren zu betrachten, welche die Missionen anführten, sondern all ihre Fährnisse, Irrungen und Wirrungen samt der inneren und äußeren Konflikte von unten her zu schildern: aus dem Blickwinkel eines Simplicissimus. Der wie jener des Grimmelshausen zwar schelmisch ist, aber dabei allmählich klüger wird – wenn auch nicht eremitenhaft weise. (Schrott n.p.)

Schrott's and Kloeble's protagonists navigate land, sea, and society horizontally and vertically, deceiving their expedition leaders and higher-ups by defying coercion through mischief. As a rogue picaresque hero, Bartholomäus mocks Victorian ideals and subverts British power when naming the colonizers "Vickys": "the English call everything and everyone in India as it pleases them. Therefore, it is only fair that I call them what I please" (*Museum* 5). Bartholomäus' mischief comically lays bare the stiff conventions of the Victorian Age but also takes on a distinct political agenda when he becomes a spy for the rebellion forces and the Chinese government, working several sides at once while evaluating their motives, goals, and means. At the conclusion of the novel, Bartholomäus rejects the Schlagintweits' offer to follow them to Germany and instead decides to join the widespread but ultimately unsuccessful Indian Rebellion in 1857. Unlike previous nonfictional renderings of the expedition, Kloeble does not end his novel with the Schlagintweits' return to Germany. And unlike the ensuing historical record, Kloeble does not depict the brutal dissolution of the Indian Rebellion and inception of the British Raj. Instead, the picaresque form allows Kloeble to close his novel open-ended, with a hopeful Bartholomäus renouncing his name along with the use of German and English and affirming his Indian identity as Eleazar.

III

As a self-assured and brazen protagonist, Bartholomäus refuses to be subjugated to the role of a servant by the Schlagintweits and the colonial British Empire whose interests they represent. Pursuing his own agenda, he instead turns the scientists into objects of his own museum. At the orphanage in Bombay, Bartholomäus was schooled by the Jesuit Father Fuchs who acts as a loving father to the boy, teaches him German and the Bavarian dialect, and names him Bartholomäus after one of the twelve Apostles who went to India but also after Bartholomäus Ziegenbart (1682–1719), a Protestant missionary who established schools in India and translated the Bible into Tamil. The novel begins with Father Fuchs' disappearance (as we later find out, he suffered from severe tuberculosis and likely died of an Opium overdose) and Bartholomäus leaving the orphanage with the

Schlagintweits. Even though Bartholomäus initially sets out to look for his beloved mentor, he eventually comes to view Father Fuchs' naming, Christian education, and withholding information about his biological parents more critically. Over the course of the expedition, Bartholomäus becomes attached to the middle Schlagintweit brother, Adolph. As Bartholomäus learns more about the brothers and their project, however, and encounters unforeseen situations and new people and surroundings, his alliances begin to shift. In a surprising turn at the end of the novel, Bartholomäus learns that Father Fuchs baptized him at birth in order to protect him, given that he was an illegal offspring of a German soldier recruited to fight along the British in India and an Indian mother who died in childbirth. Bartholomäus must learn to live with this legacy. In Kloeble's version, it is the Indian orphan who, at the beginning of the novel in October 1854, finds, collects, and describes artifacts, people, flora and fauna, smells, and experiences named and numbered as "remarkable objects" 1 through 94 that form the chapters of *Das Museum der Welt*. Even before the Schlagintweits arrive at the orphanage to take him along as a translator, Bartholomäus had already begun collecting items for "India's first museum. I call it the Museum of the World" (*Museum* 3), a large-scale project inspired by Alexander von Humboldt's holistic vision, modeled after the British Museum, and named in antithesis to European colonial history. In his essay "Welt/Reisen: Zur Poetik des Globalen in Reisetexten des 21. Jahrhunderts," Bay tracks the epistemologically ambiguous yet totalizing claim of the term "world." In light of such global claims, the Indian orphan's "world" museum in Kloeble's novel robs the Schlagintweits, and European explorers in general, of their agency, upends traditional power structures, and questions Western hierarchies of knowledge.

While the Schlagintweits endeavor to establish an archive of India from the perspective of the colonizers by sketching landscapes, gathering plants, collecting rocks, measuring faces and bodies, taking pictures, and procuring face masks, Bartholomäus assembles his own museum made up of memories, dreams, notes, and small items. In stark contrast to the valuable items taken from the colonies and exhibited in the Western world, Bartholomäus' collection is deemed worthless and exists mainly on paper and in his mind. He selects and sorts the objects for his museum according to his own value system, including "exceedingly small objects that were collected on the street; they were thrown away or forgotten like orphans" (*Museum* 15). Drawing a parallel between the discarded items and his own identity as an Indian orphan, Bartholomäus seeks to make visible and elevate both, so that the museum becomes a personal and political quest. With his collection, Bartholomäus thus rewrites a material and cultural history of India from a decolonizing perspective, reordering and restructuring colonial patterns and practices.

Compared to the Schlagintweits, Bartholomäus is far superior at his task: He speaks a host of local languages such as Hindi, Gujarati, Punjabi, Marathi, and Farsi in addition to English and German, enabling him to understand and communicate not only with the influential politicians and businessmen they meet but also with local citizens, guards, and prisoners. He is intimately familiar with India's diverse religions and cultural traditions, conventions, and foods; at the same time, he is also well versed in Western thought, including the works of Humboldt and Goethe, among others. Unlike the Schlagintweits, Bartholomäus is also in constant communication with all expedition members. When Bartholomäus, at several points in the novel, wishes to depart from the expedition, the Schlagintweits desperately beg and then order him to stay. The fictional form here allows Kloeble to emphasize facts that are easily dismissed, namely Western travelers' utter dependence on Indigenous guides, cooks, porters, and merchants, resulting in an inversion of traditional power structures.

In his role as an often unwilling and poorly compensated translator, Bartholomäus begins to devise his own goals for the journey: these goals partly overlap with the Schlagintweits, partly with the Indian struggle for independence, and partly with his personal quest of finding Father Fuchs and creating his museum of India. In this multifaceted endeavor, he develops several strategies as a translator, underscoring the forceful potential of multilingualism: Bartholomäus adds his own questions regarding Father Fuchs' whereabouts into conversations with local officials, he mistranslates phrases like "soon" into "later" in order to extend the brothers' time in Bombay, he omits sentences he dislikes such as when he is ordered to be quiet, he changes names ("Nrupal" into "Nobody" (*Museum* 50)), and alters statements: "I transformed the precise instructions given by an official into diffuse statements" (*Museum* 40). In all these examples, Bartholomäus cleverly and successfully uses acts of mimicry to undermine the Schlagintweits' agenda for his own purposes. Even after he is caught and punished for his translation liberties, Bartholomäus continues more carefully, still fashioning translation into an act of defiance.

Overall, the novel illuminates the imaginative but also material power of translation as mimicry. Through his multilingualism, Bartholomäus enjoys hitherto unknown privilege and access: he is served imported frozen ice cubes and rides in horse-drawn carriages and on elephants, he is allowed to enter buildings and partake in gatherings frequented by Europeans, and even meets the Governor of Bombay, the Scottish Thirteenth Lord Elphinstone (1807–1860), the Governor-General of India, the Scottish First Marquess of Dalhousie, James Broun-Ramsay (1812–1860), and the head of the opium trade, Sir Jamsetjee Jejeebhoy (1783–1859), all authentic historical figures. Later in the novel, multilingualism becomes a means of survival when Bartholomäus acquires mysterious powers through his use of German that remains unintelligible to the porters and is able to convince them to cross over a mountain pass rather than stay behind in fear of the Hindu Goddess Nanda Devi.

Through the tool of translation, Bartholomäus has the power to expand or restrict the transfer of knowledge, and to deliver his own thoughts. Knowing languages thus renders power, and multilingualism becomes a tool of the resistance, granting Bartholomäus first hope and later literal aids for the Indian Rebellion:

> Every language gives me another home. And all of them together give me the confidence to know that the Vickys will soon go away. They will never be able to plant their English over our innumerable languages. (*Museum* 58)

As Bartholomäus provocatively predicts monolingualism to be the downfall of Empires, it is no coincidence that Eleazar, the character who eventually convinces him to join the resistance, is also a translator, speaking Malayalam, Hindi, English, Portuguese, Dutch, Chinese, and Hebrew. Moving between privileged and unprivileged spaces, knowing different languages provides Eleazar and Bartholomäus the freedom to remain understood, misunderstood, or not understood altogether in each of these spaces, an immense advantage and tool of mimicry for both adaptation and resistance.

IV

In the novel, the Schlagintweit brothers come across as sometimes likable, sometimes pitiful, but mostly arrogant, preposterous, and privileged travelers hopelessly overextended and unprepared for their proposed task. Bartholomäus terms Hermann *Haarbüschel* (Tufty) for his quivering moustache, Adolph *Pausbacke* (Chubby Cheek) for his puffed cheeks, and Robert *Fledermaus* (Bat) for his pointed protruding ears. Moreover, he mocks their white skin, flushed red faces, impractical clothing and constricting footwear, their measured steps and gesticulating arm movements, as well as their verbosity.

Even though Bartholomäus initially becomes impressed with the Schlagintweits' scientific quest, he recognizes both its unsound dimension and inherent racism. In this vein, he wonders why the so-called explorers exclusively pursue accommodation and company with fellow Europeans rather than locals (*Museum* 45) and choose to spend more time at official receptions and celebrations rather than in the remote areas they seek to explore (*Museum* 189). As a picaresque hero, Bartholomäus is given agency to expose the Schlagintweits' preposterousness and hypocrisy, as they judge and evaluate from an isolated position those they call "natives" (*Museum* 32) or "the Indians" (*Museum* 38). This becomes evident when Bartholomäus is tasked with reading a portion from Hermann Schlagintweit's notebook at Consul Ventz's residence in Bombay. The account describing "all races in India" (*Museum* 35) as lacking ambition and work ethic is as denigrating as it is ludicrous when the literate and multilingual boy is forced to read aloud a characterization of his race penned by someone who has not spent more than a few weeks in Bombay and does not speak local languages. Even in his third year on the subcontinent, Hermann Schlagintweit holds on to his derogatory beliefs when stating "that Indian cities have a uniform appearance and that it is difficult to distinguish between the races as well as the individuals" (*Museum* 345) in letters to his brothers from Bhutan and Assam that Bartholomäus once again reads (and translates) aloud. In both of these examples, Kloeble uses Bartholomäus as an interlocutor to recast historical sources and refute traditional topoi of exploration.

While the Schlagintweits engage in brotherly quarrels and competition, they are united in their bigotry and discrimination when deeming "natives" unclean, deceiving, and incapable of strong values and deep emotions. Unsurprisingly, this conforms to the racial reasoning of Western philosophy of the time, and Kloeble has Hermann quote from Kant's lectures: "In hot countries man matures earlier in all aspects, but he does not achieve the perfection of the temperate zones" (*Museum* 128). While alike in privilege, self-importance, and condescension, Kloeble endows each of the brothers with different personality traits. Hermann as the oldest is domineering and considers himself entitled to lead the expedition. Adolph as a more sensitive and artistic character grows closest to Bartholomäus but disappoints the child repeatedly. Robert is more reserved and chiefly concerned about his photographic mission and camera equipment; as the youngest brother (who was officially only hired as an assistant), he continuously seeks to prove himself and can be particularly callous. Harboring deep-seated jealousies, insecurities, and obsessions, the brothers appear stiff, out of place, and boastful.

Bartholomäus begins to realize that the scientists' incessant measuring and naming fails to capture his country's peculiarities: "By subordinating places I had always known to his numerical system, he [Hermann Schlagintweit, C.S.] was taking them away from me" (*Museum* 37). While the act of counting cities' square feet and inhabitants appropriates the land and its people, Bartholomäus questions both the numbers themselves ("Who had counted them [the residents of Bombay, C.S.]?" *Museum* 37) and their validity in representing the country. He also registers the Schlagintweits' disregard for Hindu religion and culture when the brothers scavenge corpses from the sacred Hooghly River for their studies. With the unabashed bluntness and simplicity in the voice of a child, the narrator exposes and questions European science's biases and practices during colonial times.

Bartholomäus however remains a more unconcerned observer in one of the most uncomfortable passages of the book, which describes the brothers' ethnographical practices at a prison in Calcutta. As such, the naked Urdu prisoner, by the force of cane beatings and with the help of Bartholomäus' translations, is photographed by Robert Schlagintweit, then measured by Hermann using pliers painfully pinched deep in the flesh, and finally, still in great fear and under more gentle instructions by Adolph, subjected to a gypsum facial casting. Surprisingly, Bartholomäus views the latter procedure not as denigrating but empowering, recalling that at the orphanage, Father Fuchs likewise produced facial casts of every child, then painted and collected them.[6] The passage reveals that the ethics of scientific research methods greatly depend on power relations and particular contexts. If for Bartholomäus the procedure became a festive celebration of his racial identity on his tenth birthday, for the prisoner it is a coerced and terrifying violation of his subjectivity and well-being.

Once again, the novel's description of the above procedures fictionalizes historical records, which reveal that the Schlagintweits indeed took many photographic portraits of prisoners, became preoccupied with measuring the bodies of various races they encountered,[7] and took facial plaster casts from living persons.[8] These artifacts objectify Indigenous subjects and foreground colonial violence, racism, and power relations. They also provide vivid images and names of those encountered. In this way, the Schlagintweits' immense collection of sketches, photographs, and human facial casts provides insights into deeply disturbing practices in early ethnography and colonial science, while also giving some evidence to the brothers' collaboration with and reliance on Indigenous laborers, assistants, and companions.

As part of their scientific mission, the brothers sought to climb various Himalayan mountains. In August 1855, Adolph, Robert and eight unnamed companions advanced to 6,788m on Abi Gamin in their attempt to summit what they believed to be Mount Kamet – a height that broke Humboldt's previous altitude record of

---

6 In a footnote, Kloeble details that Father Fuchs learned this technique from the Scottish scientist and editor of the *Bombay Times*, Dr. George Buist (1805–1860).

7 As is evident in Robert Schlagintweit's photographs and his chart "Measuring of Human Races" (n.p).

8 This was a new practice as facial casts had only been taken from dead persons. There is no evidence that these facial casts were taken under force, but the procedure was quite arduous, involving 4–5 pounds of gypsum on one's face and having to lie still with closed eyes and paper rolls in the nostrils for several hours. Breaking with Humboldt's beliefs that integrated Europeans and non-Europeans into one common system of human cultures and languages, the newfound interest in facial features reflected contemporary anthropologists' research on "race theories." For more information, see Moritz von Brescius, Friederike Kaiser, Stephanie Kleidt.

5,760m on Mount Chimborazo.⁹ They abandoned their attempt in deteriorating weather conditions, greatly exhausted from the onset of altitude sickness (H. Schlagintweit 348–349). The descriptions of their ascent in the 1920 entry of the *Alpine Journal* (Meade) but also the current Wikipedia page fail to mention guides and companions. In Trenker's retelling in *Helden der Berge*, Adolph and Robert likewise act on their own, focused on their advances on the Himalayan mountains that are depicted as a grander extension of the European Alps:

> Dies war nun der höchste Punkt, bis zu dem Menschen emporgedrungen waren, und die Leistung der beiden Brüder blieb auf viele Jahre hinaus zweifelsfrei der Höhenrekord der ganzen Erde. Sie waren die ersten Bergsteiger, die mit alpiner Erfahrung an die „Weltberge" herangingen, aber doch noch nicht über die Himalajaerfahrung und die besondere Ausrüstung und Taktik verfügten, denen die Pioniere der jüngsten Zeit ihre Erfolge verdanken. (*Helden* 80)

In a similar vein, Rudi Palla's recent description of the ascent in *In Schnee und Eis* celebrates Robert and Adolph as pioneers of high-altitude mountaineering, barely mentioning their companions (*Schnee* 104–110).

Conversely, in his fictional recasting of this mountaineering achievement, Kloeble makes Bartholomäus the person who reaches a world altitude record on Abi Gamin. In the literal high point of the novel, Bartholomäus rests on Adolph's shoulders and proclaims: "I am the highest point of the world. [. . .] One of the smallest Indians has reached the hitherto highest points in the world" (*Museum* 295). In another fictional reversal, Bartholomäus is carried by the German scientist rather than the other way around, as was customary. Using once more acts of mimicry, Bartholomäus' words echo the boastful posturing of many mountain conquests. By juxtaposing the superlative language of mountain feats ("highest") with superlative diminutives ("smallest"), Kloeble heightens the importance of travel companions who are often excluded from historical records and even many recent depictions of mountaineering. At the same time, the novel's mimicry subtly mocks and undermines the record-seeking Western tradition of scientific exploration in the manner of Alexander von Humboldt.[10]

---

9 As has been established, however, twenty-one Andean peaks above 6,000m bear signs of Inca occupation on or near their summit, making Humboldt's claim obsolete. See Echevarria 48.
10 See also Schaumann 2020, 48–72.

V

In his chapter "The Inner Life of a 'European' Expedition: Cultural Encounters and Multiple Hierarchies" in *German Science in the Age of Empire,* Moritz von Brescius meticulously researched various travel companions and the complex network of diverse languages, religions, and cultures that formed the Schlagintweit expedition. As von Brescius makes evident, the Schlagintweits were often not the main actors of their own undertaking. Kloeble's novel embellishes this historical information to imbue each travel companion with their individual backstory, caste, religious beliefs, languages spoken, and other characteristics, from the Hindi physician Harkishen, the caretaker of the collection Mr. Monteiro, the draughtsman and surveyor Abdullah, to the Sikh mountain guide Mani Singh. The novel's representation strives to remain historically accurate: according to von Brescius, Harkishen was employed as a "Native doctor" who saved Hermann's life through a surgery that removed an abscess (von Brescius 189). The Indo-Portuguese Mr. Monteiro served as the "general superintendent of the collectors" (von Brescius 183) and continued his scientific work independently after the Schlagintweits left India. The Muslim assistant called Abdul provided valuable data and sketched landscapes and river systems. Mani Singh mediated and guided the illegal forays into Tibet.

Going beyond the historical record, however, Kloeble outfits his narration with stories and fictional figures not found in historical documents, such as the illiterate cook Maasi Smitaben who arrives at the orphanage after being beaten by her husband, and the Parsi bookkeeper Hormazd whose mysterious death is apparently the result of Bartholomäus' imprudent actions. The translator Eleazar is both a historical and fictional character: he was indeed a travel companion working as a guide and personal assistant for the Schlagintweits,[11] but in the novel, he becomes a child abused by Catholic priests at an orphanage in Cochin. Kloeble fashions Eleazar into a fellow orphan and early friend of Mr. Monteiro who adopts a Jewish name and later collaborates with the Chinese to fight for independence from the British Empire, pressuring a reluctant Bartholomäus to join him. Toward the end of the novel, readers learn about Eleazar's former life and path into the resistance, which in turn prompts Bartholomäus' decision to actively collaborate with the movement. This implausible resistance narrative remains removed from the more realistic narrative of

---

[11] Von Brescius describes Eleazar Daniel's important role, quoting from the Schlagintweits that he was "a coloured Jew from India [. . .] entrusted with the superintendence of the transport of our instruments and collections" (187).

the expedition itself but significantly widens the novel's focus, further decentering the Schlagintweits' mission.

While the fictional characters and stories allow Kloeble to include, albeit peripherally, intersecting layers of oppression such as domestic violence and abuse by pedophile priests, they sometimes overburden the narrative, further stretching its credibility. In this way, the author's aspiration to deliver information on colonial India can become overloaded by too many fictionalized details and backstories, and the novel's child perspective can seem forced, especially in the latter half of the novel. Nevertheless, Kloeble succeeds in drawing attention away from the Schlagintweit brothers to elucidate the expedition from below and pay tribute to some of the many companions and collaborators.

The novel also provides readers with details about influential historical figures in India to elucidate both colonial oppression and instances of subversion and resistance. For instance, the Scottish Thirteenth Lord John Elphinstone, the Governor of Bombay, in Kloeble's rendering speaks Hindi and is smart but cruel, with signs of encroaching tuberculosis – the historical Elphinstone put down attempts at an Indian uprising by seizing their leaders during his governorship of Bombay. The General-Governor James Broun-Ramsay is depicted as a condescending despot with an expansionist agenda. Kloeble directly quotes the infamous words from the Governor's single-handed, unauthorized annexation of the Punjab: "Unwarned by precedent, uninfluenced by example, the Sikh nation has called for war; and on my words, sirs, war they shall have and with a vengeance" (*Museum* 153). Indeed, as is explained in the novel, Broun-Ramsay's Doctrine of Lapse legitimizing British control over any Indian state where the male heir lineage had "lapsed" led to the illegitimate annexation of numerous princely states. However, as Kloeble shows, power and influence were not exclusively held by the British. In the novel, Bartholomäus receives information about Father Fuchs from the Parsi drug lord Jamsetjee Jejeebhoy and his Chinese assistant. The historical record shows that Jeejeebhoy, in another example of subversive mimicry, made a fortune as a merchant in the cotton and opium trade with China and became the first Indian knighted by the British. Growing up poor – he lost both parents at age 16 and received no formal education – Jejeebhoy became a philanthropist who donated a substantial portion of his wealth to the poor and advocated non-violence; he was commemorated on a 1959 stamp of India. *Das Museum der Welt* freely employs these historical figures to illustrate hierarchies of Europeans, Indo-Europeans, Chinese, and Indians, but also to provide a glimpse into India's diverse and manifold cultures and religions that determine dietary restrictions, work schedules, languages and even intricacies such as currencies and weight systems.

In addition, the novel illuminates little-known facts of the German involvement in British colonialism when explaining Bartholomäus' family history. As revealed in a (fictional) letter by Father Fuchs, Bartholomäus' father belonged to the group of 2,000 Hanoverian soldiers recruited by George III (1738–1820) who was concurrently King of Great Britain and Ireland and Elector of Hanover. As the latter, George III provided two regiments of German volunteers fighting along the East India Company in the Anglo-Mysar Wars (1869–1799) that resulted in much of the Mysorean territory annexed by the British (Historisches Museum Hannover). Germans from the Kingdom of Hanover thus actively aided colonial expansion in India.

VI

Historical accounts of the Schlagintweit expedition invariably culminate in the ill-fated conclusion of the Schlagintweit journey and Adolph Schlagintweit's premature death. In December 1856, the brothers parted ways: Robert, with the majority of the immense collection carried by hundreds of camels, horses, and porters, embarked on a monthlong trek via Karachi back to Bombay, where he boarded a ship back to Alexandria. There he met Hermann who had traveled to Lahore and Nepal, and the two brothers returned to Berlin in June 1857. Adolph had remained in Asia; his plan was to return to Germany via Central Asia and Russia, crossing war-besieged Turkestan despite safety warnings not to do so. In August 1857, he and his companions were captured by the Turkestan warlord Wali Khan during the Kashgar uprising, and Adolph was swiftly beheaded as a presumed spy without being granted a hearing. Most of his travel companions were also killed or forced into slavery, and only a few were eventually able to flee and preserve some documents.[12] Robert and Hermann were left not only with the tragic loss of their brother but also the examination of their extensive research collection, a task that proved insurmountable. As the Schlagintweits' expertise, methods, and findings were increasingly questioned in the British press and beyond, they tried to salvage their scientific reputation and financial standing by unsuccessfully lobbying for an Indian museum in Berlin. Eventually, they sold or auctioned many

---

12 There had been longstanding conflicts between the Chinese military and Muslim clans, with Wali Khan seizing a short but violent control over Kashgar. With his European instruments and official letters of the British Empire, Adolph immediately raised suspicion – he was taken hostage and beheaded in front of Kashgar's gates on August 26, 1857.

pieces from their collection that, as a result, remains dispersed over various countries and continents, with many artifacts missing to this day.

Adolph Schlagintweit's death usually comes front and center in biographical portrayals of the Schlagintweits' expedition: in Trenker, a depiction of its gruesome details follows the exclamation "Adolf's Schicksal war besiegelt!" (*Helden* 44) at the heart of the essay. The execution is also mentioned on the cover of Palla's book and forms the introduction of von Brescius' study. Conversely, the violent death receives only brief mention in a short chapter at the end of Kloeble's fictional rendition. In it, Wali Khan's troops capture Adolph, Eleazar, Abdullah, Mr. Monteiro, and Bartholomäus, and violently inquire whether they are spies for the British, Russians, or Chinese. When the soldiers start to break Bartholomäus' fingers one by one, Adolph admits to being a spy for the East India Company to spare Bartholomäus further torture and is then promptly beheaded. Mr. Monteiro is likewise killed for being a Christian, Abdullah is sold into slavery, and Bartholomäus and Eleazar are imprisoned. As Eleazar grows weaker, Bartholomäus recalls the objects of his museum in his memory, in a passage that echoes the first chapter verbatim when Bartholomäus explained his museum to Father Fuchs before his death. Eleazar dies in captivity shortly before the Chinese reconquer Kashgar and free all prisoners. In the novel, Adolph Schlagintweit died to save Bartholomäus, and the latter succeeds where the Schlagintweits failed, in the creation of an Indian Museum. Yet in another turn of events, Bartholomäus becomes skeptical of the universal scale of priorities leading to a "museum of the world" altogether and instead decides to join the Indian resistance. The final chapter concludes with Bartholomäus affirming his Indian identity, swearing off speaking English and German, and naming himself Eleazar.

As a European author intimately familiar with and knowledgeable about the subject matter, Kloeble writes from a position of power and privilege.[13] In the picaresque tradition and from the perspective of Bartholomäus, Kloeble embellishes a precocious and imagined perspective of the Schlagintweit expedition, the country they cross, and people they meet. While this move cannot adequately deliver the realities and consequences of oppression from the perspective of the colonized, it brings into focus historical and fictional travel companions, shedding light on how guides, informants, and translators creatively used their skills to serve and at the same time subvert the expedition's goals and the colonialist agenda in general. Employing historical and fictional characters with and without power, the novel conveys information about life under the colonial rule of the British East India Company and elucidates the German complicity in the colonial

---

13 See also Nora Koldehoff's review of Kloeble's book.

system, while also calling into question the very process of historical transmission. Through Bartholomäus' fictional travels with the Schlagintweits, Kloeble's work encourages readers to realize and imagine European exploration and its aftereffects, providing insights into how aesthetics, science, and colonialism became intricately and unpredictably intertwined.

Works Cited

"Abi Gamin." *Wikipedia*, en.wikipedia.org/wiki/Abi_Gamin. 20 March 2025.

Bhabha, Homi K. "Of Mimicry and Man: The Ambivalence of Colonial Discourse." *Discipleship: A Special Issue on Psychoanalysis* (Vol. 28, Spring 1984), pp. 125–133.

Bay, Hansjörg. "Going native? Mimikry und Maskerade in kolonialen Entdeckungsreisen der Gegenwartsliteratur (Stangl; Trojanow)." *Ins Fremde schreiben. Gegenwartsliteratur auf den Spuren historischer und fantastischer Engdeckungsreisen*, edited by Christof Hamann and Alexander Honold, Wallstein, 2009, pp. 117–142.

Bay, Hansjörg. "Literarische Landnahme? Um-Schreibung, Partizipation und Wiederholung in aktuellen Relektüren kolonialer ‚Entdeckungsreisen.'" *Literarische Entdeckungsreisen. Vorfahren – Nachfahrten – Revisionen*, edited by Hansjörg Bay and Wolfgang Struck, Böhlau, 2012, pp. 107–132.

Echevarria, Evilio A. *The Andes: The Complete History of Mountaineering in High South America*. Joseph Reidhead, 2018.

Historisches Museum Hannover. "Britain – Master of the World." kolonialismus-hannover.de/britain-master-of-the-world/. 20 March 2025.

Holdenried, Michaela. "Von der Unermesslichkeit der Welt. Historische Forschungsreisen in der Gegenwartsliteratur." *Reiseliteratur der Moderne und Postmoderne*, edited by Michaela Holdenried, Alexander Honold, and Stefan Hermes, Erich Schmid Verlag, 2017, pp. 289–309.

Kloeble, Christopher. *Das Museum der Welt*. Deutscher Taschenbuch Verlag, 2020.

Kloeble, Christopher. "Presentation at the Center for European Studies." *Brandeis University*, 8 April 2024, brandeis.edu/cges/webinar-recordings/authors-in-conversation2.html, 20 March 2025.

Kloeble, Christopher. *The Museum of the World*. Translated by Rekha Kamath Rajan. Harper Collins, 2022.

Koldehoff, Nora. "Wissenschaft und Rebellion. Christopher Kloeble: *Das Museum der Welt*." *Deutschlandfunk*, 28 February 2020.

Lickhardt, Maren. "Pikareske Reise." *Handbuch Literatur und Reise*, edited by Hansjörg Bay et al., Metzler, 2024, pp. 192–194.

Lützeler, Paul. "Neuer Roman von Christopher Kloeble: Ein Widerständler gegen den europäischen Kolonialismus." *Der Tagesspiegel*, 6 May 2020.

Meade, C.F. "The Schlagintweits and Ibi Gamin (Kamet)." *Alpine Journal*, vol. 32, 1920, pp.70–75.

Palla, Rudi. *In Schnee und Eis: Die Himalaja Expedition der Brüder Schlagintweit*. Kiepenheuer & Witsch, 2019.

Schaumann, Caroline. "'Calamities for Future Generations': Alexander von Humboldt as Ecologist," *Ecological Thought in German Literature and Culture*, edited by Gabriele Dürbeck et al., Lexington, 2017, pp. 63–76.

Schaumann, Caroline. "Humboldtian Writing for the Anthropocene." *German-Language Nature Writing from Eighteenth Century to the Present: Controversies, Positions, Perspectives*, edited by Gabriele Dürbeck and Christine Kanz, Palgrave Macmillan, 2024, pp. 103–120.

Schaumann, Caroline. *Peak Pursuits: The Emergence of Mountaineering in the Nineteenth Century*. Yale UP, 2020.

Schellbach, Miryam. "Weltaneignung in klein." *Frankfurter Allgemeine Zeitung*, 27 February 2020.

Schlagintweit, Hermann. *Reisen nach Indien und Hochasien*, Vol. 2. Hermann Gostenoble, 1871.

Schlagintweit, Robert. "Measuring of Human Races." *Royal Asiatic Society Archives*, royalasiaticarchives.org/index.php/measuring-of-human-races. 20 March 2025.

Schrott, Raoul. "5 Fragen an . . . Raoul Schrott." *Hanser Literaturverlage*, hanser-literaturverlage.de/buch/raoul-schrott-eine-geschichte-des-windes-oder-von-dem-deutschen-kanonier-der-erstmals-die-welt-umrundete-und-dann-ein-zweites-und-ein-drittes-mal-9783446263802-t-2961. 20 March 2025.

Schuhen, Gregor. *Vir inversus: Männlichkeiten im spanischen Schelmenroman*. Transcript, 2018.

Spivak, Gayatri Chakravorty. "Can the Subaltern Speak?" *Marxism and the Interpretation of Culture*, edited by Cary Nelson and Lawrence Grossberg, Macmillan, 1988, pp. 271–313.

Trenker, Luis. "Die drei Himalajabrüder: Adolf, Hermann und Robert Schlagintweit." *Helden der Berge*, Kanur, 1935, pp. 82–93.

von Brescius, Moritz. *German Science in the Age of Empire: Enterprise, Opportunity and the Schlagintweit Brothers*, Cambridge UP, 2018.

von Brescius, Moritz, Friederike Kaiser, and Stephanie Kleidt, eds. *Über den Himalaya. Die Expedition der Brüder Schlagintweit nach Indien und Zentralasien 1854 bis 1858*, Böhlau, 2015.

Hanna Maria Hofmann
Dinçer Güçyeters *Unser Deutschlandmärchen* im Dialog mit Scheherazade, Loreley und Dorothea Viehmann

Abstract: Der Artikel liefert eine Analyse des literarisch hochkomplexen Anspielungshorizontes auf Märchen in Dinçer Güçyeters preisgekröntem Debütroman *Unser Deutschlandmärchen* (2022), nämlich ‚deutsche' Volksmärchen wie die *Kinder- und Hausmärchen* der Brüder Grimm, Heinrich Heines Exil-Versepos *Deutschland. Ein Wintermärchen* (1844) sowie die Märchen aus *Tausendundeiner Nacht* und deren literarische Rezeption in der Wiener Moderne (Hofmannsthal). Der Beitrag macht die tiefgreifende intertextuelle Bedeutung und Funktion dieser ‚Märchen'-Referenzen für die transkulturelle Schreibweise des Romans sichtbar und liest vor diesem Hintergrund dessen spezifische Thematisierung, Deutung und Inszenierung familiärer, gesellschaftlicher und insbesondere auch weiblicher Migrationsgeschichten und -erfahrungen in Deutschland. Dabei entsteht – so die These – ein migrantisch-kritisches Gegennarrativ sowie ein schöpferisches Schreiben zwischen Okzident und Orient, wobei Güçyeters *Deutschlandmärchen* eine transnationale, postmigrantische Erinnerungskultur entwirft und sich in eine Literaturgeschichte des Märchens und des Exils einschreibt.

I

Dinçer Güçyeters Debütroman *Unser Deutschlandmärchen*,[1] 2023 mit dem Preis der Leipziger Buchmesse ausgezeichnet, trägt die Gattungsbezeichnung Märchen im Titel, ohne den Gattungskonventionen zu entsprechen. Jedoch organisiert der Text seine Themen und Bedeutungsebenen sowie seine Konzeption als transnationale, postmigrantische Literatur über die Schaffung eines literarisch komplexen, intertextuellen und transkulturellen Anspielungshorizonts auf Märchen und literarische Märchenrezeptionen, vom deutschen Volksmärchen über Heinrich Heines Exil-Werk *Deutschland. Ein Wintermärchen* (1844) bis hin zu orientalischen Märchenrezeptionen in der europäischen und deutsch-türkischen Literatur. Gü-

---

1 Im Folgenden zitiert als *Deutschlandmärchen*.

çyeters Text ist eine dialogisch strukturierte, autofiktionale Erzählung der familiären Migrationsgeschichte, die Gattungsgrenzen zwischen Prosa, Drama und Lyrik, Familienalbum und Liedersammlung paradigmatisch unterläuft. Zentral ist die Geschichte und Erzählstimme der Mutter Fatma, die Mitte der 1960er Jahre als anatolische ‚Gastarbeiterin'[2] nach Deutschland kam und aus heutiger Sicht auf ihre Migrationsgeschichte schaut. Mit der unterrepräsentierten Nebenfigur des Vaters Yilmaz stehen diese Eltern und Eheleute symbolisch für eine andere Erinnerungsgeschichte der türkischen Arbeitsmigration aus innerfamiliärer Perspektive, in der die Frauen die eigentlich starken Stimmen und Protagonist:innen sind. Fatma leistet in ihrer „Big-Mama-Rolle" (*Deutschlandmärchen* 88) tagtäglich Übergroßes als Arbeiterin in Mehrfachschichten und Hausfrau, Hauptverdienerin und Mutter, zusätzlich noch in der verschuldeten Kneipe des Ehemanns. Zugleich ist sie immer hilfsbereit und solidarisch mit anderen Frauen und deren Familien. Trotz ihrer Stärke hat Fatma Rollenzuweisungen männlicher Willens- und Lustdominanz und weiblicher Passivität internalisiert und ihre Erfahrungswelten sind in der Türkei ebenso wie in Deutschland gesellschaftlich geprägt durch männliche Gewalt und Unterdrückung gegenüber Frauen.

Abschnitt II der folgenden Analyse zeigt, dass der Roman in dem skizzierten Themen- und Spannungsfeld Gattungsregeln des ‚Volksmärchens'[3] zitiert und subvertiert, um vom *Bruch* der Illusionen zu erzählen und die Vorstellung Deutschlands als ein ‚märchenhaftes' Einwanderungsland kritisch zu hinterfragen[4] und als ein gesellschaftliches Lügen- und ‚Ammenmärchen'[5] zu entlarven: von persönlichen Enttäuschungen und Konflikten über gesellschaftliche Verletzungen und Ausgrenzungen bis hin zu sozialen Ungerechtigkeiten und politischem Versagen in Deutschland. Ironisch gebrochen, konturieren insbesondere die märchentypischen Erzählmuster einer glücklichen Migration (Tokponto 123–124) sowie der glücklichen

---

2 Siehe zu dieser „von der Wissenschaft lange übersehen[en]" Thematik Schreiner 195. Einen migrationshistorischen Überblick gibt Mattes 2008. Zur literarischen und filmischen Darstellung von ‚Gastarbeiterinnen' wie etwa *Shirins Hochzeit* (1975) der Regisseurin Helke Sander-Brahms s. Ezli 116–139, 506.
3 Zur Problematik der – dennoch geläufigen – Kontrastbegriffe ‚Volksmärchen' und ‚Kunstmärchen' s. Klotz 7–9, Neuhaus 1–11.
4 Diese zur Zeit des deutschen ‚Wirtschaftswunders' kursierende Vorstellung von der BRD wurde bereits 1985 von dem türkisch-deutschen Autor Yüksel Pazarkaya zur Formel des „verschlossenen Paradies[es]" umgewendet, s. Pazarkaya 33. Ein Beispiel jüngsten Datums, das sich auf genau diese Zeit rückbezieht, ist die Autobiographie *Es war einmal Deutschland: Gelobtes Land* (2022) des 1965 von Italien nach Deutschland emigrierten Arbeiters Nello Simeone.
5 Bereits bei Heine sind die erinnerten deutschen Volksmärchen, die für dessen Deutschlandkritik eine zentrale Rolle spielen (s. Gille), buchstäblich Ammenmärchen, nämlich Lieder seiner Amme (*Wintermärchen* 455).

Braut Fatmas individuelle Erzählung und kollektive Erfahrung einer weiblichen Arbeits- und Heiratsmigration nach Deutschland. Thematisiert wird ferner die Auseinandersetzung zwischen der Mutter Fatma und dem Sohn/Schriftsteller Dinçer als Aushandlungsprozess verschiedener Lebensentwürfe zwischen erster und zweiter Einwanderungsgeneration[6] sowie als Ausdruck der Notwendigkeit, im Dialog zu einem neuen Deutschlandmärchen und einer gemeinsamen Erzählung zu finden.

Im folgenden Abschnitt (III) wird erörtert, wie im Roman das Schreiben sowie das solidarische, dialogische ('Märchen'-)Erzählen zwischen Mutter und Sohn, aber auch zwischen solidarischen Frauenfiguren und -stimmen, zu einem postmigrantischen Medium und literarischen Mittel nicht zuletzt der weiblichen Selbstermächtigung wird. Insbesondere wird gezeigt, welche Rolle dabei dem transkulturellen Bezug auf Märchen[7] sowie dem intertextuellen Bezug auf eine ‚orientalische' Märchenrezeption einerseits im europäischen Orientalismus der Wiener Moderne (Hofmannsthal), andererseits in der postmodernen, deutsch-türkischen Literatur der Gegenwart (Özdamar) zukommt. Der letzte Abschnitt (IV) legt den Fokus auf Güçyeters Verfahren der literarischen Fortschreibung einer deutschsprachigen und deutsch-türkischen, transnationalen und kosmopolitischen Literatur- und Erinnerungsgeschichte, für die der intertextuelle Bezug auf Heinrich Heines Exil-Versepos *Deutschland. Ein Wintermärchen* (1844) von zentraler Wichtigkeit ist.

II

Im ironisch-dekonstruierenden Rekurs auf märchentypische Motive, Figuren und Gattungsgesetze, wie sie etwa aus den *Kinder- und Hausmärchen* der Brüder Grimm weltbekannt sind, wird die vermeintliche ‚Märchengeschichte' einer Einwanderung nach Deutschland als falsch entlarvt. Dabei partizipiert der Text an einer auch allgemeinen Vorstellung des Märchens: sowohl im positiven Sinne von Träumen, Sehnsüchten, Utopien und „Geschichten persönlicher und gesellschaftlicher Wunschwelten, die der zeitgenössischen Umwelt trotzen" (Klotz 9) als auch

---

6 Siehe auch zum Beispiel Fatma Aydemirs Roman *Dschinns* (2022).
7 Gemeint ist der Bezug auf Märchen als eine ‚quer' durch alle Kulturen und Kontinente existierende Textgattung, deren Formen, Motive und Stoffe insofern beständig ‚migrieren'. So könnte das bei Güçyeters auf Fatma als ‚Dornröschen' verweisende Kapitel *Der Dorn im Auge* ebenso auf das türkische Märchen *Die Geschichte vom Kristallpalast und Diamantschiff* (Spies 5–16) oder auf das italienische Märchen *Die goldene Wurzel* aus Giambattista Basiles *Pentameron* (1634/1636) (Massenbach 154–164) verweisen, in denen jeweils ein Dorn im Auge bzw. Gesicht ein wichtiges Motiv sind. Siehe zu diesem Begriff von Transkulturalität Mecklenburg 13.

im negativen Sinne der Verdrängung von Wahrheiten bis hin zur Erzählung von Unwahrheiten. Dabei zeigt sich eine interkulturelle Dimension in Fatmas Verstrickung zwischen einem türkischen Deutschlandmärchen vom Wohlstand für alle und einem deutschen Türkeimärchen vom traumhaften Urlaub.[8]

> [U]m die gebrochenen Knochen kümmert sich [im türkischen Heimatdorf, HMH] keiner, alle glauben, die Fatma pflückt die deutsche Mark wie Birnen von den Bäumen. [...] Und Fatma darf wieder am Gaskocher stehen, was soll's! Zurück in Deutschland, erzähle ich den Kolleginnen, wie wunderbar und erholsam die Reise war. (*Deutschlandmärchen* 94)

Diese selbstschutzbedingte Verkehrung und „Lüge ins Gegenteil" (ebd.) korrespondiert mit einer Verkehrung des Märchenhaften in gattungsstruktureller Hinsicht, um umgekehrt die Realitäten der weiblichen Arbeitsmigration und der „gebrochenen Knochen" zu benennen. Die geradezu gattungsdefinierende Märchenhandlung von Verbannung und Vertreibung, Heimkehr und Erlösung, Auszug in die Welt und „märchenhafte[m] Erlebnis der Entheimatung" (Haase 45; s. auch Klotz 10) hält normalerweise für den Helden oder die Heldin am Ende stets den verdienten „Gewinn" bereit, der „ein für allemal glücklich macht" (Klotz 11). Das Weltbild des Volksmärchens ist eine „Ordnung der Harmonie" (Klotz 15), in der die moralischen Pole von Gut und Böse klar gekennzeichnet sind. Selbst der ‚materielle' Gewinn, „ein Liebespartner, eine Königskrone, Reichtum – oft alles zusammen" (Klotz 11), ist symbolischer Ausdruck einer insofern immer gerechten Belohnung der Märchenheldin für ihre Handlungen, Anstrengungen und Entbehrungen: häufig ein besonderer Fleiß oder wundersamer Erfolg bei scheinbar unlösbaren Arbeitsaufträgen, und „immer geht die Rechnung auf" (Klotz 15). Im *Deutschlandmärchen* hingegen wird Fatma vom „Gastarbeiterchor" schon früh vorgewarnt, dass das materielle und moralische Preis-Leistungsverhältnis aus dem Gleichgewicht geraten und sie am Ende die Betrogene, ewig Vertröstete sein könnte: „Lerne zuerst, mit der Zunge die Suppe zu rühren, wir reden dann später, Fatma ... wir reden später" (*Deutschlandmärchen* 26). Rückblickend heißt es im Kollektiv der „ausgewanderten Mütter":

> Keinen einzigen Tag hat das Schicksal selbst meine Haare geflochten oder den Schnee vor meiner Haustür geschaufelt oder die Kohle in meinen Ofen geworfen. Und wenn da jemand war, war die Rechnung untragbar. (*Deutschlandmärchen* 193)

---

[8] ‚Interkulturell' im Sinne einer Beziehungskomponente zwischen deutscher und türkischer Kultur, s. hierzu Mecklenburg 13.

In dieser Anti-Märchenwelt der verkehrten Ordnung gibt es keine wunderbaren Helferwesen, und die Schwächeren bleiben immer die Schuldner:innen.[9] Gegen diese Position des Stillhaltens und Schweigens begehrt „Das Lied der Mütter vor dem Parlament" aktiv auf, insofern diese im Chor ihre Stimmen erheben:

> AYSE (SOLO): [I]n Fabrikhallen mit Metallstaub werden wir weiter schweigen/sag uns, Deutschland, was gehört dir, was uns? Wie viel schulden wir? CHOR: Gesparte Pfennige, ausgegebene Sehnsucht, Überstunden, Arbeitsunfälle, befristete Aufenthaltserlaubnisse, Angst vor dem Vorarbeiter, Angst vor Arbeitsunfähigkeitsbescheinigungen, Angst vor den Beamten, Angst vor den Regeln, Angst vor Gewerkschaften. Schweigen. [...] CHOR: [...] Können wir abrechnen, Alamanya? Was kostet die Steuer! (*Deutschlandmärchen* 130)

In einem ‚märchenhaften' oder auch nur gerechten Einwanderungsland Deutschland wäre der Preis für die Arbeitsmigration die volle Teilhabe an den Errungenschaften des demokratischen Wohlfahrtsstaates BRD, faire Angebote und Ausbildung, Versicherung und Rente, rechtliche und soziale Anerkennung und Sicherheit für alle, einschließlich seiner seit 1955 gezielt angeworbenen zugewanderten Arbeiter:innen und steuerzahlenden Bewohner:innen. Deren gegenteilige Realität besteht aus der „Angst vor Gewerkschaften", unversicherten „Arbeitsunfälle[n]" und einem „Behinderungsgrad" von „70%" als „Ergebnis der letzten 35 [Arbeits-]Jahre" (*Deutschlandmärchen* 187). Im Kapitel *Der Dorn im Auge*, dessen Titel mit der vorangegangenen Bezeichnung Fatmas als „Dornröschen" (*Deutschlandmärchen* 48) korrespondiert, rekapituliert Fatma ihre Situation als junge Frau, die im Jahre 1965 auf Ansage des Onkels und entgegen dem Wunsch ihrer Mutter in die Arbeits- und Heiratsmigration nach Deutschland geschickt wird:[10] „*Fatma soll den Weg für ihre Brüder pflastern!* [...] Verliebtsein, für mich war es ein fremdes Gefühl. Sowas hab ich viel später in Filmen mit Türkan Şoray gesehen" (*Deutschlandmärchen* 123). Dabei ist Fatmas rückblickende Selbstbeschreibung als goldbestückte Braut auf dem Weg in die Fremde ein häufiges, transkulturell verbreitetes Märchenmotiv und ebenso gekennzeichnet als eine kollektive Migrationsrealität der Frauen:

> Auf meinem Hals die Goldtaler [...], besteige ich das Pferd und verlasse das Elternhaus, folge als Braut meinem Mann mit dem riesigen Kopf nach Deutschland. Fremde, flüstere ich, die Fremde, die uns [Frauen, HMH] seit drei Generationen hin- und herweht [...]. (*Deutschlandmärchen* 19)

Eine transgenerationale Linie der ‚Nomadinnen', beginnend bei der einst aus Griechenland in die Türkei eingewanderten „Nomadin Ayse", Dinçers Urgroßmut-

---

9 Schuld und Schulden, Schuldgefühle und Unschuld sind wiederkehrende Motive und Begriffe im *Deutschlandmärchen*.
10 S. hierzu Samper und Kreyenfeld.

ter, manifestiert sich bereits vor der erzählten Arbeitsmigration der Enkeltochter Fatma aus der Türkei nach Deutschland im Sprechen der Großmutter Hanife, die „euch kurz meine Geschichte erzählen, dann meine schwere Zunge meiner Tochter Fatma übergeben [wird]" (*Deutschlandmärchen* 9).

Die Konstanten dieser weiblichen Erfahrungen sind Armut und Vertreibung, harte Arbeit und Ausbeutung, weibliche Ehepflichten und die Dominanz durch Männer, die in einem patriarchalen Regelsystem der „Männerschwänze[]" gerne „[e]in obdachloses Weib behüten" (*Deutschlandmärchen* 9), Tränen und Schmerz, Tod und Verlust, aber auch die Mutter als beschützende Überlebenskämpferin. In diesem weiblichen Kontext steht Fatmas doppelte ‚Verdammnis', die als mehrfach Diskriminierte zuerst in der Türkei, dann in Deutschland ein Leben voller Hindernisse bewältigen muss: „Kein Vater, kein Vaterland, der zweite Schritt der Entwurzelung begann. [...] Eine Frau, eine Waise, eine Arbeiterin, eine Migrantin; Ich war von so vielem gezeichnet!" (*Deutschlandmärchen* 124).

Auf paradoxe Weise findet sich Fatma im ‚Gastgeberland' Deutschland in einer Welt wieder, die dem ‚Regelsystem' der ‚Obdach' gebenden Männer in der ländlichen Türkei gleicht. Die Ankunft im Ruhrgebiet bedeutet nicht nur die Anpassung an eine fremde Sprache und Kultur, sondern ebenso an einen fremden Mann. Über ihren von der krankmachenden ‚Gastarbeit' „ausgeschabten Körper" sagt Fatma zu Dinçer: „Lach mich bitte nicht aus, die deutschen Ärzte haben mehr an mir rumgefummelt als dein Papa. [...] Von OP zu OP wurde ich zu einem größeren Krüppel" (*Deutschlandmärchen* 130, 61). Dabei wird hier eine sexuell konnotierte, ‚lächerliche' Nicht-Dominanz des Ehemanns angesprochen: Fatma sieht sich in Beziehung zu ihrem Mann wenig als ‚geschundene Suleika' (s. Yesilada). Doch obgleich weder sie dem Bild des weiblichen, hilfebedürftigen Opfers entspricht noch ihr Ehemann Yilmaz, der häufig in den Tag träumende „Mann mit dem riesigen Kopf", dem des gewalttätigen Patriarchen, gehören beide einer Alltagswelt an, in der „fast alle [Männer] [...] ihr Gehirn im Schwanz [tragen]" (*Deutschlandmärchen* 69), in der Frauen Objekte der Lust sind und eine von Fatma kritisierte Doppelmoral der Familienväter herrscht, die weibliche Prostitution genießen, jedoch die eigenen Töchter fallen lassen, wenn sie sich prostituieren (vgl. *Deutschlandmärchen* 69–70). Diese männliche Doppelmoral von der unbedingten ‚Unschuld' der Frau als (zukünftige) Braut weist der Text als eine transkulturelle aus: Sie wird im Selbstbild Fatmas als in die Fremde ziehende Märchenbraut, einem transkulturellen, hier allerdings mit Attributen der muslimischen, jungfräulichen Braut kombinierten Märchen- und Weiblichkeitsmuster (vgl. *Deutschlandmärchen* 19), ebenso transportiert wie in der Assoziation Fatmas mit „Dornröschen" (*Deutschlandmärchen* 48), also *der* bürgerlich idealisierten Frauenfigur sexueller Unschuld in den *Kinder- und Hausmärchen* der Brüder Grimm schlechthin (s. Mazenauer und Perig). Bereits Elfriede Jelinek hat diese

Figur in den *Prinzessinnendramen* (2003) einer literarisch-feministischen Märchenkritik unterzogen. Dinçers Vergleich seiner im Wochenbett liegenden Mutter mit dem schlafenden Dornröschen birgt insofern eine Ironie, verweist aber auch auf einen kurzen Moment des echten Glücks. Der Wochenbett-Schlaf des Fatma-Dornröschens ist ein allzu kurzes Ausruhen, wie ein im Roman abgedrucktes Foto der erschöpften Wöchnerin zeigt (*Deutschlandmärchen* 53), bevor Fatmas ‚dorniger' Alltag weitergeht: „Die Klinken sind dornig, die Klinken sind dornig, die Schlösser verrostet. *Leider, Fatma, leider, Fatma* […] *Leider, Schwester, leider, Schwester*" (*Deutschlandmärchen* 32). Das ewige Hinhalten im unverschuldeten Schuldner:innen-Dasein – hier durch die Schuldner ihres Ehemannes, die umgekehrt Fatma in höchster Not nicht helfen – scheint ebenso endlos wie das pausenlose Arbeiten im Klima gesellschaftlicher Abwertung und Ausbeutung: „Unsere einzige Option war, mehr zu arbeiten, und jeder abwertende Blick hat größeren Ehrgeiz ausgelöst" (*Deutschlandmärchen* 124). Eine weitere Bedeutung hat das Dornröschen in Kombination mit dem aus *Dornröschen, Rapunzel* und *Schneewittchen* bekannten Märchenmotiv des zunächst unerfüllten Kinderwunsches und Betens der Mutter um ein Kind (*Deutschlandmärchen* 38, 43). Jedoch ist der Sohn Dinçer, das lang ersehnte erste Kind, in der Wunschvorstellung der Mutter der ‚rettende' Prinz,[11] mit dem eine gelungene Verwurzelung in der Fremde noch möglich wäre, da mit seiner Geburt „[m]eine vierzehnjährige Leere [des Exils, HMH] ihre Fülle [findet]" (*Deutschlandmärchen* 38, 43). Indem das lange Bitten und Beten der Mutter um ein Kind nicht umsonst war, ergibt sich eine „zweite Chance" (*Deutschlandmärchen* 168), Fatmas Deutschlandmärchen doch noch zu einem guten Ende kommen zu lassen: Dinçer, der Prinz, soll der Mutter Ersatz und Trost sein für seinen nutzlosen Vater, den „Sultan mit nacktem Hintern" (*Deutschlandmärchen* 43). Der Sohn hätte seine Mutter für die Verluste, die gebrachten Opfer und die harte Arbeit entschädigen können,[12] hätte wenigstens er, anders als sein Vater, nach Fatmas Vorstellungen in der Migration und trotz Migration sein Glück gemacht: „Als Ausländer, Gastarbeiterkind hast du schon als Verlierer angefangen. Mit Aktien, Eigentum, Sparbuch und als gestandener Familienvater hättest du der Welt zeigen können, dass du nicht kleinzukriegen bist", aber „für solche Sensibilitäten wie deine gibt es im wahren Leben keinen Lohn" (*Deutschlandmärchen* 169). Der internalisierte und an den Sohn weitergegebene Auftrag, es in Deutschland ‚schaffen' und sich be-

---

11 Ein im Roman abgedrucktes Foto zeigt Dinçer als Baby-Karnevalsprinzen, s. *Deutschlandmärchen* 47.
12 Im Kapitel „Du warst mein verlorener Mann" sagt Fatma zu Dinçer: „Als Frau habe ich mir nichts anders als ein wenig Schutz, Geborgenheit gewünscht. Du warst meine zweite Chance im Leben, du solltest die Entschädigung für das Unvermögen deines Vaters sein" (*Deutschlandmärchen* 168).

weisen zu müssen, in Klasse und Wohlstand aufzusteigen, vermischt sich mit Männlichkeitserwartungen aus dem anatolischen Heimatdorf: Fatma wirft Dinçer vor, dort als Junge über eine zu schlachtende Kuh in Tränen ausgebrochen zu sein: „In dem Moment wusste ich, [...] ich hatte dich nicht zu einem richtigen Mann erziehen können" (*Deutschlandmärchen* 169). Dinçer widersetzt sich den Erwartungen der Mutter, ihr ‚Prinz' im Sinne eines ‚richtigen Mannes' zu sein,[13] ebenso derjenigen, im Sinne eines konventionellen ‚Deutschlandmärchens' ein ‚guter' und erfolgreicher Einwanderer in zweiter Generation sein zu müssen:

> Hier werden wir nicht mehr auf einen Nenner kommen, dafür habe ich die Unschuld längst verloren. Wie Großmutter vor Jahren auf einer Pferdekutsche alles an Heimat, Besitz, Beziehungen verloren hat, das Gleiche wünsche ich mir. [...] Ich möchte allen fremd bleiben, die von Sicherheit reden, für diese Welt habe ich keine Zugehörigkeit übrig. (*Deutschlandmärchen* 173)

Es ist ein Beharren auf eigener Identität, auf einem eigenen Lebensentwurf auch jenseits der Welt der ‚Gastarbeiter:innen', auf allem, was der Mutter (an ihm) fremd sein mag, ein Aufbegehren gegen die in Märchen und Legenden festgeschriebene Rolle des ‚guten Sohnes': „Ich wollte in meinem Leben mehr als die Geschichte des *guten Sohnes*. Eine eigene, meine Geschichte schreiben" (*Deutschlandmärchen* 172). Die Befreiung von Zugehörigkeitsfragen ist eine Reaktion auch auf die mütterlichen Ängste vor Identitätsverlust und Entfremdung von ihren Kindern, wie sie im Märchenmotiv der weggenommenen Kinder (*Deutschlandmärchen* 33, 54) und im „Lied der Mütter über ihre geflohenen, verlorenen Kinder" Gestalt annehmen: „[I]ch gebäre gesichtslose Kinder auf diesem kalten Boden [Deutschlands, HMH]"; „[I]ch musste das Kind, das ich mit wunden Warzen gestillt hatte, der Ferne verpfänden" (*Deutschlandmärchen* 192–193). Es ist aber auch eine Reaktion auf die Gesellschaft, auf eine von der ersten Einwanderungsgeneration und deren Erfahrungen ererbte Angst, niemals anzukommen, sowie auf die *gemeinsame* Angst und Erfahrung, als Migrant:innen in Deutschland niemals in Sicherheit zu sein und geachtet zu werden. „Der Dorn im Auge" (*Deutschlandmärchen* 122–128), der Verlust der Unschuld, die Lüge von der Sicherheit in Deutschland, all das meint auch die Pogromstimmung gegen Migrant:innen in den frühen 1990er Jahren, die tödlichen Brandanschläge auf Familien und deren Wohnhäuser durch Rechtsradikale in den Städten Mölln 1992 und Solingen 1993, auf die Traumata, die die Ermordung unschuldiger Menschen und Familien für die Einwanderungsgesellschaft und -gemeinschaften bedeuteten.

In diesem bedrohlichen gesellschaftlichen Klima, das sich nicht zuletzt auf die deutsch-türkische Literatur auswirkte (s. Schreiner 226–229), ist für Fatma der

---

[13] „*Verzeih mir, Mutter, ich bin nicht der Mann, den du für eine Front großgezogen hast, verzeih mir*" (*Deutschlandmärchen* 162).

Segen, Kinder bekommen zu haben, noch ein weiterer Grund für Sorge und Angst: „Solingen brennt, Menschen brennen, die verdammten Nazis verbrennen Menschen bei lebendigem Leib. [...] Das ist also die Gegenleistung für die Arbeit, für all die Schichten, für alle die Müdigkeit ... die Angst ... " (*Deutschlandmärchen* 126). Wenigstens „die [Kinder, HMH] sollen in dieser Gesellschaft ihren Frieden haben, war der Gedanke meiner Generation. Aber in diesen Flammen [von Solingen, HMH] verkohlten auch unsere Hoffnungen, diese Flammen umzingelten nun auch euch" (*Deutschlandmärchen* 126).

Unser *Deutschlandmärchen* ist die kritisch-retrospektive, postmigrantische Bestandsaufnahme der im Vergleich zur Realität allzu naiven Wunsch- und Märchenvorstellungen einer ‚glücklichen' Migration in das deutsche Wirtschaftswunder ebenso wie die kritische Bestandsaufnahme letztlich des heutigen, seit 1989 wiedervereinten Deutschland mit über 50-jähriger Einwanderungsgeschichte als ein Land, in dem nach wie vor Ausgrenzung bis hin zu rechtsradikalen Mordanschlägen Teil der Realität sind. Insofern wird auch die Beschreibung einer postmigrantischen Gesellschaft, in der Herkunft keine diskriminierende Rolle mehr spielen sollte, im Abgleich mit der Realität als ein ‚Märchen' entlarvt.[14] Leeres Gerede anstatt Solidarität, Ignoranz der gesamtgesellschaftlichen Dimension, denn „[n]icht nur wir, auch die Täter stehen mit uns in Flammen, auch dieses Land" (*Deutschlandmärchen* 126), das zum ‚Lügenmärchen' wird, indem die Bedrohungen und Verbrechen mit Schweigen bedacht, geleugnet oder gar gezielt vertuscht werden. „[V]om Traum gepeitscht, von Märchen betäubt" (*Deutschlandmärchen* 116), heißt es im Kapitel „DJ Dinco legt in der ELIF-Disco auf." In Gestalt eines poetischen RAP bringt es tägliche Ausgrenzungserfahrungen und Bedrohungen zur Sprache, die Wut über die Brandanschläge ebenso wie über die Missachtung der Opfer durch das Verhalten des Bundeskanzlers und die Reden seines Regierungssprechers, die Wut über ein jahrzehntelang polizeilich und politisch nicht aufgehaltenes rassistisches Morden des selbsternannten „Nationalsozialistischen Untergrundes", eine durch Vorurteile gegenüber den Opfern fehlgeleitete Aufklärung, Akten unter Verschluss, ein Versagen der Öffentlichkeit und auch der Medien. Genau hier zeigt sich, im Verweis auch auf Güçyeters eigenen Verlag „Elif", ein postmigrantisches Selbstbewusstsein im Dreh zum eigenen Lied, zur eigenen Stimme und Erzählung der Geschichte(n) als befreiendes Gegenmittel. Dieser Wunsch und Beginn einer eigenen, machtvollen Erzählung, als dessen Symbol ein erwachender Drache erscheint (*Deutschlandmärchen* 118),

---

14 Im Sinne eines *Postmigrant Turn* wäre und ist es allerdings die Aufgabe, genau auf diese Widersprüche in der Gesellschaft hinzuweisen mit dem Ziel, diese zu überwinden. S. hierzu Cramer, Schmidt und Thiemann.

wird nun auch von der Mutter Fatma geteilt, als Bitte an den Sohn, mit dem Schweigen ihrer Generation zu brechen:

> Wir haben uns das nie getraut, wir sahen Offenheit als Schwäche. Ihr, deine Generation, wird vielleicht all das Aufgestapelte hemmungslos lüften, in die Welt streuen. Glaub mir, auch wenn ich es spät begriffen habe, was dein Schreiben bedeutet, es füllt in mir eine Leere, bitte, schreib weiter, auch das hier, das alles musst du aufschreiben. (*Deutschlandmärchen* 125)

Doch Dinçer hat mit diesem doppelten Auftrag als Sohn und Schriftsteller zu kämpfen. In der verkehrten Ordnung des Anti-Märchens wird er zum ‚Schuldner' seiner Mutter. Dabei muss auch er sich schon früh vielfach bewähren, mit Diskriminierungserfahrungen zurechtfinden, zwischen den Sprachen und in den verschiedenen Welten einrichten: zuhause, als mehr oder minder freiwilliger kindlicher Hilfsarbeiter auf dem Arbeitsfeld der Mutter, in Kindergarten und Schule, später als Lehrling in der Fabrik, dann in der Welt des Theaters, die ihm als ‚Gastarbeiterkind' doppelt fremd ist. Als Lehrling im „Werkzeugbau" muss er „[d]ieses verrostete, verbogene Stück [...] so lange feilen, bis alle Flächen zueinander in 90 Grad stehen" (*Deutschlandmärchen* 139) – eine Aufgabe, die in ihrer sinnlosen Mühsamkeit mit dem einzigen Zweck der Bewährung an eine typische Märchenaufgabe erinnert. Ähnlich mühsam erscheint der ganz andere Weg zum Schriftsteller, da „[d]eine Stimme, Mutter, die Stimme meines Vaters, die Stimmen aus der Kneipe, die Geräusche der Maschinen [...] mir ein Rohmaterial auf die Werkbank gelegt [haben], an dem ich immer noch feile" (*Deutschlandmärchen* 191). Existenziell für das Schreiben der eigenen Geschichte ist gleichzeitig die Befreiung vom projektiven Zugriff und den Ängsten der Mutter, überhaupt von einer bisweilen recht übergriffigen Familie: Bereits den neugeborenen Dinçer wollen Verwandte für sich haben und seiner Mutter wegnehmen (*Deutschlandmärchen* 52) und im Kapitel „Der Pascha" berichtet er, wie er sich als Baby durch vorgetäuschten Schlaf „ein wenig Ruhe" verschaffte, da „[d]ie Verwandtschaft wartet, um mich quälen zu können" (*Deutschlandmärchen* 52). Ein wenig erscheint die wiegenliedsingende Hanife auch als eine böse Großmutter aus dem Märchen (*Deutschlandmärchen* 49). Einen starken Wunsch nach Entlastung verspürt Dinçer aber vor allem gegenüber den Erwartungen seiner Mutter an ihn. Deren ‚Leere' zu füllen, die „[schwere] Fracht" Fatmas und ihrer Generation weiter zu tragen im Leben und in der Literatur, erscheint ebenso notwendig wie unmöglich: „Dich wollte ich entlasten, nun spüre ich eine Fracht in mir, die unmöglich zu tragen ist. Darüber zu schreiben, versetzt mich in Scham, aber ich muss darüber schreiben, es gibt keinen Ausweg mehr" (*Deutschlandmärchen* 171). Schon das Kind wollte seine Mutter, die ‚geschundene' Gastarbeiterin, heilen, so wie „das heilende Wasser [eines Badeortes in der Türkei, HMH] [...] dem zusammengeschraubten Körper meiner Mutter guttun [soll]" (*Deutschlandmärchen* 158). Das Erzählen von Märchen erscheint dazu als das geeignete, märchenhafte ‚Heilwasser', ja als „Heilerde" der Verwurzelung in Geschichten, jedoch „nicht um die Wahrheit zu kaschieren" (s. *Deutschlandmärchen* 41), denn „[d]er Wahrheit ins Gesicht zu schauen, ist oft schwieriger, als den Salzsack auf den Berggipfel zu tragen" (*Deutschlandmärchen* 41). Es ist ein wahrhaftiges, *gegenseitiges* Erzählen der gemeinsamen und doch verschiedenen ‚Deutschlandmärchen' im Dialog mit der Mutter, das als heilsame, aber schwerste Aufgabe ausgesprochen und angekündigt wird, zu deren Zweck ein eigenes, selbst definiertes, nicht fremdbestimmtes märchenhaftes Erzählen beitragen könnte. „Wir werden [...] unser eigenes Märchen schreiben, Mutter", verspricht Dinçer Fatma bereits im "Lied des ungeborenen Kindes" (*Deutschlandmärchen* 41). Gegenläufig lassen sich die späteren, vom Wunsch nach Abnabelung angetriebenen (Angst-)Träume über den Tod der Mutter (*Deutschlandmärchen* 171–172) psychoanalytisch als Wunsch deuten, diese als Erzählerin ihrer wenig märchenhaften (Lebens-)Geschichte zum Schweigen zu bringen. Damit würde Dinçer in gewisser Weise zum Stellvertreter seines Vaters, der Fatma durchaus zum Schweigen bringt (*Deutschlandmärchen* 80–81) und nähme eine als Sohn und ‚Prinz' männliche (Macht-)Position des Ehegatten/Königs ein. Denn Dinçer weist seiner Mutter die Rolle der „Scheherazade" zu (*Deutschlandmärchen* 186), jener Braut und Erzählerin aus den *Märchen aus Tausendundeiner Nacht,* die bekanntlich unermüdlich und schließlich erfolgreich um ihr Leben erzählt, damit ihr Gemahl, der Sultan, sie nicht wie ihre Vorgängerinnen tötet. Statt seine Mutter zum Schweigen zu bringen, stellt sich der autofiktionale Sohn und Autor[15] in eine Traditionslinie des weiblichen Erzählens in seiner Familie und positioniert insbesondere die Mutter, das migrantische, müde gewordene ‚Dornröschen',[16] als „Scheherazade", um sie zum erzählenden Subjekt, zur aktiven, lebendigen, transkulturellen ‚Märchenerzählerin' und letztlich Gestalterin ihrer eigenen Geschichte und ihrer wirklichen Wünsche und Sehnsüchte, Enttäuschungen und Ängste zu machen. Im Folgenden wird aufgezeigt, wie diese Genese eines transgenerationalen, ursprünglich weiblich assoziierten Erzählens in Zusammenhang steht mit der Genese von Güçyeters transkultureller, postmigrantischer Schreibweise, die er aus dem literarischen, intertextuellen und interkulturellen Spiel mit Märchenbezügen zwischen Orient und Okzident, europäischer, arabischer und deutsch-türkischer-Literatur heraus entwickelt.

---

15 *Unser Deutschlandmärchen* ist daher eine Auto(r)fiktion. Siehe zu diesem literarischen Konzept Wagner-Egelhaaf 2013.
16 Fatma sagt an einer Stelle: „Dinçer, ich bin müde, setze diesem Märchen einen Punkt" (*Deutschlandmärchen* 211).

III

Güçyeters Roman setzt Mutter und Großmutter nicht nur als Erzählerinnen seines türkisch-deutschen *Deutschlandmärchens* ein, sondern positioniert sie auch als türkische, ‚orientalische' und zugleich deutsche Märchenerzählerinnen ihrer Geschichten. Die autofiktionale Figur des Dinçer/Güçyeter erscheint als ‚Sammler' ihrer Geschichten, die er später durch Eigenes ergänzt und die er ins Schriftliche und Literarische und zu einem nicht genau bestimmbaren Teil wohl auch aus dem Türkischen ins Deutsche überträgt. Zumindest wird ein Prozess des Hineintragens der türkisch-deutschen Familiengeschichten in die deutschsprachige Literatur und den deutschen Buchmarkt impliziert, das heißt also auch eine Übersetzung der türkischsprachigen Familien- und Frauenstimmen ins Deutsche. Es ist zugleich eine transkulturelle Erzähl- und Erzählerinnenkonstellation des intertextuellen Märchenerzählens: Die von Dinçer als Scheherazade vorgestellte Fatma (s. *Deutschlandmärchen* 186) übernimmt den Erzählstab von der Großmutter Hanife Duymuş, deren Porträt im Buch abgebildet ist (siehe Abb. 1). Fatma löst deren „schwere Zunge" ab, ein Verweis auf die literarisch ungeformte Sprache der mündlichen Erzählung Hanifes, die hier ausdrücklich allein auf Bitten Dinçers erzählt (s. *Deutschlandmärchen* 9). Als erste mündliche Erzählerin des *Deutschlandmärchens*, deren Erzählung der ‚Märchensammler' Dinçer aufschreibt, ist die türkische Großmutter assoziiert mit der Grimm'schen Erzählerin deutscher ‚Volksmärchen', Dorothea Viehmann, die Jacob und Wilhelm Grimm in ihrer Vorrede zur zweiten Auflage der *Kinder- und Hausmärchen* 1819 als Gewährsfrau der ‚Authentizität' ihrer ‚Volksmärchen' anführen (s. Neuhaus 133–135). Das von Ludwig Emil Grimm angefertigte Porträt (siehe Abb. 2) jener „Frau Viehmännin" in Kleid und Haube, von den Grimms vorgestellt als eine „Bäuerin" aus dem „bei Kassel gelegenen Dorfe Niederzwehren"[17], wird bereits dort erwähnt (s. Grimm 26) und hat mit der weit verbreiteten und oftmals reproduzierten Neuausgabe durch Otto Ubbelohde 1922, der es programmatisch als Bildabdruck vorangestellt ist (s. Grimm), Berühmtheit erlangt.

Güçyeter bezieht sich auf diese märchenhistorische Vorlage aus der deutschen Literaturgeschichte, indem er eine humorvolle Konstellation des *crossing cultures* auf die Bühne seines von Frauen erzählten *Deutschlandmärchens* bringt:

---

[17] Dorothea Viehmann war jedoch weder eine Bäuerin noch war sie „nach ihrer Herkunft [...] Hessin, sondern eine Hugenottin", die „als Kind zuhause französisch sprach" und „mit Mädchennamen Pierson" hieß (Weber-Kellermann 12–13). Bereits in der Idealisierung Dorothea Viehmanns zur hessischen Märchenerzählerin aus dem Bauernvolk zeigt sich die literarisch-fiktionale Umdeutung mündlich überlieferter, transkultureller Märchenerzählungen zum Schriftgut deutscher Volksmärchen.

Abb. 1: Porträt von Hanife Duymuş (*Deutschlandmärchen* 12).

Abb. 2: Porträt der Märchenerzählerin Dorothea Viehmann, Radierung von Ludwig Emil Grimm aus dem Jahr 1814.

die Großmutter Hanife, die in Anatolien in Haus, Hof und Feld arbeitete, in der Rolle der hessischen ‚Viehmännin'; die seit Langem im Ruhrgebiet lebende und arbeitende ‚Gastarbeiterin' Fatma in der Rolle der ‚Scheherazade'. Sie sind Figuren einer literarischen Maskerade und eines transkulturellen Spiels des Austauschs von Rollen und Sprechpositionen. Zumal sich dieses Konzept eines überlappenden, transkulturellen Märchenerzählens und -schreibens zwischen Orient und Okzident, Mündlichkeit und Schriftlichkeit mit der Figur des Sohnes/Schriftstellers Dinçer fortsetzt: Anfangs quasi in der Rolle der Grimm-Brüder, schlüpft Dinçer zeitweise in die Rolle des „orientalischen Märchenerzählers", indem er sich metaphorisch eine Art „Schnäuzer" über seine „beiden Wangen [hing]" (*Deutschlandmärchen* 181). Der implizierte Übersetzungsprozess der mündlichen Erzählerinnen ins Schriftliche und Deutsche ist außerdem bedeutsam, insofern er den Gründungsmoment des ‚deutschen' ‚Volksmärchens' um 1800, der als ein (von Jacob und Wilhelm Grimm nachhaltig inszenierter) doppelter Migrationsprozess des Märchens vom Mündlichen ins Schriftlich-Fixierte sowie vom Transkulturellen ins Nationale beschrieben werden kann,[18] sozusagen unter türkisch-deutschen, transnationalen Vorzeichen neuschreibt und damit auch desavouiert. *Unser Deutschlandmärchen* hält seine mündlich-dialogische, vielstimmige und transkulturelle Struktur gezielt präsent, um unter Bezug auf die Transkulturalität der Märchenwelten (vgl. Volkmann; Neuhaus 135–136; Tawfik) mit dem Mythos eines ‚rein' deutschen Volksmärchens auch den einer ‚reinen' Nationalliteratur und -kultur zu dekonstruieren.[19] Dabei sind Güçyeters Umgang mit dem Märchenerzählen und seine intertextuell-interkulturelle Bezugnahme auf Märchen(-rezeptionen) auch aus einer postmigrantisch-feministischen Perspektive heraus zu verstehen, nämlich als eine Zitation und Dekonstruktion, Infragestellung und Hybridisierung tradierter Fremdheits- und Weiblichkeitsdarstellungen. Der Roman macht darauf aufmerksam, dass die weiblichen Erzählerinnen und Protagonistinnen nicht zuletzt auch Projektionen des Autors sind.

In „Glücksmomente[n] der Kindheit" imaginiert Dinçer im „Prinzenumhang" seine Mutter als wunderschöne „Prinzessin" und „Scheherazade" (*Deutschlandmärchen* 86, 186). Seine kindlichen Fantasiewelten sind geprägt von fantastischen Figuren der Kinderliteratur (s. *Deutschlandmärchen* 60, 69) sowie von *Fantasy*- und Märchenfiguren aus Fernsehen und Disney-Filmen und enthalten typische Versatzstücke ‚orientalischer' Märchen in der Popkultur. In der so ausgestatteten, poetischen Erhöhung seiner Mutter zur Märchenfigur verzaubert Dinçer sein eigenes Umfeld mit: Fatmas Arbeiten in der Gaststätte, in der Fabrik und im Haus werden zu wunderbaren Aktivitäten in „Märchenländern" und „Zauberküche[n]", in denen

---

[18] Volkstümliche Märchenerzählungen, obgleich ein „Medium der Transkulturalität" (Tawfik), werden mit der Märchensammlung der Grimms zu einem „Medium nationaler Geistesbildung" (Steinlein 12–14).

[19] Eine ähnliche Richtung schlägt Yoko Tawada in ihrem ‚Grimm-Essay' *Wortarbeit* (2015) ein, in dem sie sich als eine deutsch-japanische, europäisch-asiatische Schriftstellerin zu der „nationale[n] Angelegenheit" der *Kinder- und Hausmärchen* in Bezug setzt, die bereits im Moment ihrer Entstehung eine Fiktion war, da der „Märchenstoff" sich wie ein „wässerige[r] Redefluss" und „wie Asche im Wind bis nach China verteilt" (Tawada, 236, 233–234).

auch ein „Kilim aus *Tausendundeiner Nacht*" nicht fehlt (*Deutschlandmärchen* 86–87).

Grundiert werden die Fantasien des jungen Kindes, später des bereits pubertierenden Sohnes von den fürsorglichen Wünschen des Sohnes für seine Mutter, diese möge einmal *ihren* Sehnsüchten und Wünschen folgen, würde Liebe, Freude erleben bis hin auch zur erotischen Lust: Die Stöckelschuhe, die in Dinçers Vorstellung direkt ins Märchenland führen (s. *Deutschlandmärchen* 86), landen bei Fatma ungetragen im Keller der aus dem Alltag verdrängten Sehnsüchte von Liebe, Luxus und Schönheit. Bestandteile dieser „Aussteuer der unvollendeten Träume" sind „verpackte[] Schätze[] von AMC, BOSCH, SIEMENS" (*Deutschlandmärchen* 94) ebenso wie „Wandteppiche mit Motiven aus *Tausendundeiner Nacht*, Bodenteppiche mit imitiertem Orient" (*Deutschlandmärchen* 90): All der „Kram", der „viel zu schade" ist, um ihn „im vergänglichen Deutschland-Leben auszupacken" und der für das „richtige[] Leben" (*Deutschlandmärchen* 94, 91) aufgehoben wird, das eigentlich erträumte, das niemals kommt: „[D]er Tag wird auch kommen und wir werden die Königinnen dieses Lebens sein, erst dann darf alles ausgepackt werden" (*Deutschlandmärchen* 95). Um davon zu erzählen, greift der Roman auf literarische, bereits zum Klischee gewordene, buchstäblich ‚verstaubte' Orient-Klischees wie den fliegenden Teppich zurück. Der größte Traum aber, den Dinçer in den „glänzenden Augen" der Mutter beobachtet, wenn sie Lieder türkischer Sängerinnen und Filme wie *Die bezaubernde Cevriye* hört und sieht, ist der von einer „unendlichen, bedingungslosen Liebe" (*Deutschlandmärchen* 159–160).

In seinem besonderen Mix aus Stilen und Stimmen ist der Roman zugleich lyrisch und ironisch, derb und poetisch, dabei literarisch wie politisch provokant und geeignet, allzu ‚märchenhafte' Darstellungen der Gesellschaft auf eigene Art offenzulegen, wie etwa das Kapitel „Pierburg in Nettetal: Das Wunderland der Gastarbeiter" zeigt. Besonders provokativ ist die imaginäre Verbindung und Vermischung Dinçers von Fatma/Scheherazade mit einer Pornodarstellerin aus den Videofilmen, die sein Vater nachts im Familienwohnzimmer schaut – ein Geständnis, das der Schriftsteller seine Leser:innen möglichst gleich wieder zu vergessen bittet, jedoch im imaginären Dialog mit seiner Mutter begründet:

> [I]ch hätte es dir wirklich gewünscht, dich wie diese Frauen auf dem Bildschirm zu fühlen, frei von Scham, nah dieser obszönen Lust. Einmal in deinem Leben nicht die schweigende Ehefrau, nicht die aufopferungsvolle Mutter, nicht die funktionierende Fabrikarbeiterin zu sein [...]. Alle Verpflichtungen, jede Moral in den Müll zu kippen und jeden, der einen Teil deines Lebens für sich beansprucht hat, zu enttäuschen[.] (*Deutschlandmärchen* 184)

Statt um den männlichen Blick (des Vaters) auf die Frau als erotisches Objekt geht es ihm um seine Mutter als Frau, die er sich vorstellen möchte als *Subjekt* der Empfindungen von Lust jenseits von Moral und Verpflichtungen, jenseits der Festlegungen von außen auf „geliehene Rolle[n] im geliehenen Leben" (*Deutschlandmärchen* 90). Er wünscht der Mutter, dass sie ihre große Fähigkeit zur Aktivität auch (sexuell) freisetzen könne, um die eigenen Lüste, Wünsche und Sehnsüchte zu erfüllen. Diese Befreiung zum Leben, zur Liebe und auch zur Lust, an der Dinçer schreibt und die er nicht nur an seiner Mutter schmerzlich vermisst, sondern die er auch für sich selbst wünscht, führt in der provokativen Gegenbewegung beim Sohn zu umso exzessiveren, sexuellen Ausschweifungen: „Alles an Liebe, Neigung, Treue wollte ich aus meinem Leben wischen und dem Animalischen näherkommen" (*Deutschlandmärchen* 172). Im Widerstreit zwischen dem Animalischen und den fürsorglichen, liebenden Wünschen des Sohnes für seine Mutter verweist der Text auf eine Transkulturalität der Pornofilme sowie auf eine Erotik und Exotik verbindende Darstellung orientalischer Märchenfrauen in der Orient-Rezeption der deutschsprachigen Literatur. Dinçers/Güçyeters poetische Imagination der Fatma-Figur als Scheherazade steht in einer Parallele zu einem Gedicht, das Hugo von Hofmannsthal 1890 unter Pseudonym in der Wiener Presse veröffentlichte, ein „frühestes literarisches Zeugnis seiner Verarbeitung einzelner Erzählungen aus *Tausendundeiner Nacht*" (Sander 13). Der Titel „Gülnare"[20] spielt an auf eine Märchenfigur der versklavten Braut, die an den König von Persien verkauft wird, der sich in die wunderschöne Frau verliebt und sich einen Thronfolger von ihr wünscht. Im Gedicht spricht das lyrische Dichter-Ich die „märchenhaft[e] und fremd[e]" „Schönheit" an:

„Auf dem Teppich, Dir zu Füßen, spielt der Widerschein des Feuers,/Zeichnet tanzend helle Kreise, Flammenbogen um Dich her;/Und die Uhr auf dem Kamine, die barocke, zierlich steife,/Tickt die Zeit, die süßverträumte, wohlgewogen um Dich her" („Gülnare" 11). Bedeutungsvoll sind weniger die – unverkennbaren – motivischen Parallelen in Dinçers „Scheherazade"-Fantasie über seine Mutter[21] als insbesondere die Wendung am Ende von Hofmannsthals Gedicht: „Nur die Liebe fehlt dem Märchen, die das Schönste doch im Märchen:/Laß' es mich zu Ende dichten, gib Dich, Märchen, mir zu Eigen" („Gülnare" 11).

Sander sieht darin „den Wunsch nach der Produktion eines erotischen Märchens, in dem die Vereinzelung überwunden wird" (Sander 12). Diese Imagination der Frau als (literarisches) Subjekt, das sich aus selbstempfundenem Gefühl und eigenem Antrieb einer erotischen Liebesbeziehung ‚hingibt', übersteigt den Rah-

---

20 Im Folgenden zitiert als „Gülnare".
21 Wie Hofmannsthals Gedicht beschreibt auch Güçyeters Roman an dieser Stelle den Blick auf eine wunderschöne Prinzessin „aus einem fremden Land", weitere Elemente sind der „feurige[] Teppich", der „Kilim aus *Tausendundeiner Nacht*" sowie auch hier die Uhr als Übergangsmedium in eine märchenhafte, vermeintlich ‚orientalische' Welt (*Deutschlandmärchen* 86–87).

men des exotisierenden Blicks auf die ‚schöne Orientalin' als bloßes Objekt und stellt eine Märchenpoetik der fehlenden Liebe einer solchen Braut zu ihrem Gemahl in Frage. Der Sohn/Schriftsteller Dinçer wünscht seiner Mutter ebenfalls eine lustvolle Subjektivität und erfüllende Erfahrung der (auch erotischen) Liebe und sein literarisches Anliegen ist das einer Fürsorge durch ‚Wunden heilendes' Märchenerzählen, welches die passive Rolle der Frau als Braut überwindet. Hofmannsthals literarische Rezeption orientalischer Märchen durchbricht stereotype Darstellungsweisen und setzt sich kritisch mit der eigenen orientalistischen Ästhetik auseinander. Seine Erzählung *Das Märchen der 672. Nacht* (1895) ist „eine ‚Abrechnung' [...] mit dem Ästhetizismus", deren Held ein „Antitypus normativer Maskulinität" (Sander 19, 21) und die ekelerregende Darstellung von dessen Tod durch den Tritt eines Pferdes in den Lendenbereich ein radikaler „Verstoß gegen die Märchenkonventionen" (Kreuzer 294).

Das wichtigste Vorbild für Güçyeters experimentierendes, subversives literarisches Spiel mit interkulturellen Fremdheits- und Weiblichkeitszuschreibungen in Anspielung auch auf arabische Märchen und orientalische Märchenklischees ist jedoch das Werk Emine Sevgi Özdamars, der deutsch-türkischen Schauspielerin, Dramatikerin und virtuosen Schriftstellerin von kanonischem Rang. Bereits das pränatale Versprechen zum gemeinsamen *Deutschlandmärchen*, das Dinçer seiner Mutter gibt (*Deutschlandmärchen* 41), verweist auf diese ‚zweite', literarische ‚Mutter', auf Özdamars Werke und die darin beschriebenen Kinder der deutsch-türkischen Literatur.[22] Das auch in intertextueller Hinsicht vielstimmige *Deutschlandmärchen* ist insofern ein Dialog, mehr noch ein erzählerisches Zusammenspiel mit Özdamar: als türkische ‚Gastarbeiterin' der ersten Generation und ermutigende ‚Freundin', die sich den deutschen Literatur- und Kulturbetrieb ebenfalls erst erobern und erschließen musste.[23] Özdamar, in der deutschen Literaturkritik immer wieder als ‚orientalische Schönheit' objektiviert, steht bei Güçyeter Patin für eine literarische sowie interkulturelle Sprachermächtigung, da sie in ihrem Werk eine „Mischung aus Märchenhaftem und Realistischem, [...] Osmanischem und Deutschem" und „im literarisch-ästhetischen Spiel mit den Versatzstücken des Orientalismus eine komplexe Position artikuliert, die Tradition und Innovation in eigentümlicher Weise verbindet und eine weibliche Identität schafft, die sich allen starren Zuordnungen verweigert" (Hofmann 246, 250).[24] Im von der Jugend in der Türkei der 1950er Jahre inspirierten Blick erzählt Özda-

---

22 Zum Motiv des Erzählens aus dem Mutterbauch bei Özdamar s. Ezli 306–307, 330, 387, 401, 505.
23 Siehe Dinçer Güçyeters sehr persönlichen Artikel *Epen in der Muttersprache* zur Würdigung der Verleihung des Georg-Büchner-Preises an Özdamar im Jahr 2022.
24 Die vielfältigen Einflüsse der von Michael Hofmann dargelegten literarischen Techniken Özdamars – insbesondere „Hybridisierung", „Karnevalisierung", „eine weibliche Perspektive ‚von

mar von einer sogar durch die Großmutter befürworteten weiblichen „lustvolle[n] Erkundung des Körpers" (Hofmann 250).[25] Auch in dieser Hinsicht ist Özdamar als selbstbewusste weibliche Erzählerin und Autorin ein Vorbild für die in *Unser Deutschlandmärchen* zum Erzählen ihrer eigenen Geschichte aktivierte Figur der Fatma/Scheherazde. Es geht um die Freisetzung von deren eigentlich immer schon aktivem Wesen als eine erzählerische (Selbst-)Befreiung zum Leben, zur Lust, auch zum Genuss am Reichtum der eigenen, weiblichen und familiären Geschichten und Erinnerungen. Hier (siehe Abb. 3) ist Fatma die endlich einmal im Scheinwerferlicht sitzende (und erzählende) Hauptprotagonistin, während der erwachsene Sohn und Schriftsteller unterstützend an ihrer Seite im weniger ausgeleuchteten Hintergrund

Fatma und Dinçer, 2022. Foto: Studio Özgür, Uşak / Türkei

Abb. 3: Familienporträt Fatma und Dinçer (*Deutschlandmärchen* 212).

---

unten'" sowie ein „subversiver Humor" (Hofmann 249–254) – zeigen sich in Gücyeters Roman sehr deutlich.
25 Hofmann bezieht sich auf Özdamars Roman *Das Leben ist eine Karawanserei* (1992) als Darstellung „widersprüchliche[r] Rollenerwartungen an Frauen" entgegen der Klischees einer unterdrückten ‚orientalischen' Weiblichkeit und Sexualität (246).

einen Schritt hinter ihr steht, neben den beiden die symbolisch als ‚Schatztruhe' der eigenen Geschichte zu lesende Brautkiste der Mutter.

Am Ende zeigt sich so ein nicht nur transnationales und interkulturelles, sondern auch ein liebevoll miteinander versöhntes, solidarisches Erzählen von Mutter und Sohn, eine aktive, positive Bezogenheit auf die eigenen Familien- und Migrationsgeschichten mit allem Schönen und Schrecklichen, Derben und Komischen, mit Hoffnung auf eine befreite, angstfreiere Zukunft für die Jüngeren, aber auch dem Schlussstrich einer müden ersten Generation (vgl. *Deutschlandmärchen* 211). Im Zuge des Romans entwickelt sich dementsprechend ein poetisch befreites postmigrantisches Erzählen, dass die familiären Stimmen der eigenen interkulturellen Familiengeschichte als „Rohmaterial" nutzt (*Deutschlandmärchen* 191), sie aber auf eine andere Ebene hebt und sich loslöst vom Ballast des ständigen, ‚blinden' Aufrechnens (s. *Deutschlandmärchen* 211). Es ist eine archetypische Vergegenwärtigung der Migration nach Deutschland, aber auch Anatoliens als dem Land der Kindheit und Jugend Fatmas, das in ihr und gemeinsam mit ihr zu sprechen beginnt: „Hier ist Anatolien, hier ist die Steppe. Hier werden die schönsten Märchen erzählt, hier müssen die Kinder früh ihre Flügel ablegen" (*Deutschlandmärchen* 204). Im Zuge eines magischen Realismus, in dem die Kinder und jungen Frauen wie Fatma gemeinsam mit den Kräutern, den Eidechsen und selbst den Steinen erzählen und der nun ganz ohne ironische Brechungen Märchen- und Sagenmotive inhaliert, wird die junge Fatma selbst zu einem ‚Märchen', zugleich aber zur eigenmächtigen, ‚wahren' Ich-Erzählerin und sinnlich-nachsinnenden Beobachterin ihres Selbst, ihrer Vergangenheit und ihres Weges nach Deutschland mit all den durchaus widersprüchlichen Gefühlen und Erinnerungen:

> Ich war einmal ... ich war einmal ... ich war einmal in einem Land, wo die Wasser in die Risse der Erde mündeten, ich war in einem Märchen, wo der Schnee bis zur Brust lag. [...] [Ich] hörte [...] aus der Ferne die Tanzmusik [.] Ich sah mich [...], in einem Brautkleid neben einem Mann [...], mit einem ängstlichen Blick in einem *schwarzen* Zug, [...], in einem blauen Kittel vor einer donnernden Maschine. So habe ich mein Märchen im Licht einer Kerze gestrickt. (*Deutschlandmärchen*, 206)

Durch die zum „Ich" transformierte Es-Perspektive des Märchens (*Es war einmal*) vereinigen sich individuelle und kollektive weibliche Erfahrungen. Es ist eine märchenerzählerische Erweiterung des Ichs zu einem kollektiven Unbewussten/Es, für das Fatma nun *Worte* findet. Mit der poetischen Wortfindung wird eine Opferposition überwunden und verabschiedet, es entsteht eine ‚selbst gestrickte', selbstermächtigende, eigene Erzählung. Die Schlüsselbotschaft der Befreiung zum eigenen Leben und Risiko, zum angstbefreiten Erzählen der ‚eigenen Geschichte', zum lustvollen anstatt ‚schweren' Einsatz der eigenen Sprache und ‚Zunge' (s. *Epen in der Mutterzunge*; auch *Deutschland-*

märchen 9, 26) ist eine weibliche Selbstbotschaft im transnationalen Dialog: Im Kapitel „Ein Traum oder ein Deutschlandmärchen" spricht *Ophelia*, eine berühmte Frauenfigur der Weltliteratur und des Theaters, damit aus ihrer eigenen Opferrolle heraustretend: „Fatma, das Leben kannst du nicht in Truhen schützen" (*Deutschlandmärchen* 208). Als Hommage an die Stärke der Mutter Fatma und Frauen wie sie erzählt *Unser Deutschlandmärchen* von einer „Solidarität und Harmonie gerade unter Frauen" (Hofmann 254), die wie im Falle der starken Freundschaft zwischen der türkischen Fatma und der griechisch-türkischen Zeynep jenseits „kulturelle[r] Homogenität" wie selbstverständlich „intrakulturelle Differenz[en]" integriert (Hofmann 254–255). So bestünde für Dinçer und seinen Bruder die Gefahr, sich selbst überlassen zu sein wie Hänsel und Gretel, wären da nicht die immerfort im Einsatz befindlichen Frauen, die sich über Arbeitsplätze, Haushalte und Nationen hinweg gegenseitig unterstützen: „*Der Teig ist bereit, lass uns an die Arbeit gehen, bevor die kizanlar (Kinder) vor Hunger die Wände anknabbern*" (*Deutschlandmärchen* 66). „Unsere Vergangenheit ist aus gleichem Holz geschnitzt", so spricht Zeynep, die als Angehörige der griechischen Minderheit einst als Zehnjährige aus ihrer Heimatstadt Istanbul brutal vertrieben wurde und wie Fatma „allein nach Deutschland" kam (*Deutschlandmärchen* 64–65). Der mit Scheherazade assoziierten Fatma stellt *Unser Deutschlandmärchen* die ‚Schwester' Zeynep als griechisch-türkische ‚Loreley' an die Seite. Heines bekanntestes Gedicht, eine lyrische Liebeserklärung an die rheinische Märchen- und Sagenfigur (s. Höhn 67–69), ist bei Güçyeter transferiert zum „Lieblingslied aus Anatolien", in dem „ein Mädchen namens Zeynep" ihre Lockenpracht mit einem „Kamm aus Gold" kämmt (*Deutschlandmärchen* 65). Welche zentrale Rolle darüber hinaus die Referenz auf den Exil-Autor Heine und dessen Versepos *Deutschland. Ein Wintermärchen* für Güçyeter *Deutschlandmärchen* spielt, wird im Folgenden erörtert.

IV

Der autofiktionale Autor fordert seine Leser:innen geradezu auf, den verschiedenen literarischen Einflüssen und intertextuellen Referenzen seines *Deutschlandmärchens* nachzuspüren. Einige der Vorbilder, die Dinçers Weg vom Leser zum

Schriftsteller und die Genese des Romans prägen, werden explizit genannt,[26] auf andere verweist der Text implizit.

Im literarischen Bezugsfeld, das die Stimmen der Arbeiterinnen und der eigenen türkischen Familie mit einbezieht, spielt auch ein deutscher Anwalt und Freund der Familie eine Rolle als erster Leser und zweiter ‚Vater' im Sinne einer „interkulturelle[n] Quasi-Generationenfolge", über die sich Dinçer nicht nur „in den deutschen kulturellen Zusammenhang [einschreibt]" (Holdenried 94). In Assoziation dieses ‚Vaters' mit Heine und dessen Gedicht *Aus alten Märchen winkt es* (1822/1823) wird ein Erweckungsmoment geschildert, mit dem die Genese Dinçers zum Schriftsteller sowie seines *Deutschlandmärchen* beginnt: „Die Figur Hans Hoeke gibt dem schweigenden Märchen eine Hand, das Märchen beginnt, seine zukünftige Stimme zu suchen" (*Deutschlandmärchen* 152). Hoeke führt Dinçer nicht nur in die Welten deutsch- und türkischsprachiger Literaturen sowie in die transnationale Welt der Weltliteraturen ein, er legt ihm auch die literarische und transkulturelle Inspiration der Weltstadt Istanbul nahe. Als Symbol für dies alles erscheint „ein Istanbul-Buch aus seiner Bibliothek [mit Büchern u. a. von Novalis, Rilke, Eichendorff, Fried, Lasker-Schüler, HMH]" (*Deutschlandmärchen* 151), zu denken wäre sehr vage an Orhan Pamuks international rezipiertes, vielfach übersetztes autobiografisches *Istanbul*-Buch von 2003. Als gefühlter „Bürger keines Landes" (*Deutschlandmärchen* 175), der seine Heimat und Freiheit in einer eigenen literarisch-politischen Sprache sucht, die transnational und deutsch zugleich ist (vgl. *Deutschlandmärchen* 177), ähnelt Dinçer aber weniger Pamuk als vielmehr Heine. Der autofiktionale Schriftsteller Dinçer reist nach Istanbul, in die Hauptstadt des Herkunftslandes seiner Eltern, um sich mit allen Widersprüchlichkeiten inspirieren zu lassen und gerade deshalb „weiter an Märchen zu glauben" (*Deutschlandmärchen* 198). Das autofiktionale, wie Heine selbst nach Paris emigrierte Dichter-Ich aus *Deutschland. Ein Wintermärchen* (1844) unternimmt eine Deutschlandreise, um seine ambivalente Position zum Heimatland als Inspiration und Grundlage zu nutzen für seine literarisch-politische Kritik an einer deutschen Kultur nicht zuletzt der Sagen und Märchen, die es zugleich liebt (*Wintermärchen* 442). Eine formale Verwandtschaft zu Heines Versepos zeigt sich auch im provokanten Stilmix zwischen lyrisch und prosaisch, derber und poetischer Sprache. *Unser Deutschlandmärchen* ist, bei allem historischen Abstand und der sehr unterschiedlichen politischen Kontexte, nachhaltig inspiriert von Heines literarisch virtuoser, politisch und kulturell nuancierter Deutschlandkritik, die nicht zuletzt über eine politische Aufladung von Märchen und Sagen sowie eine komplexe

---

[26] Darunter Nazim Hikmet, Hesse, Frisch, Lasker-Schüler, Dostojewski, Whitman, Bukowski, Bachmann, Lâle Müldür, Novalis, Rilke, Eichendorff, Erich Fried; Thomas Brasch, Octavio Paz und Konstantinos Kafavis (*Deutschlandmärchen* 149, 151, 174, 190).

literarische, kritische und satirische Rezeption von Texten der *Kinder- und Hausmärchen* der Brüder Grimm funktioniert (Gille).[27] Darauf rekurriert auch der Titel von Heines *Deutschland – ein Wintermärchen*, an den *Unser Deutschlandmärchen* erinnert. Auch die in Heines *Wintermärchen* entfaltete Metaphorik der Kälte und des Winters als Ausdruck eines *politischen* „deutschen Klima[s]" (*Wintermärchen* 421, 428–429, 456)[28] taucht bei Güçyeter in verschiedenen Kontexten auf: bezogen auf Fatmas Aufwachsen in Armut in der Türkei (*Deutschlandmärchen* 16–20), auf die Angst als Folge der Brandanschläge in Mölln und Solingen („ein Frost wehte nun durch unsere Zimmer", *Deutschlandmärchen* 41), auf die Krankenhäuser, in denen Fatma die vielen Operationen durchstehen muss (*Deutschlandmärchen* 41, 61), auf „die Kälte der Bahnhöfe" und ganz allgemein auf „die Realität da draußen" (*Deutschlandmärchen* 147, 145). Aus dem preußischen Wappenadler, der in Heines *Wintermärchen* dem Dichter ein Dorn im Auge ist (*Wintermärchen* 429, 464–465), wird in *Unser Deutschlandmärchen* der deutsche Bundesadler, der als alles beherrschender „Adler auf den Geldscheinen" (*Deutschlandmärchen* 129) oder als märchenhaft-gefährliches Raubtier erscheint, das den Müttern ihr Kinder zu rauben versucht (*Deutschlandmärchen* 33).

Die flammende Rache des Dichters, in Heines *Wintermärchen* ein wichtiges Motiv (s. Höhn 126), erscheint bei Güçyeter indirekt etwa in der Figur des erwachenden Drachens als Schöpfer „neue[r] Geschichten [...], die diesen Eisberg zersprengen sollen" (*Deutschlandmärchen* 118). Deutlich ist vor allem die ‚flammende' Wut der Mutter über ihre gesellschaftliche Ausgrenzung, auch weil sie nicht für „diese Rednerpulte" tauge, weshalb der Sohn „das ewige Feuer" der Mutter in einen öffentlichkeitswirksamen Text überträgt (*Deutschlandmärchen* 127–128, 185). Dieser ‚männliche' Einsatz als Erzähler für seine Mutter findet ironischen Ausdruck in Dinçers Kostümierung als „orientalische[r] Märchenerzähler" und enthält eine versteckte Heine-Referenz. Denn der „Schnäuzer", den er sich zu diesem Zweck über seine „beiden Wangen [hängt]" (*Deutschlandmärchen* 181), ähnelt dem ‚neuen' „Kostüm" des preußischen Militärs, dessen soldatische Männlichkeit Heine satirisch dekonstruiert: „Der lange Schnurrbart ist eigentlich nur/Des Zopftums neuere Phase:/ Der Zopf, der ehmals hinten hing,/Der hängt jetzt unter der Nase" (*Wintermärchen* 428–429). Dinçers „Schnäuzer" hingegen ist der Haarzopf seiner Mutter, den diese 25 Jahre lang aufbewahrte und ihm dann schenkte: jener wunderbar starke Zopf der schönen „Scheherazade" (*Deutschlandmärchen* 186), den Fatma in Deutschland der Arbeit in der Fabrik opfern und abschneiden

---

27 Konkret verweist Heines *Wintermärchen* auf die Barbarossa-Sage und das Märchen *Die Gänsemagd*, vermutlich auch auf das Märchen *Die klare Sonne bringt's an den Tag* (s. Gille).
28 Zur Wintermetaphorik im *Wintermärchen* s. Höhn 116; zur ‚kalten' Welt bei Heine s. Höhn 66.

musste. Seine Weitergabe an Dinçer (*Deutschlandmärchen* 187) ist eine symbolische auch des Erzählfadens der verborgenen Geschichten von Stärke und Verlust.

Von Wichtigkeit für Güçyeters Heine-Rezeption ist auch dessen eigentümliche Statusmischung als enorm wirkungsmächtiger, politischer deutschsprachiger Schriftsteller, der als deutscher Exilant und Jude dennoch eine Außenseiterposition markiert. Als solcher wurde der Autor des *Wintermärchens* zur zentralen Identifikationsfigur bereits für Autor:innen des antifaschistischen deutschen Exils ab 1933 (Neuhaus-Koch 654–657). Güçyeter wiederum knüpft an eine deutsch-türkische Traditionslinie des transnationalen literarischen Schreibens an, des Dialogs „between such exilic voices as those of Heine, Hikmet, Özdamar [...], thus mapping ways in which these writers deepen our understanding of the power of language against censorship, persecution, and human mortality" (Seyhan 115). *Unser Deutschlandmärchen* entwirft auf dieser Grundlage ein literarisches Modell der postmigrantischen, transnationalen Erinnerungskultur verschiedener, jedoch miteinander verschränkter Geschichten Deutschlands: Die Erinnerung an Weltkrieg und Holocaust, an „menschengefüllte Waggons, [...] Arbeitslager, [...] Gaskammern, alle, die schwach, nutzlos, anders waren, wurden hier entsorgt" (*Deutschlandmärchen* 174) ist verschränkt mit der Erinnerung an fremdenfeindliche Tendenzen unter den Deutschen der Nachkriegszeit, an Pogrome gegen Migrant:innen in den 1990er Jahren und rechtsradikale Verbrechen in der BRD bis heute. Die Metaphorik des ‚brennenden' 20. Jahrhundert (*Deutschlandmärchen* 114) reaktiviert eine Flammensymbolik, die schon bei Heine nicht nur als Ausdruck eines gerechten Dichterzornes gegenüber politischer Unterdrückung, sondern auch für den Schrecken der Scheiterhaufen, der brennenden Menschen und Bücher steht (*Wintermärchen* 488–489, 431). Sie verweist bei Güçyeters auf die Flammen von Mölln und Solingen ebenso wie auf den Militärputsch in der Türkei 1980 mit seinen vielen unschuldigen Opfern und Geflüchteten (*Deutschlandmärchen* 105). Hier schlägt *Unser Deutschlandmärchen* eine Brücke zu den übergenerationalen Konflikten des ‚deutschen' Familienromans, dessen „Kernelement die nationale Geschichte" und hier insbesondere „die Auseinandersetzung mit der Zeit des deutschen Nationalsozialismus" ist (Holdenried 91): in der Thematisierung eines interkulturell zwar variierenden, dennoch letztlich gemeinsamen Gefühls der übergenerationalen Verantwortung der jüngeren Generation gegenüber der ihrer Eltern und Großeltern (*Deutschlandmärchen* 173–174), das zwar belastet, aber auch immer wieder die Chance bietet, Deutschland „ein neues Lied, ein besseres Lied" zu singen (*Wintermärchen* 425). „Wann wirst du dein eigenes Lied singen, Alamanya?", heißt es daran anknüpfend bei Güçyeter im „Lied der Mütter vor dem Parlament" (*Deutschlandmärchen* 131). Denn während die nationale Geschichte Deutschlands in Büchern und Filmen vielfach beschrieben ist (*Deutschlandmärchen* 174), müssen die transnationalen, mündlich kursierenden Geschichten Deutschlands vielfach erst noch gehört und aufgeschrieben werden.[29] Dabei ist *Unser Deutschlandmärchen* vor allem auch ein besonders prägnantes und literarisch eindrucksvolles Beispiel einer Tendenz in der aktuellen postmigrantischen und postkolonialen Gegenwartsliteratur, unter Bezug auf Märchen als ein *mündlich* konnotiertes „Medium von Transkulturalität" (Tawfik) Konzepte des Transnationalen und Transkulturellen zu entwerfen sowie sich kritisch mit Mythen und Stereotypen ‚deutscher' Volksmärchen auseinanderzusetzen.[30]

Literaturverzeichnis

Aydemir, Fatma. *Dschinns*. Hanser, 2022.
Cramer, Rahel, Jara Schmidt, und Jule Thiemann. *Postmigrant Turn. Postmigration als kulturwissenschaftliche Analysekategorie*. Neofelis, 2023.
Ezli, Özkan. *Narrative der Migration. Eine andere deutsche Kulturgeschichte*. De Gruyter, 2022.
Gille, Klaus F. „Falada und Rotbart. Zur Verwertung und Funktionalisierung von Sagen und Märchen in Heines Deutschland. Ein Wintermärchen". *Götter, Geister, Wassernixen entlang der Oder*. Hg. von Hannelore Scholz-Lübbering. Leipziger Universitäts-Verlag, 2012. S. 15–28.
Grimm, Jacob und Wilhelm. *Kinder- und Hausmärchen gesammelt durch die Brüder Grimm*. Mit den Zeichnungen von Otto Ubbelohde und einem Vorwort von Ingeborg Weber-Kellermann. 3 Bde., Bd. 1. Insel, 1984.
Güçyeter, Dinçer. *Unser Deutschlandmärchen*. 3. Auflage, mikrotext, 2023.
Güçyeter, Dinçer. „Epen in der Muttezunge". *Republik*, republik.ch/2022/11/02/epen-in-der-mutterzunge. 7. Mai 2025.
Haase, Donald. „The Politics of the Exile Fairy Tale". *Wider den Faschismus. Exilliteratur als Geschichte*. Hg. von Sigrid Bauschinger und Susan L. Cocalis. Francke, 1993. S. 61–76.
Heine, Heinrich. „Deutschland. Ein Wintermärchen". *Werke*. 4 Bde., Bd. 1: *Gedichte*. Hg. von Christoph Siegrist. Insel, 1994. S. 421–488.
Höhn, Gerhard. *Heine-Handbuch*. 3. Aufl., Metzler, 2004.
Hofmann, Michael. „Postmoderne Inszenierungen weiblicher Körper in Räumen der Tradition und der Modernisierung: ‚Orient' bei Emine Sevgi Özdamar." *Morgenland und Moderne. Orient-Diskurse in der deutschsprachigen Literatur von 1890 bis zur Gegenwart*. Hg. von Axel Dunker. Lang, 2014. S. 243–259.
Hofmannsthal, Hugo von: „Gülnare". *Sämtliche Werke. Kritische Ausgabe*. Bd. 1: *Gedichte 1*. Hg. von Bernd Schöller. Fischer, 1984. S. 11.

---

29 Zur transnationalen Erinnerung und dem Aufbrechen nationaler Geschichtsschreibungen im deutsch-türkischen Kontext und in der deutschsprachigen Literatur s. Konuk 2007 und 2016.
30 Sharon Dodua Otoos Roman *Adas Raum* (2021) etwa dekonstruiert eine in den *Kinder- und Hausmärchen* typische Semantik der Gleichsetzung von weiß mit gut, schwarz mit böse, indem die Geschichte einer kolonialen Verschleppung erzählt wird in Gestalt eines „schaurige[n] Märchen[s] von dem Jungen, dessen Haut weiß wie Kokos wurde, weil er viel zu lange jenseits des Wassers geblieben war" (*Adas Raum* 109). Zu der genannten Tendenz s. auch Fußnote 19.

Hofmannsthal, Hugo von. „Das Märchen der 672. Nacht". *Erzählungen. Erfundene Gespräche. Reisen.* Hg. von Eugene Weber. Fischer, 1979. S. 15–30.

Holdenried, Michaela. „Eine Position des Dritten? Der interkulturelle Familienroman Selam Berlin von Yadé Kara". *Die interkulturelle Familie. literatur- und sozialwissenschaftliche Perspektiven.* Hg. von Michaela Holdenried und Stefan Hermes. Transcript, 2012. S. 89–106.

Jelinek, Elfriede. „Der Tod und das Mädchen II (Dornröschen)". *Der Tod und das Mädchen I-IV. Prinzessinnendramen.* BvT, 2003. S. 25–40.

Klotz, Volker. *Das europäische Kunstmärchen. Fünfundzwanzig Kapitel seiner Geschichte von der Renaissance bis zur Moderne.* Metzler, 1985.

Konuk, Kader. „Taking on German and Turkish History: Emine Sevgi Özdamar's *Seltsame Sterne*". *Gegenwartsliteratur. Ein Germanistisches Jahrbuch/ A German Studies Yearbook* 6 (2007): S. 232–256.

Konuk, Kader. „Genozid als transnationales Erbe? Literatur im Kontext türkischer und deutscher Geschichte". *Gegenwart schreiben. Zur deutschsprachigen Literatur 2000–2015.* Hg. von Corina Caduff und Ulrike Vedder. Fink, 2016. S. 165–175.

Kreuzer, Stefanie. „‚Märchenhafte Metatexte': Formen und Funktionen von Märchenelementen in der Literatur". *Metaisierung in Literatur und anderen Medien.* Hg. von Angelika Corbineau-Hoffmann und Werner Frick. De Gruyter, 2007. S. 282–302.

Mecklenburg, Norbert. „Die Interköpfe und die Transköpfe. Interkulturalität und Transkulturalität in kulturtheoretischer und literaturwissenschaftlicher Sicht." *Transkulturalität/Interkulturalität. Konzepte, Methoden, Anwendungen.* Hg. von Martina Engelbrecht und Gabbriela Ociepa. Lang, 2021. S. 11–27.

Massenbach, Sigrid von, Hg. *Es war einmal. Märchen der Völker.* Holle, 1958.

Mattes, Monika. „Migration und Geschlecht in der Bundesrepublik Deutschland. Ein historischer Rückblick auf die ‚Gastarbeiterinnen' der 1960/70er Jahre". *Femina Politica* 17.1 (2008): S. 19–28.

Mazenauer, Beat, und Perig, Severin. *Wie Dornröschen seine Unschuld gewann. Archäologie der Märchen.* Kiepenheuer, 1995.

Neuhaus, Stefan. *Märchen.* Francke, 2005.

Neuhaus-Koch, Ariane. „‚Heine hat alle Stadien der Emigration mit uns geteilt.' Aspekte der Exilrezeption 1933–1945". *Aufklärung und Skepsis.* Hg. von Joseph Kruse. Metzler, 1999. S. 649–665.

Otoo, Sharon Dodua. *Adas Raum.* Fischer, 2022.

Özdamar, Emine Sevgi. *Das Leben ist eine Karawanserei, hat zwei Türen, aus einer kam ich rein, aus der anderen ging ich raus.* Kiepenheuer und Witsch, 1992.

Pazarkaya, Yüksel. „Das verschlossene Paradies". *Zeitschrift für Kulturaustausch* 35.1 (1985): S. 33–35.

Samper, Cristina, und Michaela Kreyenfeld. „Marriage Migration and Women's Entry into the German Labour Market". *Journal of Family Research* 33.2 (2021): S. 439–466.

Sander, Gabriele. „‚das eigene in einem geheimnisvollen Spiegel anschauen' – Hugo von Hofmannsthal und Tausendundeine Nacht". *Textzugänge ermöglichen. Gattungsspezifische und methodische Perspektiven.* Hg. von Katrin Kloppert, Stefan Neumann, und Verena Ronge. Schneider, 2020. S. 9–24.

Schreiner, Daniel. *Vom Dazugehören. Schreiben als kulturelle und politische Partizipationstechnik. Mexikanisch-Amerikanische und Türkisch-Deutsche Literatur im Vergleich.* Königshausen & Neumann, 2019.

Seyhan, Azade. „Looking for Heinrich Heine with Nâzım Hikmet and E. S. Özdamar". *Germany from the Outside: Rethinking German Cultural History in an Age of Displacement.* Hg. von Laurie Ruth Johnson. Bloomsbury, 2022. S. 109–128.

Simeone, Nello. *Es war einmal Deutschland: Gelobtes Land*. Sparkys, 2022.
Spies, Ott, Hg. *Türkische Märchen*. Eugen Diederichs, 1991.
Steinlein, Rüdiger. „Das Volksmärchen als Medium nationaler Geistesbildung in der literaturpädagogischen Diskussion des 19. Jahrhunderts". *Kinder- und Jugendliteraturforschung* 6 (2000): S. 11–25.
Tawada, Yoko. „Wortarbeit". *Die Grimmwelt. Von Ärschlein bis Zettel*. Hg. von der Stadt Kassel in Zusammenarbeit mit Annemarie Hürlimann und Nicola Lepp. Sieveking, 2015. S. 232–237.
Tawfik, Shaimaa. „Das Märchen als Medium der Transkulturalität. Kontrastive Studie anhand ausgewählter Texte aus der deutschen und arabischen Literatur". *Unterrichtspraxis/Teaching German* 45.1 (2021): S. 103–117.
Tokponto, Mensah Wekenon. „Zur Problematik der Migration in deutschen und afrikanischen Märchen". *Weltengarten. Deutsch-Afrikanisches Jahrbuch für Interkulturelles Denken* (2010): S. 123–134.
Volkmann, Helga. „,Und an den Bäumen hingen als Früchte lauter kostbare Edelsteine'. Gärten in den orientalischen Märchen". *Zauber-Märchen*. Hg. von Ursula Heindrichs. Diederichs, 1998. S. 45–52.
Wagner-Egelhaaf, Martina. „Was ist Auto(r)fiktion?" *Auto(r)fiktion. Literarische Verfahren der Selbstkonstruktion*. Hg. von Ders. Aisthesis, 2013. S. 7–22.
Weber-Kellermann, Ingeborg. „Vorwort". *Kinder- und Hausmärchen gesammelt durch die Brüder Grimm*. Mit den Zeichnungen von Otto Ubbelohde und einem Vorwort von Ingeborg Weber-Kellermann. 3 Bde., Bd. 1. Insel, 1984. S. 9–18.
Yeşilada, Karin. *Die geschundene Suleika – Das Eigenbild der Türkin in der deutschsprachigen Literatur türkischer Autorinnen*. Orient-Institut der DMG, 2000.
Zipes, Jack. *Fairy Tales and the Art of Subversion. The Classical Genre for Children and the Process of Civilization*. 3. Aufl., Routledge, 2012.

III **Rezensionen/Book Reviews**

Harald Gschwandtner

Aust, Robin-M. „*Im Grunde ist alles, was gesagt wird, zitiert*". Die kreative und intertextuelle Thomas-Bernhard-Rezeption

Bielefeld: Transcript Verlag, 2025. 494 S. € 58,00/Open Access.

Wenige Autor:innen der deutschsprachigen Literatur nach 1945 wurden so ausführlich beforscht wie Thomas Bernhard. Bereits Mitte der 1970er Jahre, als zentrale Texte wie *Beton*, *Alte Meister* oder *Auslöschung* noch nicht veröffentlicht waren, erschienen erste Monographien zu Leben und Werk; heute ist die Fülle der Publikationen längst nicht mehr zu überblicken. Zugleich wurde sein Werk schon zu Lebzeiten von zahlreichen Schriftsteller:innen produktiv rezipiert und weitergesponnen. Die in den letzten Jahren entstandene Online-Plattform „GlobalBernhard" (globalbernhard.univie.ac.at) verzeichnet eine beeindruckende Anzahl internationaler Rezeptionszeugnisse: von Imre Kertész bis Jon Fosse, von Antonio Tabucchi bis Stefanie Sargnagel.

Das „Ausstrahlen" hat Thomas Bernhard selbst ausdrücklich zu einem Ziel seines Schreibens erklärt: „Und das nicht nur weltweit, sondern universell." Dass ihn manche Zeitgenoss:innen zum literarischen Vorbild erkoren, schmeichelte ihm – zugleich hatte er die Befürchtung, damit seine Unverkennbarkeit im literarischen Feld einzubüßen: „Soviele Bücher, die ich aufmache, beweisen mir, wieviele Schriftsteller meine Prosa gelesen haben", klagte Bernhard 1973 in einem Brief an Siegfried Unseld. „Ich ziehe die Furchen, die andern ernten die Kartoffel!"

Dem anhaltenden Erfolg von Bernhards „Ausstrahlen" widmet sich nun Robin-M. Aust in einer umfangreichen Studie, die auf seiner Promotion an der Heinrich-Heine-Universität Düsseldorf beruht. Er nimmt „ein breites Spektrum intertextueller wie intermedialer Schreibweisen" (21) in den Blick: Kontrafakturen einzelner Bernhard-Texte stehen ebenso im Fokus wie stilimitatorische Weiterschreibungen und satirisch-parodistische Literarisierungen von Bernhards Autorpersona. Austs Theoriesetting stützt sich auf diverse Ansätze der Intertextualitätsforschung (u.a. Gérard Genette), die er um Konzepte der Digital Humanities ergänzt, um philologische Argumente durch quantifizierende Erhebungen zu stützen.

Nach einer Rekapitulation des Forschungsstandes (29–34) untersucht er in drei großen Abschnitten ausgewählte Beispiele der Bernhard-Rezeption. Unter

Harald Gschwandtner, *Universität Salzburg*, harald.gschwandtner@plus.ac.at dem Titel „Bernhard umschreiben" analysiert Kapitel I „hypertextuelle Transformationen" von Thomas Bernhards Erzählung *Gehen* (1971) in Büchern von Barbi Marković und Gabriel Josipovici. Marković hat mit ihrem Debüt *Ausgehen* (2009), das dem „Prinzip der Überlagerung" folgt (59), einen sprachlich fulminanten Remix von Bernhards Erzählung vorgelegt, der die Geschichte in die Belgrader Clubszene transferiert.

Kapitel II, „Bernhard weiterschreiben: Einfluss, Imitation, Weiterentwicklung", stellt zwei Autoren ins Zentrum, die sich über Jahre hinweg mit Bernhard auseinandergesetzt haben: Hermann Burger und Andreas Maier, für die Aust „zwei grundverschiedene Einflussdynamiken" (457) beschreibt. Als theoretische Basis beruft er sich auf den von Genette geprägten Begriff der „Mimotextualität", der verschiedene Formen nachahmender oder auch persiflierender Textverfahren umfasst. Zunächst liefert er jedoch einen Abriss zentraler Topoi, Themen und Stilmerkmale von Bernhards Werk und zeichnet Entwicklungen und Brüche innerhalb seines Œuvres nach. Das „Bernhardeske", auf das sich die intertextuellen Antworten Burgers und Maiers beziehen, hat sich, wie Aust betont, erst allmählich geformt: Von den „heterogene[n] literarische[n] Gehversuche[n] eines jungen Autors, die zwischen diversen Stilen, Ästhetiken und Schreibweisen oszillieren" (99), bis zu einem originären, leicht wiedererkennbaren Stil musste Bernhard einen weiten Weg zurücklegen. Gerade am Beispiel von Andreas Maier zeigt Aust, dass affirmative Nachfolge und prononcierte Abgrenzung (mit Harold Bloom: „Einfluss und Einflussangst", 86–91) mitunter Hand in Hand gehen.

Kapitel III, „Bernhard schreiben: Transfiktionale und allofiktionale Rezeption", widmet sich Thomas Bernhard als Protagonist literarischer und biographischer Texte. Der buchlange Bericht des Bernhard-Vertrauten Karl Ignaz Hennetmair, *Ein Jahr mit Thomas Bernhard* (2000), wird ebenso einer genauen Lektüre unterzogen und behutsam kontextualisiert wie Alexander Schimmelbuschs Roman *Die Murau Identität* (2014). Wie bereits in Kapitel II bildet eine detaillierte Untersuchung von Bernhards eigenem Text- und Paratext-Kosmos eine wichtige Grundlage für Austs Argumentation, hat Bernhard doch zeitlebens intensiv an seiner biographischen Legende gestrickt und sich als „Kunstfigur" inszeniert (349–363). Aust hat auch hier seinen „analytische[n] ‚Werkzeugkasten'" (27) gut bestückt und stützt sich etwa auf die Studie *Der öffentliche Autor* (2014) von Caroline John-Wenndorf, deren begriffliche Kategorien er umsichtig für die eigenen Forschungsfragen adaptiert. Im Zuge dessen führt Aust auch den Begriff „Allofiktion" ein, der, in Abgrenzung zum Konzept der Autofiktion, literarische Fortschreibungen des Lebens nicht durch den Autor selbst, sondern durch andere meint.

Eine überraschende Leerstelle bildet dabei Bernhards eigenes ‚allofiktionales' Schreiben. Die pointierten Fort- und Umschreibungen von Künstler-Viten, in denen Bernhard auch poetologische Fragen verhandelt – etwa das Glenn-Gould-Porträt in *Der Untergeher* (1983) –, bezieht Aust nicht in seine Überlegungen ein. Auch Bernhards wohl prononciertester ‚allofiktionaler' Text, seine hintersinnige Erzählung *Goethe schtirbt* (1982), hätte ein Bezugspunkt für die Einordnung der späteren Rezeptionszeugnisse sein können, weil sie gewissermaßen das Modell für diese bereitstellt.

Freilich will Aust mit seiner verdienstvollen Arbeit keinen vollständigen Überblick liefern; vielmehr widmet er sich in detaillierten und textnahen Interpretationen einzelnen Beispielen der Rezeption von Bernhards Werk und Autorschaft. Er konzentriert sich dabei weitgehend auf Prosatexte und, abgesehen von dem Roman *Moo Pak* (1994) des britischen Autors Gabriel Josipovici, auf die Rezeption im deutschsprachigen Raum: eine im Sinne der Arbeitsökonomie notwendige Beschränkung, obgleich der Autor natürlich weiß, dass es sich bei Bernhards „Ausstrahlen" um ein „gleichermaßen intermediales wie internationales Phänomen" handelt (456).

Aust setzt grundsätzlich nicht auf quantitative Fülle, sondern auf konzentriertes *close reading*, um pars pro toto Prinzipien der intertextuellen Bezugnahme herauszuarbeiten. Er rekapituliert zunächst stets den Bernhard'schen „Hypotext", erläutert dessen ästhetische Merkmale und Eigenheiten, bevor er sich dem Rezeptionszeugnis zuwendet. Ziel der Argumentation ist die genaue „Analyse von Analogie und Differenz zwischen Vorlage und Transform" (457). Angesichts des Umfangs der Studie von beinahe 500 Seiten hätte man sich allerdings ein Personen- und Werkregister gewünscht, zumal Erläuterungen zu manchen Autor:innen und Texten nicht über das Inhaltsverzeichnis zu finden sind.

Mit seiner Dissertation erweist sich Robin-M. Aust jedenfalls als versierter Bernhard-Kenner. Auf gesicherter Basis der etablierten Forschung zeichnet er detailreiche Bilder von Bernhards anhaltender Wirkung – und bringt sich dabei auch kenntnisreich in Debatten der Intertextualitäts- und Autorschaftsforschung ein. Seinem Plan, damit künftige Forschungen anzustoßen – zu Thomas Bernhard, aber auch darüber hinaus –, ist alles Gute zu wünschen.

Necia Chronister

Brockmann, Stephen. *The Freest Country in the World: East Germany's Final Year in Culture and Memory*

Rochester: Camden House, 2023. 339 pp. $130.00 (hardcover), $29.95 (ebook).

The German nation, going on thirty-five years in its current iteration, is in crisis. 2024 saw failed governing coalitions at the national and state levels and a no-confidence vote of the German Chancellor, in part due to the influence of the far-right party *Alternative für Deutschland* (*AfD*). The fact that *AfD* supporters have appropriated the slogan from 1989/1990 "Wir sind das Volk!" for their own ethno-nationalist purposes indicates that the current discontent might be traced, at least in part, to the sense of erasure that many Eastern Germans have felt since unification. To comprehend what is happening currently in Germany, we must better understand the hopes and disappointments of the revolutionary year 1989/1990. That is the aim of Stephen Brockmann's newest monograph.

The book's title, *The Freest Country in the World*, refers to Brockmann's thesis that in the last year of the German Democratic Republic (GDR), East Germans experienced an unprecedented sense of political agency and personal freedom, coupled with the security that the socialist state still provided, all of which ended with unification with the Federal Republic of Germany (FRG). Brockmann contends that the differences in the way this year is remembered – fondly by many Easterners and hardly at all by Westerners – is key to how both populations recall the GDR today: "This is a book about the GDR and the space that it once occupied, but the GDR that it examines – which existed for much of 1989/1990 – is different from the one that is usually commemorated in museums, public ceremonies, and political speeches. It is a GDR that began as a dictatorship but ended as probably the freest and most open society that Germans have ever experienced" (2).

In his introduction, Brockmann paints a picture of that unexpected, exhilarating, and transformational time, drawing on documentary films and sociological studies to include voices from the government (like Joachim Gauck), popular culture (like the punk band Feeling B), religion (like the pastor Renate Wegner), and everyday citizens. He also sets the priorities for his study: to explore the feelings of 1989/1990 in East Germany and to assess how that year has been preserved (or not) in cultural memory. The first three chapters focus on cultural products made during that year or soon after. Chapter 1 surveys East German documentary films that show the messiness of the time, the optimism and hope, but also the worry and disappointment as the realities of capitalism set in. While a few of the films that Brockmann discusses are well known, for example Andreas Voigt's *Leipzig im Herbst* (1989), or at least accessible through the DEFA Film Library, such as Kurt Tetzlaff's *Im Durchgang: Protokoll für das Gedächtnis* (1991), Jörg Foth's *Letztes aus der DaDaeR* (1990), and Petra Tschörtner's *Berlin-Prenzlauer Berg: Begegnungen zwischen dem 1. Mai und dem 1. Juli* (1990), most of the films analyzed are largely forgotten or unavailable either commercially or in libraries. However, Brockmann provides helpful tips for accessing some of these materials, which he contends are likely absent from cultural memory because they cause friction with the more triumphalist, more easily digestible narratives about the telos of freedom that tend to dominate mainstream depictions of the revolutionary year.

Chapters 2 and 3 are stand-out chapters, focusing on the punk and neo-Nazi scenes respectively, two opposing subcultures that had grown throughout the 1980s and saw in the virtual disappearance of governmental apparatuses in 1989 the possibility of furthering their own goals. Brockmann draws together a number of sources to provide a view into these scenes, including the documentary films *flüstern & SCHREIEN: Ein Rockreport* (Dieter Schumann, 1988) and *Unsere Kinder* (Roland Steiner, 1989), existing scholarship in German studies on the punk and neo-Nazi scenes, and literary depictions such as in Peter Richter's novel *89/90* (2015). Of particular note is how Brockmann presents the flaws in standard celebratory narratives of the Monday demonstrations, revealing the (ethno-)nationalist undertones in the people's marches once unification became the goal.

While the first half of the book shows the messiness of 1989/1990, the second half outlines how specific narratives have since been established to remember that year. Chapters 5 and 6 trace a trajectory in film and television from the early 1990s into the 2010s: after productions depicting the quotidian struggles of Eastern Germans proved commercially unsuccessful (a notable example being the eight-part television series *Wir sind auch ein Volk*, conceived and written by the distinguished East German author Jurek Becker, dir. Werner Masten 1994–1995), film and television found in the Stasi a much more appealing villain to western audiences. With this version of the GDR in the public imagination, the narrative that unification led directly from oppression to freedom was further cemented. At the same time, chapters 4 and 7 demonstrate that counternarratives are emerging. Chapter 4 surveys novels by Thomas Brussig and Ingo Schulze before focusing in a more sustained way on Lutz Seiler's *Kruso* (2014), Clemens Meyer's *Als wir träumten* (2006), and Peter Richter's *89/90* (2015). Brockmann argues that these novels from the early twenty-first century counter triumphalist narratives about unification by depicting the GDR as a place of innocence and relative happiness, if also boredom and predictability, through their focus on young people. Perhaps the most telling evidence of Germany's ongoing disunity, in Brockmann's estimation, is the discord on how 1989/1990 should be commemorated in public spaces, in memorial rituals and structures, which he traces in chapter 7.

Given the book's title, one might expect a meditation on the concept of freedom: what it means and what Germany's revolutionary year might teach us about it. Brockmann selected texts for his study that discuss freedom, but he never delves far into the question itself. Only toward the end of the book does he take a moment to contemplate it. When comparing the two slogans of 1989/1990 – that of liberalization "Wir sind das Volk!" and that of unification "Wir sind ein Volk!" – Brockmann notes that freedom, typically an individualist notion, is in many ways incompatible with unity, a feeling of being bound to others. In retrospect, the friction between these two concepts has been an implied thread in Brockmann's readings throughout his study. One wonders if this reflection on freedom versus unity could have come in the book's introduction, perhaps in a more extended form, to frame a deeper investigation of what was (and still is) at stake for Germans competing for recognition in the memory culture.

The book's subtitle, *East Germany's Final Year in Culture and Memory*, indicates the real aim of the book, and the survey of texts, films, television productions, commemorative events, and monuments that Brockmann provides is a stunning accomplishment. Brockmann demonstrates with this book that taking a second look at more obscure cultural texts can be extremely valuable for gaining a truer, more nuanced sense of a time once a standardized narrative has been established. This volume could serve as a foundation for any number of deeper investigations into that turbulent year and its impact on Germany today. Written in an eminently accessible and engaging style, this book would be suitable for the graduate or even advanced undergraduate classroom and would be a fantastic starting point for anyone seeking an orientation to unification discourses for their own research.

Roberto Di Bella

Catani, Stephanie und Christoph Kleinschmidt (Hg.). *Popliteratur 3.0. Soziale Medien und Gegenwartsliteratur*

Berlin/Boston: De Gruyter, 2023. 262 S., mit Illustrationen, € 39,95/Open Access.

Die Digitalisierung wälzt nicht nur unseren Alltag um, sondern verändert zusehens auch den zeitgenössischen Literaturbetrieb. Doch wie prägen insbesondere soziale Medien die deutschsprachige Gegenwartsliteratur? Auf welche Weise adaptieren Autor:innen digitale Formate wie Chats, Tweets oder Instagram-Beiträge bzw. welche neuen ästhetischen Formen und Schreibweisen entstehen im Netz? Diesen und weiteren Fragen geht der Sammelband *Popliteratur 3.0* nach.

Der Titel verweist implizit auf Diedrich Diederichsens inzwischen als geradezu klassisch geltende strukturgeschichtliche Periodisierung von Pop I und Pop II, mittels derer er Ende der 1990er Jahre zugleich das Ende der Popkultur als historisch-progressiver Kraft verkündete. Der Kulturwissenschaftler reagierte damit auch auf die inflationär gewordene Verwendung des Begriffs und den Hype um die Popliteratur. Pop sei insbesondere ab 1995 zum begrifflichen Passepartout einer unübersichtlichen Gesellschaft geworden, habe als „zeitdiagnostischer Dummy-Term" seine subversive Distinktionsfähigkeit verloren. Wiewohl seitdem oftmals totgesagt, ist die Geschichte des Konzepts Pop seit 1955 (vgl. hierzu auch Thomas Heckens umfassende Studie von 2009) noch nicht auserzählt. Bereits 2014 hatte eine von Diederichsen mitveranstaltete Wiener Tagung zu „Pop III" angesichts der fortschreitenden Akademisierung und Musealisierung des Diskurses Möglichkeiten ausgelotet, das Sprechen über Pop für die Gegenwart anschlussfähig zu halten: ästhetisch ebenso wie sozial, medial und nicht zuletzt auch politisch. Im Zeitfenster von den 2010er Jahren bis heute entstanden auch die meisten der in der vorliegenden Publikation untersuchten literarischen Fallbeispiele, mit deutlichem Schwerpunkt auf der Prosa.

Habe die dem Sammelband zu Grunde liegende Tübinger Tagung von 2021 mit dem Titel „Popliteratur 3.0?" noch unter der Frage gestanden, ob man überhaupt von einer dritten Phase der Popliteratur sprechen könne, „liege deren Legitimation drei Jahre später auf der Hand" (1). Eine ambitionierte Setzung, welche die Herausgeber insbesondere aus dem Boom digital inspirierter Literatur ableiten, die längst

Roberto Di Bella, *Universität Siegen (SFB 1472 Transformationen des Populären)*, roberto.dibella@uni-siegen.de

auch eine Fülle entsprechender Forschungsarbeiten angestoßen habe. Dabei tun Catani und Kleinschmidt in ihrer Einleitung mit dem Untertitel „Eine Positionsbestimmung" gleichwohl gut daran zu betonen, dass es sich beim Zusammenhang von Popliteratur und Digitalisierung keineswegs um eine Gleichung handele.

Zum generationsübergreifende Spektrum der behandelten Autor:innen zählen sowohl einem breiteren Publikum (noch) weniger bekannte Namen – u. a. Rafael Horzon (*1968), Joshua Groß (*1989) und Lisa Krusch (*1990) – als auch feste Größen des Literaturbetriebs, darunter Sibylle Berg (*1962), Christian Kracht (*1966) und Benjamin von Stuckrad-Barre (*1975). Hinzu kommt Leif Randt (*1983), der die Tübinger Tagung als Gast begleitet hatte. Nicht weniger als fünf Beiträge und ein Podiumsgespräch mit dem Autor widmen sich mehrheitlich seinem Schreiben, so dass der Band fast den Charakter eines Randt-Readers erhält. Zwar nimmt der Autor seit dem Erfolg seines Romans *Schimmernder Dunst über Coby County* (2011) eine herausgehobene Rolle im Diskurs über jüngere popaffine Literatur ein, doch ob und inwiefern sein Werk auch als mustergültig im Sinne einer „Popliteratur 3.0" gelten kann, wird leider eingangs nicht begründet.

Die 15 Aufsätze in *Popliteratur 3.0* sind nicht näher unterteilt, doch gibt es drei deutliche Schwerpunkte. Den Anfang machen Beiträge mit Überblickscharakter, die thematische Konstellationen von Popliteratur beschreiben bzw. Fluchtlinien zu Pop I und/oder Pop II folgen. So untersucht Christoph Kleinschmidt „popliterarische Krisennarrative" bei Benjamin von Stuckrad-Barre und Julia Zange (*1983); Timo Sestu wiederum erörtert die „rhizomatische Weltaneignung" in Rolf Dieter Brinkmanns Materialheften der 70er Jahren, Rainald Goetz' wegweisendem Internet-Roman *Abfall für alle* (1999) und Jan Böhmermanns *Twitter-Tagebuch 2009–2020*. Weitere Aufsätze loten „Pop-Nachbarschaften 3.0" aus (Pola Groß, Hanna Hammel) oder untersuchen den Weg von der „Marken- zur Datensubjektivität" (Karl Wolfgang Flender).

Eröffnet wird der Interpretationsteil mit Jano Sobottkas Beitrag zur Anthologie *Mindstate Malibu*, die bereits bei Erscheinen 2018 vielen als Rückblick auf ein literarisches Jahrzehnt erschien. Zu Recht stellt Sobottka sie deshalb in die Tradition stilbildender Kompilationen wie Brinkmanns und Rygullas Reader zur US-Counterculture *ACID* (1969) oder auch *Tristesse Royale* (1999), das diskursprägende Gesprächsprotokoll aus dem Berliner Hotel Adlon. Demgegenüber machen, so Sobottka, die Herausgeber in *Mindstate Malibu* „ein eigenständiges, aber nicht traditionsloses Angebot, Pop und Kritik zusammenzudenken, das als Pop 3.0 bezeichnet werden könnte" (19). Paradigmatisch wirkt *Mindstate Malibu* für Sobottka vor allem im Hinblick auf die den versammelten Texten (und zahlreichen Fotostrecken, Zeichnungen wie auch Screenshots) eingeschriebene verdeckte politische Agenda, die mit den Begriffen „Kapitalismuskritik und Kritik am Neoliberalismus, aber auch das Einstehen für feministische Positionen" (19f.) zu umreißen sei. Indem Bildcodes und Schreibweisen der sozialen Medien aufgegriffen und gleichsam ästhetisch überinszeniert werden, zeige sich in den Beiträgen eine Art affirmatives Problembewusstsein.

Diese Einschätzung ließe sich auch für weitere Werke im Kontext von Pop III produktiv machen. So nimmt Katja Kauer Leif Randts Roman *Allegro Pastel* (2020) über die Fernbeziehung eines Paares aus dem Mittelklasse-Milieu zum Anlass, um in ihrer vielschichtigen Analyse mit Hilfe von Theoremen aus Psychoanalyse und Gender-Studies das Thema der Selbstobjektivierung zu erörtern. Hierbei kommt sie zu dem Schluss, das „Selbst-Sein popkultureller Subjekte [sei] an ein medial generiertes Bild (von sich) gekoppelt." (121f.) Die Ich-Erkenntnis bedürfe also eines digitalen Mittlers – Kauer arbeitet hierbei mit dem Begriff des *Digital Other* – in Form von Facebook, Instagram oder Twitter, durch den die Figuren sich ihrer Subjektivität und sexuellen Identität vergewissern könnten.

Zentral ist auch das Konzept der Ironie bzw. Postironie, dem sich Marvin Baudisch am Beispiel von Leif Randts Roman *Planet Magnon* (2015) widmet. In Anschluss an das in einem Buch wie *Tristesse Royale* minutiös inszenierte Scheitern, einen Ausweg aus der ‚Ironic Hell' zu finden, meine Postironie nämlich ausdrücklich kein erneutes Ende, sondern eine Wende gegenüber der ubiquitären Ironie hin zu einer „PostPragmaticJoy"; dies ein Begriff von Randt.

Mit diesem Spannungsmoment arbeitet auch der Berliner Autor, Konzeptkünstler und Unternehmer Rafael Horzon (*1968), dem sich Matthias Schaffrick widmet. Schaffrick untersucht Horzons autofiktionale Erlebnisberichte – 2020 gesellt sich das in der dritten Person erzählte *Das neue Buch* hinzu – gemeinsam mit der Website horzon.de und Horzons Instagram-Präsenz, um die ästhetischen Praktiken des erklärten „Nicht-Künstlers" präzise zu beschreiben und grundlegende Überlegungen zum Verhältnis von Pop und (prätendierter) Popularität anzustellen. Dabei folge der passionierte Nietzsche-Leser Horzon einer ebenso paradoxen wie konsequenten Umwertungslogik, bei der z. B. auf Instagram „Popularität zugleich beansprucht, angestrebt, behauptet und ignoriert wird" (180).

Schaffrick leitet damit zur dritten ‚Sektion' des Bandes über, in der einzelne Social-Media-Plattformen und ihre wachsende Rolle im heutigen Literaturbetrieb im Mittelpunkt stehen. Mit den Beiträgen von Catharina Richter zu Gedichtposts auf Instagram und Manuela Ruckdeschel über digital generierte Poesie wird hierbei dankenswerterweise auch die Gattung Lyrik zum Thema, findet diese doch in der Popliteraturforschung meist nur wenig Beachtung. Abschließend lenkt Jasmin Pfeiffer – am Beispiel populärer (englischsprachiger) YouTube-Kanäle wie *A Clockword Reader* oder *polandbananasBOOKS* – den Blick auf neue Formate der Literaturkritik. Indem dort im direkten Austausch mit den User:innen Konventionen von ‚Professionalität' und Journalismus hinterfragt werden, zeige sich einmal mehr, so Pfeiffer, „das die Gegenwärtigkeit immer auch mitgestaltende, grenzüberschreitende Potenzial von Pop" (242).

Ist nun aber Pop III nur alter Wein in neuen (digitalen) Schläuchen oder doch der notwendige Paradigmenwechsel, der den bereits so oft ins Museum verabschiedeten Pop zurück in die Debatten holt, um auch in der Literatur das zu leisten, was Diederichsen 1999 am Ende von „Ist was Pop?" einfordert: den Diskurs anzureichern, Machtstrukturen zu kritisieren, neue Räume (auch der Partizipation) zu öffnen? Viele der in *Popliteratur 3.0* vorgestellten Werke bzw. Akteur:innen haben das Potenzial dazu. Dabei ist es letztlich zweitrangig, ob dies begrifflich unter Pop III, ‚After-Pop' oder auch Post-Postmoderne verhandelt wird. „Pop ist tot, es lebe der Pop. Man muss eben gucken, welcher Pop", konstatierte Johannes Ullmaier bereits 2001 in seinem wichtigen Kompendium *Von Acid nach Adlon*.

Bemerkenswert an *Popliteratur 3.0* ist neben der Bandbreite an methodischen Zugängen auch, wie schnell die Germanistik inzwischen auf neue und neueste Autor:innen, Tendenzen und Texte reagiert. Dies gilt ebenfalls für weitere, ähnlich konzipierte Sammelbände der letzten Jahre. Jedenfalls ist die Popliteratur- und Popkulturforschung, zu Beginn des Jahrtausends noch eine nerdige Nische, inzwischen fest in der Academia verankert. Vielfach erforscht von Vertreter:innen des wissenschaftlichen Nachwuchs, sind diese damit auch vom Alter ‚näher dran' an den Lebenswelten der neuen literarischen Akteur:innen. Das macht die zumeist gut lesbaren Analysen speziell dieses Bandes auch geeignet als Seminargrundlage für den Einstieg in eine äußerst lebendige Gegenwartsliteratur und ihre Themen und Verfahren.

Michael Braun
Jürgensen, Christoph und Michael Scheffel (Hg.). *Günter Grass Handbuch*

Berlin/Boston: De Gruyter, 2025. 795 S. $219.99 (Hardcover) $240.00 (E-book).

Um die Günter-Grass-Forschung braucht man sich wenig Sorgen zu machen. Neben vorzüglichen Biografien (Volker Neuhaus, Per Øhrgaard, Dieter Stolz) und umfangreichen Begleitbänden zum Werk (wie Stuart Taberners *Cambridge Companion to Günter Grass*) liegen drei Erläuterungs- (bei Reclam), fünf Materialienbände (bei Steidl) und vier einführende Werkkommentare (bei De Gruyter) vor. An Dissertationen herrscht kein Mangel, in den Schulen ist zwar vieles von Grass verschwunden, aber die Vertreibungsnovelle *Im Krebsgang* als Schullektüre (2002) angekommen. Die Editionslage ist seit dem Erscheinen der 24-bändigen *Neuen Göttinger Ausgabe* (NGA, 2020) so gut wie sie nur sein kann, und die internationale Rezeption lässt, zumal nach der Nobelpreisverleihung an den Autor (1999), wenig zu wünschen übrig. Schließlich bietet der reichhaltige, wenn auch über verschiedene Archive in Lübeck, Berlin, Bremen und Göttingen verstreute Nachlass genügend Anreiz zur Beschäftigung mit Grass' Werk. Was bislang fehlte, war ein umfassender Überblick über seine künstlerischen Werke, ein Kompendium mit Informationen zu Themen, Genese, Wirkung und Perspektiven, kurzum: ein Handbuch. Das ist nun, herausgegeben von Christoph Jürgensen und Michael Scheffel unter Mitarbeit von Dieter Stolz, in der renommierten Reihe des De Gruyter Verlags erschienen und kommt mit fast 800 Seiten seinem Anspruch als umfassender Wissensspeicher sehr nahe.

Im einleitenden Biografie-Kapitel wird schnell klar, dass die Wahrnehmung des Autors Grass stark beeinflusst ist von seinem eigenen und dem öffentlichen Umgang mit Grass' Lebensgeschichte, in der die späte, manchen Kritikern zufolge: zu späte Enthüllung seiner Mitgliedschaft als Panzerschütze in der Waffen-SS 1944/45 in einem Vorab-Interview mit der *Frankfurter Allgemeinen Zeitung* anlässlich der Veröffentlichung seines autobiographischen Buches *Beim Häuten der Zwiebel* (2006) eine prägende Rolle spielte. Die Schatten, die dieses ‚Geständnis' geworfen hat, sind auch in diesem Handbuch vielfach dokumentiert; sie ragen freilich aus der Biografie heraus in die literarische Inszenierung des Autor-Erzählers, der sich in dem oben genannten Buch, zwischen erster und dritter Personenanrede schlingernd und im Irrealis abtauchend, als „Jungnazi" und „Mitläufer" apostrophiert

Michael Braun, *Universität zu Köln,* braunm1@uni-koeln.de

(NGA 17, 39). Wer mit Grass' Vita vertraut ist, wird in dem siebzehnseitigen biografischen Überblick von Katrin Wellnitz wenig Neues finden – die wichtigen Stationen sind indes benannt, von der Danziger Kindheit über die Kriegszeit und das Kunststudium bis zur literarischen Erfolgskurve, die mit der *Blechtrommel* (1959) steil begann, dann in der Kritik, nicht aber bei Verlagen und Lesern abfiel und mit dem Nobelpreis den verdienten Höhepunkt erreichte.

Der dominante Teil über das Werk bringt hingegen Nuancen und nahezu Neues an Forschungsergebnissen und -perspektiven; Kritik an mancher wissenschaftlichen Bewertung eingeschlossen, wie etwa an Volker Neuhaus' These vom Modernisierungsschub der Novelle *Katz und Maus* (1961, vgl. 49) oder an der ambivalenten Heidegger-Parodie in der Materniade der *Hundejahre* (1963). Hervorzuheben sind der inspirierende Beitrag von Heinrich Detering über Grass' Post-Katastrophen-Roman *Die Rättin* (1988) als „Pionier-Werk einer ökologisch reflektierten Literatur" (115), vierzehn Jahre vor der programmatischen Ausrufung des Anthropozän durch Paul Crutzen und Eugene Stoermer in der Zeitschrift *Nature*, Uwe Schüttes Würdigung des Journals *Aus dem Tagebuch einer Schnecke* (1972) als Wendepunkt von der Rollenprosa ins autobiographische Schreiben und Stefan Neuhaus' geschickte Zusammenfassung von Konzeption und Rezeption des umstrittenen Nachwende-Romans *Ein weites Feld* (1995). Torsten Hoffmanns eingängige Vorstellung der literaturgeschichtlich, narratologisch und heteronormativ ambitionierten Anlage von *Der Butt* (1977) lässt sich mit der Feststellung, dass dieser Roman von Problemen der Männer mit dem Feminismus handle, gut an das Themenkapitel von Julia Ingold über Geschlechterfragen anschließen, in dem Grass wiederum eine einschränkende und präskriptive Gestaltung von Genderkonstellationen bescheinigt wird. Überhaupt sind die Kapitel des Handbuchs spannend miteinander vernetzt, und es ist auf jeden Fall rühmenswert, dass über alle öffentlichen Debatten hinweg, die Grass provoziert und geführt hat, die ästhetische und künstlerische Seite seines Schaffens in den Mittelpunkt gestellt wird.

Zu den Nebenthemen von Grass, die in seinen zwölf Theaterstücken (1957 bis 1970) und weitgehend auch in der Lyrik vorkommen, zählen die Kritik des Arrangements mit dem Status quo, die deutsche Unfähigkeit zur Revolution und die Zurückweisung der Verantwortung gegenüber der nationalsozialistischen Unheilsgeschichte. In den Kapiteln zu den Lyrikbänden von Grass leuchtet der enge Zusammenhang von Prosa, Lyrik und Zeichnung ein: Es handelt sich, so Julia Ingold, um ein „multimodales" Werk (450) mit vielfältigen „Verweisspielen" (345), bei dem insbesondere die Kunst der Buchgestaltung eine nähere Betrachtung wert ist (wegweisend dazu wiederum ein Beitrag von Detering, 460–465). Grass legte, zumal seit der Zusammenarbeit mit dem Verleger Gerhard Steidl seit den 1980er Jahren, großen Wert auf die Materialität des Kunstschaffens, auf Umschlagfarbe und Schriftgröße, auf Papierqualität – und eben auf das kreative Zusammenspiel von Text und Graphik: ein schreibender Zeichner, der in beiden Medien bei der Tinte blieb und es liebte, Zeilen von Zeichnungen zu illustrieren und Gezeichnetes von Zeichen unterbrechen zu lassen. Zu den Essays, die in stattlichen vier Bänden der NGA gesammelt sind, steuert Paul Ingendaay eine von Staunen grundierte Einführung in einen ganz und gar nicht barock erzählenden Autor bei, der sich oftmals als „nüchterner strategischer Kopf mit glasklaren Sätzen" entpuppt habe (350).

Besonders interessant sind die Abschnitte des Handbuchs, die sich mit den Gesprächen und den größeren publizierten Briefwechseln von Grass befassen. Hier kann man nachlesen, warum Uwe Johnson 1968 Günter Grass zwei Hüte schenkte (und weshalb die Johnson-Forschung mehr für ihren Autor getan hat als die Grass-Forschung für ihren), auf welche Weise die Nobelpreisträger Grass und Kenzaburo Ôe wechselseitig ihre „Gegengeschichten" im kulturell diversen „Spannungsfeld von Schuld und Scham" kommentierten (407) und wie Grass den asymmetrischen Briefwechsel mit Willy Brandt als beflissener Berater und übermotivierter Helfer, und manchmal auch als ungebetener Anwalt, nur scheinbar dominiert. In diesen Abschnitten geht es um die im Gespräch entwickelten, über Jahrzehnte hinweg stabilen Strategien einer ästhetischen, politischen und kanonischen Selbstverortung des Autors. Etwa in dem 1999 geführten Gespräch mit Pierre Bourdieu, mit dem Grass im Erzählen der Geschichte von unten, nicht aber in der Frage des politischen Engagements und im Urteil über eine „Komik des Scheiterns" (440) übereinstimmte.

Für die Forschung ergiebig sind die Handbuchartikel, die sich mit den Strukturen und Schreibweisen des Werks von Grass befassen. In diesen Beiträgen geht es um die fortschreitend komplexe Codierung des Fiktionsstatus des Erzählpersonals (Christian Baier), um die Kommunikation des Autors mit seinen literarischen Vorbildern (mit Fontane, den Brüdern Grimm und, nicht zu vergessen, mit ihm selbst; Gabriele Sander), um Formate von Medienwechsel und Medienkombination im Werk (Viktoria Krason), was wiederum mit den Handbuchartikeln über Buchgestaltung und Text-Bild-Werke korrespondiert, über verwachsene, vergessene, belehrte und erlebte Kindheitsnarrative in der Prosa (Nicole Thesz), um „Essen / Kochen" (Anselm Weyer) und „Gefühle in Suppen" (NGA 4, 511).

Was von Autor und Werk bleibt, dokumentiert dieses Handbuch schließlich im Teil über die Rezeption in der literarischen Welt. Grass tritt uns da als exzentrischer und von sich bis zur Unbelehrbarkeit überzeugter Schriftsteller von Weltrang entgegen, der die deutsche Nachkriegsliteratur von Anfang an bestimmt hat, besonders in den Debatten um seine öffentliche Zeitgenossenschaft, ein Autor, der die „Gruppe 47" so sehr geprägt hat wie sie umgekehrt auch ihn, ein Kulturstaatsbürger, der das Bildungsbürgertum maßgeblich zu politisieren half, etwa in der wegen der bereits vergangenen Wahl verschleppten Wahlkampfrede zum Büchnerpreis 1965. Grass war Auslandsrepräsentant der deutschen Kultur, vielfacher Stifter von Preisen und Projekten in der Zivilgesellschaft, findiger Netzwerker und einer, auf den das Wort ‚Großintellektueller' zutrifft, weil er sich selten scheute, sich, frei nach Sartre und mit hegemonialem Habitus, auch in Dinge einzumischen, die ihn vorderhand nichts anzugehen schienen. In Frankreich gilt er nach wie vor als „Schlüsselfigur" (697) der französischen Betrachtung der deutschen Literatur, in Dänemark und in Schweden fand er, anders als in Polen und in Russland, schnell seinen Weg zu den Lesenden, in China kam er früh als politischer Kämpfer an.

Das Handbuch liefert einen willkommenen Überblick über Grass' vielfältiges Werk. Es führt auf der Grundlage der internationalen Forschung verlässlich in die einzelnen Werke, die übergreifenden Themen und die Selbstdarstellungen als Autor und Zeitgenosse ein. Und es eröffnet neue Forschungsperspektiven: beispielsweise auf den Film (die vier Roman-Adaptionen kommen hier auf knapp zehn Seiten etwas zu kurz) und auf die in der NGA ausgeklammerte praxeologische Analyse der Bildgestaltung und der Gespräche. Eine Gesamtbibliografie fehlt leider; dafür ermöglichen eine Zeittafel, Verzeichnisse der Werkausgaben und Erstdrucke, sowie ein Personen- und Werkregister eine Orientierung der Leser:innen.

Dora Osborne
Meyer, Christine und Anna Gvelesiani (Hg). *Postmemory und die Transformation der deutschen Erinnerungskultur*

Berlin/Boston: De Gruyter, 2024. 287 S. $114.99 (E-book/Hardcover).

Nearly thirty years since its introduction, Marianne Hirsch's concept of postmemory remains hugely influential and of particular relevance to German memory culture. This edited volume, on the one hand, probes the significance of Hirsch's work in this context, and, on the other shows postmemory as driving various transformations in *Erinnerungskultur* itself. This duality reflects how postmemory functions both as concept and practice, "Begrifflichkeit und Methode" (17), and, moreover, as positionality. In their attentiveness to postmemory's various modes, the combined essays provide a rich understanding of a range of literary and other works as constitutive of, and in dialogue with, German memory culture. Their engagement with Hirsch's work also shows how postmemory maps onto broader understandings of history and memory, tracing connections to Walter Benjamin's concept of "Eingedenken" as well as to Michael Rothberg's "multidirectional memory" and "implicated subject," interventions in Memory Studies and wider public discourse that could be said to have overshadowed Hirsch's were it not for Rothberg's own indebtedness to postmemory.

Following the editors' introduction, which provides an excellent overview of the shifting discourses – public and academic – that have shaped the landscape of *Erinnerungskultur*, the volume is divided into four sections reflecting how the framework of German memory culture has expanded to include different perspectives – on the violence of National Socialism, on other violent histories and on their intersections: "Begriffliche und theoretische Grundlagen"; "Neuverhandlungen des NS-Erbes"; "Fluchtlinien der Shoah"; "Postimperiale und postkoloniale Zusammenhänge". The contributions that appear under these headings focus on a range of topics and primary material, including the documentary film project *Diese Tage in Terezín*; there are two essays on Ursula Krechel as well as discussions of work by Ulrike Draesner, Marion Welsch, Esther Dischereit, Eleonora Hummel, and the Hungarian writer Alexander Lenard. The scholarly essays that make up most of the volume are prefaced by a conversation between Hirsch and the Berlin artist Silvina Der Meguerditchian, which as well as being extremely informative, has a programmatic function. It shows precisely how postmemory of-

Dora Osborne, University of St Andrews, do38@st-andrews.ac.uk

fers a framework of understanding, functions as a mode of (here, artistic) practice, while also describing the position from which subsequent generations – to which both Hirsch and Der Meguerditchian belong – attempt to remember past traumas. The essays that follow consider how postmemory operates along multiple lines: for example, Axel Dunker traces Draesner's self-reflexive use of the term in *Sieben Sprünge vom Rand der Welt,* while Katja Schubert, in her moving discussion of two of Dischereit's texts, considers the effect of "die literarische *postmemory"* in public space (163). The embeddedness of postmemory both as concept and mode also allows for the reappraisal of authors and their works, or of earlier works in the light of more recent ones, where the "memory of the first postmemory" (161), as Schubert terms it, has inscribed itself. Postmemory emerges here, then, as a mode of re-reading.

The contributions embrace postmemory's broad definition and applicability, while recognizing that this wide-ranging use has itself been subject to criticism (see Brigitte E. Jirku, 137). In particular, its 'affiliative' form allows for empathetic connection to past traumas and traumatic histories to which one has no personal or familial connection. Crucially expanding the scope of the term from its original focus (reflecting Hirsch's personal situation) on descendants of Holocaust survivors allows for discussion of under-represented victims of the Nazi regime (chapters on Roma and Sinti, including an excellent contribution by historian Eve Rosenhaft, and on victims of 'euthanasia'), of generational negotiations of identity in the context of *Erinnerungskultur* (chapters on postmigrants, Olga Grjasnowa, Nino Haratischwili) and the emergence of transnational connections between histories of violence that emerge from a postmemorial perspective.

The interview between Hirsch and Der Meguerditchian also highlights an important shift in the discourse of postmemory – something set out already by Christine Meyer in her introduction – namely a move away from trauma's gaps, absences, silences and disconnections to gestures that would overcome these aspects: repair, healing, sharing and collaboration. The subsequent essays trace these gestures, but they are also alert to the limits of postmemory and to what Myriam Geiser terms "das postmemoriale Unbehagen" (261) that affects those responsible for remembering something they did not experience. Several of the contributions engage in nuanced ways with key elements of Hirsch's work, such as questions of belatedness and its concern for other 'post'-concepts, allowing for sensitive readings of works that are themselves sensitive to postmemory and its discontents.

This is a very timely contribution to Memory Studies and German Studies that demonstrates the complexity of cultural responses to violent histories. It will be an invaluable resource to scholars and students in setting out the continuing shifts in *Erinnerungskultur* and the roles that artists and authors have in both driving and critically reflecting these changes.

Anna Seidel

Pasewalck, Silke (Hg.). *Shared Heritage – Gemeinsames Erbe. Kulturelle Interferenzräume im östlichen Europa als Sujet der Gegenwartsliteratur*

Berlin/Boston: De Gruyter/Oldenbourg, 2023. 312 S. $43.99 (auch als E-book).

Wie erinnert zeitgenössische Literatur kulturelle Interferenzräume in Mittel- und Osteuropa und welche Rolle spielen diese Räume auf motivischer, struktureller und poetologischer Ebene? Diese Fragen stehen im Zentrum des von Silke Pasewalck in Zusammenarbeit mit Jan V. König entstandenen Bandes, der die Ergebnisse einer gleichnamigen, 2020 im *Literaturhaus Berlin* veranstalteten Konferenz versammelt. Der Band macht den ‚Shared Heritage'-Begriff aus Kunstgeschichte und Denkmalpflege für literaturwissenschaftliche Analysen produktiv. Dabei geht es darum, die topologische und ästhetische Ebene der Reflexion von Orten des geteilten Erbes (z.B. Denkmäler, Städte) und entsprechender (divergenter) Erinnerungsnarrative in literarischen Texten zu diskutieren und Tendenzen, Brüche und Parallelen in der historischen Entwicklung jener Repräsentationen offenzulegen.

Der Band ist in drei Abschnitte unterteilt. Der erste Teil, „Kulturelle Interferenzräume als Orte des Shared Heritage", geht anhand von Fallstudien den Entwicklungen literarischer Darstellungen von unterschiedlichen kulturellen Interferenzräumen nach. Katarzyna Śliwińska stellt den Erfahrungsmodus und das ästhetische Modell des Unheimlichen als ein der zeitgenössischen polnischen Literatur inhärentes Spezifikum fest. Hans-Christian Trepte reflektiert in seinem Aufsatz eine „Renaissance der Mitteleuropa-Problematik", die insbesondere in der sog. Wurzelliteratur und in realen wie fiktiven Reisetexten erkennbar wird. Sabine Kyora stellt die These auf, dass Literatur dadurch, dass sie Vielstimmigkeit und räumlich-semiotische Überlappungen produzieren kann, Konfliktforschung am Objekt (nach Sigrid Weigel) ermöglicht. Joanna Jabłkowska wiederum fragt, wie die polnische (Post)Identität im Erzählprozess und Kontext der räumlichen Fremdheitserfahrung an Orten des Shared Heritage mit der Entropie des Nationalen umgeht, und kommt zu dem Schluss, polnische Literatur zeichne ein trübes Bild der Möglichkeiten von echtem „geteilten Erbe".

Der zweite Teil, „Das Verhältnis zum geteilten Erbe in literarischen Texten der Gegenwart", versammelt Beiträge, die analysieren, in welcher Relation sich Literarisierungen zu Interferenzräumen und kulturellen Aspekten des Shared He-

Anna Seidel, *Humboldt-Universität zu Berlin*, seidelay@hu-berlin.de

∂ Open Access. © 2025 bei den Autorinnen und Autoren, publiziert von De Gruyter. [CC BY-NC-ND] Dieses Werk ist lizenziert unter der Creative Commons Namensnennung - Nicht-kommerziell - Keine Bearbeitungen 4.0 International Lizenz.
https://doi.org/10.1515/9783112218631-018

ritage positionieren. Gudrun Heidemann unternimmt eine poetologische Annäherung an unterschiedliche Textformen (Comic, Prosa, Lyrik), die sich mit schlesischen und galizischen Räumen beschäftigen. Alina Molisak legt den Fokus auf den Umgang mit dem jüdischen Erbe in polnischer Literatur und nimmt eine literaturhistorische Einordnung vor, die zeigt, wie sich die Literarisierung der jüdischen Kultur in den 1990ern verändert. Silke Pasewalck diskutiert Adoption als literarisches Motiv und ästhetisches Verfahren in Gusel Jachinas *Wolgakinder* und Olga Tokarczuks *Die Jakobsbücher* und zeigt, wie beide an einer Adoption des Anderen im Rahmen eines ‚affiliativen' (nach Marianne Hirsch) Nach-Erinnerungsprozesses arbeiten. Ästhetische Verfahren des Teilens von kulturellem Erbe zeichnet auch Eszter Propszt in Zsuzsa Bánks *Schlafen werden wir später* nach und bestimmt darin die Produktion eines virtuellen Raums sowie die Einbettung der Kommunikation zwischen den beiden Protagonistinnen in einen endlosen ‚Redeschwall' als Hauptcharakteristika für die Integration von unterschiedlichen Erinnerungen an mitteleuropäische Räume (Ungarn, Böhmen) zu einer kollektiven, polyphonen Erfahrungsnarration. Sabine Egger wiederum führt Tanz als eine Möglichkeit der Subversion von monolithischen, homogenisierenden Erinnerungsnarrativen ein und belegt dies in Analysen von Katja Petrowskajas *Vielleicht Esther* und Anna Burns' *Milkman*.

Im letzten Abschnitt des Bandes „Zur Poetologie literarischer Shared Heritage-Texte" wird die Suche nach derselben fortgeführt, und zwar mit einem regionalen Fokus auf Böhmen/Mähren, Schlesien und Galizien, Siebenbürgen/Banat und Kärnten. Anne Hultsch zeigt, wie neuere Texte über Nordböhmen an einem An-eignen des deutschen Erbes arbeiten, anstatt wie zuvor die Enteignung der ehemaligen Bevölkerung in den Fokus zu stellen. Dabei wird Literatur zunehmend durch den Einsatz visueller Medien (Fotografie, Frottagen) ergänzt, wodurch der Topos von Spur und Landschaft als erinnerungstragendes Subjekt in den Vordergrund tritt. Jan V. Königs Analysen zeigen, wie in Radka Denemarkovás *Ein herrlicher Flecken Erde,* Jan Štifters *Kathy* und Kateřina Tučkovás *Gerta* Figuren des Dritten im Vordergrund der Erzählungen stehen, die als intermediäre Personen zwischen den Kulturen den Aufbruch monolithischer nationaler Erinnerungsnarrative ermöglichen. Aleksandra Burdziej skizziert in ihrem Beitrag eine literaturhistorische Entwicklung der Repräsentation von schlesischen Vertriebenengeschichten in der deutschsprachigen Literatur und sieht Sabrina Janeschs *Katzenberge* und Ulrike Draesners *Sieben Sprünge vom Rand der Welt* diesbezüglich als Wendepunkte: sie erzählen nicht mehr von einem geteilten – im Sinne eines zerteilten – Erbe, sondern von einem gemeinsamen, fluide ineinander übergehenden. Draesners Text in den Fokus nimmt auch Erik Schilling, der zeigt, wie der Roman Multiperspektivität einsetzt, um subjektive Geschichtswahrnehmung darzustellen, dadurch lineare Historiografien subvertiert und an einer Öffnung von Geschichtsverständnissen arbeitet. Michaela Nowotnicks Beitrag fokussiert als einziger rumänische Regionen und analysiert zeitgenössische deutschsprachige Prosa hinsichtlich der Darstellung des rumäniendeutschen Exodus. In der Diskussion von Nadine Schneiders *Drei Kilometer* und Thomas Perles *wir gingen weil alle gingen* stellt sie zwei unterschiedliche Verfahren heraus: bei Schneider wird der Exodus als Notwendigkeit und Flucht vor einer desintegrierten rumänischen Gesellschaft dargestellt; bei Perle wiederum steht Rumäniens positiv konnotierte Multikulturalität in einem starken Kontrast zu monokulturellen Bestrebungen in Deutschland. Csongor Lőrincz zeigt, wie durch eine kunstvolle Verdichtung von Zeichenhaftigkeiten in Ádám Bodors *Verhovina madarai* die Latenz des Erbes der k.u.k-Monarchie repräsentiert wird, wobei Religion, Natur und historisches Erbe miteinander verflochten werden. Jacqueline Gutjahr fokussiert schließlich Kärnten als Ort des Shared Heritage. In ihrem *close reading* von Maja Haderlaps Versepos *karantanien* zeigt sie, wie der Text Strategien und Wirkungsmechanismen von Erinnerungskulturen reflektiert und damit ein Bewusstsein für erinnerungskulturelle Prozesse transportiert.

Der Band überzeugt durch den Ansatz einer Adaption des ‚Shared Heritage'-Begriffs für die literaturwissenschaftliche Analyse – ein Begriff, der Aushandlungsprozesse und damit auch Konflikte impliziert –, wodurch Literatur nicht nur die Rolle eines Repräsentationsmediums, sondern eines Aktanten in erinnerungskulturellen Negotiationsprozessen zugesprochen wird. Der Band legt einen klaren Fokus auf Schlesien, Galizien und Böhmen, wodurch eine Häufung der Analysen einzelner Texte bemerkbar wird und stellenweise Redundanzen entstehen. Umso bereichernder sind die Beiträge, die den räumlichen Kontext wechseln und Perspektiven auf österreichisch-slowenische, österreichisch-ungarische oder rumänisch-deutsche Interferenzräume eröffnen.

Besonders produktiv sind meines Erachtens jene Kapitel, die auf ein ökokritisches Potential literarischer Texte hinweisen, darunter die Beiträge von Lőrincz und Hultsch. Beide zeigen, wie die nicht-menschliche Umwelt durch ihre ‚Neutralität' hinsichtlich anthropozentrischer Erinnerungsdiskurse entweder zu einem Ort der Aushandlungsprozesse wird oder aber auf die Gewaltsamkeit kultureller (Erinnerungs-)Prozesse und dadurch auf die Bedeutsamkeit von Erinnerungskulturen in der Produktion anthropozäner Realitäten hinweisen kann.

Auch die Oszillation von migrantischen Narrativen, die im Kontext von ‚Shared Heritage'-Texten entstehen, zwischen Romantisierungs- und Abwertungstendenzen (der Herkunfts- oder Ankunftsregion), worauf u.a. Kyora und Nowotnick hinweisen, schafft wichtige Anknüpfungspunkte für weitere Studien. Sie deuten auf Aushandlungsprozesse von Multikulturalitätsentwürfen hin, die insbesondere vor dem Hintergrund postmigrantischer Theorien zu fokussieren sind und für die

Analyse von literarischen Repräsentationen zeitgenössischer, vor allem urbaner, Interferenzräume von Bedeutung sein können.

Insgesamt ist das Bestreben aller Beiträge hervorzuheben, die ‚Shared Heritage'-Literatur poetologisch zu bestimmen und in diesem Rahmen Topoi, Motive und Verfahren herauszuarbeiten, die genutzt werden, um kulturelle Interferenzen auf ästhetischer Ebene zu repräsentieren und zu diskutieren. Eine Sammlung und Aufgliederung entlang der von den Autor:innen identifizierten Verfahren hätte womöglich die Trennschärfe der thematischen Strukturierung des Bandes und der Zuordnung der einzelnen Beiträge zu den Teilabschnitten etwas klarer gemacht. Der Band stellt dennoch eine produktive Annäherung an eine Poetologie der Literatur des geteilten Erbes in Mittel- und Osteuropa, womöglich sogar einen ersten Schritt in der Bestimmung eines eigenen Genres der ‚Shared Heritage'-Literatur dar. Jedenfalls zeigt er, dass transregionale, komparatistische Studien in Hinblick auf Literatur über kulturelle Interferenzräume notwendig sind, um das multikulturelle und multilinguale Erbe Mittel- und Osteuropas und seine Einbettung in aktuelle erinnerungskulturelle Diskurse zu reflektieren.

Anna Horakova

Pinkert, Anke. *Remembering 1989: Future Archives of Public Protest*

Chicago: University of Chicago Press, 2024. 360 pp. $35.

What kind of violence is concealed when the revolutions that swept across East Germany and Eastern Europe in 1989/1990 are (mis)labeled as "peaceful"? Anke Pinkert's terrific new book joins the ranks of recent scholarship on the subject of the *Wende* years, notably Stephen Brockmann's *The Freest Country in the World* (2023; see the review in this *Jahrbuch*). Pinkert's intervention in the field lies primarily in showing that the term "peaceful" suppresses the radically democratic potentialities of events that proved disruptive to the narrative of German reunification and hindered the spread of neoliberalism. The notion of "peaceful revolutions" disregards the real violence that accompanied them in, for instance, Romania, Georgia, and later, the Yugoslav republics. While in Germany, the uprising did resolve without a large loss of life, "peaceful revolutions" – rather than the more accurate terms "rebellion," "revolt," "uprising," or "unrest" that Pinkert suggests – also serves as a taming mechanism.

The term disregards the immense force of the hundreds of thousands of East Germans who "participated in a process of self-determination" that toppled an unpopular SED leadership but also attacked "the legitimacy of Western capitalism itself" (24, 22). The irruptive, anarchic force that underpinned the collective unruliness of 1989/1990 envisioned the future as open-ended, often not inimical to reformed socialism, and shaped by genuine forms of anti-colonial and anti-racist struggle. These agendas are all too often obscured by post-*Wende* commemorations of East Germany as a totalitarian state against which the "gently courageous" (*sanftmutigen*) citizens rose only to affirm the superiority of Western liberal democracy. Three decades later, a similarly simplistic narrative declares this alleged affirmation to have failed, positing causal links between the end of socialism in the former East and the staggering rise of the *Alternative für Deutschland* (*AfD*) in the new federal states because the protests had supposedly "harbored right-wing, anti-statist elements from the start" (22).

Remembering 1989 effectively walks a tightrope on a number of topics. It espouses a defense of the promise of democracy in light of Russia's imperial attack on Ukraine and the ongoing descent of several Western democracies into rightwing

Anna Horakova, *University of Connecticut*, anna.horakova@uconn.edu

populism, while not shying away from exposing the limits of existing forms of democracy. Joining Wendy Brown and Ann Stoler in their critiques of neoliberalism and its attendant evacuation of liberal democracy's content, Pinkert's book proposes to revisit the late GDR as a moment of rupture between the two antagonist systems of the Cold War; as a historic moment when the meaning of democracy was being radically reinterpreted and propagated across numerous public fora, institutions, and movements that her book helps to bring back into the spotlight.

Much of the volume thus focuses on critiquing the ongoing impulse to "pacify" the revolutions of 1989/1990 by erasing their traces from public memory, documenting instead more productive spaces for commemoration, public memorials, and artworks. Building on Jacques Derrida and Hal Foster, Pinkert coins the key term "future archives" to designate alternative, underground, and often intermedial spaces that refuse to consolidate the neoliberal status quo in Germany's memorial culture.

The first chapter, "Erasing '89–90 from the Capital" critiques several Berlin-based memorials, including the permanent exhibition "Topography of Terror" (2010) and the Berlin Wall Memorial at Bernauer Straße (1998). While the former simply conflates the ideological projects of Nazism and Communism, the Berlin Wall Memorial, by focusing on those killed at the Wall, marks a shift in the official public memory of the GDR towards "narratives of authoritarian oppression and victimization" as opposed to the more recalcitrant memories of hope, activist struggle, or political projects rooted in collective solidarities. The chapter also discusses an inconspicuous stela at the Schlossplatz, designed to commemorate a site of the Peaceful Revolution. Although this memorial features photographs that may contradict hegemonic narratives, it does not afford enough visibility to the events that it sets out to commemorate. The chapter concludes with a critique of the planned grandiose Monument to Freedom and Unity at the Berlin Stadtschloss, a walk-in, dish-shaped memorial designed to honor the peaceful revolution of 1989 and German reunification. Pinkert notes that the initial design of the monument as proposed by the choreographer Sasha Waltz who later withdrew from the project, had more aptly captured the civic movements' fearless occupation of public space and might have been more conducive to rethinking the movement's legacy.

The volume's second chapter, titled "Pacifying Memory," uses both historiography and oral history to document the complex circumstances of the Leipzig demonstrations, in which Pinkert, a Leipzig native, had participated. The chapter likewise reexamines the globalized notion of the revolutions' "peacefulness" in the Leipzig-based memorials to the civic movement. It argues that even though the demonstrations were guided by pacifist principles and originated in the peace prayers that various grassroots movements held at the *Nikolaikirche* throughout the 1980s, the demonstrations ought to be fundamentally remembered for their disruptive power. Pinkert describes the tense atmosphere of the peace prayers, which were often met with police brutality and shows that the peaceful nature of the Leipzig demonstrations did not necessarily reflect personal moral beliefs of ordinary GDR citizens but resulted from what was in fact a conflict between local pastors, the Saxon Church administration, and various oppositional groups who aimed to transform the *Nikolaikirche* into a radical political space. Thirty-five years later, the protesters leave behind "unfinished business" in that their aspirations have not been honored in the post-reunification, neoliberal order.

The subsequent two chapters are dedicated to several filmic and intermedial responses to commemorating 1989/1990 and the GDR. Titled "Possible Archives," Chapter Three analyzes the documentary *Karl Marx City* (2016), co-directed by Petra Epperlein and Michael Tucker. Straddling the personal and the public, the film tackles the role that the *Bundesbehörde für die Stasi-Unterlagen* (*BStU*) played in post-reunification memory. The documentary is based on the story of Epperlein's late father whose potential collaboration with the Stasi and suicide in 1998 is being probed when the director pays a visit to the Stasi archives during the shooting of the documentary. Pinkert argues that in its use of self-reflexive filmic techniques, including "pensive" and "indeterminate" photographic stills, Epperlein's documentary unsettles the authoritative role that the Stasi archives played in Germany's official memory politics, which imposed a shroud of "collective guilt" on East Germans (Heiner Müller). Chapter Four uses the term "prospective archaeology" as a way of theorizing the experimental films of the recently departed documentary filmmaker Thomas Heise (1955–2024). On the basis of a detailed analysis of Heise's films, especially *Material* (2009) that was compiled entirely from leftover footage shot for Heise's other films, Pinkert demonstrates the late filmmaker's remarkable ability to generate future-oriented, non-melancholic narratives through the past.

The final Chapter Five, "Futures of Hope," takes on the topic of the *AfD*'s gains on the territory of the former GDR and the parallel success of rightwing nationalist parties in Eastern Europe by critically examining – as opposed to accepting – their link to the socialist past. What factors determine whether a crowd of protesters becomes the anti-immigrant, xenophobic, and racist *Volk* or coalesces into "*the people* claiming sovereign self-rule, performing the community as negotiated and differentiated *Gemeinschaft*?" (206), the chapter asks. Pinkert argues that the combined phenomena of the demise of state socialism, the sidelining of the former GDR, leftwing melancholia, and the "perpetual now" of neoliberal Germany altogether ceded alternative, counter-public spaces to the far right. The chapter reviews the ambivalent legacies of the GDR's international solidarity schemes as well as various migrant archives (such as the exhibition *BİZİM BERLİN 89/90* that brought into relief the perspectives of Turkish Berliners on the fall of the Berlin Wall) and offers as an alternative the notion of "post-migrant allyship." The latter especially has the potential to inspire a renewed public commons as we persist in addressing issues related to race, gender, and the planet's survivability.

Namensregister/Index of Names

Abel, Julia 32, 78, 84, 92
Achternbusch, Herbert 63

Bay, Hansjörg 205–206, 211
Becker, Heike 194
Berger, Frauke 75, 89, 92, 98
Bhabha, Homi K. 205
Brenner, Hildegard 6
Brescius, Moritz von 207, 215, 217, 220

Cheng, Anne Anlin 133, 139
Chute, Hillary L. 103–104
Crumb, Robert 104, 114

Daggett, Cara 81, 98
Dieck, Martin tom 150, 154
Ditschke, Stephan 57, 113
Doucet, Julie 151

Eisner, Will 19, 21–24, 143–144
Enzensberger, Hans Magnus 6

Feuchtenberger, Anke 2, 29, 115, 149–167
Fitzpatrick, Zach Ramon 141–142
Franck, Julia 6
Frank, Anne 21, 36

Gemünden, Gerd 63–64
Goblet, Dominique 115, 151
Groensteen, Thierry 33, 111, 114–115, 118, 135, 138
Grünewald, Gernot 173, 176–177, 184, 196
Güçyeter, Dinçer 223, 225, 231, 233–236, 238–240, 242, 244–245
Gueneli, Berna 133, 141
Gundermann, Christine 34–36, 54, 56, 103

Haft, Hertzko 1, 31, 37–40, 42–48
Haraway, Donna Jeanne 82, 86, 89, 92, 96, 98
Hatfield, Charles 130
Heer, Jeet 127–128
Hein, Christoph 6
Heine, Heinrich 223–225, 242–245

Hirsch, Marianne 38–39, 267–268, 270
Honigmann, Barbara 6
Horn, Dara 69
Huber, Markus 150
Humboldt, Alexander von 203–204, 207–208, 211–212, 215–216

Illich, Ivan 75, 78, 90–92, 99

Kahn, Lisa 61
Kleist, Heinrich von 154, 162, 165–167
Kleist, Reinhard 1, 31, 33–34, 37, 39–46, 48, 58, 164
Kloeble, Christopher 2, 203–221
Klotz, Volker 224, 226
Köhler, Barbara 6, 10
Kolesch, Doris 175, 184–185
Konuk, Kader 246
Kunka, Andrew J. 144

Landry, Olivia 175, 191–192
Lefèvre, Pascal 32–33, 40, 113
Lust, Ulli 27, 113, 115, 228, 237–238, 240

Mahler, Nicolas 29
Marcks, Marie 2, 103–121
Mazzucchelli, David 24–27, 29
McCloud, Scott 32–33, 129, 132, 136
Melber, Henning 173, 181
Mikkonen, Kai 32, 35, 39–40
Miller, George 2, 75, 78–79, 81
Mills, Robert 129
Modan, Rutu 151
Morrison, Toni 125–126, 145
Moses, Dirk 65

Ndjavera, David 176–177, 181, 187, 189, 192, 196
Nguyen, Hami 130, 139–140

Özdamar, Emine Sevgi 225, 239–240, 245
Oskamp, Nils 1, 51–71
Oziewicz, Marek 92

Palandt, Ralf 54–55, 70
Palla, Rudi 207–208, 216, 220
Pateman, Carol 129
Pinkus, Yirmi 151
Platthaus, Andreas 1, 19–29, 57
Postema, Barbara 130, 139
Produktionsgenossenschaft des Handwerks
    (PGH) „Glühende Zukunft" 150

Rheinsberg, Anna 6
Rifas, Leonard 129, 143–144
Rothberg, Michael 175, 185, 267

Schlagintweit, Adolf, Hermann und
    Robert 203–221
Schneider-Özbek, Kathrin 77
Seyhan, Azade 245
Smith, Sidonie 144
Spiegelman, Art 20–21, 27, 38–39, 54, 71, 104,
    107, 113–114, 117

Spivak, Gayatri Chakravorty 206
Stanišić, Saša 5
Stein, Daniel 104, 117
Sterling, Brett 112

Trenker, Luis 207–208, 216, 220

Vieweg, Olivia 2, 75, 84, 89, 98, 125–145
Volkmer, Steffen 56
Vries, Katrin de 149

Walser, Martin 6
Ware, Chris 26–27
Weyhe, Birgit 2, 29, 103–121, 151, 161
Whitted, Qiana 127
Wyatt, Robert 153

Yelin, Barbara 115

Zimmerer, Jürgen 174, 176, 199

www.ingramcontent.com/pod-product-compliance
Lightning Source LLC
Chambersburg PA
CBHW061707300426
44115CB00014B/2595